A Harem Boy's Saga
II
Unbridled

A Memoir by Young

A Harem Boy's Saga

II
Unbridled

A memoir by

Young

A Harem Boy's Saga II: Unbridled

Copyright © 2013 by Young

Solstice Publishing – www.solsticepublishing.com

All rights reserved. No part of this book may be used or reproduced in any manner whatsoever including Internet usage, without written permission of the author.

Author's Website:

www.aharemboysaga.com

Author's email:

young@aharemboysaga.com

The contents of this book constitute a work of NONFICTION. It documents the author's experiences, and is not intended as an expose'.

No portion of this book may be transmitted or reproduced in any form, or by any means, without permission in writing from the author or publisher, with the exception of brief excerpts used for the purposes of review.

This book contains substantial sexually explicit material and language which may be considered offensive by some readers.

Book design by Maureen Cutajar

www.gopublished.com

Young 3

This book is dedicated to 'big brothers', 'big sisters', mentors and guardians around the world.

"They (teenagers) don't really listen to speeches or talks. They absorb incrementally, through hours and hours of observation."

- Rob Lowe

Foreword

In the process of writing *A Harem Boy Saga* - **Initiation**, a veil of curiosity shadowed me; I continued to ponder to Andy's whereabouts. It had been forty two years since I had last connected with my ex-lover. I had moved on with life, and with it my numerous fashion adventures had kept me busy throughout the years. Although our separation was mutual, it had been an extremely difficult decision for us (especially when we know we are soul mates in our present and past lives). As much as I welcomed the idea of being Andy's life partner living in New Zealand, foregoing my fashion ambition at 18 was too heavy a sacrifice. I couldn't live in the shadow of a passionate bridge-building engineer, especially when destiny called me to be a fashion designer since six years of age. In order for our individual ambitions to take flight, we had to separate, letting love pass. I am sure fate will unite us, if we truly are to be inseparable.

Sparks to locate Andy is within my soul with each passing day, since writing *A Harem Boy's Saga*; yet, within my being, I continue to be unsure if the time is ripe for us to reunite. I am in a loving relationship with Walter Bissett, a delightfully understanding and spiritually enlightened gentleman of panache and integrity. We have been together for 16 years. Our love continues to grow with every passing day. Is it wise to rekindle a previous love relationship while living in the loving presence of another? I don't know the answer but I am curious and inquisitive to know what happened to my beloved Andy.

A Sairam Boy's Saga JJ: Unbridled

Contents

PART ONE:
Germany –
Tübingen, *Stuttgart, Rottenburg am Neckar, Nuremberg,* Vaduz, Füssen.
Switzerland – Lucerne.
United Kingdon – London, Isle of Wight.

Chapter 1   Curiosity Takes Flight
Chapter 2   A Moment In Time
Chapter 3   Love Letters From The Heart
Chapter 4   Lots Of ChocolARTs For Me To Eat
Chapter 5   The Art Of Loving
Chapter 6   Hello Dollies, Well Hello Dollys!
Chapter 7   Run Baby Do Run, Run!
Chapter 8   Honesty Is The Best Policy
Chapter 9   A Silent Confession
Chapter 10 Yuletide Hell Broke Loose
Chapter 11 To Love Unceasingly
Chapter 12 Yodelling Our Way To LOVE
Chapter 13 The Perfumed Chalet
Chapter 14 A Happy New Year My Trusted Friends

PART TWO:

The United Arab Emirates –
Dubai, Bahriji School.
Abu Dhabi, The SEKHEM Household.

Chapter 15	A Friend In Need Is A Friend Indeed
Chapter 16	The I AM!
Chapter 17	The Sekhem Mansion
Chapter 18	A Game Of Thrones
Chapter 19	In The Olive Garden
Chapter 20	A Forbidden Sharia
Chapter 21	Bring In The Bacha Bereesh
Chapter 22	Work & Play
Chapter 23	The Harem Girls
Chapter 24	The Masks We Wear
Chapter 25	Drama At The Sekhem

PART THREE:

Italy –
Venice, Rome, Vatican City.

Chapter 26 The Count, The Professor & The Habiibi
Chapter 27 Vanquish The Jealous Heart
Chapter 28 Rome Is Burning
Chapter 29 The Holy City Of God
Chapter 30 The Fountains Of Rome
Chapter 31 Love Among The Ruins
Chapter 32 Shrouded In Mystery
Chapter 33 A Love Story
Chapter 34 The Room Of Mysteries
Chapter 35 Under The Blessed Knife
Chapter 36 Christo Salvatori - "Christ The Savior"
Chapter 37 Osiris-Dionysus = God-Christ
Chapter 38 Holy Father "John VIII" alias "Pope Joan"
Chapter 39 The Call Of The Wild
Chapter 40 Tie Me

PART FOUR:

The United Arab Emirates
Abu Dhabi, The SEKHEM Household.
Italy, Rome.
France, Paris.

Chapter 41 Sunnat Of Rasulullah Sallallahu Alayhi Wasallam
Chapter 42 Are Marriages Made In Heaven?
Chapter 43 Which Coin Will The Fountain Bless?
Chapter 44 From Grey To Pink
Chapter 45 The Butterfly Experience
Chapter 46 I Hope Your Troubles Are Few
Chapter 47 The Wedding
Chapter 48 'P'
Chapter 49 "Prince Alberts" & "Cock Rings"
Chapter 50 Hey Big Spender
Chapter 51 Money Can't Buy Me Love
Chapter 52 Worship The Creator
Chapter 53 The Wonder In Everything I See
Chapter 54 A New Generation

PART FIVE:

United States –
Nevada, Las Vegas, Arizona, Grand Canyon, California, Los Angeles.

Chapter 55	Viva Las Vegas
Chapter 56	Let Your Spirit Soar
Chapter 57	Cat Fight & The Kokopelli
Chapter 58	To Get & Beget
Chapter 59	Communing With Animals
Chapter 60	Wise Men Say, "Only Fools Rush In"
Chapter 61	I Asked God . . .
Chapter 62	Myth Is More Potent Than History
Chapter 63	An Omen
Chapter 64	Guess Who's Coming To Dinner
Chapter 65	To The Place Where I Belong
Chapter 66	Life's An Experience
Chapter 67	The Playboy Club
Chapter 68	Pride & Prejudice
Chapter 69	War & Peace
Chapter 70	From Hollywood To Bore-ywood

PART SIX:

The United Arab Emirates, Abu Dhabi,
The SEKHEM Household, Makkah, Mecca.

Chapter 71   Questions & Answers
Chapter 72   The Secret Hideaway
Chapter 73   The Profane & The Profound
Chapter 74   The Pilgrimage
Chapter 75   The Hammam
Chapter 76   Missing You, Missing Me
Chapter 77   A Time For Us
Chapter 78   Ma'a salama ل قطاس م‍ع - Goodbye Sekhem

Part One

Germany - Tübingen, Stuttgart, Rottenburg am Neckar,

Nuremberg, Vaduz, Füssen.

Switzerland – Lucerne.

United Kingdom – London, Isle of Wight.

1

Curiosity Takes Flight

"A journey of a thousand miles must begin with single step."
Chinese Proverb

January 2012

As I sat on my computer, formulating the outline for Book II and sorting through a box of old photographs of handsome Andy, thoughts of finding my ex-lover raced through my mind incessantly. Should I take a chance and locate this man on Facebook or should I let the past settle into distant memories? What should I do? I typed my Valet's name into the social networking site. Curiosity got the better of me. With trembling fingers, I scoured the search engine. A few seconds after typing Andy's name, a number of corresponding profiles appeared on the screen next to some portraiture, while others on the list had each individual person's descriptions. I ventured down the list, looking at the profiles and photographs which might match the description of my soul mate. Throughout the exercise I felt the urge to withdraw, yet my fingers continued scrolling down the page. My search for Andrew Samson Finckenstein had begun.

Das Jagdhaus (The Cabin)

I remember the photograph well, Andy in his red and black wool flannel bathrobe. We had just stepped out of a warmth bath at Ludwig and Oberon's rented cabin in the outskirts of Tübingen after the professor had collected Andy and me at the train station. We had flown from Heathrow to Stuttgart Echterdingen Airport before hopping onto a train to Tübingen for the start of our 1966 Christmas vacation in Germany and Switzerland. Ludwig, driving a brand new Jaguar Mark X (a gift from his wealthy Bedouin father for obtaining his professorship position at the prestigious Tübingen University), was waiting for us at the station. It was early evening and Oberon, Ludwig's partner was at Das Jagdhaus (The Cabin) preparing a delicious dinner for Ludwig, Andy and me. Being a superb cook, he had painstakingly prepared a scrumptious meal for us before we ventured into the nearby woods behind their cabin for an after dinner stroll. It had been snowing heavily the last few days in Tübingen, and the grounds were covered with a thick blanket of glimmering white. It was three days before my birthday, and I had never seen so much snow in my adolescent life; I was mesmerized by the beauty and quietness of this winter landscape as we went exploring.

Inside Das Jagdhaus

Entering Das Jagdhaus, I was greeted by the immense coziness of the lodge. Warmly-lit fireplaces invited us into every room. The cabin resembled a fairytale storybook cottage where Goldilocks and the Three Bears could live happily and comfortably together. I felt like Goldilocks with Ludwig, Oberon and Andy masquerading as the 3 bears. We sat down to a deliciously cooked meal and finished dinner with Griessbrei for dessert, specially crafted by Oberon's expert culinary hands. The wooden floors were strewn with an assortment of fur rugs, welcoming Andy and me with a generous dose of German hospitality. In a corner of the living room sat a freshly cut 6 ft. tall Christmas tree, decorated with an abundance of fairy lights. Beneath the pretty pine was Buff, a large, friendly Great Dane lying next to several beautifully wrapped gifts. As soon as Buff saw us, he rushed to our welcome with licks and kisses. He was extremely delighted to have visitors fawning over his lovely doggy self, and before long we became best buddies.

A Walk on the Wild Side

After dinner, we strolled into the woods because I wanted to experience the winter scenery. With the glow of the evening sun casting an enchanting spell within the thick forest, Andy and the boys chatted. I decided to trail a short distance behind and explore the beauty of the serene landscape. I had never been inside a German forest, and was curious to experience everything within this white winter wonderland. Observing a nibbling and scratching squirrel a few yards away, I was curious to see what this furry animal was doing. I stopped to observe its actions. Burying its tiny head in the snow, the squirrel emerged with a pine nut in each paw. Knowing it was being watched, the animal scrambled in the direction of a tall tree, turning to see if I would follow. Curious to see where the squirrel was heading, I followed quietly. This little fellow was as inquisitive as I, stopping every few seconds to stare at its stalker, challenging me to continue. Before long, I had lost my friends but I was determined to follow the animal wondering where it would lead me? Before the squirrel disappeared up a tree, I noticed a fire burning in a clearing, but did not see anyone present at the camp site. I drew close to the fire for warmth, and four rugged-looking men in ragged clothes suddenly jumped out of the shadows towards me, looking horrifyingly menacing and dangerous. I got on my feet to run when one of the heavy-set men cornered me. Speaking in German, he commanded, *"Wer sind Sie? Was tun Sie hier (Who are you? What are you doing here)?"*

Since I did not speak or understand German, I did not answer. I started to run when one of his mates shouted at me, *"Halten Sie an (Stop)!"* I continued running, and before he could finish his sentence, one of his mates had pounced, pinning me to the snow; he called to his mates, *"Er sieht reich aus, wollen wir nehmen, dass er hat (He looks rich, let's take what he has)!"*

Scared To Death

Sensing imminent danger, I was scared and I knew I had to escape. Struggling to get free, the man who threw me to the ground forced my hands behind my back while one of the ruffians threw his friend a leather belt to bind my wrists. Fearful images of the bullying gang of four from my primary school rushed to the forefront of my mind, and I was afraid that I would be molested and possibly raped by these villains. As I struggled desperately to loosen from the man's grip, his friends joined him and pinned me down brutally, forcing me into submission. Covered with snow, I wriggled crazily.

I was screaming, *"Help! Somebody help me!"* One of the thugs had cupped his filthy hands over my mouth to muffle my cries. Pointing a knife at me, the bully threatened to mutilate my face if I continued to scream. I was a frightened rabbit with thoughts of death looming large on my mind. Wiggling and kicking with all my strength, memories of the school bullies flashed across my eyes, reminding me that these men will kill if I didn't do as they commanded. No way could I escape their hurtful grip. My captors had already tied my wrists, gagged me with a piece of cloth in my mouth, and bound my ankles securely so I could not scream, run or escape. I was in a state of terror by the time these men turned me around, pushing me roughly against a tree. I didn't care if they robbed me; they could take whatever I had! My greatest fear was being raped and be murdered under their brutal hands. Searching my pockets, they found nothing since I carried no money or valuables. They decided to strip my clothing and boots, leaving me to freeze. I was in complete agony and completely petrified! Oh no! I thought; I am going to be raped by these villains! My heart was thumping hard and fast; I was desperately trying to struggle away from their rough, prying hands.

Petrified

Terrified, I began to sob. The leader of the pack pulled at my hair and spoke in a rough voice, *"Was tun duim Wald allein achts (What are you doing in the woods alone at night)?"*

At the time, I had no idea what he was saying, so I kept quiet while my heart thumped with fear. I was desperately trying to figure out an escape route from these bullying gypsy vagabonds.

Just then I heard a gunshot. The robbers stared at each other in bewilderment, wondering if they should stay or scramble. Another shot fired; this time, the sound was closer. From the corner of my eyes I saw a Great Dane rushing out of the woods towards the clearing, launching at one of the thugs when several figures came running towards the campfire.

My captors scattered, disappearing as fast as they could with my clothes and shoes into the darkness as Buff chased them and gnarled at their heels. I sat stunned, watching the scenario unfold in slow motion. Ludwig, Oberon and Andy were rushing towards me to untie the hurtful bonds. Seeing me naked, my Valet took off his fur jacket immediately to shield me from the freezing temperature. I was like a scared and startled faun as my lover carried my limp body, holding me tightly against his chest as tears streamed down my face. He was here to carry me back to Das Jagdhaus.

Ludwig and Oberon had brought a hand gun into the woods, knowing it to be dangerous at night with salacious gypsy vagabonds lurking to rob naïve and innocent prey. I owned my saviors 3 huge favors (which I repaid handsomely during the course of my stay in Germany and Switzerland).

2

A Moment in Time

"A truth spoken before its time is dangerous."
Greek Proverb

Surprisingly it was my delightful partner, Walter who spearheaded my search for Andy. Throughout the course of writing **Book 1 – Initiation**, Walter had been following my autobiographical story, querying me about Andy constantly.

"What happened to lover boy?" He would ask? "Where is your Valet now?" He would ask curiously. Since I could not provide my partner with answers, I told him truthfully, *"I have absolutely no idea where or what happened to my beloved Andy. I don't know."*

During one of our conversations, Walter suggested I initiate the search for my ex-lover, after we separated in 1970. I resisted the idea – in the past, I had found it best to let sleeping dogs lie. It is often the case, the person whom I hold near and dear do not conform to my expectations when we meet again many years later. Our cherished moments had dissipated, run their course and dissolved into the unconsciousness of time. Often both parties have changed, grown apart and moved forward, or, in some cases, backward to separate pastures (be they greener or otherwise). To me, re-living the past often brought disastrous results and heartaches. Personally, I would prefer to remember those cherished relationships as moments of passionate pleasures instead of recreating the glories of the past in the now. I prefer to remember Andy as he was between the years of 1966 and 1970.

Searching For Andy – January 2012

Under Mr. Bissett's relentless urging, I scrolled down the Facebook profiles that resembled my soulmate's description. Five candidates came close to his profile but none resided in New Zealand except one: a Mr. Andy S. Finckinstene, 62, construction engineer living in Wellington. There was a retired Andrew Samson Finckenstein 66 years old from Newport, Oregon, U.S.A.; a 3rd gentleman Dr. A. S. Finckenstein aged 63 residing in Frankfurt, Germany and the 4th, a Mr. Andre Samsun Finckensteen, 64, living in Perth, Australia. Last but not least the 5th man by the name of Dr. Andee Finckeenstein was a 66-year-old retiree stationed in Phuket, Thailand. Scratching my head, I wondered which of these five is Andy? Should I try solving this riddle, or should I pass the search baton to Mr. Bissett since it was his idea to locate Andy, not mine?

Looking at the profiles of these candidates, I couldn't help but remember Uncle James' valuable advice when we met in London before my 1966 Christmas vacation with my Valet to Tübingen, Germany.

The Ritz London

I had recently returned from Paris from the Haute Couture fashion shows with the Kosk ladies. Before long, I was on the ferry and train to London from Daltonbury Hall to spend 3 days at Uncle James' residence during my Christmas break. I was sad to leave Oscar and sadder to leave Andy even though we would see each other in a span of few days, before flying to visit the two professors, Ludwig and Oberon, at Tübingen, Germany.

I was delighted to see my guardian and to have him with me. The following day Uncle James suggested having Afternoon Tea at a special restaurant I had not been to before. His chauffeur drove towards Piccadilly and arrived at a luxurious 5 star hotel, aptly named The Ritz. The grandeur of The Ritz reminded me of the Singapore Raffles Hotel and The Savoy at the Strand; high ceiling interiors trimmed ornately with gold awnings around the periphery welcomed us into the hotel. I could smell the sophistication of this grand dame the moment I stepped through its front doors. Memories of enjoying High Tea at Raffles' Tiffin with Mother came flooding to my mind.

Conversation with Uncle James

After we sat and ordered, James inquired, *"Every time I see you, you grow more into your own. How are you doing, my boy?"*

I replied happily, *"I'm well and enjoying everything life is offering. I'm glad I decided to take up the scholarship and have absolutely no regrets joining E.R.O.S."*

"Good, that's wonderful to hear. I know you will do well in their various programs. I haven't seen you for 4 months; tell me all that transpired since our last meeting." Uncle James smiled delightfully.

"I don't know where to begin; so much has happened over these past months. I can't remember everything; but I know I'm having a great time and learning a great many things along the way.

"I do have some questions for you." I replied happily.

My guardian smilingly said, *"What questions do you have that your Valet or professors cannot answer? Tell me and I will do my best to fill in the gaps."*

With that encouragement, I related to James everything that had happened during the course of the past four months, beginning from my acceptance into the student exchange program to my initiation into E.R.O.S., my education at the Bahriji School, to my experiences at the Kosk. Last but not least, I discussed my field trips to Florence, Venice, Tuscany and Paris. I also told of my loving relationship with Andy.

My guardian listened attentively before responding, *"Andy sounds like a wonderful person. You'll have to invite your Valet to* stay with us in London. I would like to meet him, since you are so fond of him and he is infatuated with you. Young, I want you to be happy; you are like my adopted son."

"Thank You Uncle James. I adore you!" I was moved by my guardian's kindness and acceptance of my sexual preference, and I was deeply grateful that Mother had handed James the task of being my mentor and guardian.

During our conversation, I asked my uncle further details about E.R.O.S. Looking about him, he said, *"There are many things you will learn and discover throughout your journey at the various Arab Households. Each harem is unique and you'll be expected to perform different duties. My advice to you: tread with caution. Andy, your Valet, will make sure you are protected and looked after. An important aspect – you must be mindful, to reveal none of your E.R.O.S. experiences to anyone."*

Out of curiosity I questioned, *"Why is everything about E.R.O.S. so secretive?"*

With a sigh my uncle replied, *"Many people don't understand the nature of this society, and most will consider this program an unorthodox method of teaching our young. The enlightened, whose worldviews are accepting and open-minded, will understand the educational system that E.R.O.S. is offering. Unfortunately, majority of people are neither sophisticated nor sufficiently accepting to view our society's methods as positive educational tools for young people like you and Andy.*

"There are many people who are afraid of homosexuals, blacks or any minority groups that are different. Personal beliefs or cultural practices that don't conform to regular accepted practices or behaviors are often considered a threat to our so-called 'advanced civilization.' My advice to you, Young: "A truth spoken before its time is dangerous." Although our society is changing, the level of sophistication, understanding and acceptance in the ways of other cultures are not in keeping with the Ancient methods of adolescent mentorship, which have been pushed underground in the name of

progress. E.R.O.S. members must proceed with caution until the correct moment in history presents itself to again and apply our methods of education as accepted norm in our common culture."

Mr. Koo and Janet

As I was taking mental notes of Uncle James' advice, an Asian couple entered the restaurant, noticed my guardian and waved to him. James proceeded to greet them before introducing me to David Koo, a banking business acquaintance of my uncle, and his lovely girlfriend Janet Fonda, who were in London on vacation. Thus, my conversation with my guardian terminated when the lovely couple joined our table.

Mr. Koo was a senior executive at the Hong Kong & Shanghai Banking Corporation and Janet was involved in her family's entertainment business. Many years later, when I was teaching at the fashion department in the Hong Kong Polytechnic (now a University), I had the privilege to design Janet's wedding ensemble for her marriage to a well-known Hong Kong television and movie producer.

London, Winter 1966

Spending time with Uncle James was wonderful; I learned plenty about the Enlightened Royal Oracle Society as well as about my guardian's life. James had spent time in several Middle Eastern Households from mid-1920s to early 1930. He related many of his harem experiences with the various Household women and the occasional male whom he serviced. It was a vastly different world in the 20s and there were many perils and dangers; yet he gained an abundance of valuable experiences throughout the course of his adolescent years as an E.R.O.S. member. When he met my mother on the RMS Queen Mary, she had mentioned about my effeminacy and my negative relationship with my dad. James suggested for her to enroll me into Daltonbury Hall, secretly hoping I would be selected for E.R.O.S. He believed the scholarship student exchange program would assist me in finding my life's path. And Uncle James was correct, I did find many loving families away from home together with an abundance of love along my harem way.

I am extremely grateful to Mother in heeding Uncle James' advice by enrolling me into Daltonbury Hall instead of subjecting me to Father's wishes to enroll me into a quack experimental homosexual reform institution which would undoubtedly have forced me to change my effeminate behavior to become a 'normal' dude. Most likely, had I entered one of these reform establishments, my experiences would have been devastating, making me into a depressed, suicidal person for the rest of my life. My heart reaches out to the unlucky boys whose parents knew no better.

Thank you, dear Mother, for standing your ground, insisting I enter Daltonbury Hall. With the fine assistance of Sir James R. Pinkerton, I had grown unscathed and unscarred into adulthood, finding my voice and enjoying an artistically fashionable career to this day.

The day I received the devastating news of Uncle James' passing in June 1980, a terrible sense of loss washed over me for my enlightened guardian, an amazing gentleman of honor, integrity and godliness. His mentorship is greatly missed. The amazing times we spent together will continue to live within my heart forever.

Thank You, Sir James R. Pinkerton, Thank You Sir!

3

Love Letters from the Heart

*"Love and magic have a great deal in common.
They enrich the soul, delight the heart,
and they both take practice."*

Nora Roberts

January 2012

After much thought, I decided to compose a generic letter to send the five Facebook gentlemen whom Walter, my life partner had suggested I contact. The written content:

Dear Sir,

I hope this message finds you well. You may or may not know me. I decided to write to you because many years ago I lost touch with a very dear and intimate friend, who shares a similar name as your good self. The last time we met was in London, England in the summer of 1970. I was then in my late teens and Andy, my friend was 22. I had recently been accepted into the Belfast College of Art & Design, Northern Ireland to commence my 1st year of Foundation Art studies while Andy was on his way to Christchurch, New Zealand to further his engineering studies at the University of Canterbury. He was my 'Big Brother' when we were stationed in the United Arab Emirates for a period of 4 years (1966 to 1970) and shared many wonderful times together.

It has been 39 years since we connected. If you are the Andy I am hoping to locate and might consider renewing our long lost friendship, please contact me through my Facebook page or at this email address...I will be delighted to reconnect and renew our friendship. Andy has been on my mind throughout the years and I miss the delightful times we shared. I look forward to your response.

Sincerely and my best wishes!

Young,

Alias Bernard Foong.

(Fashion Designer)

With a click on my mouse, the message went to these 5 candidates; while I waited with bated breath for the universe to bring forth the results. As I read through the contents of my message, my mind drifted to the winter of 1966, the day after my attack in the woods by the gypsy thugs...

A Loving Liaison

Oscar, my temporary 'big brother' had spent the night with me before my departure to London and Europe. It had been a sad parting since we disliked the thought of not seeing each other for the next few weeks. We did our best to keep ourselves in good spirits when we said our goodbyes the following morning. As much as Oscar did not welcome the idea of spending our holidays separately and me going with my Valet, he donned a brave face and wished me an enjoyable vacation; reminding us that I would be on his mind throughout our time apart. As much as I wanted to spend the holidays with Oscar, I had responsibilities to fulfill: spending a little time in London with Uncle James and the rest of the two and half weeks with Andy, and visiting our professor friends, Ludwig and Oberon, in Baden Württemberg, Germany. I had also promised Andy to visit his parents in Vaduz, on Christmas and Boxing Day.

The evening after my saviors rescued me from the horrific clutches of the robbers, we had spent the night sleeping together on the same bed. None of my 3 'bears' wanted me alone. I was petrified during the frightening assault and was glad my protectors were next to me on either side as if they were guarding a precious jewel. Andy had washed and cleaned me in a hot bath before wrapping his cozy red and black checked flannel bathrobe around my shivering body. He tucked me between Ludwig, Oberon and him in the king-size bed. Sandwiched between my 3 sexy 'bears,' their warmth radiating from their naked bodies, I felt safe. Wrapped in Andy's hairy chest a peaceful loving sensation fell across my tired eyes before sensual and sexual thoughts began drifting through my mind. The evening's excitements were too terrifying and I was lucky to be saved by these 3 hunky angels now keeping watch, holding and caring for my safety. Their masculinity aroused as I held tightly onto my lover while his intoxicating scent drifted up my nostrils. Before long my Valet had lowered his face to mine, gently kissing my longing lips and desiring mouth. Surrendering to his loving touch, I was grateful for his protection.

Oberon lay against my back, his muscular hands wrapped around my slender waist, and his palms began inching towards my throbbing erection. His blonde pubic hair gliding against my backside, I couldn't resist tilting my lower back towards my rescuer's groin, his erection sliding against my opening. Feeling his breath on the back of my neck, he stuck his tongue out and lapped at my ear lobes. The erotic sensations were too tantalizing for the three of us. Turning on my back, I offered access to Oberon's wet lips, nibbling on my ears. Moving slowly down my left nipple the blonde angel munched, licked and ate at my tiny nob until it resembled a little ripe cheery on top of a delicious cake.

Andy, imitating the blonde's actions on my other side, caused me to moan in rapturous ecstasies in the quiet night. Ludwig, having lowered himself between my legs, was busy lapping, eating and nibbling at my globes before plunging his mouth on my straining erection. Delighted to repay my saviors, I gave myself willingly to their loving caresses. That night, the 'bears' and I took turns making love with each other, happily surrendering to each other's tantalizing touches, not wanting these ecstatic sensations to end. We copulated many times over until the wee hours before succumbing to sleep in each other's embrace. I was indeed the luckiest boy at Das Jagdhaus that winter's evening.

Showering Together

We did not leave the comfort of the bed until late afternoon. The beauty of our endless lovemaking was too invigorating to get out of bed into the cold of Tübingen city for nourishment. But our tummies needed feeding, so we reluctantly left the comfort of the King and showered together under a blanket of warm tinkling water in our host's spacious bathroom. The closeness of our nakedness was too irresistible for us not to make love again. The entanglements of our body parts too titillating to forgo another intimate session, and we continued where we left off on the King.

It seems I could never repay my saviors enough. Longing to please every part of their enticing bodies, I went to town sucking and suckling their engorged 'lollipops,' which were pointing at my face. Each mouthful was as yummy as the next. We took turns wrapping our lips and mouths on each other's length, savoring every drop of our oozing liquid while warm aqua rained down our dripping heads. None of us wanted these intoxicating simulations to end as we rotated in front of each other, savoring the human 'bratwurst' delicacies offered us. Leaning against the shower wall, I gave myself to my angels; tilting my longing sex towards their engorged organs as they mounted their faun with passionate devotions. Before long they were sowing their juicy seeds within my sweet offering. I wanted them, I needed them and I loved them; I was eager to reward my heroes with love and gratitude for their unwavering grace.

At Weinstube Forelle

By the time we got into Oberon's candy-apple red 1966 Mercedes Benz W110, we were famished. Andy and I had situated ourselves warmly at the back of the vehicle as we drove to Weinstube Forelle, a historical German restaurant in old Tübingen city for a scrumptious Gulaschsuppe (Goulash soup) and Knackwurst w/krauf meal, followed by a delicious Apfelstrudel (Apple Strudel) dessert.

Over brunch, Andy inquired, *"When does ChocolART start?"*

Ludwig replied wickedly, *"It starts tomorrow. There will be plenty to do and lots of sweet delicacies to eat! It's an all you can eat buffet."* He was licking his lips; already planning our erotic liaisons for when we returned to the cabin.

Oberon chimed in adding flavor to his lover's naughty remarks, *"By the end of the festival, you guys will be so full, and you'll not want to get out of bed."*

"You two have everything planned, haven't you?" Andy joked.

Ludwig laughingly continued, *"Tomorrow we'll go to town for brunch and do some sightseeing before proceeding to the ChocolART Festival. How does that sound?"*

"Fabulous!" I chirped, *"That sounds absolutely delicious. Everything is so sex-citing. What are we doing after brunch?"*

Both hosts and Andy laughed at my childish exuberance before Oberon spoke, *"Well, young man, you'll have to wait and see. Whatever we are doing will be very sex-citing,"* he continued laughing.

By now their contagious laughter had me in stitches, amused at my own childish naiveté.

Our scrumptious food arrived and I gobbled everything before me. Ravished from our excessive lovemaking, I was game to paint Tübingen red.

Love Letter from the Heart

After the delicious meal, Ludwig suggested we visit the Eberhard Karls University where he and Oberon taught. The campus consisted of several outlying buildings; some were located in the old town while other faculties were on campus. As the two professors showed us the institution, I reached into my shoulder bag to locate my camera for some photo-ops. Instead I found an envelope tucked between my camera and a book. Since I didn't want to open the letter in front of my friends, I waited, suspecting the letter to be from Oscar. At Ludwig's office, while they were busy chatting, I excused myself to the rest facility. Inside a locked stall, I peeled open the envelope and a sparkling Christmas card emerged. It read:

Young, my dearest boy,

I miss you terribly. Life isn't the same without you. By the time you open this card, you will be in Germany and I in Scotland. I wish I could spend Christmas and New Year with you, Andy and your friends. It would be fun! Unfortunately my parents required my presence during the holiday season, leaving me little choice but home in Edinburgh with family. I look forward to seeing you at Daltonbury Hall in a couple of weeks, holding, caressing and making love to you again. Your sexy groans never fail to excite my horny self and I'm a selfish lover. I hope you are thinking of me daily. Be safe and have a wonderful Christmas and a Happy New Year!

Love and kisses to my teddy bear!
Yours Truly,
Oscar.

How could I not fall in love with my angelic BB when he wrote so romantically? We were playing an emotionally dangerous game and I felt terribly guilty not telling Andy the truth about my affair with this deliriously loving beau.

4

Lots Of ChocolARTs for Me To Eat

"You have to see the sex act comically, as a child."
W. H. Auden

January 2012

Two days after I sent the five messages, I received a reply from Mr. André Samsun Finckensteen, 64, currently living in Perth, Australia. Since there was no photograph of him posted on his Facebook page, I didn't have a clue how he looked. He wrote:

Hello Young,

I am not sure if I am your intimate friend you are trying to reconnect but I would like to renew our friendship. If I recall correctly we met many years ago at a chocolate festival in Europe. Please email me at…and we can discuss further.

Regards,

André, otherwise known as Samsun (when we met).

I was surprised to receive this response and couldn't help wondering who this person was. Instead of replying immediately, I left the message for a couple of days. Throughout the course of two days, I racked my brain to remember if I had met an André at a chocolate festival in Europe? There were a number of chocolate events I had attended over the years and wasn't sure at which festival I had met this person or if I had ever met André at all. As I sat contemplating, memories of my first Tübingen ChocolART Festival came sweeping across my mind.

At The Concert

December 6th 1966 was a beautiful winter's day at Tübingen as my 3 friends and I journeyed towards Hollderlin Tower. Back then, a section of the tower was designated to showcase cultural exhibitions and concert performances while the ground floor of the building was used by the Hölderlin Society. The tower was also an office while a lower room was designated as Mr. Hölderlin's Room (a miniature museum).

Oberon had bought us tickets for a matinee concert of Mozart's Die Zauberflote, which was performed at the tower that day. I had never been to a life concert and was excited for an opportunity to attend a masterwork, within a historical setting. When we arrived at the auditorium, a small crowd had gathered. While Ludwig and Oberon greeted people they knew, Carol and his fiancé Finny came over to acknowledge our hosts. Introducing us, our friends informed the couple that Andy and I were visiting from England. Before the concert was over, we had received a dinner invitation from our acquaintances at their apartment the following evening. They had also invited several guests and a lesbian couple to celebrate the holiday season. We were delighted to accept their invitation.

Tübingen ChocolART Festival

The annual Tübingen ChocolART Festival, known to the world as the premiere chocolate event, was held at the old town center. In the winter of 1966, unlike today, there were more chocolate retailers than wholesalers marketing their cocoa products at the fair. But this did not derail the event's homey, festive atmosphere and the exquisite taste of hand crafted chocolates offered by the vendors. To me, these artistic delicacies were more enticing to look at than our mass-produced 21st century commercialized products were. Like many public festivals, this one had street performers, musicians and a great variety of activities to see and do. As the name ChocolART suggest; anything and everything to do with chocolates was represented. There were tents selling different brands of chocolates, enclosed booths set up within buildings offering chocolate messages, facials, body rubs, manicures and pedicures. Chocolate sculptures, chocolate body painting, chocolate cooking and eating contests, together with chocolate seminars, lectures, and talks were held at this expo.

There was also a Chocolate Theatre Production by the name of Chocohaar; resembling the rock musical production of Hair where nude performers danced and rolled around in gooey masses of brown sticky melted chocolates, reminiscent of bodies covered in a heap of deep s*#t. Yet the actors were happily singing and dancing on stage. I had a funny feeling they were on heavy doses of LSD as observed from a layman's point of view. Nevertheless it was 1966 going on 1967 where free love, free sex and free everything were the norm of the day. For me, it was a fun outing, painting Tübingen red or psychedelic, whichever the case.

Chocoholic's Delight

This fair was definitely a haven for chocoholics like me. I loved the varieties of chocolates available for savoring. Each vendor offered free chocolate tasting, and, as we progressed down booths, I was positively and affirmatively in love with ChocolART. As Ludwig had mentioned over brunch, this was an all-you-can-eat buffet.

When we arrived at a life-sized chocolate gingerbread house covered with berries, raisins and other delicious goodies, I was bewitched. Never had I seen anything remotely resembling such an enticing savior faire as I stood admiring this large chocolate gingerbread creation. Through the doorway of this scrumptious cottage appeared a man dressed from head to toe in white. His hair, face and hands were partially covered in a layer of flour, and he resembled a life snow man without the button eyes, carrot nose, scarf, and hat. He carried a broom, which he used to sweep the interior of this fascinating building. Seeing Oberon, he came to greet us and introduced himself as the creative baker Olaf. He was just finalizing the assembly of this edible structure when we strolled by his stall.

Wiping his hands on his apron, the man extended his hand to shake ours before plunging into a lengthy German conversation with Oberon. By the time we left Olaf's Hansel & Gretel's cottage, we had received an invitation to a chocolate celebratory party at the baker's private hangout, which our blond professor, Oberon termed as Olaf's 'Persönliche Enklave' (personal enclave). We were informed that the evening's party will commence at 10pm.

Olaf's 'Persönliche Enklave'

It was close to 11pm when we arrived at a large farm house outside Tübingen city. The parking areas were filled and disco music blared from the inside of the heated barn, specially converted into a discotheque for the evening's festivities. The 'rave' (a term I used before today's rave, an all-night raucous party, became popular) was already in full swing when we passed through the oversize doors. The building had been partitioned into a series of rooms. The large rooms had thick mattresses on the floors where party guests were already in different stages of undress, passionately entwined in varied sensual and sexual positions. Several of the mid-size rooms had queen or king size beds, already occupied by groups of three, four or five people; enthralled in the heat of passion. A handful of voyeurs mingled around, watching the unfolding erotica.

We were at a Gay SEX Party.

Wet Chocolate Wrestling

The party was in full swing. Several exhibitionists were performing their not-so-private dances on tables and service bars where beers and liquor flowed unceasingly throughout the night. The partiers, some fully clothed and others half naked, were cheering the dancers and encouraging them to discard the remaining items on their almost nude physiques.

A special room with a bathtub in the middle was the wrestling arena for nude participants to combat in a pool of gooey chocolates. Gamblers were betting on the winners and losers. The winner was the aggressor, who got to take his human spoils for his personal pleasure. The losers were the oppressed, who were subjugated to their Masters' wishes and commands.

Party Time

Another room was for human sculpturing. Anybody could participate. All he had to do was strip naked and allow buckets of melted chocolates to be poured over his body until he was transformed into a dripping brown liquid work of art. The moving artwork would than proceed to strike a variety of erotic poses while the audience cheered. Throughout the ordeal, any member of the audience could titillate the live chocolate sculpture with erotic fingering, licking and poking on any area of his anatomy. If the human sculpture felt sexually liberated, he could have his penis and or his sexual orifices worked on until ejaculation. His chocolate-covered semen could be devoured by one or a group of lickers and suckers who wished to have a taste of the sculpture's release on any part of his chocolate-coated anatomy. Upon the completion of the human art project, the sculpture could shower in two of the communal shower areas especially installed for this event, before proceeding to other areas of Olaf's 'Persönliche Enklave' for other sexual activities. The shower facilities were also sexual enclaves in and of themselves, which I will leave to your active imaginations to decipher.

Before long, Oberon and Ludwig had disappeared into the various orgy rooms while Andy guarded me like a hawk and would not let down his guard, in case I disappeared on him. This party was definitely an eye-opener for an adolescent like me. The decadent display of unbridled sexual freedom was too awesome to witness. What did I do? I took out my automatic camera and started clicking at the explicit wantonness gyrating before my eyes. Although photography was officially not permitted, I snapped away when no one paid attention.

Outside The Barn

Fascinated by the party, I longed to explore the orgy rooms to witness firsthand the sexual happenings, but Andy, my protector, would not leave me alone, afraid I might be accosted if left to my own devices. It was my Valet's honorable duty to protect my wellbeing, making sure I was safe by all accounts. Although I encouraged my guardian to explore and have some fun on his own, he did not relent to my gentle persuasions; instead, he clung to me like a Siamese twin.

A man standing next to us at the hall started a conversation with my guardian and me, but the music was deafening, so we proceeded outside the barn. Samsun was a charming 20-year-old medical student from Brussels, Belgium studying at the Université libre de Bruxelles. Like us, he has been visiting his friend Jason before being invited to Olaf's party at ChocolArt. Although Sam's mother-tongue was French, he spoke sufficient English to strike up a conversation. Jason was an archeology student at Tübingen University and was busy having fun in one of the orgy rooms. Since Sam preferred intimate encounters, he distanced himself from the sexual debauchery, waiting for his friend to finish before heading back to their apartment. By the time we left the party, a luncheon invitation two days later has been extended to us by Sam.

5

The Art of Loving

"The great difference between voyages rests not in ships but in the people you meet on them."
Amelia Barr

January 2012

Hello André alias Sam,

Thank you for responding to my message in regards to finding my friend Andy. If I recall correctly, are you the guy whom we met in Tübingen at Olaf's 'Persönliche Enklave's' in the winter of 1966? I remember you well. You were a med student in Brussels visiting your friend Jason who was studying archeology at Tübingen University. Shortly after Olaf's party we travelled together to Stuttgart, Rottenburg am Neckar and Nuremberg. Back then, you went by your middle name, Sam. It took me a while to register the name André, as I know you as Sam. Are you the Sam I'm referring to above? If you are, I do recall the times we spent together.

Tübingen To Stuttgart

It was two days after Olaf's party, and we had scheduled a lunch meeting before travelling by bus to tour Stuttgart and Rottenburg am Neckar. Ludwig and Oberon were to join us, but unfortunately they had to cancel due to urgent matters on campus. Sam was expecting Jason to join us on the tour but he was down with a bout of influenza after a night of sexual debauchery. Too much sex, drugs and rock certainly did not roll well, so he fell ill and stayed home in Tübingen. Andy, Sam and I were eager to see Germany so we hopped on an old fashion tour bus and away we went.

To Heidelberger Schloss

On the bus, Andy asked our English-speaking German guide, Logan, *"Where is our first stop? Is it Bebenhausen Abbey?"*

Sam chimed in, before our guide could reply, *"First stop, Heidelberger Schlossis (Heidelberg Castle); am I correct?"* turning towards Logan for confirmation.

Logan smilingly answered, *"You're right, wise guy! In approximately half an hour we'll be at Heidelberger Schlossis. We'll stay at the castle for an hour before departing for Stuttgart. On our return to Tübingen from Nuremberg the day after tomorrow, we will stop at Bebenhausen Abbey."*

During the journey, we got to know Sam. He was born into a family of intellectual professionals; his father was a Belgium heart surgeon and his mother a political satirist. He was the eldest of two children and his younger sister was studying at a private school in Antwerp. Without telling his family that he was gay, Sam met Jason a few months prior to our meeting while travelling in Holland. An affair followed soon. Our friend hoping to develop a deeper relationship with his fling came to visit Tübingen. Unfortunately for Sam, Jason preferred his sexual freedom to settling into a long term relationship. The Belgian was left to play out the rest of his visit alone before meeting Andy and me at the party. He was delighted to have us for company; he didn't have to spend the rest of his vacation alone. My Valet and I were glad to have Sam accompany us since we didn't want to be a nuisance to our hosts, Ludwig and Oberon during our entire stay at Das Jagdhaus. Travelling with Sam was indeed a blessing.

The moment we met Sam, I had a hunch that he fancied my lover. Since I was Andy's charge, our new friend had little choice but to accept my presence. I didn't mind if Andy and Sam were to have a sexual liaison, as I knew my Valet would not abandon me for another. Andy was too responsible to do anything dishonorable, let alone abandon his beloved charge. My immature adolescent mind reasoned, if I played my role as 'Puck' like in *A Mid-Summers Night's Dream* to hook up my lover and Sam, maybe I might feel less guilty about my secret affair with Oscar. Possibly, in some minute way, my score with Andy might be considered even. That was my limited reasoning at that young age. So I went about creating situations for them to have time alone. Unfortunately, my plans backfired and I was back to square one, feeling guiltier than ever.

At Heidelberg Castle

Heidelberg Castle was breathtaking. Since there were 8 people on our tour and Sam, Andy, and I were the only young men, we decided to explore every part of the castle ruins. In order to create opportunities for my friends I would either run ahead or trail some ways behind; hoping that Sam would seize the opportunity to break the ice with my Valet and possibly solicit a sexual rendezvous before we were due back aboard the bus.

A part of the castle was a long flight of winding stairs, which I presumed led into the castle dungeon where prisoners were kept in ancient times. Sam and Andy decided to explore the darkness. I followed behind. Although there were sufficient light at the top to see where we were going, it got progressively darker as we descended. Without telling my friends, I fell behind, intending for Sam to have his chance with Andy. Every so often my Valet would yell to check if I was alright? I responded, *"I'm right behind you."* In reality, I was halfway between light and darkness. A few minutes passed, I didn't hear noises so I presumed my friends were making out in the dungeon below.

In The Dungeon

It might be true to say that curiosity kills a cat. I plucked up the courage to quietly descend the winding stairs, to see if, in some weird way, I could witness the erotic scene I imagined unfolding below. It was pitch dark by the time I descended the steps. I had to steady myself with my hand against the stone wall. From nowhere, a hand reached out and cupped my mouth, muffling my scream. I had no idea who the intruder was! I struggled for release. Scary images of my forest assault flashed across my mind, and I thought the worst. I was again in deep trouble, and I panicked but could not free myself. Suddenly a thought flashed across my mind and I did a full-strength back kick, hitting the intruder's groin with a powerful force. Letting out a painful yell, the man released his hold. Taking the opportunity to scramble up the stairs, I fled as fast as I could without looking back, afraid my abductor might catch up. Fortunately I made it into the open and darted towards the tour bus. My heart pounded fast and I was panting for breath. Logan saw me dashing towards the bus before catching hold of me. Eager to find out why I was running like a madman he inquired if I was alright. Breathing heavily, I told him I had been assaulted while descending into the dungeon stairs.

Logan wagged his finger and said, *"You are lucky they didn't get you. There had been cases where young people had been abducted never to be seen again. Lurking in the woods are many treacherous, out-of-work illegal refugees and gypsies, left over from Hitler's war. Rumors abound of tourists being robbed and the defenseless young being abducted. These lecherous scoundrels are also dealing in illegal drugs and are slave traders. You, young man, are a prime target for these unsavory characters."*

The guide continued, *"Where are your friends? My advice is never venture anywhere on your own. It is always safer to travel with a group. You're lucky you are unharmed. From now on, stay on the bus and wait. Don't go anywhere without company."*

I was too frightened to leave the bus or argue with Logan. A few minutes later Sam and Andy appeared. My Valet was in a state of panic searching for me. Since he and Sam couldn't find me they returned to the bus to inform Logan to dispatch a search team to locate missing me. My guardian was terribly relieved when he saw me sitting in the bus and I felt safe to have him at my side again. The remainder of our time at Heidelberg Castle, I stayed on the bus with Andy holding me close.

Stuttgart

The Stuttgart Christmas Market was already busy before nightfall. The city had laid out charming displays of Christmas lights and festive fireworks to celebrate Advent. Deutschland is known to take its Christmases seriously. Every corner of the city had festive decorations, especially in the old town square where a massive Christmas Market was in full swing. There were all kinds of fun and games that catered to the young and old. For the rest of our travels I dared not leave my Valet's side in case I got abducted. Andy being more protective than usual made it difficult for me to arrange alone time for him and Sam.

As acrophobic as I was, I wanted to go on the prettily lit Ferris wheel in the center of the fair. Normally each gondola accommodated 2 people. The ticket master refused to allow the 3 of us in one capsule. So, I happily offered Sam to go in my place with my guardian, but Andy refused to leave me alone. *"If Young is not going, I will not go,"* he said. After much hustling, bustling and persuading, we came to an agreement that I would wait for them in a busy cafe where they could see me from their gondola. Andy could keep a watchful eye from afar, making sure nothing terrible would befall me. At last I thought I had finally created an opportunity for them to be together, if only for a while.

Settling into the warmth of my café seat, I looked up at the Ferris wheel, watching Sam chatting happily with my lover. A sense of self-satisfaction enveloped me. Maybe I was finally learning the Art of Loving as taught by my beloved Andy when we had our discussion at the 'Hanging Gardens of Babylon' five months earlier. *"The beauty of loving a person is to love unselfishly,"* Andy had said. I was beginning to understand the meaning of true love. My Valet had also said, *"I love you because I love myself."* In that brief moment, I loved Andy as much as I loved myself and felt an irreproachable contentment in seeing my lover's happy face way up high. The deeper I loved my protector, the more I desired him to have a superb time with Sam. That moment, I was contented to be a distant observer of a laughing couple on a Ferris wheel. I wanted Andy and Sam to be happy more than anything.

Back In January 2012

…I will be delighted to catch up with you, Sam. Did you finish medical school in Belgium? How did you end up in Sydney, Australia? Let's connect.

Looking forward to hearing from you.

Young.

With a click on my mouse, my reply to André went to his Facebook page.

6

Hello Dollies, Well Hello Dollies!

"Follow love and it will flee, flee love and it will follow."
Bernard Tristan Foong

January 2012

The following day after I replied Sam's Facebook message, an email arrived from the one and the same. Attached with his mail were several recent photographs of him. Sam aged gracefully, although a few lines marked his youthful-looking 64 year old face; he still looked as handsome as I remembered him 44 years ago. His email message read:

Hi Young,

I'm glad you remember me. Yes I am indeed 'the' Sam you mentioned in your reply. I remembered you tried hooking me with Andy, although I did not realize he was your Valet and lover at the time. You created opportunities for Andy and me to be alone but the harder you tried, the more Andy wanted you.

After our German trip, I stayed in touch with your Valet for a number of years until he moved to New Zealand. We lost touch after I was involved with David (my ex-boyfriend) in 1972. David and I were together for three years before we separated. There were several occasions I had thought of locating Andy but never did, due to my busy schedule. Back in the 70s and 80s it wasn't easy to locate a lost friend compared to the present, where facile are the norm.

I stayed in touch with Sybil and Abigail, the lesbian couple you introduced me to at the Toy Museum in Nuremberg. You remember them? You met them at Carol and Finny's dinner party in Tübingen and I believe they enlisted your design services on a collection of dolls' dresses and houses after we left the Nuremberg Toy Museum. They remember you...

Sybil & Abigail

I had indeed met the lesbian couple at Carol and Finny's dinner party the following evening after the Mozart's Messiah concert at Hollderlin Tower. In the winter of 1966, Sybil and Abigail had been together for two years and they were assisting Sybil's parents in their doll business at Balthasar-Neumann-Straße, Gößweinstein. Over dinner that evening, I had mentioned to the women that I had designed and fashioned dolls' clothing for my own doll collection. Fascinated by my youthful enthusiasm and knowledge of dolls, they suggested that Andy and I visit the Toy Museum in Nuremberg. They would be there with Carol, conducting research on historical dolls; if I was interested we could visit the museum together. I jumped at the opportunity and scheduled to meet the ladies in Nuremberg. Since I would be discussing dolls with the women, I suggested for Andy and Sam to go sightseeing. After all, I would be safe in the company of the three females. But my Valet refused to hear of my suggestion.

Andy's Command!

"No, Young! I am not leaving you on your own after what happened with the two attempted abductions. I will go with you to the Toy Museum. I don't trust you alone.

"I am responsible for your safety, so don't try to persuade me to stay away. I know what's up your sleeves; you are trying to hook me with Sam, you tricky fellow. That isn't going to happen. If anything happens between Sam and me, you will be involved in the rendezvous. I'm not leaving you out of the picture." My Valet commanded sternly.

"But, but you don't understand? Sam prefers you alone. He doesn't want me around when he is having sex with you," I argued.

Andy continued annoyingly, "*I don't care what Sam prefers or not prefer. You, my boy, are not going to be out of my sight for the rest of our trip. You are my charge and I'll have to be vigilant with you. So, young man you better skip your nonsense in playing Puck!*"

"*Andy, I want you to have a nice time. That's why I'm hooking you with Sam.*" I said meekly.

My lover looked me in the eyes before responding, "*I'm happy being with you, so don't second guess what I want or don't want. You are the person I love; I don't need to have sex with another unless E.R.O.S. duty calls for me to do so. If we have liaisons, we are in it together. Therefore, stop creating alone time for me with Sam.*

"*Don't get me wrong, I like Sam and he is a great guy. Maybe, if fate crosses our paths in the distant future, I might consider having a relationship with him. But for the present moment, I am yours unless you are not agreeable to my proposal.*"

I couldn't disagree with my lover because I loved him as much as he loved me, so I promised Andy I would let life proceed as he meant it to, and would not create situations for him and Sam to be alone again.

Hello Dollies!

Housed within the Nuremberg Toy Museum was a large section devoted to the history of dolls and doll houses. The moment I walked into the dolls' section, I felt at home. There were beautiful dolls, exquisite antique dolls, fabulous wind-up dolls, musical dolls, singing dolls, talking dolls, mechanical dolls, and, of course, Ken and Barbie dolls. There was also a basement solely devoted to ugly and scary dolls. For a brief moment, the private doll collection housed in my fairytale room came flooding into my mind and I began missing my dolls and my mother. Tears began trickling down my cheeks. Sybil saw my watery eyes and handed me a handkerchief. I had to compose myself for a minute before continuing our tour.

Sybil enquired with concern, "*Why are you crying, Young?*"

Andy replied adoringly, *"Because this sentimental fella misses home, especially his mother. He started crying inside a doll shop in Venice when we visited the city recently. I had to stop him from sobbing and banging his head against a wall."*

Abigail added, *"How sweet of him to miss his mother. I wish I could cry when I am around dolls. As much as I enjoy looking at these interesting displays, they don't bring tears to my eyes. I thought girls were moved to tears by dolls; I didn't know they have similar effects on boys!"*

Andy continued amusingly, *"Young is not an ordinary fella; he is a very unique boy! That's why I love and adore him. He is the sweetest person I know and the most sentimental by far."*

The women were smiling at Andy's comments before Carol chirped, *"Shall we proceed? I really want to check out the Barbie collections. The museum is organizing a Ken and Barbie lookalike contest. It starts in a couple of hours; maybe we should wander through the rooms before attending the pageant."*

Sybil queried, *"Where is the pageant?"*

"The brochure says it's held at the Ken and Barbie room," Carol replied.

"Let's use our time wisely and check out the various exhibition halls by categories. Who will like to join me at the Barbie section?" enquired Abigail.

The women went with Abigail while Andy, Sam and I checked out the antique dolls section before adjourning to the pageant location to watch the contest.

Well Hello Dollys!

Fascinated by the antique dolls, I took my time reviewing each display. There were dolls made during the reign of French Queen Marie Antoinette, there were genuine period costume Elizabethan dolls and a fine selection of Spanish dolls crafted during the reign of Queen Isabella of Spain. There were also military and civilian dolls produced during the First and Second World Wars.

A different section was devoted to Asian dolls. Dolls wearing elegant kimonos, dolls in traditional Chinese cheongsams, Balinese and Javanese sarong wearing dolls, Indian sari dolls to Middle Eastern dolls. There were dolls exquisitely crafted for wealthy children to adore and there were simply sewn-together rag dolls made of hemp and jute for less privileged kids.

The ugly, scary and evil looking dolls were allocated to the basement. These macabre looking creations were locked in glass cases; my guess was that the glass was psychological protections by the museum authorities to prevent evil entities from possessing these play objects. Personally I would be afraid to handle these weird-looking dolls. As Andy had mentioned, *"Young is no ordinary boy, he is a special fella."* And this special fella definitely would not design or play with scary toys such as those I saw in the museum that day, even if they were exorcised.

The Barbies

A catwalk was constructed in the middle of the Ken and Barbie room. Lots of activities were already buzzing backstage when we arrived. The separating walls made of fabric draped against a plywood backdrop and divided the contestants' male and female changing rooms. On the left was the changing area for the living 'Barbies' who were already queuing at the wings, ready to sashay down the runway. To the right were the human Kens, awaiting their cue to parade on stage. As soon as the judges took their seats, the Barbie look-alikes appeared. Displaying their outfits, hairdos, make-up, and Barbie mannerisms, they twisted, turned and posed to selected music, corresponding the era and style to the doll they were carrying in their hands. A couple of competitors wore 1950s rock and roll skirts with fitted blouses. One contestant donned a long evening gown reminiscent of Art Deco style. Another went way overboard in a Cinderella ball gown, completing the look with a fake diamond tiara similar to the one on the princess Barbie she was holding.

Carol sat in the front row, jotting down notes on a note pad as each contestant made their appearance. Curious to find out what she wrote, I asked, "What are you scribbling on your pad?"

She laughingly replied, "Besides keeping mental tabs, I like to keep written scores on contestants that best resemble their dolls. This way, I can select my personal winner regardless of the judges' decisions."

"How are you doing with your scores thus far?" I asked inquisitively.

"I loved the girl with the rock and roll ensemble. I think she is a carbon copy of her Barbie. Don't you agree?" Carol asked my opinion.

"Personally, I prefer the gal in the one-piece swimsuit and the one in the black slinky evening dress. The swimsuit Barbie looked like the doll I have at home. Maybe that's the reason I feel connected to her. If my assessment is correct, I believe Miss Slinky Evening Dress will take home the trophy," I commented.

Ken Dolls

Some of the male contestants were as cute as the miniature Kens they portrayed. The men in our entourage were more interested in the human 'Kens' than the female 'Barbies.' One person in particular, who was glad he joined us on the museum tour, was Sam, who cheered and wolf-whistled while the male competitors were doing their twirls. One contestant in particular caught our friend's fancy: a Mr. Bowtie Ken who sashayed in front of Sam and gave a flirtatious wink. Before I knew it, Mr. Bowtie had returned Sam's eye signal and chemistry flew between the two.

Before the winners were announced, Sam fidgeted wildly in his seat, rearing to proceed backstage to introduce himself to Mr. Bowtie. Seeing him in a state of anxiety, I leaned across and said,

"Calm down Sam, Mr. Bowtie isn't going anywhere. He's waiting for the results, so relax and be cool. You'll have a chance to meet him."

Sam gave me an innocent glance as if he didn't know to whom I was referring before answering, "What are you talking about?"

I smilingly said, "Your eyes don't lie. I saw you and Mr. Bowtie winking at each other."

"I was being friendly, encouraging the contestants," my friend replied.

"It's OK; you can tell me the truth. Your secret will be safe and I can be your ally if you're truthful. I might even help you when you require my assistance," I whispered in Sam's ear.

Just then, Andy asked, "What are you boys talking about?"

Sam responded quickly, "Nothing! I am just guessing which 'Ken' is going to take home the trophy."

"Oh! I know which 'Ken' is taking the trophy," I said giving Sam a wicked wink when Andy wasn't watching.

"It's either Mr. Bowtie or Mr. Necktie. Those two cuties caught somebody's fancy." I proudly announced to my friends.

The Winning Streak

Of course, my predictions were correct; Miss Barbie Slinky Dress and Mr. Ken Necktie won hands down. As soon as the contestants returned backstage, Sam shot out of his chair and headed straight into the men's dressing room, while Andy and our female friends waited for the winners to finish their photo-ops before congratulating them on a job well done.

As soon as Sam emerged from the changing room I quietly cornered him to deliver a word of advice.

Whispering into his ear I said, "Follow love and it will flee, flee love and it will follow."

"What do you mean?" Sam asked inquisitively.

"You know what I mean. Let Mr. Bowtie come to you; don't be so eager, be patient and he will follow."

January 2012

Do you remember my words of wisdom, Sam?

7

Run Baby Do Run, Run!

"Security is mostly a superstition. It doesn't exist in nature, nor do the children of men as a whole experience it. Avoiding danger is no safer in the long run than outright exposure. Life is either a daring adventure, or nothing."
Helen Keller

January 2012

I continued reading Sam's email.

"Young,

You haven't changed much over the years and you're looking as delightful as always. I wish I could provide you with further information on Andy; unfortunately I have no idea where he is. The last time we corresponded was in 1973 when he was studying engineering at the University of Canterbury in Christchurch, New Zealand. I heard from Barry Finnigan, a mutual friend of ours, that Andy was in a relationship with a guy named Toby whom he met at university. This was back in 1975 and that is the extent I have of his news. I will be happy to contact Barry to inquire if he has further information on Andy Finckenstein. When we were introduced, I wasn't surprised to find that Andy shared an almost identical last name to mine. Finckenstein and Finckensteen are popular Jewish German surnames and we did derive from similar ancestry.

Do you remember Barnaby Filip Zachausson, whom we met at the Ken and Barbie competition? The guy you referred to as Mr. Bowtie Ken? We were together for 8 months after the adventurous evening at Nuremberg Frauenkirche (Nuremberg Cathedral). You kept vigilance while Filip & I went exploring the crypts...

To Kriskindlesmarkt

Of course I remembered the adventurous evening at Nuremberg Frauenkirche. After the Toy Museum, Andy suggested we attend a late afternoon Brahms organ recital at Nuremberg Cathedral before strolling along the massive Kristkindlesmarkt (Christmas Market) located outside the church. We hopped onto two horse-drawn carriages taking us to the Cathedral of Light (Nuremberg Cathedral). It was fun riding in an enclosed carriage beside Andy. I felt like 'Cinderfella' accompanied by my prince charming on our way to a Christmas ball. Sitting opposite us were our handsome courtiers, Sam and Barnaby, who preferred to be called Filip (Mr. Bowtie Ken). Our friend had picked him up after the Ken and Barbie competition. Carol, Sybil and Abigail followed behind in a different carriage.

As the horses trotted down the cobblestone streets, an air of exuberant excitement rushed to greet me, brushing its chill against my flushed cheeks. Nuremberg was a fairytale city come alive during the festive seasons and I was absorbing the pretty sights and the melodic sounds of bells as we trotted towards our destination. It is of little wonder that many fairytale stories are set in German towns; Nuremberg was definitely a place where fantasy meets reality.

Nuremberg Frauenkirche

The Nuremberg Cathedral was a huge gothic structure. Inserted high above the main entrance was a huge clock that chimed on the hour. During Hitler's Nuremberg Rally, this was the venue where the dictator filmed his propaganda movie, glorifying Nazi troops saluting to the madman. It was inside this historical building where we attended the Brahms music recital. Part of this massive Cathedral was under renovation in the winter of 1966 and certain sections of the building were off limits to visitors. Before we situated ourselves in one of the pews for the concert to begin, I was eager to view the religious relics, icons, and stained glass windows lining the aisles of this imposing structure. Our entourage decided to take a brief tour before the recital started. As Sam, Filip, Andy, and I wandered around the church's periphery; I decided to fall in step with Sam while Andy was talking with Filip.

"How's your new beau? Do you like him?" I asked inquisitively.

Sam smiled at my boyish curiosity and said, "He is a nice guy, and I'll like to get to know him better. I hope we can spend more time together."

I replied, "You can invite him to join us to Rottenburg am Neckar; then you'll have more time to get to know him."

My friend, charmed by my comment, continued "I had already invited him to join us, but he has to return to work tomorrow. Since we only have this evening together, I want to make the most of it. Yet I don't want to appear too eager, as you advised me at the museum."

I was already scheming in my head to bring them closer together. I said, laughingly, "I can help."

"What's up your devilish sleeves, you little schemer? Tell me your crafty plans!" Sam smiled.

"During the concert, the two of you can secretly disappear into the renovation section of the cathedral and find a secluded spot to conduct your naughty business. I'll excuse myself from our group to discreetly follow the both of you and be your watchdog if anyone is suspicious of your whereabouts. I'll keep my eyes and ears open, so nobody will approach your space while you are at 'it.' I'm happy to assist the both of you if you'll accept my offer."

Finding my suggestion funny, Sam gave a loud, yelping laugh, causing Andy and Filip to turn around wondering what was so amusing. I shrugged my shoulders, smiled and pretended not to have any knowledge as to Sam's sudden outburst. As soon as they returned to their conversation, I continued, *"Don't worry, I am a good watchdog and a superb keeper of secrets. Whatever you do with Filip, it'll be a well-guarded secret. You have my promise."* I said this crossing my heart and finger zipping my mouth shut.

Sam found my pledge amusing and replied, *"You are quite the little Puck, playing the role of the devil's advocate. I'm sure you get away with murder with that naughty smirk on your face, don't you?"*

Grinning cheekily I responded, *"Well, you'll find out soon enough if you decide to solicit my assistance. I'm at your humble service."* I gave my friend a 'Puss in Boots' trickster bow, which made him laugh louder than before.

Sam gave me a sly look and said, *"OK! I'll take up your offer to go exploring with Filip while the concert is in progress. You, boy, better keep your promise and be an excellent watchdog so no one will suspect what we are up to!"*

In The Crypt

Halfway through the concert, Sam and Filip snuck out to the back of the church, disappearing into a side door within the cathedral. Making an excuse to visit the washroom, I quietly followed the men. Down the corridor I went as they progressed down a steep spiral staircase. I shadowed behind, unnoticed. Below the stairs, I saw large transparent plastic sheets covering the walls with words *Gefahrenzone Kein Zugang* (Danger Zone No Entry) printed on them. Next to the words of warning were black skull images crossed over in red paint, marking the area a danger zone.

Although this section of the Cathedral was dimly lit, it was unguarded. If not for the distant haunting organ music eliminating from the auditorium, this space would be extremely quiet. As I continued following Sam and Filip, who were nowhere to be seen, I noticed a gaping entrance between two of the plastic sheets. Venturing through the gap, I saw a series of ancient tombs encased within the walls of a large catacomb. At the far end was a series of crypts with German inscriptions etched on top of each burial chamber. Unafraid of this creepy subterranean hideaway, I tried to seek out Filip and Sam. Deep in the recess of a better lit room was an adjoining doorway; the shadows of two figures in passionate embrace danced behind the transparent drapes. Suspecting them to be my friends, I did not interrupt their intimacies. Instead I went exploring the smaller antechamber to the side.

Large wooden crates stacked on top of each other filled the entire room. The space smelled like an old basement storage facility. Walking closer to the sealed boxes, I noticed black Nazi swastikas etched onto the sides of these crates. One of the open crates had its lid pushed ajar. As I took a closer look, I heard footsteps approaching the corridor. I stood frozen, yet my curiosity urged me to peek inside the box. Pushing the cover apart, I was stunned to discover varieties of precious jewels and artifacts neatly packed inside the container. The footsteps were now approaching the direction of the chambers. Without hesitation, I quietly tiptoed to warn the lovers. They had also heard the sound and stopped in mid action. Pointing my finger towards the direction of an exit, we maneuvered noiselessly towards the opening. Just a few steps short of reaching our escape route, the overhead lights came on. Scrambling like hunted rabbits, we ran as fast as we could through the open doorway. Voices yelled at us from behind, *"Halten Sie an, oder wir werden schießen (Stop or we'll shoot)!"* Not caring to be captured, we scattered like wild rabbits scampering in all directions.

As soon as we made it out of the catacomb we rushed up the spiral staircase towards the corridors. No gunshots were heard nor fired, but racing footsteps approached in different directions. On top of the staircase, we split, scattering down two different corridors. Sam and Filip headed down one while I took another, leading to the doorway into the concert auditorium. Turning round to see who was chasing behind I saw a man in rector's garb limping and waving his cane, shouting at me to stop. Once through the arched doorway, I slapped the door shut and locked it before discarding the key into a nearby donation box.

Flustered from my great escape, I did my best to remain composed before returning next to Andy, praying I would not be recognized by the church authorities. Thank God the auditorium was nearly filled to capacity. When the recital finally drew to an end I noticed Sam and Filip had entered the church from the rear door; they relocated themselves to the back pews while catching their breaths. The three of us had narrowly escaped the clutches of the church officials. As the audience began filing out of the cathedral, I was glad to be out in the open. My adventurous escape had flushed my face a shade of red, leaving Andy tell-tale signs that I had been up to no good.

His eyes filled with intensity, he asked, *"Why are you flushed? What have you been up to and what secrets are you hiding from me?"*

"Nothing! The church is hot and stuffy I'm glad to be out in the cold," I lied.

"You are lying. You were gone for a while. Where did you disappear to?"

I did my best to appear nonchalant and answered, *"It took me a while to find the rest facility, that's why I was gone for some time."*

"Why do I not believe you? You are a terrible liar, you naughty fella. What secrets are you keeping from me? Own up, before I find out. You better own up." My lover threatened.

Not uttering a word, I smiled and ran to join Sam, Filip and the ladies, leaving Andy to puzzle over my evening's adventure.

January 2012

I continued reading Sam's email:

...That was quite an adventure, wasn't it? When Andy found out, he was furious until I intervened on your behalf. Did you tell Andy about the Nazis' stolen treasures you witnessed that night?

I moved to Australia with David in 1976 after completing my medical studies in Brussels. I have been living in Sydney since I opened my private practice in 1980. You are most welcome to stay with me and Jonathan, my partner of 8 years, when you visit Australia. Jonathan is two years younger than me and he's a chartered accountant. I'm sure he will like to meet you. Are you currently single or are you in a relationship? Let's stay in touch. It's been too long and I'd like to catch up on your news.

Be well, my friend, and stay safe!

Sam.

8

Honesty Is the Best Policy

"Honesty is the first chapter in the book of wisdom."
Andy

January 2012

After reading Sam's email, I wrote him a respond a few days later:

Hi Sam,

I am glad you emailed me. I didn't expect to connect with you when trying to locate Andy but I'm glad we did. I remember all the wonderful times we spent in Germany. Your message brought back many cherished memories. I remembered our episode at Nuremberg Cathedral as if it happened yesterday. And our visit to the Teddy Bear Museum in Rottenburg am Necker before our return to Tübingen...

Rottenburg Am Necker

Our tour bus arrived at Rottenburg am Necker old town in the early hours of the morning and dropped its passengers at the terminal. Most of the shops were not open, except for the breakfast cafes. Rottenburg am Necker reminded me of a toy town, the perfect birthplace for Pinocchio. As Sam, Andy and I sat at a charming cafe ordering our waffles and crepes, a man and a woman whom I presumed to be his girlfriend came over to chat with us. They were dying for some young company instead of talking with the retired travelers on our tour.

Nick & Sue

The man introduced himself as Nick and inquired, *"Where are the three of you from?"*

Andy replied, *"Young and I are travelling from England and Sam is studying in Brussels."*

Sue answered, *"We are from New York and Nick is my theatre colleague. We are here researching puppets for an upcoming musical production of 'The Adventures of Pinocchio.'"*

Excited to hear that they were theatre researchers, I asked, *"What do you expect to find in Rottenburg Am Necker for your upcoming production?"*

"We are fascinated by the architectural styles of old German towns and we have made progress in our research. Nick is an artist and set designer, and he's done some remarkable idea sketches for the show's sets."

I continued, *"I heard there is a well-known Teddy Bear Museum in the vicinity; will you be checking it out?"*

"Yes, we'll be there. We also have permission to visit a puppet maker's workshop," answered Sue.

Fascinated by this information, I couldn't help but blab out excitedly, *"Can I visit the puppet maker's workshop too?"*

Andy quickly added with embarrassment, *"Young, you can't impose an invitation on our acquaintance, whom we just met!"*

Nick and Sue laughed loudly before replying, *"Not a problem, Andy, we'll be delighted to have you guys join us on our visit. This young man seems very interested in our production of Pinocchio."* Turning to me, she asked, *"Are you involved in the theatre in England?"*

Before I could respond, my Valet answered, *"This fella is always so exuberant and wants to learn and see everything connected with the arts. He is quite a handful."*

Our friends continued laughing and Nick interrupted, *"He is so spirited. I haven't seen anyone that keen and excited for a while. It'll be great if you guys can join us to the puppet workshop."*

I replied with immense enthusiasm, *"Fabulous! We will be absolutely delighted! Where and when shall we meet?"*

Andy looked at me, eyes rolling as if he didn't know how to handle my impudence. Our friends noticed his gesture laughingly commented, *"Let's meet outside the Teddy Bear Museum in three hours and we'll proceed to see the puppet maker."*

Happy that I had gained an invitation to another fascinating adventure, I clapped cheerfully and yelped, *"Hooray!"* causing further laughter around.

A Teddy Bear's Panic

After a hearty breakfast, the three of us walked the old town. Since Sam didn't want to go to the puppet workshop, Andy and I arranged to meet him for high tea after our visit. The Teddy-Museum was situated off a main street and an illustrated sign of an eye-glassed old fashion teddy bear reading a newspaper welcomed visitors to its wooden revolving entrance. The museum consisted of several stories and housed a decent selection of antique teddies as well as newly crafted bears. There was a gift shop selling different sizes and types of costumed bears. From historical teddies to children's story book bears, there were teddy souvenirs, teddy knick knacks, teddy keepsakes to a variety of bear illustrations and paintings. I was impressed by the abundance of teddy bear information and memorabilia that were available. While the three of us were touring the rooms, I couldn't but feel a panic attack coming on for keeping secrets from my guardian. It was there and then I revealed my Nuremberg Cathedral great escape to Andy.

No More Lying

"Did you enjoy the concert last evening?" I asked Andy timidly.

"Yes, thank you very much for asking. Did you?" asked my Valet.

I took time to answer his question, "To be honest, the little I heard of the organ recital was fantastic."

Andy sensing I had some hidden agenda up my sleeves continued probing, "Do you have something you'll like to tell me, young man? I sense you are hiding some secrets from me. You should know that honesty is the first chapter in the book of wisdom."

As we passed an exhibit of two hugging bears, I plucked up courage and confessed, "I am a terrible liar and want to ask your forgiveness."

Andy and Sam stopped strolling, looked my direction and waited for me to speak. "Last evening, I lied about having a difficult time finding the toilet. To be honest I was acting as a watchdog for Sam and Filip (looking at Sam with guilt in breaking my promise and revealing his secret) when they were in the restricted area of the cathedral," I confessed.

Andy said nothing while Sam stared at me spitefully as I continued. "I followed them into a forbidden area below the church's subterranean catacomb."

"And?" my guardian encouraged me on. "And we were discovered and chased by several guards and a rector who threatened to shoot us," I cowered, afraid to face the consequences of my confession.

"Did the guards and rector catch you?" asked my concerned Valet.

"No, the rector was limping and couldn't catch up. I escaped." I said, not daring to tell my Valet that I locked the door and threw the key into the donation box. Nor did I dare confess seeing the Nazi's treasures hidden in the antechamber.

Andy looked at me sternly and spoke firmly, "*I leave you on your own for a moment and you're up to no good. Now sit down and tell me everything that transpired!*"

I told him as much as I dared mention with Sam listening, keeping certain details from the equation (such as witnessing the Nazi's stolen treasures and my secret longing for Oscar). Andy, angry that I ignored his explicit instructions not to go exploring alone, lectured me on unethical conduct and consistently taking dangerous initiatives into my own hands without his approval. Most importantly, he was angry with my blatant dishonesty. Since I knew I was in the wrong, I listened attentively to my lover's reprimands, not daring to answer back. Sam did his best to shoulder the blame but Andy would not hear of it. Seeing my lover's beguiled state, I conjured up my boyish charm and vowed never to wander off on my own again, especially in this dangerous country.

My protector held my hands firmly while lecturing me with concerned conviction, *"Young, you must do your best to understand that Germany is not Daltonbury Hall or the Bahriji; it is a dangerous place for a young man to be out alone, even though the war is over. You must, and I stress, you must have me with you at all times. Do you understand?"* making me promise that I would never reenact what I did.

"Yes, I understand and I give you my solemn promise." I said meekly, desiring to tell Andy the whole truth but afraid to continue. Instead I decided to seek another opportunity to confess the guilt that was consistently gnarling me with each passing day.

Sam did his best to calm my Valet's displeasure and blamed himself for getting me into this nasty puddle. Andy, not an angry person by nature, forgave me after his stern reprimanding. From that moment forward, I dared not leave his side for the remainder of our vacation. I was an obedient dog strapped onto my Master's leash. After my confession Andy would not allow me out of his sight under any circumstances.

At The Puppet Workshop

At our appointed time, we met Nick and Sue to go to the puppet maker's studio and workshop, which was within walking distance of the Bear Museum. On the door of a charming house was an un-descriptive wooden plaque with the words: *World renowned Puppeteer and Puppet Maker – Albrecht Roser.* Nick knocked several times on the brass knocker before a young apprentice came to answer the door, leading us to a sitting room reminiscent of an illustrated fairytale story book chamber. I was sure Pinocchio would feel at home sitting attentively on one of the oversized chairs, waiting for his maker to approach.

Herr Roser was a middle-aged man with a dark colored mustache. Although he was officially based in Stuttgart, he had maintained lodging and a workshop in Rottenburg am Necker, where he felt artistically inspired to craft his string puppets. Had I met Albrecht Roser on the street, I would never have guessed him a puppet maker. Appearances could be deceiving, and I was definitely fooled in those young years by images of Pinocchio's creator as a silvery, white-haired elderly man wearing thick-rimmed glasses as portrayed in Walt Disney movies and books. Herr Roser led us up several flights of stairs to his workshop; the floors below were shared with his wife and children. His family assisted Albrecht in his puppet business with an indisputable degree of puppetry excellence.

Pinocchio

Herr Roser spoke English well, but Sue, fluent in German, chose to communicate with the puppeteer in his native tongue. As Albrecht babbled about the various types of string puppets, Sue asked, *"Der Hauptgrund wir kamen, um Sie zu besuchen, soll über die Marionette Pinocchio lernen. Einschnitt und ich arbeiten an* einer Theater-Produktion 'Der Abenteuer von Pinocchio' und möchten weitere Kenntnisse der Ursprünge dieser Marionette haben. Können Sie erleuchteten uns (The main reason we came to visit you is to learn about the puppet Pinocchio. Nick and I are working on a theatre production of 'The Adventures of Pinocchio' and would like to have further knowledge to the origins of this puppet. Can you enlighten us)?"

Albrecht smiled and replied in English, "My English is not good, but I will do my best to tell the story of a little boy who told lies. Since our friends (indicating to the rest of us) don't speak German, I will tell the story in English."

As Mr. Roser related the story of Pinocchio, my guilty conscious began festering, much like Pinocchio's nose and ears growing longer and longer with each lie. As Albrecht continued to the protagonist's tail growing in length on his rear, I knew I had to come clean to my guardian. Yet, I did not want to interrupt the story teller from relating his tale, so I was vigilant and listened attentively. When he finally finished, I was 101 percent ready to confess my secrets to my lover. The opportunity arrived when we were enjoying a delightful sleigh ride below the foothills of Vaduz Castle a couple of days later.

January 2012

I continued my email to Sam:

...Did you remember how angry Andy was when I told him about our secret? Sam, you were truly scrumptious for being a trooper and stepping in to ease the situation so he wasn't so harsh in lecturing me. The episode seems hilarious, but it wasn't at the time. I must admit we had a wonderful time in Germany, didn't we?

I am in a great relationship with my life partner, Walter and we had been together for 16 years. When we visit Australia, I hope we can meet to renew our friendship and have the opportunity to meet David, your partner. If you visit Maui, you're most welcome to stay with us.

Please let me know if you have information on Andy; I will like to connect with him.
Aloha and Best Wishes!
Young.
A click of my mouse and off my email flew to Sam.

9

A Silent Confession

"As for me, to love you alone, to make you happy, to do nothing which would contradict your wishes, this is my destiny and the meaning of my life."

Napoleon Bonaparte

Mid – January 2012

During the time when I received André's (Sam's) Facebook response, I also received a message from another gentleman: a Dr. A. S. Finckenstein aged 63 residing in Frankfurt, Germany, who wrote:

Hello,

This might come as a surprise to you. I received your message enquiring whether I am your friend Andy, with whom you had lost touch over the years. I looked at your Facebook profile and am intrigued that you are a fashion designer. Many years ago when living in England I met a young man who was planning a career in fashion design. In a conversation, he mentioned that his father did not approve of him pursuing a fashion career. I cannot recall the boy's name, but I had a similar experience with my parents (now deceased) regarding my career and sexual preference. My parents, especially my father, were anti-gay. When he discovered that I preferred the company of males to females, he and my mother severed ties with me for over a decade. Thanks to my sister, my parents and I reconciled under more favorable circumstances before my father's death. The young man's story is similar to my personal experience and it stuck with me over the years. When I received your message and viewed your profile, memories of this chap returned, so I decided to write…

A Harem Boy's Saga IV: Unbridled A Harem Boy's Saga IV: Unbridled

1966/67 Vaduz, Germany

Andy rented a car to drive us from Tübingen to Vaduz to spend Christmas and Boxing Day at his parent's home. By the time we arrived at Vaduz, it was late afternoon on Christmas Eve. As we drove past the town square, a beautiful sight welcomed us. A circle of brightly lit Christmas trees greeted visitors to Vaduz with joy and good cheer. The town's signs were covered with a layer of soft powdery white, heralding neon messages of peace and goodwill towards all men.

The Finckensteins

Herr und Frau Finckenstein's cottage was situated on top of a hill overlooking Vaduz city. Fraulein Maria inherited the house from her maternal grandmother, who passed in the late 1940s, leaving her favorite granddaughter a piece of prime real estate (which the Finckenstein used as their vacation home). Every Christmas and New Year was their family's annual gathering. Andy's parents, especially his father, often asked his youngest if he had a girlfriend or girlfriends. My Valet had tactfully brushed away the questions with a smile and no definitive answers, changing the topic to subjects that did not reveal his sexual inclinations. My lover dreaded spending time at home. Ari and Aria, Andy's siblings (who were twins), often came to their brother's rescue; they interrupted their father by telling him their latest adventures and saving their little brother the embarrassment of their father's constant harassments.

Ari & Aria

Two years older than Andy, the twins frequently experienced similar premonitions and thought patterns. Both were outstanding pupils studying at Ludwig-Maximilians-Universität München. The boy was majoring in physics and she in biology. Although Andy had never admitted his orientation to his siblings, I sensed they knew without being told. They accepted Andy as he was and loved him unconditionally, unlike their dad, who wanted all his children to settle down and start a family.

Ari said he was seeing a girl from university and Aria was dating a banker gentleman, although their dates were never present at the Finckenstein's Christmas celebrations. I was the only invited family guest that year. Andy had mentioned to his parents that I was his school chum and would be spending the holidays alone because I wasn't returning to Malaya. It would be a friendly gesture to invite me to spend Christmas with his family. Little did his parents know we were lovers (or members of a clandestine society); in their eyes I was their son's platonic pal. Ari had his own room and so did Aria, while Andy and I shared a room with 2 single beds.

A Finckenstein Christmas Eve

That evening, after the family's Christmas Eve dinner, Ari, Aria, Andy and I took a stroll in the city. Since Ari and Aria hadn't communicated with their brother for over a year, we found a cozy cafe to catch up on each other's news and for the twins to be acquainted with me.

After ordering our beverages, Aria asked, "Andy, *what have you been up to and where is your friend from?*"

My Valet, delighted to see his brother and sister, said, "*I am well and enjoying school as usual. Young (looking at me adoringly when he spoke) is from Malaya. I am acting as his Big Brother, teaching him the ropes.*"

Ari asked, "*Where is Malaya?*" turning to his brother and me, "*How did you end up as a coach to this little guy?*"

Before Andy could respond, I replied merrily, "*Malaya is in S.E. Asia and it's a tropical country. There is no snow in my country, unlike the abundance you have here.*"

Not wanting to lie to his siblings, my guardian answered, *"I was put in charge of Young because I applied to the school board to be his BB. This fella is intelligent and full of zest, and I love him dearly."*

The twins smiled, looked at me and said simultaneously, *"This boy is indeed very adorable and spunky. We like him too."*

Andy & His Teddy Bear

Ari turned his attention to Andy, *"When and where are you planning for university?"*

"No plans yet. For now, I want to be with Young, and when he is ready for college or university, I'll decide what to do next. How are your studies coming along?" inquired my Valet.

His brother answered, *"I'm doing great, enjoying physics as always. Why are you so attached to this kid?"*

Aria replied before Andy could answer, *"Let me guess? Can I be honest and tell you my opinion from observation?"*

"Go ahead, Aria, speak; you know the three of us don't hide from each other. I don't have to answer if I don't want to."

"I think the both of you are lovers. I can see the sparkle in your eyes when you look at each other," continued Aria.

Andy and I smiled but said nothing. Ari teasingly chirped, *"Really! Is that true?"*

"Remember, bro, when you were 6 years old, you had a teddy bear that you adored to death; you refused to let the bear out of your sight even when it was falling apart. You cried so hard when Mum threw it out. Come to think of it, I see the similarities between the bear and Young. Admit it; you are head over heels with this boy aren't ya?" he ruffled Andy's hair as he teased his younger brother.

My lover tried changing the topic, but the twins were pursuing for answers. Neither Andy nor I admitted we were lovers, but I guessed our avoidance in answering was sufficient prove that their speculations were correct. Little did they mind their brother being gay – they were cool in accepting our intimate relationship. Andy's parents were 'horses of a different breed;' when they discovered the truth about their son's sexual preference, all hell broke loose.

Mid-January 2012

...*If you don't mind my being inquisitive, was Andy your ex-lover and you're hoping to renew your intimacies? I am intrigued to learn more about you and hope we can be friends. I hope to hear from you and wish you the best in finding Andy.*
Yours Sincerely,
A. S.

10

Yuletide Hell Broke Loose

"Your time on earth is limited; don't waste it living someone else's life. Don't be trapped by dogma, which is living the result of the other people's thinking. Don't let the noise of other's opinion drowned your own inner voice. And most important, have the courage to follow your heart and intuition, they somehow already know what you truly want to become. Everything else is secondary."
Steve Jobs

January 2010

The following day, after I received a reply from Dr. A. S.', I wrote to the stranger:

Hi Dr. A. S.

Thank you for your message, which came as a surprise. We do share similar experiences with our conservative fathers when it comes to our sexual preferences. Andy, my lost friend, also had similar experiences with his parents, especially his dad. It was difficult for their father/son relationship to rekindle and I have no idea if they made up over the years.

To answer your question regarding Andy and me being lovers, the answer is yes. During our four inseparable years, we loved each other unconditionally. We separated because of our career choices; he went to New Zealand Canterbury University, and I to fashion college in London. It was an extremely difficult decision for us to make. There were numerous instances when I regretted my decision and wished he was back in my life. But I grew through these heartbreaking periods and came into my own over the years.

I still remember that day when Andy's parents found out their son was gay...

1966/67 Cross Country Skiing

It was a sunny Christmas Day in Vaduz. After a hearty home cooked breakfast by Fraulein Maria; the twins, Andy and I decided to go cross country skiing. Arriving on a horse-drawn sleigh in the foothills of Vaduz Castle, we decided to ski back to the Finckenstein's cottage, which was approximately 3 miles south of the castle. Since Ari and Aria were avid skiers, they went ahead, opening a chance for me to talk with Andy of the issues that were gripping me hostage.

I ask, *"Are you enjoying home?"*

Side stepping my question, my Valet answered, *"It's great to take time away to enjoy our holidays together. I'm glad my family likes you, although I can't tell my parents the truth about us. On the surface they are very polite to you, but I don't know what they are thinking."*

"Your parents seem nice. I know your brother and sister are fine with us being a couple."

Andy continued with a sigh, *"There are times I want to tell my parents I'm gay, but I don't think they will take kindly to my honesty. I hate not being open about our relationship. I love you dearly and will certainly like them to love and accept you as I do."*

"I'm sure the correct moment will reveal itself for you to come clean. After all, we are here another day before returning to Daltonbury Hall. It seems pointless to stir up problematic resentment during our visit." I replied comfortingly.

"But Father pesters me about girlfriends whenever I'm home. I wish I could find the right moment to confide the truth about my sexuality, but it is none of my parents' business."

As we skied, I was figuring out how best to break my secret to Andy, so I responded calmly, *"I'm sure it will be a shocker if you confess. Maybe it's best for them to find out for themselves; then* they can decide how best to cope with the situation. You know I love you dearly and will never intentionally hurt you in any way."

Andy stopped skiing looked at me said, "Uuh, Oh! What confessions do you have to make this time? I can tell you are up to something when you start professing your love for me and not wanting to hurt me. Well, boy, what dark secrets are you hiding, you better own up Mr.!"

The Cat's Out Of the Bag

"I've been meaning to tell you the truth, but the right moment, never seems to manifest. My guilt has been festering like a sore and I can't hide it anymore. Will you promise not to be angry with me?" I finally spoke.

Andy said in a loving voice, "You know I am not the angry type and I don't harbor resentment for long. I am glad you are plucking up the courage to confess whatever you are hiding. Go on; spit it out, boy! I'm all ears. I'm listening."

With that encouragement, I told my lover the truth about my affair with Oscar. I told Andy repeatedly that I loved him very, very, much and nobody could ever replace him. He listened attentively as we slowly progressed along the ski trail, saying nothing. I kept apologizing for not being truthful, asking his forgiveness. After going some distance, my Valet stopped and spoke, "I'm not mad at you for loving Oscar. I've always had my suspicions regarding the two of you. It is noble to love, but definitely not honorable to lie. I am terribly angry with you for lying, but not for loving Oscar. Love is a noble act, but lying – lying is a dreadful sin!"

I kept quiet, lost for words while figuring how best to respond. Finally I plucked up my courage and said, "My dilemma is; I love the both of you equally. I don't know what to do! I don't want to give up either of you; I want you both in my life."

Andy broke up with roaring laughter, replied, "That's an easy solution; we can have a triplet relationship. I don't blame you for loving Oscar; he is a charming guy and since he loves you and I do too, the three of us together we can have a huge love fest. Do you think him agreeable to that? I am!"

I was caught speechless, not knowing how to respond to this unorthodox suggestion. I certainly did not anticipate such an unusual response. This was an unexpected surprise and certainly a solution to consider seriously; a solution I had never thought of before. Before I could find the appropriate words to respond, Andy continued lovingly, *"I am definitely open to loving Oscar and you; if we all agree. That way, we can be happy together without having to keep secrets from each other.*

"But you, young man, I am terribly disappointed in your constant dishonesty. This is a serious issue you must overcome. I have always told you that the truth will set you free. You can always confide in me. Let there be no secrets between us anymore, you understand?"

Feeling irresponsibly guilty, I nodded, informing my lover that I would seriously consider his triplet relationship suggestion and would have an answer for him before our vacation was over. I also solemnly promised my lover not to keep secrets from him in the future.

Yuletide Dinner

It was a tradition in Andy's German-Jewish family to celebrate Yuletide (even though they weren't Christian) with an elaborate family dinner. Fraulein Maria and her daughter had been busy preparing a delicious meal for her family that evening. Herr Finckenstein, the patriarch, was happy to have his children home and asked about their dating lives over dinner. When it came to Andy's turn, my Valet diverted the topic to other newsworthy events of the day instead of providing his father answers. Ari tactfully came to his brother's rescue, *"Dad, if Andy isn't ready to divulge any information, don't pester him about whom he is dating. I'm sure he will inform you when he is ready."*

Herr Finckenstein, turning to Andy, said impatiently, *"Son, you can tell this old man."*

A Harem Boy's Saga JJ: Unbridled

I could detect annoyance in my Valet's voice when he replied sarcastically, *"It's none of your business, dad, whom I am dating. I do not want to discuss this topic anymore,"* he turned a deaf ear to his father's further questioning.

The room fell awkwardly silent for several seconds, before Aria changed the subject to break the errie silence, *"Dessert is ready; shall we sit by the fire to have some liquor?"*

The family's high spirits returned after we retreated to the living room. Andy, tipsy from drinking the wines and liquors, started dancing with his mother and sister to the radio's dance tunes. When a piece of romantic music came on the air, my lover pulled me off the sofa and we began slow dancing cheek to cheek; while his father desperately averted his gaze with much chagrin. Although the patriarch did not stop our dancing, I could detect extreme discomfort toward his son's act of defiance. As the evening drew to a close, the siblings politely bid their parents Gute Nacht and retired to their respective chambers. Thinking Andy had securely locked our bedroom door, I fell into any intimate embrace with my lover on one of the single beds, snuggling close to his warm, muscular chest. That night I gave myself unselfishly to my lover as we consummated our love many times over, until exhaustion overshadowed our youthful bodies in a holy night of restful slumber.

The Morning After

Neither Andy nor I heard the knocking on our bedroom door until a loud crushing noise shook us from our sleep. Fraulein Maria stood, shocked and stared at our naked bodies intertwined on her son's bed. Her breakfast trays lay shattered and the contents spattered all over the carpet. For a brief moment, I thought I was dreaming, but reality soon set in. I realized my lover had not locked the bedroom door; had it been his intoxication, or had he purposely wanted his parents to discover us in bed? An answer I would never know. His mother had knocked, and, hearing no answer had pushed open the door intending to wake us gently for our respective breakfasts in our individual beds. Shocked by the sight of two naked interlocking boys on the same bed, she dropped the trays and woke the entire household in the process. Her husband and twins rushed to her aid, only to witness a naked Andy and me cuddled together. Yuletide hell had broken open its doors at Herr Egon Finckenstein home; he now bore concrete evidence of his son's love interest, witnessing firsthand a shocked and scared boy wrapped in his son's arms, face buried in his lover's chest.

"What are the two of you doing?" Egon demanded angrily.

Andy, awakened rudely by the commotion, rubbed his tired eyes uttered, *"What do you think we are doing?"* As soon as my lover came to his senses he grabbed the blanket; covering our nakedness from his parent's view.

The fuming patriarch spoke spitefully in a thunderous roar, *"Get dressed immediately and get the hell out of my house! NOW!"* He didn't give his son a chance to speak. Andy's mother pleaded with her husband not to make such any irrational decision, but the angry man refused to listen to his wife. Instead he stomped into his den, locked the door and stayed there until we left the house. The twins stood speechless, staring blankly at us. Finally Aria went over to console her mother while Ari cleaned the splattered mess.

Flashes of my clash with my father over my affair with KiWi returned with a vengeance. I knew the agony my lover was experiencing and did my best to console him with love and understanding. I quickly packed our belongings, ready to depart the Finckenstein home for good.

Dressed, Andy turned to me said, *"Let's get out of here now."*

Without further ado, I did as was told. The twins tried to persuade us to stay but their brother refused, muttering that he would not set foot in his father's house unless the old man apologized. If he couldn't accept his homosexuality, then they would never see each other again. As we loaded our luggage into our rental Volkswagen Beetle, Maria ran to embrace her son, pleading with him not to leave. Facing her tear-filled eyes, Andy said, *"Mum, I love you very much and will miss you terribly but I cannot stay after what happened. Dad obviously doesn't want us here. I will write you as soon as I return to school. I'll be in touch,"* kissing his distraught mother on her cheeks and forehead, he held my hand and led us to the car.

Ari and Aria bid us sad farewells before Ari spoke, *"Bro, I'll catch up with you in Lucerne – see you in Switzerland in a couple of days. Take care and drive safe."*

Looking in my direction, he continued, *"Young, take super care of him. He needs your support and love more than ever. Love our dearest brother. See you soon."*

On a sad note, we drove towards the direction of Neuschwanstein, Bavaria our next destination after Vaduz.

January 2012

...I hope Andy reconciled with his father like you did with yours. A number of my gay friends also had unfavorable experiences with their parents because of their homosexuality. It's a shame that there are many people who cannot live and let live or love and let love. It is my sincere prayer that men will live in peace and goodwill towards their compatriots instead of hating their fellow men because of their sexual differences.

Best Wishes to you, A. S., and thank you for connecting with me. A question; what do the initials A. S. stand for?

Regards,

Young.

My message went into cyberspace in the direction of Dr. A. S.'s computer.

11

To Love Unceasingly

"Love is like the wild-rose briar; friendship is like the holly-tree. The holly is dark when the rose briar blooms, but which will bloom most constantly?"
Emily Bronte

Towards The End-January 2012

A reply arrived from Dr. A. S. a couple of days after my response to his Facebook message. He provided his email address so we could connect on a more personal level. He wrote;

Hi Young,

I'm glad to hear from you. I am a retiree, but am affiliated with several New Zealand universities when writing my doctorate thesis in Physiology some years ago. I might be able to assist in locating Andy if you can provide me with further information to the university and department where he was studying from 1970 to 1976. I can try checking their list of alumni to see if there is information on him. I cannot promise it will be fruitful, but I can try.

*I have been following **"Initiation,"** your Facebook blog. You have blocked it with a username and password. I am not able to continue reading your memoir and I hope you can provide me access to the site. Your life is fascinating and I'd like to stay in touch.*

Like you, I have friends that fell out with their parents. Several had made peace with their families and I'm sure there are many that are going through similar experiences as ours with our parents. I am contemplating starting an online grassroots support system for folks who are going through tough times with their sexuality and their family's rejection of them being gay. It might provide solace and assistance if they have mentors to guide them to reconcile themselves and their families. Would you be interested in collaborating with me on such a project? From reading your memoir, you seem to share a positive worldview in human relationships, which would be wonderful to share with others who are experiencing difficult family dynamics. I hope you will give this idea some serious consideration. We can continue to brainstorm if you are interested.

From your descriptions of Andy, he seems an enlightened young man of 19, especially during the mid-1960s when the youth revolutionary culture and open sexual experimentations were actively prohibited. Andy seems to have had remarkable insights, and he envisioned a larger picture in human relationship dynamics. I look forward to reading more about yours and Andy's relationship.

1966/67 Füssen

Finally, Andy and I arrived at the village of Füssen and checked into the Schlosshotel Lisl (Castle from Lisl hotel), an intimate lodging for a couple in love. Andy was, to say the least, not in the best of mood that day. I did my best to provide him with good cheer along our lengthy journey. I knew full well the difficulties we had with parents, especially when we had to keep secrets regarding our involvements with E.R.O.S. Yet Andy and I were glad we had each other in our lives. With the enlightened and supportive advice from our clandestine members, we were able to cope and adjust pretty well to the demands of our teenage lives.

Since our vacation, I finally had Andy to myself, not having to share him with friends or his family. Sitting by the cozy fireplace, we required no dialogue; we were contented to be in each other's company enjoying the peace, tranquility and joy emanating from our inner beings. Nobody was present to interrupt our blissful happiness and despondent contentment.

For the first time since Andy shared my bed, we were blissfully one with each other.

Loving You Is Easy To Do

Loving Andy was natural and easy, much like well-oiled equipment churning smoothly as the gears fitted together effortlessly. After a light dinner at the hotel restaurant, we retired to our villa for a quiet evening – just the two of us. Seated comfortably in front of the fireplace, I leaned against my lover's chest as he lovingly stroked my hair with his nimble fingers. Feeling his intoxicating breath against the back of my neck, I voluntarily tilted my ear to receive his transcendent breathing, which was decisively stirring my loins to wake. Andy's closeness encased me in an aura of indescribable passion, wrapping me in a cocoon of sensuality as I surrendered willingly to my lover's gentle caresses. Before long, his sensuous tongue was nibbling at my ear lobes, sending electric currents to my arching spine. As he turned me to him, we kissed longingly, prying each other's lips open as we gave in to our intimate desires. His manliness overwhelms me still; darting chills of enraptured kisses pleasured my body, tempting me to surrender my nakedness to his alluring masculinity. Slowly but surely our love dance took flight, inhaling and releasing our life forces into the cores of our inner beings. We were inseparable; we were merging into an undecipherable entity of love.

Inside Me, Inside You

Pieces of clothing lay discarded on the floor as we moved with sensual precision to our rhythmic love tango. Andy's intoxicating scent held me captive while my unconditional love sealed our union, propelling us into blissful states of transcendent nirvana. The fiery warmth captured by our innumerable body heat took flight as we sealed our earthly bond; we were spiraling upwards to meet the heavenly Gods of Olympia. My lover needed no lubricant to slide inside me; neither did I require added stimulation to surrender to my handsome Apollo. Lustful orgasmic releases were not required to satisfy our human longings, I was happy to feel his love deep within and he was utterly delighted to bathe in my glowing warmth. Together we lay in our overflowing nectar of sweet contentment rocking ourselves into a lullaby of peaceful slumber. I was one with my beloved and he with me. United, we did not wake until the following morning. I didn't want his stiffness to leave, neither did he desire to release from my core. We stayed entangled until our hungry stomachs called to be fed. We finally disengaged, vowing to be together again as soon as we have an opportunity.

Sleigh Ride

After a delicious breakfast, we rented a horse-drawn sleigh to Neuschwanctein Castle. This fairy tale castle had forever been etched into the walls of my childhood room and my unforgettable memories. Now, I was on my way to see the original specimen located high above the alpine slopes. My fairytale dream had manifested into reality but unfortunately, due to heavy snowfall, our visit was canceled. The treacherous winding roads up the mountain slopes were closed; they were deemed too dangerous to travel. Instead Andy and I went round the foothills of Neuschwanctein Castle, en route to King Ludwig II's childhood home; Schloss Hohenschuangau (Hohenschwangau Castle). When my guardian sat snugly with reins in hand, I took the opportunity to discuss the logistics of a triplet relationship between Oscar, him and me.

Triplet Relationship

Covered in thick blankets of fur, we set off round the mountain with 2 strong black horses pulling our sleigh. As the horses trotted towards the direction of Hohenschwangau Castle, a wonderful sensation rushed over me. I was transported to the winter scene as portrayed in the famous 1965 *Doctor Zhivago* movie; where Omar Sharif and Julie Christie, wrapped in luxurious furs, rode a similar horse-drawn sleigh on the Russian steppes. For a brief moment I also imagined being King Ludwig II of Bavaria on his sleigh, gliding towards Neuschwanctein Castle, towards his fantasy sanctuary.

"*I love you.*" I couldn't help whispering to Andy as our horses trotted away.

My beloved smiled, returning a loving gaze in my direction as I continued, "*I've been thinking seriously about the triplet relationship you proposed and have questions; I need clarifications.*"

"*What do you not understand, my sweet one?*" asked Andy.

"*Can three people love one another without being jealous of each other?*" I asked.

"*Well, that depends on how loving and giving the three parties are. You see, Young, in order for this type of relationship to work; each member of the trio must be secure within himself and not feel threatened by one or the other. Oscar, you and I must love one another unconditionally and contribute our best interest to all within the triangle.*"

"*Can you provide me an example?*" I asked.

"*Let's take for instance our love making last evening; if I am with you and we are in passionate throes of intimacy, not wanting a 3rd party involvement, if Oscar loves us unconditionally, he will allow us time alone and not be jealous or demand participation in our love duet unless we invite him into our inner sanctum. Similarly if I see you and Oscar in the act of passionate lovemaking and if the two of you don't want to be intruded upon, I will retreat without jealousy, knowing full well that the both of you love me nonetheless, but at that particular moment, the two of you want to be alone* together. The same applies to you if you witness me and Oscar during our moments of intimacy.

"I understand this can be difficult for us and one might suffer the feeling of rejection. That is why I stress that the individuals must be secure in themselves in order not to feel threatened by the other two lovers."

Looking adoringly at my Valet, I commented, "You are so enlightened and light years ahead in your ideology of love. I wish I could be more like you."

Andy, finding my remark amusing, said grinningly, "My darling Young, you are the sweetest person I've ever met and I love you because you are you, and I love you no other way. In regards to being more like me, I believe you are doing just fine without imitating my philosophies. You will realize that when you love a person unconditionally, you will automatically open yourself to his happiness. The happier that person or persons are, the more joy will flow into your own life."

"How do you control jealousies?" I was curious to find out my Valet's response on this topic.

He laughingly answered, "Young one, jealousy is a choice, like all other choices. You can either change your thought patterns when the green-eyed monster rears its ugly head or let the beast control every fiber of your being. It is up to you to determine if you want to be the victim or the victor.

"Any more questions, my dear?"

I smiled contentedly, keeping quiet until we arrived at the various historical destinations we were visiting that day. One of them was the Museum of the city of Füssen. That day was one of the most pleasant and memorable experiences in my young life. I was coming into my own by just being with Andy.

Towards the end-January 2012

I continued reading A.S.'s message;

...Enclosed is my email address, please feel free to contact me. I look forward to your reply. Be well; be of good cheer and best wishes.
In regards to your question about my initials A.S., see below.
Das ganze Beste (All the best)!
Dr. Arius Sigrid.

12

Yodelling Our Way To LOVE

"Your task is not to seek for love, but merely to seek and find all the barriers within yourself that you have built against it."
Jalal Rumi

Towards End January 2012

Around the time when I was corresponding with Arius Sigrid, I also received an email from Sam's friend Barry Finnigan. I was flabbergasted to receive messages from these two unlikely sources in my quest of locating Andy. The universe had certainly opened doors when an intention is set in motion. For my intention to manifest, I'd have to allow the universal energy to flow unobtrusively. Without expectations, I wrote to Barry and Arius with an open heart. Barry wrote;

Hi Young (Bernard),

André (Sam) mentioned that you are trying to locate Andy Finckenstein, your lover at boarding school. I knew Andy for many years when we were university students in New Zealand. After graduation, we kept in touch for a number of years. At university he was in a relationship with a Portuguese Fillippino student named Toby. To my knowledge, he and Toby separated before his departure to Canada. That is the last I have of Andy's news. I haven't heard from him since 1978. At this juncture I cannot provide you with further information regarding either of them. I received a New Year's greeting card from Toby some years back, in which he enclosed his email address that I am now forwarding you. You can try emailing Toby to enquire if he has any information on Andy?

I wish I could assist further but will keep my ears open for any leads to Andy. Sam said that you guys met when you were on vacation in Europe in the winter of 1966/67...

1966/67 Hotel Chateau Gütsch

Two days later after our visit to Füssen, Andy and I drove to Switzerland on the last leg of our European holiday before returning to England to welcome the New Year with Uncle James. Arriving in the sparkling city of Lucerne, we were greeted with grace and beauty by the hotel staff at the historical Chateau Gütsch where we lodged for a couple of nights. This magnificent hotel, situated high above a hill overlooking the city, offered breathtaking views of Lake Lucerne.

Ari had arranged to have dinner with us at Gault et Millau, a fine dining establishment located inside the fancy Palace Luzern Hotel. Ari was staying with a recently married couple, Sabrina and Yann, owners of Chalet Marmont. The newlyweds were in the beauty products business. Ari introduced his friends over dinner and Andy and I took a liking to the couple immediately. They had met Ari through a mutual friend, and since their meeting six months ago, Ari had become a regular fixture at the couple's Munich home. Our dinner conversation soon drifted to the topic of the fateful morning when Andy and his father had their falling out.

At Gault Et Millau

Ari turned to Andy, asked, *"How are you coping? I know it must be stressful for you with dad being such a pain."*

Ari had obviously mentioned the episode to his friends and they were sympathetic towards Andy and me.

Sabrina said, *"You know, boys, it is difficult for parents to understand the way our generation lives. They experienced the difficult war years and their expectations of themselves and their children are vastly different from our needs."*

Yann added, "That's why we don't confide to our parents either. As long as we have a successful career and everything on the surface look rosy, that's all they care about, which is very superficial. We don't tell them anything personal other than what they see on the surface."

Out of curiosity, I asked, "What do you not tell them?"

Andy quickly chirped in, "Young, you can't go prying into our friend's personal matters!"

Sabrina found my childlike exuberance amusing and said, "This young man is so full of life. It is hard not to fall in line with his innocent ways of viewing the world." Turning towards me she continued, "I will answer your question as best I can."

"This guy is always asking the most inappropriate questions. You don't have to tell him anything. He is just a little inquisitive devil," Andy responded with embarrassment.

"It's okay; there are no secrets. Besides, I feel I already know the both of you after everything Ari told us."

Ari said immediately, "Don't worry, we are all young people and we are in similar circumstances and situations. There is nothing to hide between us, right?"

Now I was more curious than ever, so I asked, "What sort of similar circumstances and situations are you referring to, Ari?"

Sabrina, Ari and Yann laughed out loud. When Yann calmed, he turned his attention to Andy and said, "We might as well be honest with you. Like your love for Young; Ari, Sabrina and I are in a three-way love relationship. It might come as a surprise to you, but if I am not mistaken, Ari informed us you are open-minded and will understand our triangle liaison."

That indeed was a surprise to me and I was sure my Valet wasn't expecting this piece of news either. Andy, looking a little dazed, composed himself before replying, "I am rather surprised by this information. Ari never mentioned that the three of you were lovers!"

Ari answered quickly, "I didn't mention this because I didn't want father to start asking unnecessary questions. Neither did I want mum to worry unnecessarily about my sexuality. Now that you have been told, I presume you are ok with it?"

"Off course I am. Ari, you should know by now, I don't judge your sexuality, nor does it matter one way or another what your sexual inclinations are. You are my beloved brother and whoever you choose to love is fine by me. I hope you feel the same about me and Young." Andy told his brother calmly.

"Good, now we have cleared the air, let's eat." Yann said cheerfully, "Tomorrow afternoon you guys are invited to spend the afternoon with us at Chalet Marmont. We can frolic at the hot springs behind our house and enjoy a beautiful day together. How does that sound?"

A day in Lucerne

The following day we meet Ari for breakfast and took a city tour together. As we walked the famous old bridge across Lake Lucerne, Andy said, "You crafty guy, you never mentioned you were having a relationship with a married couple! When and how did it happen?"

Ari leaned against the side of the wooden bridge, smiled and answered, "I didn't tell you or sis because you might leak my secret to our parents. I don't want them to know.

"It was lust at first sight when I met the couple. They invited me to their Munich house for dinner and we ended up making love. I do enjoy their company, and our sex is great. They are open and accepting, without any trace of snobbishness, even though they come from money. Our triangle relationship is built on unconditional love."

"I bet Aria must have guessed; she knows you better than any member of our family. I'm glad you are happy."

"Maybe Aria knows, and maybe not. Either way I know you two wouldn't mind," Andy's brother replied.

My Valet said, "In many ways I am glad mum and dad know about my relationship with Young. I hate having to lie about not being gay. Now that they know, it's up to them to accept us or not. They will have to come to terms with my sexuality.

"But don't worry Ari, I wouldn't tell on you, since dad is not speaking to me anyway. If mum pries, I'll tell her to go directly to you, but I doubt she will."

"You remember when we were kids and I used to tease you about your undying love for your teddy bear? I was secretly envious of you; I wanted to be like you, to love someone or something so passionately that I would break down rather than give it up, which was what you did with your bear. When it was falling apart, you held onto it for dear life, not letting it go. Is your love for Young like the love you had for that bear?" Ari asked, looking at his kid brother lovingly.

My lover smiled before replying, "I'm afraid so. I love my young charge just like I loved my teddy bear. I hope Young and I will not separate, and if we do I will be totally devastated. It will be extremely difficult for me to forget this guy," he said, staring at me adoringly before continuing.

"I wish the best in your relationship with Sabrina and Yann. Are you planning to move in with them?"

Since the conversation was between the two brothers, I did not interfere. Instead I listened attentively on the side. "Lucerne is so peacefully tranquil. My dream is to migrate to a place where I can enjoy its natural beauty and be away from our parent's dating and marrying nags," muttered my guardian.

As we proceeded to the Dying Lion Monument before progressing up the Swiss Alps, I found myself humming the tune, the 'Lonely Goatherd' from The Sound of Music. It seemed Ari, our lonely goatherd, had finally yodeled a married couple into his life; while Andy and I were about to yodel ourselves into a triplet relationship upon our return to England and The Middle East with Oscar.

Towards end January 2012

...*Feel free to email me. I'll be delighted to hear from you. Will keep you posted if I have further information on Andy.*
Regards,
Barry.

13

The Perfumed Chalet

"To love for the sake of being loved is human, but to love for the sake of loving is angelic."

Alphonse De Lamartine

End January 2012

A thought came for me to ask Dr. Sam. I composed an email to him.

Hi Sam,

Thank you for connecting me with Barry Finnigan. He forwarded me Toby's email and I'll be writing to thank him for the information. Did you meet Andy's twin siblings, Ari and Aria during the course of your friendship with my ex-lover? In the off-chance you did, maybe you may have their contact information or know someone who has their current information? I remembered when Andy and I were in Lucerne, Ari introduced us to a married couple, Sabrina and Yann who were in the beauty business. Do you know to whom I am referring? Did you meet them through Ari?

1966/67 Chalet Marmont

After our Lucerne tour, Ari, Andy and I proceeded to Chalet Marmont to join Sabrina and Yann for a late afternoon frolic at their hot-springs. That evening, they had organized a pre-launch party to introduce a new beauty product line to a selected group of potential clients, so Andy and I brought a fresh change of clothing to the party after our swim.

Chalet Marmont sat high above a mountain on an elegant, 6-acre piece of land secluded by tall fir and pine trees. The property was circled by a long driveway leading to the main house. A guest chalet located behind the hot springs acted as a divider between the two accommodations; ensuring privacy for guests who were staying on the property. In this instance, the guest chalet was occupied by Ari. The winter sun was glowing at 4 P.M. and our host and lady of the chalet were waiting our arrival.

Sabrina

Sabrina, a tall, elegant beauty commensurate to her intelligence as a beauty product manager was also a delightful chatelaine in her chalet. She and Yann met when he was a junior executive at the beauty company where she was hired as a sales executive. Due to her business acumen, she had swept Yann upstream like a torrential undercurrent towards the corporate ladder. Now the youngest senior product promotional manager in the Swiss firm, she had persuaded her company to revamp a traditional Indian Ayurveda essential oil; repackaging the product to coincide with the latest bohemian fashion fad made famous by the Beatles' 1966 India visit. This stupendously quick-witted beauty, herself a Beatles fan, urged her company's operational executives to develop two lines of sensual products using this Ayurveda essence; rejuvenating them under seductive Sanskrit names of 'Rata' (Sexual Union/Intercourse) and 'Mituna' (Sexual Pairing/Coupling). 'Rata,' being the essence of femininity, came in the form of tantric massage creams, make-up products, perfumes, bath oils, lotions and potions while 'Mithuna', its male counterpart appeared in the form of body colognes, shaving lotions, gels plus a series of soaps and after shave splashes. Sabrina's European aristocratic ancestry did nothing to harm her marketing ingenuity; instead it provided her access to a new generation of movers and shakers in her field. The evening's party was just one of many sensually erotic sexual soirées held at well to do establishments to promote the 'Rata' & 'Mithuna' brands.

In The Hot Springs

Before long, we were frolicking in the clothing-optional hot springs at Chalet Marmont. Preposterously, the steamy hot water was sensually titillating on my naked skin even when the temperature outside was below freezing.

At dinner the evening before, Ari had mentioned to the married couple that I enjoyed taking photographs. Andy had also added that we would be embarking on a photographic project for a couple of our Arab friends when we returned to the Middle East to continue our student exchange programs. While we were swimming in the heated pool, Sabrina seized the opportunity to say, *"Ari and Andy spoke highly of your photography. I'll love to see your portfolio."*

Surprised by her comment, I replied humbly, *"Yes, I do enjoy taking photos but it's for my personal enjoyment rather than a career in photography. But if you are interested, I will be happy to show you some of my pictures when we have a chance."*

Sabrina smilingly said, *"You should take some photos of us and the party tonight."*

"Sure, I'm honored to be of service. Thank you for inviting Andy and me to spend time with you and Yann. It's pleasant swimming in these waters. I haven't swum since we left the Middle East more than a month ago," I said appreciatively.

"The two of you are most welcome to contact us whenever you are in Lucerne or Munich and stay with us. I'm sure Ari will love to see more of you as well as his brother."

With that sincere invitation, the lady swam to join her lover and husband, who were starting to fornicate by the edge of the hot tub. Obviously, our chatelaine did not want to miss any of the action as she joined the duo. Andy, drying himself from his dip, said, *"Shall I get you your camera, you little devil? I* think you might want to snap some shots of the 'Mithuna' that's about to commence over there," pointing at the erotic trio.

I replied jokingly, "Yes Sir, hand me the camera quickly so I can capture the erotica. Hopefully she will approve of my creative photography. Who knows! I might become a photographer instead of a fashion designer."

At The Party

Guests started arriving for a light dinner before the evening's soirée began. The majority of the invitees were models, movie starlets and a host of beautiful people; they were the perfect 'Rata' & 'Mithuna' target clientele. Many were continental-speaking friends of our hosts or specially invited friends of the guests, except for an Asian couple.

Since I was the only Chinese person at the party, the Asian couple gravitated towards me. Abel, a banker from Macau, and his girlfriend, Miriam, a final year art history student at the University of Paris, had been invited to attend the function by his banking corporation to speculate about whether 'Rata' & 'Mithuna' were viable products for the Asian market. Andy and I had no problem communicating with them, since the couple spoke perfect English.

Abel remarked, "There is a good turnout of beautiful people at this party."

Before I could speak, Andy responded, "According to my brother Ari, our hostess is a shrewd PR woman." He pointed his finger at Ari, who was chatting with several guests. "And Yann has a good business head on him."

Abel said grinning, "Tell me about it, she managed to drag me all the way across the ocean from Macau to this event. And I'm glad she did, because it gave me reason to visit Miriam, killing two birds with one stone." Introducing his girlfriend to us as he spoke, he asked, "Where are you guys from?"

A Harem Boy's Saga IV: Unbridled A Harem Boy's Saga IV: Unbridled

I spoke before my Valet could answer, *"I'm going to school in England and we (glancing over at Andy) are on our last leg of our Christmas vacation, before we return to London."*

"Wonderful; I will be in London for a couple of days to visit a banker friend. He works for the Hong Kong & Shanghai Banking Corporation. We have some business to discuss before returning to Macau," the banker informed us.

The very mention of HKSBC made me think of Uncle James, so I asked, *"Is your banker friend Mr. James Pinkerton?"*

Abel exclaimed, *"Yes! Do you know him?"*

"Of course, he is my uncle and guardian. We will be spending the New Year with him, before returning to boarding school."

"Superb, I'm sure we'll see you in London if you are with James. It is a small world." He laughed.

Before the end of the party the couple had become friends with my Valet and me. Years later, Abel was instrumental in introducing me to Karen, the daughter of then Governor of Macau, for me to design her wedding ensemble.

'Rata' & 'Mithuna'

The party kicked off with an erotic massage demonstration by naked models. A sexy mustached masseur began sensually messaging a blond gal while Rata's aromatic incense, candles and massage oils filled the air with exotic smells. As their sensual rubbing progressed, the demonstration soon transformed into an erotic 'happening.' Guests encouraged by this uninhibited display of sensual sexuality and intoxicated by the aromas of 'Rata' & 'Mithuna,' began turning the soiree into a metrosexual orgy. Camera in hand, I clicked away, capturing the 'Ratas' & 'Mithunas' happening in front of my lens. Enraptured by the explicit lovemaking, I snapped many interesting pictures; although I tread with caution when I photographed people. Not every guest wanted to be the focus of attention or the object of narcissistic admiration. But this exercise proved to be a learning curve, preparing me for my apprenticeship with Aziz on *"Sacred Sex in Sacred Places."* The massage models certainly did not mind me snapping their exhibitionist display of unbridled lovemaking, but the true stars of the evening went to Sabrina, Yann and Ari, although I cannot forget several other uninhibited males and females that displayed an abundance of vigorous sexual appetites. My rolls of film had since been handed to Sabrina, but I did manage to save a few pictures for my personal portfolio.

That evening was the beginning of several metrosexual sensually and sexually-charged events that I had the opportunity to attend during my adolescent years, and I was able to photograph without reservations. This photographic experience provided me the perfect place to learn the -art of photographing the human form while in the act of heterosexual, metrosexual, bisexual, homosexual or lesbosexual (a word I invented for the act of lesbian lovemaking) copulations.

By 1968 'Rata' & 'Mithuna' had achieved great success; these 2 brands were permanent fixtures on beauty counters in most European department stores until the bohemian fad faded into obscurity, making way for other dynamic beauty products in the *'Dynasty'* and the *'Dallas'* eras.

End January 2012

...*If I can locate Ari or Aria (Andy's sister) I'm sure I will be able to locate my ex-lover.*
Sam, out of curiosity; are you currently single or attached?
Best Wishes!
Young.
With a click my email disappeared into cyberspace.

14

A Happy New Year My Trusted Friends

"Mentoring is a brain to pick, an ear to listen and a push in the right direction."
John Crosby

1966/67 London, England

Two days before 1967, Andy and I were back in London from our European vacation. Uncle James had invited Andy to stay at his Mayfair home for a couple of days before we returned to Daltonbury Hall, prior to our allocation to Wazir Thabit's household in Abu Dhabi. Elated to see Uncle James after two and half weeks of absence, I eagerly introduced my lover to my guardian. Unfortunately, James' busy schedule kept us from saying no more than a few words each morning before he had to run to his business meetings, which lasted late into the evenings. When New Year's Eve rolled round, Uncle James arranged dinner with us at the Savoy so he could get to know Andy and to catch up on our news.

The day after our arrival in London, my Valet and I decided to explore the weekend art displays along Baywater Road. That morning we set off on our walk from James's residence towards our destination. As we strolled across Kensington Gardens, I noticed a familiar silhouette accompanying two women heading towards our direction. As they approached, I recognized Oscar's familiar figure, the man who was on my mind throughout my vacation. Seeing Andy and me, he ran to us and introduced his Aunt Mary and Cousin Nicola who were visiting from Wales. My BB was accompanying the ladies sightseeing and they were on their way to Covent Garden to purchase tickets for the ballet Romeo and Juliet; danced by two premiere dancers of their day, Dame Margot Fonteyn and Rudolf Nureyev.

Kensington Gardens

Overjoyed to see Oscar after two and half weeks of absence, our lingering embrace confirmed that we missed each other terribly. Andy, forever the inscrutable gentleman, extended warm greetings to my BB and his relatives. Since we were heading in similar directions we strolled across the gardens together. My Valet engaged the women in a lighthearted conversation, giving Oscar and me a chance to talk.

"*Are you delighted to see me?*" my BB enquired, "*How was your Christmas vacation? Did you guys have a nice time in Europe?*"

Gazing adoringly at Oscar, I replied, "*Yes, and we had lots of exciting adventures throughout the holidays. Did you have a good Christmas with your family?*"

"*It's always nice to spend time with my family, even though I missed you terribly, you little rascal,*" he gave my butt a slap.

"*I miss you a lot, and I told Andy about our relationship. We have a proposition for you; when we are alone we'll tell you.*" I whispered into my lover's ear so the women couldn't hear what I was saying.

Suddenly Oscar exclaimed, "*Why don't you guys join us at the ballet? We are going to the Royal Opera House to buy tickets; are you interested in seeing a ballet this evening?*"

Andy, hearing the word 'ballet,' turned around and said excitedly, "*That would be wonderful. Shall we join them, Young?*"

"*Sure, that would be absolutely wonderful! Do you think we can get tickets at this hour?*"

"Well, let's go to Covent Garden and try our luck," said a thrilled Oscar.

Luck was indeed on our side, not only did we preposterously obtain tickets, but we also paid half price for premiere seats because some folks who bought tickets cancelled and resold them at a bargain price.

Since we had time to kill before the performance, Mary and Nicola decided to head to a pub while Oscar excused himself to join us for a stroll down Bayswater Road, providing us an opportunity to talk.

Bayswater Road

We found a café to rest our tired feet after half an hour of browsing the art that was displayed against railings along the pedestrian walkway.

Oscar couldn't wait to ask, *"What is the proposition Young mentioned at the park?"*

Andy looked at me and took his time replying, *"Oscar, I'm not angry at the two of you for loving each other, as long as you treat Young with genuine love and respect. The more love we give, the better life will be, in my thinking.*

"I also know you are a marvelous person because E.R.O.S. wouldn't have selected you into the society otherwise. You already know I am also in love with this boy," looking at me before directing his gaze towards my BB.

"My proposition is for us to have a fulfilling three-way relationship. Is that a solution you may consider?"

My BB looked surprised but listened attentively. *"To put it simply, I am suggesting that the three of us love each other unconditionally without jealousies and share our love as an entity. Do you understand what I'm trying to outline?"*

Oscar looked at me, nodding to Andy's proposal before replying, *"Tell me more, so I can better understand your proposition. I'm definitely open to your suggestions, and a triplet relationship sounds intriguing."*

A Harem Boy's Saga IV: Unbridled A Harem Boy's Saga IV: Unbridled

My guardian spoke eloquently and extensively as he explained the logistics of a three-way relationship – how it could work with ease, grace and fulfillment for all parties involved. After numerous questions and answers, Oscar agreed to put Andy's triplet relationship theory into practice. Our threesome affair had begun.

At The Ballet

It was an amazing experience to watch the legendary Fonteyn and Nureyev dance. Both dancers were at their peak of their careers, and being a ballet buff I was especially mesmerized by their breathtaking performance. After the show, Oscar suggested we congratulate the dancers backstage. Since Oscar's relatives loved to drink, they set off to the Salisbury pub leaving us boys to meet Margot and Rudolf.

A crowd of well-wishers were lining up backstage to enter the dancers' dressing rooms. By the time our turn arrived to meet Margot, I was star-struck to meet the world famous ballerina. She extended her hand to shake mine as I handed her a rose which I had bought from a flower seller outside the Royal Opera House. Grateful for the gift, she reached down and gave me a kiss on my cheek. Since I had never met a ballerina of her stature and fame I was lost for words. My lovers did most of the talking and before I came to my senses, we were standing in line to enter Nureyev's dressing room. We were the last of his fans to enter. As soon as we entered his chamber, I could tell he was delighted to see us and immediately struck up a conversation in heavy accented Russian-English. His eyes were glued on Oscar and Andy the entire time; presumably hoping to procure steamy rendezvouses with my lovers; Mr. Nureyev was notorious for his promiscuity. Before our departure, Rudolf whipped several naked photographs of himself from his dresser and handed them to us. On the backs of the pictures he gave Oscar and Andy, he wrote his private telephone number. I doubt if my lovers contacted Nureyev, but one thing I was certain, they never left me the entire time of our London stay.

We met Oscar's aunt and cousin outside the Salisbury pub before I put a call through to Uncle James requesting permission for Oscar to stay with us at his Mayfair home. James was delighted to have Oscar at his residence. The following evening, the four of us rang in 1967 at the Savoy, watching a splendid firework display overlooking the Thames.

New Year's Eve

Uncle James treated us to a marvelous New Year's Eve celebration dinner at the famous Savoy Hotel. That evening provided my uncle the perfect opportunity to get to know my lovers. As soon as we were comfortably seated at the restaurant James began, *"It's so good to have you boys celebrate New Year's Eve with me. Young is always bragging about the both of you."*

My Valet replied, *"I hope he says nice things about us."*

"Oh yes, he adores the two of you and reminds me constantly that he is happy to have two 'big brothers' who love to pamper him."

Oscar added, *"Thank you, Sir for inviting me into your luxurious residence at such a short notice. I could have stayed with my aunt and cousin, but I'd rather spend time with Young, Andy, and of course Young's beloved uncle. He speaks very highly of you, Sir."*

"This boy loves to brag. I'm just doing my best to be a good guardian when his parents are not here to attend to his needs," Uncle James answered with humility. *"Since we are E.R.O.S. members, we can speak freely. I want you boys to know I care about this chap very much. He is like my son, and you guys promise to care for him and not allow him to do anything silly, stupid and or get into dangerous situations."*

Andy said lovingly, "Don't worry Sir; we will look after him well. We love this fella very much and will protect him always."

Before Andy could continue, Oscar chimed in, "We'll do our best to mentor him well. It's our duty as E.R.O.S. members to assist our charge to grow into a responsible citizen of the world."

James said jokingly, "If I find you guys abusing him, beware; I'll be after you for revenge." He laughed heartily as he dug into his delicious celebration dinner.

As we started our countdown to 1967, Uncle James looked at me adoringly, giving me a knowing wink to tell me that he liked and trusted my lovers; as we sang Auld Lang Syne with glee. My guardian's approval meant a lot to me. It was a very good start to a brand New Year.

End January 2012

A few days after receiving Dr. Arius Sigrid's email, asking me to join his gay mentorship grassroots organization, I responded to him:

Hi Arius,

Thank you for inviting me to be on your gay mentorship team. I am intrigued, and will gladly assist to the best of my ability, although I have never done anything of this nature and have no idea where or how to begin. If you have guidelines, please forward me the information. I will be delighted to give this matter serious consideration.

I am blessed to have received positive mentoring advice and guidance from a great many magnanimous benefactors in the past and present. In return, I will be delighted to do the same with those that require guidance and directions. Please keep me posted on how best I can be of service to your gay grassroots organization – I sympathize especially with young people facing difficulties with their parents or peers.

* Arius are you currently single or in a long term relationship? I'm curious.

Best Wishes,
Young.

Part Two

The United Arab Emirates - Dubai, Bahriji School.

Abu Dhabi, The SEKHAM Household.

15

A Friend In Need Is a Friend Indeed

"You cannot do a kindness too soon, for you never know how soon it will be too late."

Ralph Waldo Emerson

Rearing to go

It was good to commence classes again at Daltonbury Hall, a week prior to departure to The Oasis and shortly thereafter to my new household at The Sekham. At Daltonbury Hall, Oscar was assigned the task of Valet to a bisexual Sri Lankan boy named Srihan. The Sekham was Srihan second household and his first deployment to Abu Dhabi.

At Daltonbury Hall, Tolkien Brotherhood, Andy and I shared a room, since he was my permanent Valet while we were there for a week. The school authorities decided that it was best for us to be together, rather than relocating Andy to the Yates Fraternity's dormitory.

Oscar shared a different Tolkien Brotherhood room with Srihan and a junior named Carl, who was not an E.R.O.S. member. Classes passed by rapidly before our group of five E.R.O.S. students with Andy, Oscar, Srihan and me were flying in the school's private jet towards the Bahriji.

At Daltonbury, Oscar would sneak into our room after Srihan and Carl were asleep. The three of us would have our sexual rendezvous before the morning bells rang for classes. My BB would be back in his bed before the boys woke. It was delightfully pleasant to be sandwiched between my Valet and BB as we played, slept, woke, played again, slept and woke until we were drained of our energies. There were many perks to a triplet relationship; instead of tiring from our overheated lovemaking, we found ourselves energized, filled with vigor and intensity and ready to begin the day's classes. A good sexual appetite translates to a vigorous workout. The more sexual exercises we performed, the more alert and aware we became. The three of us were riding high, ready for our duties at our new household.

Flying High

Before our departure to the Bahriji, I had been busy with classes with no time to get acquainted with Srihan. Now on the same flight, I seized the opportunity to have a chat with Oscar's charge. Propping myself next to Srihan, I asked, *"How are you doing? Are you excited to return to the Bahriji to start your three months at the Sekham?"*

The boy kept quiet as if deep in thoughts selecting his words carefully before replying, *"Yes, I'm excited."* His answer short and non-committal.

I continued, *"How was your first Household? Did you enjoy your time and did the Household members treat you well?"*

Srihan again took his time to respond. This time his words were calculated, *"The family members were fine and I was treated well."*

I was beginning to wonder if this adolescent was truly enjoying his mission. Thinking he was tired and didn't want to chat, I didn't probe further. We sat in silence until Oscar came over to enquire how we were doing. Oscar asked cheerfully, *"Are you boys OK?"*

I replied happily, *"I'm looking forward to my new assignments and starting on Aziz's photography project."*

Looking over at Srihan, expecting an enthusiastic response, I was taken back when the boy turned his sulky face towards the window and said nothing. I searched Oscar's reaction and found my lover shaking his head as if he didn't know what to make of his charge.

"Are you okay, Srihan?" Oscar enquired again? The adolescent did not utter a word and continued staring out the window as if he didn't hear his Valet. Oscar continued shaking his head empathetically before sitting next to me. A while passed and Srihan, looking irritated, turned towards us, mumbled something inaudible, got up and went to a seat at the back of the plane. I couldn't help asking my lover about the boy's strange behavior.

Srihan

Oscar took time to contemplate, wondering if he should discuss Srihan with me. I didn't press him to continue, but after a long silence, he began, *"Young, I am not sure whether to discuss Srihan's erratic behavior with the elders at the Bahriji. If I tell you, will you promise to keep a secret until I decide what actions to take?"*

"Sure, I give you my promise. Maybe we can discuss it with Andy; he might have a solution."

"I don't want to ring any alarm bells before I'm sure my assessments of the boy are correct," answered Oscar.

"Can I assist in any way?" I asked my lover?

"I have suspicions that Srihan may be catatonic. When we met, he behaved responsibly like an E.R.O.S. Freshman. After a few days under my care, he started showing signs of strange behavior."

Looking puzzled I asked, "What sort of strange behaviors?"

"He would plunge into sulky moods like you just witnessed. One afternoon, he started throwing a tantrum accusing me of not caring or loving him. I was shocked by his behavior and tried calming him, but he gave me a disgusting look of hatred before storming out of our dorm room. I'm not sure how to handle him." Oscar said with sadness in his voice. "You know I'll do my best to take care of my charge but I don't love him the way I love you. I care and love him like a little brother and will assist him to the best of my ability."

I advised, *"I think we should discuss this matter with Andy. Now that the three of us are an entity, if something is troubling you, we should try solving the problem together. Don't you agree?"*

"You're right; I'll speak with Andy when I have a chance."

At The Bahriji

At the Bahriji, I invited Srihan to join me at a beginners' fencing lesson with Professor Lichman. Since Srihan had never fenced, I stood at the gym's periphery observing the class while the professor provided basic fencing pointers to the new students. I was the only student in attendance who had fencing experience, so Professor Richard called on me to demonstrate with him in class. As our demonstration progressed, it came as no surprise that during the moments of body contact, our intimate body language displayed sensuality, since we were lovers and had the 'hots' for each other. We did our best to keep our cool while performing our duel professionally, but I noticed Srihan's jolly mood morphing as our demonstration came to an end. Throughout class, the boy was quietly sulking in a corner.

Professor Lichman wanted to snap some pictures of his students in their fencing garb and asked Srihan and me to pose. The Sri Lankan perked up immediately as soon as he was the center of attention during the shoot. His demeanor transformed from droll to cheerfully bubbly. He basked in every minute of adoration and attention showered him by our professor. As soon as the photo session was over Srihan turned towards me in the changing room exclaiming sarcastically, *"I can't stand you! How is it that you are so bubbly and adorable? Everyone loves you and not me?"*

I was shocked at my friend's remark, wondering how to respond to such a comment. Before I could reply, Richard entered, and, seeing me naked in the shower gave me a seductive wink. Srihan noticed the professor's sexual innuendos and without a word he dressed, before storming out of the changing room in a huff; leaving us completely aghast by his display of insolence.

Richard asked, *"What's up with him?"*

"I have no idea." I replied.

Serious discussion

I did not mention to Andy the confidential conversation I had with Oscar regarding Srihan's mental condition, nor did I tell of the boy's irrational behavior at fencing class. The day prior our dispatch to the Sekham, Oscar was in our room after his charge had gone to bed. My BB finally broached the topic of Srihan to Andy.

"Andy, I think I have a problem on my hands," Oscar said.

My Valet, looking astonished, inquired, *"What's troubling you, Oscar? Tell us; your problem is our problem. We'll do our best to find a solution."*

"Srihan is acting strange and I'm not sure what to do! He had become very erratic since our arrival at the Bahriji. I don't know if I should inform our professors about his behavior."

Oscar reiterated his observations of his paradoxical charge since becoming his Valet. Andy listened attentively and when my lover finished relating his dilemma, I added, *"Srihan was behaving strangely at our fencing class two days ago. He stormed out of the changing room after Professor Lichman conducted a photo shoot of us. During the shoot, he basked in the attention showered upon him, but when Richard glanced adoringly my direction, he started sulking. His demeanor soon turned sour and he hurled sarcastic insults at me.*

"Richard and I weren't ignoring or turning our backs on the boy. It seems he enjoys narcissistic attentions and if anyone shows love or affection other than to him, he becomes extremely jealous and throws tantrums."

Deep in thoughts, Andy turned to Oscar and said, *"As much as we love Srihan, my advice is to inform the Bahriji* authorities before his personality gets out of control. It will be disastrous if he acts up when we are at the Sekham. It's best to inform our psychology professor Angelo Linberg, so the authorities can monitor Srihan's odd behavior and have a word with the boy to assist him with his problem."

We agreed that it was best to inform the Bahriji authorities and it was indeed the most helpful solution we could provide Srihan as caring friends.

Early Febuary 2012

With Toby's email on hand, I wrote to Andy's ex-boyfriend:

Hi Toby,

You must be surprised to receive an email from me. I hope this message finds you well and in good cheer. Your email was given me by Barry Finnigan, an old friend of Andy, your ex-boyfriend. Andy and I were at boarding school together and we lost contact since he moved to New Zealand. He was my 'big brother' for many years and I am trying to locate his whereabouts and hopefully resume our friendship. Are you in touch with him? If you have his contact or has knowledge of how or whom I can contact to locate him, I will be most grateful.

Best wishes!

Young.

16

The SAQR

"Every soul innately yearns for stillness, for a space, a garden where we can till, sow, reap, and rest, and by doing so come to a deeper sense of self and our place in the universe. Silence is not an absence but presence. Not an emptiness but repletion. A filling up."
Anne Le Claire

Departure

The following day, Andy and I departed on the Bahriji helicopter to Dubai airport. Unfortunately, Oscar, as Srihan's Valet, had to stay behind to accompany the boy through therapy with Professor Linberg. The Sri Lankan was under observation by the school's authorities. We were sad to bid our lover farewell, but Oscar promised to join us at the Sekham before long.

As the helicopter ascended the cloudless skies, my heart filled with gratitude for my hallowed and wise lover, and I wondered how my Valet could be so God-like in his every action, executing his assignments with such precision and grace. I desired to be as assiduous as he and longed to learn his secrets of giving without expectations.

On The SAQR

Waiting for us in a private airstrip at Dubai airport was the SAQR (Arabic for Falcon), a highly polished black and white flying machine with three golden stripes dividing the center of its elegant body. The pilot and his assistant were already firing up the engine as our helicopter descended in the nearby air field. Male and female uniformed attendants welcomed us aboard the luxurious jet. Everything within this sophisticated machine reflected the owner's elegance. Although the Wazir was not onboard to greet us, the crew performed their task excellently on behalf of their employer. As soon as our luggage was loaded and we were comfortably seated, our short journey began. I decided to ask Andy about his secret alchemy of unconditional love.

"I want to learn your secrets on how to be calm, cool and collected in the face of adversities." I said.

My Valet burst out laughing as if it was the funniest thing he had ever heard. Looking at me, he reached over and patted my head said, "Young, you are the funniest boy I know. You're like a fluffy kitten, constantly curious about everything."

Since I didn't think my question was funny, I kept a straight face, which made Andy laugh even louder. "I don't think there's anything funny about me. This is a serious question," I responded sternly.

My lover continued laughing but did not reply until his amusement subsided. Somewhat offended, I continued, "You seem to think everything I say is amusing. Why is that?"

Andy lifted my chin towards his loving gaze and replied, "My darling boy, I'm not laughing at you; I'm glad you ask me questions. That shows your curiosity in desiring to understand the mysterious ways of the universe."

My young unsophisticated mind inquired, "What does the universe have to do with you being calm, collected and cool?"

"Oh, it does in so many ways, my curious one. Everything in this universe is connected. In order for me to be calm, cool and collected, I have to remain silent and listen to the sound of silence."

"How can silence have a sound?" I asked, scratching my head in wonderment?

"If you train your mind to mindfully listen to your silence within, your heart will show you how to behave and react to every given situation." My guardian advised.

Blowing in the wind

"Is there a method to learn that which you just mentioned – to listen to the sound of silence?" I continued.

"Easy! Just be quiet and don't chitter-chatter, like you are doing now," Andy replied amusingly.

"Well, it's easier said than done. Are there other ways to hear what your heart is saying instead of not talking?"

"Yes there are," answered my lover.

"How?"

"Pause and listen to the wind, be attentive to the roars of the ocean and intensely hear the sound of the thunderous lightning," my lover advised.

I was beginning to feel an interminable conundrum because I did not understand my Valet's riddles. I wanted black and white explanations, but I didn't get the answers I was expecting, so I kept quiet.

With a Cheshire grin on his handsome face, Andy continued, *"The answers, my friend, are blowing in the wind."* I kept silent and said nothing.

The flight attendants requested that we fasten our seat belts as the plane descended into Abu Dhabi airport.

The Sekham

A posh golden Rolls Royce sat waiting for us as we descended from the jet. The chauffeur, Sa'd had gotten out of the car and held the doors open for us to step in. We had brought our leather harnesses, but Sa'd, in broken English, informed us that we did not need to don our masks on this trip. It was nice to be free of the cumbersome contraptions, but the uninteresting scenery did nothing to stimulate my creative mind. Instead, I dozed all the way. The Sekham was an hour from the airport and there was nothing in between but heat, sand, heat, sand and more heat and sand. The Middle East had always striken me as a peculiar place, because in the midst of the heated sands are pockets of oasis where lush vegetation thrives abundantly.

I was sure the Sekham and its surrounding areas were without doubt an oasis of luscious beauty. As we drove towards the palatial mansion, a Romanesque fountain in the center of a huge man-made lake welcomed us, reminiscent of the fountains in Florence which I had seen a few months earlier.

As the Rolls stopped at the porte-cochere, several manservants appeared, carrying our luggage to the guest mansion where Andy and I would be located. This expansive property consisted of a palatial building where the Master and his male entourage lived. On both sides, separated by a large tennis and squash courts, were the female quarters, housing the suites of Thabit's two wives and female relatives. A third building was home to his five teenage children. The other two buildings near the main mansion were the guest houses, each with five or six individual suites. Andy and I occupied the suite named Maktub (Arabic for Destiny).

Maktub

The Maktub was air-conditioned with a spacious sitting room, a large bedchamber, a dining area and adjoining bathrooms with spa facilities. Beside the huge bath and shower areas there was a wet and a dry sauna. Outside the bedroom was a secluded dip pool in the indoor courtyard where residents could relax in private. The Maktub was certainly more opulent than the Peacock Suite at the Kosk where Andy and I had stayed.

In our bedchamber waiting for us was Husni, cuddled like a white love ball asleep in his basket. I was beside myself with joy when I saw the Persian. It had been a little more than a month since I last saw my beloved kitty, and he had grown furrier (and larger). For the duration of our service at the Sekham, Husni was at our side even when we were travelling on assignments for *'Sacred Sex In Sacred Places.'*

We were scheduled to meet the Wazir the next morning so Thabit could introduce us to his Household members. For the rest of that day, Andy, Husni and I spent time quietly in the Maktub. The Sekham chef, Intaj prepared a delicious meal for us to savor before Andy and I retired by the dip pool to enjoy our desserts. We had dismissed our 2 personal Abds for the evening. Now it was just my lover and me enjoying a quiet evening together.

Silence is Golden

As we sat naked by the stillness of the dip pool, I could not help but ask, *"I am still curious to know your secrets."*

"What secrets, my love? I am an open book, and I have no secrets," my beloved answered.

I replied, *"You are the only person I know who is PERFECT. I want to be like you in every way."*

My beloved smiled but said nothing, putting a finger to his lips indicating for me to be silent before brushing my eyelids closed. I sat still for a while but began fidgeting. Andy laid both hands on my shoulders gently, calming my tense wiggling movements. His caring palms seemed to emanate a soothing energy onto my physique, and slowly my body quieted itself to stillness. I could hear my rapid breathing but as my lover's energy coursed through my being; my breath relaxed and slowed. A few minutes passed and I was able to stay silently still. I understood the message my lover was teaching me on board the SAQR. I was able to hear my Maktub, my voice of God.

Andy had shown me his secrets, and that night our sexual union extended far beyond the boundaries of our souls and into the realms of our personal Maktubs. We were in Oneness with each other and with humanity!

Early Febuary 2012

I had provided Dr. Arius my Andy's details for his search through his contacts at The University of Canterbury, Christchurch. A week later I received a message from the Doctor:

Hi Young,

I did some research on Andy through some ex-college friends of mine. His name was listed in the engineering department at the Canterbury University 1976 year book graduating with honors. Professor Aaron Andropov, one of his professors remembered him well and spoke highly of him. After graduation he moved to Ottawa, Canada to work for a large engineering company. Andy kept in touch with the professor for some years before losing contact. During the years when they corresponded, Aaron mentioned that your name cropped up numerous times and you were in his thoughts. Unfortunately, that's all the information I have. I have also contacted a couple of other sources, which I hope will yield further results.

On a different note; I have enclosed some guidelines of the gay grassroots organization for your review. When you have a moment, please look through the information and let me know if there is additional information you'd like to add to or subtract from the list. Changes can be made, since we are in the preliminary development stages. Your feedback is appreciated.

To answer your question, I am currently single. I was in a relationship for twenty years, but my partner, aged 69 passed from Lupus a year ago. I had come to terms with his passing. Now I have time to assist gay men requiring mentorship; I spend time lending a helping hand, an understanding shoulder and a compassionate heart to console them through difficult times. This kept me going through my lonely periods while rejuvenating my youthful vitality.

Enclosed is my picture so you have an idea who you are corresponding with.

I look forward to your response, and I send blessings to you.

A. S.

17

The Sekham Mansion

"Today a man discovered gold and fame, another flew the stormy seas; another set an unarmed world aflame, one found the germ of a disease. But what high fates my path attend for I-today-I found a friend."

Helen Barker Parker

In Court

Early next morning, our Abds prepared our baths and breakfast at the Maktub. As soon as we finished eating, a manservant led us to our appointed venue to meet Wazir Thabit. He was in the midst of a tennis game with his physical trainer and business partner, Gabrielli Marciano Castrogiovanni. I did not recognize the Wazir, who wore a polo shirt and shorts. At our previous meeting he was dressed in a traditional Arabian thobe and headdress. Gabrielli, a good looking athletic Italian, spoke perfect Arabic and English besides his mother tongue, Italian. Aziz was seated under a shady umbrella drinking Turkish coffee, observing the game while waiting for Andy and me to arrive. As soon as the match was over, the two men came over to join us. We stood up to greet them and they gave us friendly nose rubs (a traditional Arab greeting). The manservant in attendance brought our beverages before the Wazir spoke, *"It is good to see the both of you. Did you guys have a nice vacation?"*

I replied politely, *"Yes Sir, Andy and I had a marvelous holiday and I'm ready to commence Aziz's photography project."* I didn't know if it was appropriate to mention the project's name, in case the brothers did not wish the Italian to know the nature of our collaboration.

"Very good; my personal assistant had done some research and when we return into the house I'll fill you in, after your morning's tutorial with your teacher, Gabrielli." Aziz answered.

I was surprised to learn that the Italian was my Sekham's professor, so I kept quiet when Gabrielli spoke. "You didn't expect an Italian tutor, did you?" He continued, "I am Thabit's business partner and I'm also his children's foreign language tutor. The Wazir had apportioned me to meliorate foreign students who are assigned to the Sekham. I'm so happy to meet you."

Thabit added, "This man is an excellent educator; he is very knowledgeable in international affairs and an honorary graduate from Cambridge University in international finance. I managed to convince him to be my business and financial consultant. Young, you're in good hands."

"We'll start daily tutorials from 9 A.M. to 1 P.M., except Holy Fridays. The remainder of the afternoons you are free to pursue your personal interest and projects. I believe Aziz will be keeping you busy with "Sacred Sex In Sacred Places?" My tutor commented.

The weather was getting hot, so we proceeded inside the main house.

Preparations

We assembled in a large living room in the main mansion and waited for our host and his partner to shower before our introduction to the Household members. I could hear dissonant noises and a cacophony of the Arabic language in an adjoining room while Aziz filled us in on the latest development regarding his photography project.

The Arab was the first to begin, "My assistant, Tahu, had made some contacts with a few props construction companies in America. Two of them are interested in working on the 'Sacred Sex In Sacred

A Harem Boy's Saga VI: Unbridled A Harem Boy's Saga VI: Unbridled

Places' construction project. We are waiting for their bids to arrive. A company is based in Los Angeles and the other in Las Vegas."

Andy inquired, "Once the company is selected, do we travel to America to meet with the construction team or will they come to see us here?"

"Once we finalized the confirmation, we'll decide on the next move. With Thabit and Gabrielli's involvement, it's likely that the Italian will be our representative and spokes-person for the project. Young can continue his private tutorials while we are circumnavigating the globe," Aziz announced.

"Who will be teaching Thabit's children when the professor is away?" I enquired

The Arab, smilingly, said, "Don't worry about my nephews and nieces; they attend regular Islamic schools besides their foreign language lessons and tutorials with Gabrielli. The Sekham's governor will hire a temporary teacher to substitute him when he is unavailable."

The Sekham Household

As soon as the Wazir and his partner entered the living room, the Sekham Household procession began. Much like the march of the Siamese children from *The King & I*; the youngest boy, Jasim, accompanied by his nanny, conjugated into the room followed by Mais, the boy's older sister. Behind Mais was Naira, similar in age to her half-sister. Then came the Wazir's teenage son, Sayid, and finally the last of Thabit's children, Sabiya. Marching behind the kids were the Wazir's wives, Zeba and Ula. I guessed the women's ages to be between 29 and 33 years at most. Although they didn't wear burkas, they wore hijabs and kabayas that were considered modern for Middle Eastern women in 1967.

The household agglomeration of eight males and fourteen females filed into the living room and I could not recall most of their names. I had no problem remembering the names of

Thabit's relations, as they were in daily classes with me; their mothers accompanied them regularly.

When the entire Sekham household members had assembled in the room, the patriarch formally introduced Andy and me. If Oscar had been available, he too would have been introduced with his new charge. Unfortunately, Srihan never made it to the Sekham. A week later, Oscar arrived at the mansion with an Indian boy by the name of Devaj whom I nicknamed Vaj. We became friends.

Thabit informed his household that Andy and I were foreign students on a mission, learning Arabian culture and the traditions of their country. We would also be assisting Aziz with his project since we were interested in photography; he omitted the nature of our assignment. They queried no further when the meeting adjourned.

The Tour

Photography by us, foreign students, was not permitted at the Household. For security reasons, unauthorized photography of the property would be confiscated by the Wazir, unless his permission was granted to the photographer.

After our Household introduction, Gabrielli offered to show us the property before I commenced my private tutorial with him. The Sekham covered many acres, and we took our time to cover the grounds. As per Islamic tradition the women's quarters were off limits to male visitors. My tutor led us through the main building, the children's quarters, several guest suites and the recreational facilities. He explained, *"When I arrived at the Sekham, I couldn't find my way around the property. There are many chambers and I wasn't sure which were forbidden or allowed entry. It took me a week to become acquainted with the various chambers."*

Andy asked, *"How long have you been stationed here?"*

"Close to three years. I met the Wazir when we were at a business conference in Geneva. I was a speaker at the event. Thabit

was looking for a business and financial consultant to replace Makmud, his previous assistant, a remarkably intelligent man, who now works for The Prince."

My Valet continued, "How did you end up being a teacher? Isn't looking after the Wazir's businesses and investments a full-time position?"

"If I organize my daily schedules with precision, I can always find time for other pursuits. A passion of mine is education of the young. Besides dispensing my experiences to them, I also learn valuable lessons from my students." My professor answered.

I asked, "Is your family staying on the property?" I automatically assumed that my tutor was married.

"I'm not married; that's why I can travel and follow my destiny without emotional commitments. I go whenever and wherever I'm required."

I was curious about him. I asked, "Don't you get lonely if you don't have a companion or a family?"

Gabrielli replied smilingly, "There are plenty of vibrant people to keep me occupied in this household, and there is never a dull moment in this premise. You'll soon discover that for yourselves. Besides, I enjoy spending time with the Wazir and we work and play well together."

As we continued the tour, I noticed several occupied guest suites, which Gabrielli suggested we not visit. Housed on the roof of the main building there was an Olympic-size pool and a well-equipped work-out facility located by the water's edge. Besides my regular studies, the Italian was also my physical trainer, coaching me and his other students three to four times per week.

Three large comfortable day beds surrounded the rooftop swimming pool deck. These were used mainly for the Wazir's business soirées and private functions, which there were many. I like Gabrielli Marciano Castrogiovanni. He was a funny, educated and an intelligent man. I knew I would learn much from the Italian and my wisdom expanded greatly under his tutelage. Andy also liked Signor Castrogiovanni like I did.

First Week Of Febuary 2012

A reply arrived from Dr. Sam after I inquired if he had Ari or Aria's contact information. He wrote:

Young,

You are in luck. I spoke with Carol, who has Aria's email and postal addresses. They met at a social function in Munich in the mid-70s and had kept in touch over the years. She received a Yuletide card from Aria a couple of years back with her contact information. Unfortunately she has to dig through her pile of old correspondence to locate this information. If she finds Aria's addresses, she will forward them to you. She's married to a banker and was residing in Gothenburg, Sweden.

I met Ari at his university campus in 1972 while I was working on my research paper. We were introduced by a college professor. In one of our conversations, I mentioned traveling to Germany in 1966 with a young gay couple. The older boy, Andy, was the younger Asian's BB. Ari realized the Andy I was referring to was his brother. After completing my research paper we stayed in touch for some time before losing contact.

You asked if I am single or in a relationship. I am seeing Gary, a nurse who works in my clinic. It's an on and off relationship for the past two years. To answer your query; I am sort of attached but also single. I am open to dating if you know any guys you'd like to introduce me to. LOL!

Are you in a relationship?

I will inform you if I hear from Carol. Meanwhile stay healthy and let's keep in touch.

Sam.

Xoxo

18

A Game of Thrones

"Round about them will serve boys of perpetual freshness."
Koran 56:17

The Sekham's Children

Classes with Gabrielli were enjoyable. The company of Thabit's children was equally delightful. Although the youngest boy Jasim was shy, he was extremely clever in the art of being a trickster. He often played kleptomaniacal games with us. Our possessions would miraculously reappear, just when we thought them lost. We always knew Jasim was the culprit, but he usually got away with the crime by displaying his innocent boyish look. He pretended he did not know what we were talking about; behind the cute façade, was a crafty prankster.

Mais and Naira couldn't be more different than night and day. Mais, a few months older than her half-sister, was shy, genteel and quiet. She was the epitome of a habituated obedient female, following a code of strict regimented Arabian customs. Her family predicted that one day she would become a faithful wife in an arranged marriage, bearing many children and being scrupulously subservient to her husband. Mais was the kind of girl whom male Arab traditionalists would describe as a 'perfect' wife.

Naira was the exact opposite of Mais. She had ambitions of her own. She was a witty, clever and an educated scholar. She longed to free her country's womenfolk from the confines of traditional Arab male dominance, which had been firmly ingrained within their religious faith. She was a modernist, a feminist conforming to no one but herself. This was a dangerous proposition in 1967 United Arab Emirates.

I became pals with Sayid because we were both spunky, inquisitive, and adored exploring uncharted territories. Since we were nine months apart in age, our interest lay mainly in living and experiencing life. Sayid, an intelligent boy, was constantly on the move to the next adventure. He was the eldest male heir to his doting father and was his uncle Aziz's favorite nephew. Beside these privileges, he was also next in line in the Sekham's hierarchy. Spoiled beyond redemption, the world to Sayid was a playground. And played he did. Much like his relative Ubaid from the Kosk Household, he too was destined to be a playboy of the Arab world.

Sabiya, the oldest of the siblings, like any young teenager, was blossoming into a beautiful young woman. She was conscientiously suffused with a bubbling personality. Being her father's favorite daughter, Sabiya was every inch a well-bred 'Princess' of the Wazir's castle. Rightly so: she could do no wrong in her father's eyes, since she was fresh as a rosebud blooming in her prime. Unbeknownst to her dearest daddy, she already had eyes for a foreign male, which I was sure her strict religious faith would not lend her a nodding approval. Most young people in love saw love through rose-tinted lenses; Sabiya was no exception to the rule. For the moment she was happy as a lark without stress or worries. Her carefree attitude attracted many suitors to her daddy's 'Kingdom'. On the one hand, Thabit was a happy father, seeing his eldest daugther mature into a charismatic young woman, but on the other, he was worried about unsuitable beaus manifesting like buzzing flies in his 'Kingdom' in hope of plucking his favorite rose.

The Summon

A few days after I had settled into the Sekham, I was surprised to meet two new additions to the household. They were a young Belgian girl, Anya, and her accompanying older 'big sister,' Dominique. They were introduced to Andy and me by the Sekham's governor, Wadid. Since Anya was in Gabrielli's class, I became acquainted with her rapidly. Usually, the girls had their tutorials separate from the boys, but once a week we had our meetings with our teacher together.

One day Aziz had an Abd informed us that we were required at his suite. The Arab was already in his sitting room, awaiting our arrival. As soon as the Abd served our beverages, Aziz began, *"I'll jump straight to the point. The bids from the set construction companies arrived this morning and both are similar in price. After discussing with Thabit and Gabrielli, we decided to solicit the services of both companies. The elaborate sets will be constructed in Los Angeles. I had an idea to use the Grand Canyon as a back drop. The props for the Canyon shoot will be made in the U.S. for easy transportation to location.*

"Next week, both companies will be sending their representatives to meet with us. I will keep you posted on the days when they will be here, so you can attend the meetings together. We'll most likely be meeting at my studio."

"That's splendid. We are available anytime. I didn't know you have a studio at the Sekham!" Andy commented.

Aziz replied, *"Not many household members know I have a photography studio on property. I prefer to keep it private so I can work without disturbance. Thabit had renovated a couple of guest suites as my work space and a dark room to develop my films."*

I asked, *"Will we get to see your work space and dark room?"*

The Arab said, *"Very soon; I'm planning a photo-shoot with Oscar's charge, you and another boy."*

"Who is the other boy?"

"You'll find out soon enough," answered the man. *"There's another thing I like both of you to do."*

Andy and I waited for our host to continue, *"I'd like you to entertain my nephew, Sayid. He's too shy to ask you guys directly."*

"How can we assist the young man?" My Valet asked.

"Will you take him under your wings like Oscar did with his former charge, Pi? He likes some male company, especially boys around his age. He told me he likes the two of you, but was embarrassed to approach you directly. Since I am his uncle, he asked me to speak to you."

Andy replied, "Of course. We'll be happy to take him under our wings. He can come see us anytime."

"Good, I will send him over this evening and he can stay the night at the Maktub. I think he is lonely and wants company," Aziz requested.

"Sure, he's welcome to stay the night with us," my guardian agreed.

"I'll have him come at 6 this evening. I'll tell Intaj to prepare a light dinner for the three of you. You guys can spend an entire evening together. He'll be delighted with the news." Aziz said appreciatively.

Entertaining Sayid

At the appointed time, there was a knock on our door, and standing outside the Maktub was Sayid. The bubbly boy was not as shy as his uncle had made him out to be. Over dinner he asked, "My father told me the both of you are from the Bahriji School. What's it like? Oscar told me a little about the school but I am curious to know more."

Andy responded, "It's like a regular western type school for foreigners instead of Arab boys like you."

"As much as I like going to Islamic school, I would also like to experience a foreign school's educational system."

Not desiring to give too much information to the lad, my Valet answered, "You can learn foreign subjects at the Sekham with Gabrielli. He is an excellent tutor; don't you like his teaching methods?"

"Yes, I do like Gabrielli's tutorials, but I've heard the Bahriji teaches more than regular subjects. I would like to learn those subjects," the boy said slyly.

Andy glanced at me conspicuously, wondering if the boy knew more than what he led us to believe. I asked, "What kind of subjects are you referring to?"

The boy smiled imperceptibly before replying, "Like the things the two of you do in private. I like to learn those subjects and be excellent at 'IT.'" I could hear the capital letters in his voice when he said 'IT.'

"If you are good, maybe we'll educate you in some of the 'IT' techniques after dinner," replied my Valet jokingly.

"I'll be good; rest assured. I am eager to learn the methods you'll teach me. Oscar and Pi taught me some valuable techniques when they were here. I'm not a first timer in the art of lovemaking."

A Game of Thrones

After dinner Andy suggested we play a game of hide and seek within the Maktub.

The rules of the game:

a) The seeker shuts his eyes without peeking and counts to 50, while the others hide.

b) If the seeker finds the hiders within 10 minutes, the seeker will require the hiders to remove an item of clothing.

c) If the 10 minutes are up and the seeker cannot find the hiders, the hiders get to remove an item from the seeker.

d) The loser is the person with nothing on.

e) The winner or winners will have the loser or losers perform a task of the winner's choosing.

I was left wearing my birthday suit within the next forty minutes, with Sayid coming in second, in his briefs. Andy had won.

Sitting by the edge of the dip pool with his legs dangling in the water Andy demanded his reward, *"Young, get in the pool and put your face between my crotch and inhale deeply."*

Defying my Valet's orders I playfully refused his demands and started running away naked, screaming and giggling around the suite until caught by my lover and Sayid. They tickled me unrelentingly, sending me into fits of giggles and laughter as I struggled to free myself from their forceful clutches. Kicking and screaming, Andy carried and threw me into the dip pool before plunging in. Continuing their playful torture, we elapsed into uncontrollable laughter and were sexually aroused by this Childs' play. Andy pinned me to the side of the pool and began grinding his crotch against my backside, while holding my hands spread eagle against the tiles. My lover, excited by my mock chastity, rubbed his hardness against my wiggling bottom, simulating thrusting motions. His erection was straining for release from his soaked underwear.

Sayid, excited by this domineering foreplay, leaned forward, planting his sensual lips on mine, prying my mouth open with his probing tongue, stirring my sexual desires to surrender to his urgent kisses. As he held onto my slender waist, I felt my lover's throbbing manhood, grinding against my buttocks under the splashing aqua. Sayid lifted himself off the pool, sat astride and cradled my head between his spread legs. Before I had time to inhale, the boy's throbbing hardness was jamming down my throat. I expertly suckled and lapped at his length, enjoying the rough treatment forced upon me by both Masters. Lifting his boyish bottom off the pool's edge, the Arab pushed my head onto his pulsating length, feeding its hardness into my mouth, claiming his winner's prize in our Game of Thrones. My lover, aroused by my submissiveness, was pounding my buttocks with abandon. Choking and gulping for air I savored the wild deliriousness, fed from the front while surrendering my rear to my demanding lover. I had gone to Allah's paradise, not desiring to return anytime soon.

That evening at the pool we took turns playing our nimble Game of Thrones, changing partners and positions until the wee hours passed midnight. We cuddled in comfort and contentment in each other's embrace, on the King, before peaceful slumber fell upon us. *Ahh!* The beauty of young love.

February 2012

A week after my email to Toby, a reply arrived from Andy's ex-boyfriend. It read:

Hi Young,

I was surprised to hear from you. It took me a while to realize who you were. It is nice to hear from you. Andy had told me many wonderful experiences you guys had during your teenage years. As you are aware we had broken up many years ago when he left for Canada. I did visit him in 1982, while he was still single living in Ottawa. The last time we corresponded was 1983 when he met a Hong Kong boy named Chocolate. Andy said they met at a summer camp in Vancouver.

Since he was busy with his new lover our correspondence became distant and through the grapevine I heard they broke up two years later. Andy then returned to Germany to be with his mother, who died of Leukemia in 1986. That is the last I have of Andy's news.

I am now in a long term relationship with my partner of 12 years. Andy was a loving partner, but we parted ways due to inconceivable differences in our lives. He spoke of you often; that's why I remembered you when your email arrived. If I have further information on Andy, I will keep you in the loop.

All the best!

Toby.

19

In the Olive Garden

"Passion makes the old medicine new: passion lops of the bough of weariness. Passion is the elixir that renews: how can there be weariness when passion is present? Oh, don't sigh heavily from fatigue: seek passion, seek passion, and seek passion!"
Rumi

Oscar's Arrival

Oscar's arrival with Devaj to the Sekham wasn't without fanfare. That weekend was Jasim's birthday celebration and the boy's father had organized a catered party for 150 guests at the Sekham. Thabit had invited relatives, friends, business acquaintances and elders from his religious institution to this special occasion.

This elaborate Islamic coming-of-age celebration was like a Jewish Bar Mitzvah. I was quite sure the young initiate would soon be forwarded to Oscar, Vaj, Dominique and Anya for male and female sex education or be directed to Andy and me for male-on-male tutelage, as Riqz had been at the Kosk.

About Srihan

It was wonderful to see Oscar after a week's absence and we had news to catch up on. That afternoon after his arrival, Andy and I invited our lover and his new charge, Devaj for lunch at the Maktub. We were eager to find out what happened to Srihan and be acquainted with Vaj. During lunch, Andy said, *"We are glad the both of you are here. We were beginning to wonder if you were going to appear."*

"You know I'll arrive come rain or snow. Or rather, come wind or sand in this instance," our lover laughed.

Eager to know what happened to Srihan I asked, "What happened to Srihan after we left? Pray tell."

"He went to therapy with Professor Lichman for several days. Apparently, being the only child in his family, his parents showered full attention on him and gave him everything he wanted. This excessive spoiling made him crave for more attention and when he was ignored; he turned resentful and spited whomever he thought had not given him sufficient affection.

"After much probing, Dr. Lichman discovered his parents had sent him to an English boarding school because they could no longer control his catatonic behavior. They hoped Daltonbury's Big Brothers would guide their son back to 'normal' behavior."

Andy continued his enquires, "Didn't the school know his problem before accepting him into E.R.O.S.?"

"Apparently not; the parents did not disclose the matter to the school. They were afraid that Daltonbury would refuse their son's application, so they kept it a secret." Oscar replied.

"Didn't his previous BB inform the school's authorities of the boy's erratic behaviors?" My Valet asked curiously.

"He didn't act up during observation because John (his BB) was giving him undivided attention, so he behaved excellently throughout the observation period. The authorities thought him a good E.R.O.S. candidate."

I added, "What's going to happen to Srihan now?"

"When I left the Bahriji with Devaj, he was on his way back to Daltonbury Hall. I guess he will be undergoing treatment at the 'Rabbit Hole.' I'm sure our headmaster will be talking with his parents regarding their son's behavior," Oscar explained.

"I hope he'll recover soon. I hate to see him go through life with this condition. He won't have any friends if he behaves in this weird manner." I said.

"Let's pray for his speedy recovery from this psychotic ailment. He is a nice person and I wish him well," my BB sighed.

Devaj

Over dinner we got to know Devaj. He was a direct descendant from the last Maharajah of Jammu and Kashmir. His family fled to England, enrolled Devaj into Daltonbury Hall, and he was selected into E.R.O.S. without his parents' knowledge. I nicknamed the boy Vaj. He was a pleasant soupçon of coquetry. This was his 3rd household service and he was having a ball. Oscar had been assigned to him three days before flying to the Sekham. My BB was also interested to learn more about his new charge.

Andy was the first to enquire, *"You seem like a 'Fancy' boy!"* He was referring to the red flower Vaj had in his shirt pocket.

Vaj laughed and replied, *"Nothing 'Fancy' about me, but I like to look spiffy. The flower in my pocket is my signature style."*

"Well then what are your other signature styles?" continued my Valet.

"Just because I wear a flower in my pocket, don't take me gay. I prefer females," Vaj affirmed steadfastly.

"With a rose sticking out of your pocket I'm sure you are NOT GAY. Oh! I'm sorry I misjudge your sexual preference," teased a smiling Andy, *"You could have fooled me."*

Before Vaj could reply, Oscar jokingly chimed in, *"Yeah, yeah Devaj, we know you are as straight as an arrow. But arrows do fly opposite directions sometimes,"* he teased his charge.

Vaj defended himself humorously, *"I assure you this arrow only flies in one direction."*

"OK! We believe you, Vaj. Time will tell which direction you fly," I joined in the tease.

"Time will indeed tell. You wait and see," our friend replied with firm conviction.

"Indeed we will!" Andy chirped.

During our three months at the Sekham, time indeed told us which directions Vaj flew. And flew he did, in all directions.

The Celebration

The birthday boy dressed in white descended the grand staircase with his proud father to the festive sounds of drums and gongs, followed by clapping friends and cheering relatives. The party had begun. The large dining table was laid with fabulous edible goodies, welcoming guests to dig in. Like most major Islamic celebrations, the presences of religious clerics were de-rigueur, especially in the initiation of a boy's coming-of-age, and Jasim was no exception to the rule. Unlike Riqz, who was circumcised in his early teens, Jasim had been through Khitan (Islamic circumcision) in his 7th month out of his mother's womb. This was a celebration to officially announce to the Islamic community that he was ripe for the picking. Jasim, the boy, was now Jasim, a man.

A Secret Rendezvous

Besides Jasim's Muslim classmates, his sisters' friends were also invited to partake in this joyous occasion. As the celebration progressed into the evening, I had to excuse myself from Andy to use a rest facility. As I tried finding a vacant washroom (which seemed to be constantly occupied), I decided to return to the Maktub to use our private toilet facility. While passing the gravel car park jammed full of sports cars, I noticed a couple of shadows flitting into an empty courtyard between the quiet guest chambers in the Maktub outbuilding. I followed.

In the cloud covered moonlight I trailed the mysterious shadows, which disappeared into an olive garden. Camouflaged behind an olive tree I spied on the couple. A man and a woman whispered softly in the darkness. I couldn't make out who they were but when the crescent moon reappeared, Thabit's eldest daughter and a man whose back was turned my direction were in passionate embrace. Fascinated by this scenario, I watched unmoved, even though my bladder was dying for release. Before long her veiled head was bobbing back and forth in front of her lover's crotch. I could no longer hold my urgency and urinated at my hiding place.

If it was the sound of my urination that stirred the lovers to disentangle, I would never know. Before I could stuff my trickling penis back in my pants, the lovers were scampering in different directions. Under the silvery moon Sabiya ran, and so did my teacher. The sweet teenage Arab girl was caught tasting the forbidden fruit of a thirty-seven going on thirty-eight-year-old Italian man of distinction. Though shocked by what I had witnessed, I had no desire to jeopardize the passion between the lovers so I made up my mind to keep this a secret. I did not report to Andy or Oscar and certainly not to the Wazir of what transpired within the olive garden.

February 2012

I was corresponding with Arius and my email read:
Hello Dr. Arius,
Hope this email finds you well. How's your gay online organization coming along? I looked through the materials you forwarded and made some comments and suggestions. Please view enclosed attachment for details.

Thank you for Andy's information. You mentioned you had other connections which may produce further results to his whereabouts. Are there any developments on those fronts?

If you are planning a trip to Maui, I like to extend an invitation for you and a partner to stay at our home. My partner, Walter, and I will be delighted to offer our hospitality. Our accommodation is by no means opulent but if you don't mind a modest lodging, you are most welcome at our humble abode. It will be nice to meet you in person and learn more about your online project.
Aloha!
Young.

20

A Forbidden Sharia

"Knowledge has to be improved, challenged, and increased constantly, or it vanishes."
Peter F. Drucker (1909-2005)

The Summon

One morning while Andy and I were having breakfast at the Maktub, an elegant white envelope lined in black arrived on a silver platter, bought to me by one of our Abds. Inside was a gold embossed hand crafted card. It read;

Thank you for taking Sayid under your wings. He is pleased with your tutelage and will like to continue his lessons for the duration of your stay at The Sekham.(signed) H.H.

Folded between the card was another note summoning me for a photo shoot at Aziz's studio, that same afternoon after my studies with Gabrielli. Enclosed were two cheques for the amount of US$2,500.00 one addressed to Andy and one to me.

At The Studio

At the appointed time of the photo shoot, an Abd collected Andy and me to go to the studio. Oscar and Vaj were already waiting in an adjoining room. We were told by Tahu, the photographer's adherent assistant, to wait in the lounge. The apprentice had been under Aziz's tutelage since graduating Islamic high school. Tahu's ambition was to own a photography studio. Although the young Arab was a hard worker, a creative thinker he was not. One of the reasons Aziz solicited my service was to brainstorm unorthodox methods of photographing his subjects. Besides being a model on this shoot, my host had also given me free rein to photograph the models. With the two of us photographing simultaneously, Aziz and I managed to polarize a number of unique photographs. It was proper protocol that the pictures I took belonged to Aziz especially at his photography exhibitions; my pictures would be credited in his name. This arrangement suited me since I wasn't expecting accolades as a distinguished photographer. For me, it was an ingratiating gesture and I was simply delighted to have the opportunity to learn from a professional.

Photo-Shoot

The third model joining Vaj and me was none other than Sayid. Surprisingly, Aziz's nephew was an uninhibited poser and did well in front of the camera. Vaj, like any Bahriji recruit, was a natural exhibitionist, and between the three of us, the photographer snapped a fair amount of excellent pictures of us together and as individuals. Since Oscar and Andy were not required, they waited for their charges in the living room adjacent to the studio. As with most wealthy U.A.E. palatial homes, the Sekham boasted a well-stocked library which Andy, an avid reader, had borrowed a book from and was now reading; Oscar watched the photography session.

The Perfumed Garden

It was dinner hour when the shoot finally wrapped. While Aziz stayed in the dark room developing the films, Sayid, Vaj, Oscar, Andy and I returned to the Ruba'iyat, Oscar and Vaj's suite, located next to the Maktub. Most evenings, our dinners were brought to us by our Abds and we often ate in private. This evening we gathered for dinner at the Ruba'iyat. We sat in the living room waiting for our meal to arrive; Andy, engrossed in his book, was being anti-social. I decided to lure him out of his reading trance to talk.

A Harem Boy's Saga IV: Unbridled *A Harem Boy's Saga IV: Unbridled*

"What are you reading that is so interesting?" I inquired.

Andy feeling irritated answered capriciously, "An educational book." Insensible to my question, he continued reading.

Vaj added, "Enlighten us and share the book's intrigues?"

Sayid chirped, "Yes, tell us, we want to know the contents."

Lowering the book to his lap Andy looked up said, "Are you sure you want to know?"

We replied in unison, "Yeah! Tell us."

"The name of the book is Al-rawd al-'âtir fi nuzhati'l khâtir, and it was written in the 16th century by a Muslim scholar and poet by the name of Muhammad al-Nafzawi. In English it means The Perfumed Garden of Sensual Delight and it is an Arabian sex manual."

Oscar said teasingly, "No wonder you are so engrossed, is it filled with naughty pictures?"

Andy replied testily, "This is serious literature. You mustn't make fun of it."

I asked, "Enlighten us; why is it so philosophical and beguiling?"

"Ok, I'll continue if you are truly interested. It's a mélange of sexual what and how to dos. It is also interminably lengthy so, not to be a bore, I will read excerpts from it."

Sayid answered impatiently, "Hurry and read! We don't have all night."

On Homosexuality

"I'll read you the poem on homosexuality:

"O the joy of sodomy!
So now be sodomites, you Arabs.
Turn not away from it--
therein is wondrous pleasure.
Take some coy lad with kiss-curls
twisting on his temple

and ride as he stands like some gazelle
standing to her mate.
A lad whom all can see girt with sword
and belt not like your whore who has
to go veiled.
Make for smooth-faced boys and do your
very best to mount them, for women are
the mounts of the devils."

"What do you think guys?" inquired my Valet.

"My, oh my! How sacrilegious!" Oscar hawed.

I asked curiously, "I thought Islamic law forbade homosexuality. Wait, let me rephrase; under religious Islamic law isn't any form of sexual enjoyment and freedom forbidden and outlawed? How did the author get away with such erotic writing?"

On Heterosexuality

Andy, ignoring my question, continued reading a different passage, "LEARN, O Vizir (God's blessing be upon you), that there are different sorts of men and women; that amongst these are those who are worthy of praise and those who deserve reproach.

"When a meritorious man finds himself near to women, his member grows, gets strong, vigorous and hard; he is not quick to discharge, and after the trembling caused by the emission of the sperm, he is soon stiff again.

"Such a man is liked and appreciated by women; this is because the woman loves the man only for the sake of coition. His member should, therefore, be of ample dimensions and length. Such a man ought to be broad in the chest, and heavy in the crupper; he should know how to regulate his emission, and be ready as to erection; his member should reach to the end of the canal of the female, and completely fill the same in all its parts. Such a one will be well beloved by women."

Oscar, as curious as I, said, "Okay! Ehm, ehm...I get the idea. Clearly, al-Nafzawi had significant experience and an active imagination. Good for him."

Vaj joined the discussion, *"In India, sex is not a taboo, but a celebrated jubilation. That's why we have the infamous Kama Sutra. It is strange to me that there is so much repressed sexuality in this part of the world."*

On Bisexuality

Sayid added, *"Our Sheikh preaches sharia, but behind closed doors we live differently. My father advised me that I can do whatever I desire, as long as I don't bring harm to our family. When in public we behave with morality and follow the Hadith Qudsi, but in private we do otherwise."*

Vaj questioned, *"Aren't you living a double life with double standards? Is it problematic for you to follow such strict codes of conduct?"*

"This is definitely an expository debate that can continue forever," Oscar advised. *"This can be our after-dinner discussion."*

Andy added, *"Let's not over-intellectualize the topic. As far as I am concerned, as long as you've come to terms with and accepted your personal sexual preference or preferences, what people say, do or rules and regulations imposed by men don't matter. As long as no calamitous harm is inflicted on another fellow being, it doesn't matter to me if you are heterosexual, bisexual, homosexual or any other sexual. If God didn't want the humans to be sexual beings, than he would not have created us as such, would he?"*

"I can't agree with you more," I championed my Valet's viewpoint.

Just then, our Abds brought our dinner. Without further discussion we dug in, eating to our heart's content and filling our hungry stomachs with nourishment. As far as I was concerned, food for the intellect could wait.

February 2012

An email arrived from Carol, the lady friend with whom Andy and I became acquainted in 1966 when in Germany. Dr.

Sam had forwarded her my request for Aria's contact addresses and Carol responded:

Hello Young,

I was glad when Sam informed me he had heard from you. How are you my friend? Are you still designing dolls' clothes? I continue to be an avid Barbie doll collector. Since 1966, my doll collection has grown enormously. Two rooms in my house are now filled with Barbies. I'm sure you'll be impressed when you visit.

Sam mentioned you are looking to contact Aria. I received a Holiday card from her a couple years back. She and her husband were living in Gothenburg, Sweden.

Enclosed are her latest email and postal address. These are the only addresses I have of Aria, unless they moved since 2009. Good luck and I wish you the best in locating Andy. Stay in touch; it's been a long time since we connected.

Regards,
Carol.

21

Bring in The Bacha Bereesh

"A wise boy kisses but doesn't love, listens but doesn't believe, and leaves before he is left."
Bernard Tristan Foong

Batcha

A few days after Aziz's photo-shoot I received a card from Wazir Thabit, brought to me by an Abd. The message read: *"The Wazir requests your company to perform at a special party for his friends and guests at The Grand Salon."* Written on the card was the scheduled date and time I was to be present. I showed the invitation to my Valet and he advised, *"You are summoned to be a 'batcha' (Persian meaning 'dancing-boy')."*

I asked spontaneously, *"What is a 'batcha' and what do I have to do?"*

Andy smilingly replied, *"You are requested to dance at the party. A batcha is a dancing boy."* He paused before continuing, *"Remember when you were at the Bahriji and attended Professor Mark Jobeck Arabian folk dance classes? Now is the time to apply your dance skills."*

"What else am I expected to do at the event?"

"Be yourself and dance. It is an inherent tradition in the Arab world to have 'bacha bereesh' (Persian meaning 'beardless boy') perform on special occasions. This is an all-male event, and if the men like your dancing, they will shower you with Bahraini dinar

(Abu Dhabi's 1967's currency). The money is a gratuity for your performance." Andy advised.

"What am I supposed to wear at the performance?" I inquired.

"Your Abds will supply you your performance clothes. Traditionally, the batcha wears female clothing but I doubt you'll be expected to wear girls' clothes. In the Emirates, they prefer their batcha to look like a bacha bereesh instead of dressing like a girl as they do in Afghanistan.

"You'll most likely be asked to provide Bacha Bazi (Persian meaning 'boy play' or 'playing with boys') for some of the Wazir's guests in private. Rest assured you will be rewarded well," my guardian continued.

"Can I refuse Bacha Bazi if I don't like the person?"

"Of course you can. I'll teach you some polite refusal techniques which will not jeopardize your good graces with the guest or embarrass the Wazir." My Valet replied.

The Guests

The main mansion was filled with guests and their expensive vehicles the evening of the party. Although there were women present during the dinner thoroughfare, when the plates were cleared they adjourned to the women's quarters for an evening of female entertainment while the men were left to their habitual partying. The guests were predominately men, which is the norm with most Arabian parties. There were approximately forty men and the majority held important government positions or were wealthy merchants and entrepreneurs. Impeccably groomed and dressed either in traditional Arab clothing or in authentic bespoke suits, these were the movers and shakers of the U.A.E.

When the last woman departed The Grand Salon, the men inevitably became bawdier and more brazen; as alcohol flowed freely, so did the smoking of hookahs, irrespective of the Islamic faith. Live musicians played while Vaj and I were prepped by our personal Abds for our batcha performances.

Bacha Bereesh

As the music grew louder and the men grew bolder, Vaj was ready to take center stage. Since he was a little older and more experienced than I, he mixed traditional Indian dance styles with Arabian folk techniques. The Indian swirled and twirled like a professional batcha to an audience of rowdy applause and cheers of wolf whistles. As his dancing progressed, he began disrobing without hesitation while his admirers showered Bahraini dinars at him.

My friend was authentically invigorated with the excitement surrounding his performance. Pleased with the accolades, he soon stripped down to his briefs while men stuffed and threw money at the dancer boy. The music soon ceased and Vaj was panting from his invigorating performance while guests bid for the privilege of an evening with this beardless boy. Being an experienced dancer, he charmed his suitors with seductive winks and smiles throughout the dance. Deliberately flirting and teasing his high-priced bidders, my friend proved to be, without doubt, an expert batcha in the eyes of his admirers.

The Dancing Queen

When my turn arrived I was pathologically nervous, wondering how in the world I could outdo such a remarkable performance as the one I had just witnessed. Although I had performed ballet in public, I was unfamiliar with Arabian dances especially in front of a group of impudent men. One thing I was certain; I wanted to be as good as Vaj if not better. The music commenced to the sound of joyful clapping and I knew I was off to a good start. Fear evaporated as soon as I began moving and shaking to the sound of music. I danced, danced, and danced as if there was no tomorrow. I shimmied like I did at The CLUB to whistling cat calls and men screaming for more. Unlike Vaj, who was eager to strip down to his underwear, I took time to tease and seduce. I remembered the words of Professor Andrew Henderson, my Bahriji art of seduction and flirtation teacher; his advice, *"Tease without over zealousness, seduce without blatancy and keep your devotees desiring more."* Gyrating sensually and seductively, my determination as a provocateur garnered synchronized applauds and incendiary reactions from the maniacal crowd. *Oohs* and *aahs* came from bona-fide horny men craving for more; instead I gave my admirers a show without revealing too much. This, to me, is the imperceptible art of burlesque. Contrary to Vaj's showy brassiness I offered an alternative temptation: a stratospherically classic fantasy bolstering the seduced to hunger for more.

By the end of my performance I had collected the equivalent of US$7,000.00 as compared to Vaj's 1,200.00 BHD (approximately US$3,000.00), with six bidders vying for my company. I had no idea who the guests were and had no clue who my highest bidder was. All I knew was an Arab bid 5,650.00 BHD (approximately US$15,000.00) for an evening of my company. I was the happiest batcha at the party, delighted to be desired and cherished. I didn't care who my bidder was.

Bacha Bazi

Contrary to the Bacha Bazi of Afghanistan, Vaj and I were not sold as slaves, nor were we destitute orphans auctioned to the highest bidders. We loved dancing and loved the adoration showered upon us. Neither were we polarized into granting sexual favors against our will. If we granted sexual favors, we did it because we agreed to. My compadre and I were neither raped nor abused, because if any of these illegitimate acts were inflicted upon any Bahriji students, the

Enlightened Royal Oracle Society would hold the hosting Household accountable, terminating their membership and blacklisting the Household from ever participating in the secret society. Strict rules and regulations applied to our Household Masters and their entourage that required our services; no harm was to befall any foreign students under their hospice. Our respective Valets were our twenty-four seven body guards.

To the Highest Bidder

The men who bid on Vaj and me cast ballots in an adjoining room located next to The Grand Salon. Although the bacchás (from the Persian bacheh بچه "child, young man") were auctioned to the highest bidder, we did not know who the bidders were. The only thing I knew was that the Wazir's guests were wealthy, powerful and good-looking men whom I had seen during my performance. Although I had the privilege to refuse my bidder's sexual advances, I would also have to forfeit my gratuity if I chose not to accept. Spending a night with a good-looking stranger without strings attached and a US$15,000.00 reward was reason enough for my highly charged libido to crave for sexual intercourse with my generous benefactor. What better way to offer my gratuitous services to a sexually experienced gentleman? I, for one, was delighted to oblige.

My Bidder & I

By the time the guests bid our host farewell, I was soaking in a luxurious bath at the Maktub. Andy, entering our bath chamber, announced that my highest bidder had summoned me to his suite. He was an overnight guest at Al Fayoum, a guest suite in the Sekham. Accompanying me to Al Fayoum, my Valet said, *"I have a prognostication that your highest bidder is of Royal decent."* Before he could continue, we had arrived at the chamber's large wooden entrance.

A burly Arab gentleman answered the door. Directing us into the beautifully decorated living room, he told us to wait as he proceeded to inform his Master of our arrival. A suave man in his early 30s entered wearing a white bathrobe. In perfect English he greeted Andy and me before leaning across to give my Valet a traditional nose rubbing salutation. When it came my turn, a whiff of eucalyptus greeted my nostrils as he lowered his nose to mine. What transpired next was beyond my comprehension; my bidder was tickling my nose with the tip of his tongue before savoring my delicate lips; tantalizing my boyish naiveté towards his masculine musculature. At once enchanted by the smell of fresh eucalyptus and intrigued by his beguiling protocol, I was breezed by such forwardness and at a loss for words. Releasing me, my bidder showed us to a comfortable sofa before he took the loveseat opposite my guardian and me.

He said smilingly, *"Young man, you're an excellent dancer. Will you be my 'private dancer'?"*

I thanked him for the compliment and kept silent, not knowing how to respond to his request when he continued, *"What's your name?"*

Before I could reply my guardian spoke on my behalf, *"His name is Young, your Highness."*

Stunned by my Valet's royal address I looked at him speechless while he continued, *"Sir, my charge is at your service. Shall I leave the two of you and wait outside?"*

My bidder spoke arbitrarily, *"Stay! I'll like you to do me a favor."*

Andy answered, *"How may I be of service, your Highness?"*

"Oh, you don't have to be so formal. Address me as P, I know you are looking after Young and the Wazir told me the two of you are lovers. I like to watch you make love to this baccha. It'll arouse me greatly," announced the Arab.

Before Andy could respond, P motioned me to sit by his side. Sitting close, he bends towards my neck and inhaled my adolescent aroma deeply, as if savoring the sweetness of a newborn. Whispering softly in my ear he uttered, *"Ahh! The intoxicating beauty of youth as described by the prophet: 'Round about them will serve, to them, boys (handsome) as pearls well-guarded' (Koran 52:24)."* Gently nibbling my earlobes he eased his thirsty lips down my neck before sinking in his pearly fangs as if drawing delicious nectar like a honey bee. Intoxicated by my Master's vampire guise, shocks of electric currents vibrated down my arching spine; I willingly offered my bacchá innocence to this erotic aristocrat for his inerrant enjoyment. French kisses filled my urgent provocation as his desires rendered me helpless, and Andy's tantalizing riposte replaced my bidder's sweet attraction. Laying me on the loveseat, P's obsessive glare stirred my uninhibited longing for my lover's unbridled manhood. Willingly I surrendered to my lover's sensuality before his consecrated erection encased me in a cocoon of sacramental love. Our glowing auras merged into a halo of sexual unity, bonding our sacred Eucharist, igniting a fiery passion of unimaginable bliss and filling our bodies with flowing essence of milky love. P the voyeur, sat enamored, watching a love story unfold that was as old as the creation of man.

Seduced by our tantalizing nakedness, my bidder dared himself to enter our homoerotic realm – a realm that defied time and space and only Divine Providence was left to forfeit active participation. Nothing but our lustful releases could satisfy our overwhelming genital hunger; when the cocks crowed treis, we savored our afterglow from the rising sun. This Bacha Bazi was a splendid reminder of Mario, Andy and me floating on a private gondola in Venezia's Grand Canal. I was already infatuated with my bidder before morning broke.

A Harem Boy's Saga V: Unbridled

22

Work & Play

"The three great essentials to achieve anything worthwhile are: hard work, stick-to-itiveness and common sense."
Thomas A. Edison

February 2012

On one hand, I was reluctant to write to Aria. It had been too long and I had boxed my emotional feelings for Andy, tucked our beautiful and heartbreaking memories into a tiny compartment deep within the farthest reaches of my heart, never intending to reopen the wounds except as a remembrance to the wonderful times we shared. Now I had unconsciously opened Pandora's Box while in the process of writing my memoirs. Besides cherishing our loving relationship, it had also unscrupulously released my broken heart to regrettable memories I had forsaken into the recesses of my active mind. The first couple of years after our separation were diabolical hell, which I finally managed to banish into harrowing storage. Now, I was faced with a very real possibility of connecting with the man I loved and still love, after forty two years of separation and non-communication. What am I to do? To write or not to write to Aria, requesting Andy's current information? That was the looming question I continuously asked myself.

1967: The Representatives

The 'Set Building' company representatives from Las Vegas arrived at the Sekham where Aziz had organized a meeting at a conference room adjoining his photography studio. Thabit, Gabrielli and Aziz were present together with

Andy and me. Tahu was busy acting as our gofer whenever documents and plans were required and brought to the conference table during our discussion with the two Americans, David and Eli. The men had flown from Las Vegas on the SAQR (Thabit's private jet) and were staying a couple of days at the Sekham before returning to the United States. Since it was their first visit to Abu Dhabi, Gabrielli, our hospitable spokes-person suggested we show the Americans the city. Andy and I were invited to join the entertaining entourage.

As our meeting progressed, detailed photos of actual locations were requested by the Americans for the set designs. Aziz was the first to comment, *"That's not a problem; we can supply detailed photographs. When do you require the pictures?"*

"If you want this project to commence immediately we'll need them as soon as possible. We brought all the necessary contracts for your signatures," answered Eli, the business consultant of their construction company.

Gabrielli replied, *"Give us a couple of days to review the documents and we'll finalize the contract before you leave our country."*

Andy asked, *"How long will it take to build the sets?"*

"That will depend on the number of sets and the degree of complications encountered during the construction process? Usually it takes a month to two to complete a medium size project, from the time we receive the provided architectural pictures and renderings." David answered.

Thabit turned to his brother and suggested, *"Today is Thursday, why don't you and your entourage leave for Europe the following week and photograph the sites for the set builders to commence the project at the soonest? Which sacred site do you plan to photograph first?"*

Suddenly I burst out exclaiming, *"Rome! I suggest we photograph the interior of the Vatican since it's the seat of the Roman*

Catholic Church; that's if we are starting with the Christian holy sites. Rome seems to be the ideal venue to commence the shoot, don't you agree?" I was surprised at my own outspokenness in such a serious business meeting.

"That's a great idea! Rome is my hometown and I know Vatican City better than the back of my hand. Young is correct; it's the seat of the Roman Catholic faith and Saint Peter's Basilica should be our first venue to photograph.

"I can make arrangements for us to take notes on the church. My family has connections with Vatican officials; Gaining filming permission should not be a problem for us." Gabrielli championed my proposal.

The two Arab brothers and Andy agreed and Rome became our first stop on our whirlwind research tour for "Sacred Sex In Sacred Places."

Secret Announcement

After our meeting, while the men were talking among themselves, the Wazir cornered me, said, "Young, my guests were impressed by your dance performance the other evening."

Before Thabit could continue I said appreciatively, "Thank you Sir for the compliment. It is my pleasure to be of service to you and your guests."

My host continued, "His Royal Highness, The Prince, is smitten by your performance at Al Fayoum." Deliberately grinning and stressing 'performance at Al Fayoum.'

My face turned a shade of red from childish embarrassment and I waited for him to continue, "His Highness will like to see you again. He is visiting the Sekham this Saturday; will you spend time with him?"

"Of course, Sir! I'm at your service; when will I be required?"

"His Highness will be here in the early evening and will be staying the night. I'll summon you and Andy when you'll be required. Wait at the Maktub and I'll send an Abd to fetch you," announced the Wazir.

"Yes Sir! We'll be waiting."

"Another thing: keep this conversation confidential, will you?" My host requested.

"I will, Sir," I replied.

Abu Dhabi

After our business meeting Aziz, Gabrielli, Andy and I drove into the city with the two Americans. In 1967, Abu Dhabi was just beginning its rapid transformation and many modern skyscrapers and hotels were under construction. Since it was David and Eli's first visit to the Middle East, my tutor suggested we show them a Souk. Unaccustomed to the hassle and guzzle of Souq bargainers, snorting camels and spitting bazaar commoners, our guests were intrinsically at a loss, not knowing how to behave in a Middle Eastern marketplace. Andy and I, on the other hand, found the city fascinating, especially when it came to documenting my personal journal with photographs of my Emirate experiences.

Falconry

That evening back at the Sekham, Aziz ordered some servants to set up tents in a nearby Oasis to entertain the guests. Before dinner the Sekham men began their falconry games. Falconry had been and still is a rich nobleman's pastime in this part of the world. These birds were specifically trained to hunt wild quarries in the air. Usually, a farkh (young falcon) on its first migration south is trapped in the early months of autumn and used for hunting during the winter months before being released in a healthy condition to join its flock for their spring migration to an Asian breeding ground. It is rare that the birds are kept throughout the summer, since it is difficult to care for them during the hot Arabian season.

Once a bird is trapped, it is fitted with a burka (a blindfold hood) to reduce the fowl's anxiety levels and anklets are fixed around its feet to provide control. The trainer carries the wild bird everywhere for several days to desensitize it to stressful conditions, thus creating a bond between human and bird. Falcons are almost exclusively food-motivated; the bird is fed on a falconer's leather glove and eventually sees its trainer as a reliable food source. Some falconers train their birds to fly short distances for a reward, but essentially the falcon is a bird of the lure. The tilwa (lure) is the primary tool for calling a falcon to return to its trainer. Usually the tilwa consists of the wings of the Houbara bustard or whichever bird is intended as the eventual quarry. The falcon is rewarded every time it returns to the tilwa. Once the bird is responsive to the lure, the bird can be introduced to live quarries and the hunting begins in earnest.

Invitations

Besides being a first for the Americans, attending a falconry hunt was also a first for me. Although an interesting experience, it proved tedious after an hour of watching repetitive actions performed by birds and their Masters. Picking up my pen, I began sketching the falconry happenings in my sketch pad, which I carried with me everywhere. I began drawing the birds, their trainers and owners. Aziz, watching the game in a tent, noticed me sketching and approached.

Habibi sitting next to me asked, *"What are you drawing?"*

"I'm sketching the falconers and the birds."

As we spoke Andy came to join us as I continued, *"I'm looking forward to our visit to the Vatican. It's going to be an exciting adventure."*

"I can't wait to start my photography project. It's been over a month since I had the idea, and now it's taking shape. Though I'll like to speed up the process if I can," replied the Arab.

I took the opportunity to suggest, "Maybe Mario, our photographer friend in Venice, can assist? He is acquainted with many influential people in the city and could possibly get us in to shoot the Venetian basilicas. Since we are going to Rome, maybe we can conduct a side trip to Venice to visit Mario? Is that something you'll consider?" I prayed that the Arab would agree; then I would have the opportunity to see the Italian Count again.

Before Aziz had a chance to reply, Andy spoke, "Oh! Young, I forgot to mention I received two invitations to a mask ball from Count Mario. It's a grand costume ball to celebrate Carnevale. He has also invited Habibi Aziz and a companion after we told him about his photography project." Turning to Aziz he continued, "I received the invitations yesterday, forwarded to the Sekham from Daltonbury Hall. I'll have an Abd deliver the invitation to your chambers."

Habibi was intrigued and excited that Mario had sent him an invitation, and his face lit before speaking. "That's a great idea. We can stop in Venice after Rome. I've never been to a Venetian mask ball. I've never heard of Carnevale either; when is the event?"

Andy seemed to have done his homework, and he gave us a brief orientation on the origins of this festival. "It's an old Renaissance celebration. During the two world wars, the Italian government scrapped the public masked carnivals. Lately it's making a comeback within the wealthy aristocratic circles, where elaborate fancy dress balls are held annually, forty days before Easter."

"What are we wearing to such an opulent event?" I enquired.

Andy smilingly replied, "You're the up-and-coming fashion designer; you tell us what to wear!"

Aziz added, "Yes, you advise us what to wear. You did a great job with the Kosk's ladies' wardrobes. Now I'm putting you in charge of our Carnevale costumes."

Stunned, I replied after a moment's silence, "I better put some ideas on paper and see what I can whip up." Looking to Aziz, I asked, "Who are you inviting to the ball?"

"Gabrielli is travelling with us, so I presume he'll be the one I'm inviting," answered Habibi with predilection.

Sprouting eager enthusiasm to have an opportunity to design costumes as well as a chance to see Mario, I burst out with excited exuberance, "I'll get to work immediately and will have some costume ideas to show you a.s.a.p."

February 2012

I wrote:

Hello Aria,

This may come as a surprise to you since we have not been in touch for many years. I'm not sure if you remember me. We met at your parent's home in Vaduz the Yuletide of 1966. I was the Asian boy with your brother Andy. We left abruptly on Boxing Day because your mother walked in on us, was stunned and shocked. She dropped her breakfast trays she carried. Your father was furious and demanded Andy and me to leave. Do you recall the events of that fateful morning?

You probably had knowledge that three years after that dramatic day, Andy and I separated. Since then, I lost contact with your brother. Lately, I have been corresponding with Carol and she gave me your contact information. Here I am writing to inquire after you and your brother's wellbeing. I would like to renew our friendship and any updates or methods of connecting with Andy will be most welcome.

Carol mentioned you are married and living in Gothenburg, Sweden. I wish you and your family well. Please stay in touch when you find time to correspond.

Best Wishes!
Young.

23

The Harem Girls

"There is never a time or place for true love. It happens accidentally, in a heartbeat, in a single flashing, throbbing moment."
Sarah Dessen

His Royal Highness

Saturday arrived without pronouncement or fanfare. An ordinary day but no ordinary meeting was scheduled for me and his Royal Highness. After that night of debauchery with P, I was afraid to revisit our time together. As much as I had enjoyed our sexual rendezvous, I had expected our liaison to be a one-time affair. Although I awoke that morning infatuated with his Royal Highness, I was also aware that my dazzled emotions had to be kept in check. After all, it's not an everyday occurrence that an adolescent boy gets to make love with a real prince, despite the fact that it is probably every gay boy's fantasy. In my young years, I had never dared contemplate such provocative thoughts, let alone live in that reality. Now, P had requested my company again and it certainly was a daunting nightmare for ordinary me. What am I to do or not do? Do I refrain from the temptation of meeting his Royal Highness, or should I take the bull by the horns and face the challenge head on?

A Revelation

Two Abds bathed, cleansed and dressed me in an ornate djellaba on the evening of P's visit. When the summon came from the Wazir to go to the Sekham's oasis garden, the setting sun was sparkling a fiery shade of opal against the emerging darkness over the dunes like glimmering jewels on the tranquil desert-scape. Manservants cast charades of moving shadows while lighting torches around the encampment, building a flaming fire in the midst of a sacred circle. A group of musicians were already playing symphonic melodies welcoming guests and the host to a night of jubilation. The celebration had begun.

Seated in his place of honor, The Prince, next to the Wazir and his brother, the Habibi, was smiling. As the men and their entourage conversed in indiscernible Arabic, I was led to a seat next to his Royal Highness. Unable to distinguish a single syllable of their conversation, I sat demurely, waiting to be told what to do. My Valet stood a short distance away, watching like a falcon ready to scope if anything unbecoming befell my presence, which, of course, nothing did.

As dinner progressed with an abundance of liquor and wine consumption, the party's conversation transformed from sensual nuances to sexual ribaldry. Though I did not understand the topic of their conversations, their body language spoke a million decipherable syllables. While waiting my cue to do whatever I was supposed to do, a binding euphoria flashed before my eyes.

I was at once a farkh (young falcon) trapped in a boy's body used for the pleasures of my falconers and Masters. Like a farkh I was groomed for a unique sport and gifted an abundance of gratuitous gratuity for good sexual behavior before returning to my natural environment after a few years of faithful service. Youthful hawks and falcons released to join their migration flocks were unwounded physically and unblemished psychologically despite captivity; these birds were provided opportunities to learn survival skills and rewarded by their trainers for jobs well done. What better way to learn survival skills in a protected environment than left to roam wild in the wilderness without hunting knowledge or fending skills?

Although my euphoria transpired only a brief second, it spelled out my mission in an understandable language. Nothing mattered in my universe except to be present in the now moment. The Now is a present bestowed upon me by my Creator, and we are one and the same. This revelation of omniscience was and is my claim to my universal truth that *'I AM GOD therefore I AM LOVE.'* I was reminded of the sermon Chaplin Samuel Hollinger preached the morning of my E.R.O.S. initiation; *"Tis better to have loved and lost than never to have loved at all,"* (Alfred Tennyson). In that insightful instance, I was blessed with the authentic knowledge to profoundly comprehend that I was in the right place at the right time. My Present is in the Now.

Dominique

After dinner the men sat around the campfire for liqueur, deserts and an evening of entertainment. The music transformed from symphonic melodies to transcendent Arabian tunes. All the Sekham's women were present, including the Wazir's wives, Zeba and Ula, who were seated separately from their three daughters Mais, Naira and Sabiya. Jasim and Sayid were stationed next to their father and their uncle Aziz.

Veiled in layers of colored chiffon, a harem dancer slowly emerged into the fiery circle of spectators. Unlike the night of Bacha Bazi, where the audience was predominantly rambunctious and male, tonight's affair was impassively dignified, although sensuality prevailed to the provocation of Allah's paradise; promising an abundance of Houris to serve the desires of any believing Muhammadans. As the harem dancer methodically proceeded to unveil herself, she was greeted with joyous clapping and beating drums as she performed in front of our honoree guest. Like an obedient slave she discarded each liveried veil revealing her vulnerability like a tribute to his Royal Highness. As her final veil fluttered to the ground, the dancer was no other than Anya's 'big sister' Dominique, prostrated before The Prince as if in supplication. The audience applauded loudly as showers of Bahraini dinars came raining down onto the girl, covering her from top to toe with monetary gratuities. Lifting his hand, The Prince assisted Dominique to her feet before thanking her for an enchanting performance.

Down by the River

As the crowd cheered accolades in Dominique's direction, my discerning eyes noticed Mais and Naira were missing. The places where the sisters sat were now vacant. Wondering where the siblings had disappeared to, I noticed the shadows of their unobtrusive abayas almost imperceptibly rounding into the dark periphery of the outer circle. As much as I wanted to mind my own business, my inquisitiveness got the better of me. On the pretext of going to the boys' room, I excused myself from the company of his Royal Highness and followed at an inconspicuous distance.

The women snuck to the river embankment as I hid incognito behind several date trees. Naira left her sister to proceed alone to the water's edge. Acting as Mais's unobtrusive attendant, she vigilantly kept watch, making sure nobody came near to witness what was soon to transpire. I spied with intrigue. What happened thereafter was most unconventional if discovered; indignation would surely loom large within the Sekham household and the entirety of their Islamic community – an image I dared not meticulously contemplate for the sake of these two beautiful people and their family's social standing.

The Lovers

Out of the bushes jumped a figure in the likeness of Tahu, the photographer's assistant. Before I could blink, Mais and her secret beau were clinging closely, steeped in passionate embrace, progressing to intimate caresses before flames of fiery passion soared high scorching their smoking garments until nakedness took precedent in the stifling heat. The lovers rocked their cooing lullabies in this chilly night, barely conceling their unhurried coitus under the brilliant moon, submerged in a drunken haze of loving existence. As suddenly as they had begun their anthropological incantation, they abruptly ceased in mid-flight; as if struck stiff into a pillar of salt, the youth released his love seed in an agonizing crescendo. Saved by the sounds of distant drumming, their ecstatic moans fell on deaf ears, which would otherwise sparked a search for the place from whence his cries originated. When his mournful groans subsided to whimpering whispers, the lovers plunged into the cooling aqua, washing away all evidences of their invincible love before sadly parting ways from whence they came. This two were my friends, yet they were fatally doomed to convene in secret especially in a country where strict religious laws abated to those that dare break them.

For reasons unfamiliar to me, I slumped to the ground where I stood, uttering a silent prayer, *"Please God for the beauty of love I hope their troubles are few."*

Anya

By the time I returned to my place next to The Prince, Anya was already half way through her performance. Andy and Oscar sat next to Devaj, who was obviously chosen by the Wazir as an escort to a royal envoy, was attending to the needs of his receptive messenger. Andy, noticing my return, longed to sit by my side but formal protocol demanded that he stay a distance. He could do nothing until the appropriate moment when the entertainments ceased could he again chaperone me.

Unlike Dominique, who wore a belly dancing outfit, Anya was fully clothed during her performance. I was positive that bidding for this youthful beauty had commenced in another room by the male royal entourage and the Sekham's men, away from the prying eyes of their women folk.

As the entertainment drew to a close, his Royal Highness leaned across murmuring into my ear, *"Young, come to my chambers in an hour."*

"Yes, your Highness, I will be there."

24

The Masks We Wear

"In every art beginners must start with models of those who have practiced the same art before them. And it is not only a matter of looking at the drawings, paintings, musical compositions, and poems that have been and are being created; it is a matter of being drawn into the individual work of art, of realizing that it has been made by a real human being, and trying to discover the secret of its creation."
Ruth Whitman

February 2012

I was relieved to find that my message to Aria, asking about Andy's current information was returned as 'Mail Undelivered.' I was spared the confrontation with the demons that had arisen after Andy and I had separated. The Pandora's box I had kept under lock and key for 40 years was diabolical hell, and I had no wish to revisit my past anytime soon. For the time being, I could continue reminiscing about my time at the Sekham unhindered. Staring in my face was Aria's postal address, waiting patiently for my attention. I plucked up the courage to forward my email message by mail, addressing the letter to her postal address in Sweden.

1967 Designing Costumes

The two weeks before we were scheduled to fly to Italy, I had an opportunity to corner my tutor, Gabrielli, after class tutorial. Count Mario's masquerade ball was scheduled in four weeks at his Venetian palazzo. Since my assignment to be our group's costume designer, I had not as yet started my research on this project. Who better to ask for advice in tackling my design concepts for the Carnevale outfits than my Italian professor? Since Italy was his country of origin, surely he could provide adequate information and references for me to begin my design research.

"Sir, I have several questions and I need assistance," I asked.

"How can I help you, boy?"

"Aziz may have mentioned that we are invited to Count Mario's Venetian ball. Since I have never attended a masquerade ball, can you advise me on how best to begin my costume research? I have to start preparations for these to be ready before the event." I enquired.

"The Sekham's library has a selection of pictorial history books in which you will find Carnevale costume illustrations. This will provide you references to the way people dress at masquerade balls. In regards to designing Venetian masks: we can have them custom made by master craftsmen when we are in Venice, where a lot of choices are available.

"Sabiya, Naira and Mais will be able to introduce you to their dressmaker to make the outfits. I can arrange a 3 P.M. meeting for you and the girls in the communal recreational room," my professor recommended.

Whenever my teacher mentioned Sabiya's name, I detected hints of affection from his body language and through his spoken words. I was absolutely positive the Italian was insurmountably in love with the wazir's eldest daughter.

As Gabrielli continued; memories of the couple frolicking in the olive garden came flashing across my mind. A secret lover hidden beneath an exterior of a happy-go-lucky professor provided creative inspiration for the design of his costume – an outfit that was half jolly and fun while the contrasting other side revealed a darker secret shielded in mystery. A matching mask was eventually crafted for Gabrielli by a Venetian mask maker, completing his 'Happy & Sad' costume to absolute perfection. This my teacher wore amusingly, accepting my explicit artistry 'with a grain of salt.'

Sabiya and Sisters

Meeting Sabiya and her sisters was a rarefied experience. Although we knew each other in class, we had never discussed other topics besides our studies or homework. Though I had witnessed Sabiya's and Mais's secret rendezvouses with Gabrielli and Tahu respectively, I had never openly discussed these taboo and inappropriate topics with the two women, be it in private or otherwise. On the other hand, sexual discussions with the likes of the Habibi, the Wazir, my teacher or any of the Sekham's male members were deemed acceptable.

Therefore, I stuck to my subject at hand and said, *"Gabrielli recommended I speak to you regarding making several costumes for a Venetian ball; is it possible for me to work with your dressmaker about my costume designs?"*

Sabiya was the first to respond, *"Of course I'll introduce you our dressmaker, Badra, who has a workshop in the city. I can send for her to the Sekham. When will you like to meet her?"*

"The day after tomorrow will be excellent. I'll have the designs ready when she arrives."

The girls looked surprised. They obviously had difficulty comprehending a boy's interest in fashion and costume designing. While they stared at me, speechless, I interjected, *"Don't look so shocked, I'm planning to enroll into a London Art and Design School in a few years to study fashion design.*

"I have been designing fashions and costumes for a few years and had opportunities to meet a few Paris couturiers when I was there with the Kosk's ladies."

Naira exclaimed, *"I've never met a boy who designs women's clothes."*

"Now you have," I laughed heartily.

"Will you design our clothes?" Naira continued.

"Sure, I'll love to; do you wear western fashions or only traditional abayas?" I inquired.

"I'll be going for higher education in Italy in a few months and will require western style dresses. For now we only wear abayas," Sabiya chirped excitedly.

By the end of our meeting I had become the girls' fashion designer and consultant.

Designing Costumes

The girls scheduled a meeting with me and their dressmaker a day later. Following Gabrielli's instruction, I proceeded to the library and borrowed several Italian history books for my costume research. While imbibing the illustrations and pouring over patterns, an irresistible thought dawned on me. My designs for Aziz and Andy had to evoke their personalities, so they didn't feel out of character or uncomfortable wearing their outfits. During the course of my sketching, I also contemplated the fact that the people I knew were also wearing a variety of different facial masks at every moment of every day, depending on their ever changing moods. Therefore my designs had to relate to each individual in the ways that he or she would like to project to the world. This miraculous self-discovery became the catalyst in my personal design evolution, thus starting a psychological design journey as I progressed in learning the art of my chosen craft.

For Aziz

Aziz, a pure Arabian thoroughbred, provided me inspiration for an orange and gold colored costume for this aristocrat. My creative eyes saw sparkling stars and crescent moons, national symbols of the Islamic world, appliqued as embroideries on the Habiibi's costume. His aristocratic heritage was sufficient reason to dress him as an over-the-top caricature of the infamous King Shahryar in Scheherazade of *One Thousand and One Nights*. When I showed the Arab my design sketches, he was overjoyed with the idea of becoming a supreme ruler, if only for a night. He immediately granted me full steam ahead with the construction of my design. In Venice, we had a spectacular gold crescent moon mask specially crafted to complete the look for the man who would be 'King' of the ball. Since I had done my job with flying colors, the photographer rewarded me handsomely with a gratuitous check of US$2,500.00. By the time my masterpiece was unveiled, Aziz, now a happy camper, was parading in his emperor's new robe to show it to every member of the Sekham household.

For Andy

Designing my Valet's costume was as easy as A, B, C: at least that was what I thought. He was my knight in shining armor; translating my vision into reality meant a silver costume for my beloved. An abundance of silver tulle, silver lame and metallic silver glitter gave rise to a metaphoric Sir Lancelot from the legendary Camelot. Although Andy did not view himself as such, I, the designer, was given free rein to create his costume, so my version of Sir Lancelot became his reality for a night at the ball.

Andy dreamt of being a rebellious revolutionary outcast and demanded to be dressed in black. After several successive arguments, we settled on two outfits; a silvery 'White Knight' and a sinister 'Raven King' ensemble. Being a good sport, he wore both costumes at the ball. To please me, he wore the 'White Knight' outfit before transforming into a 'Raven King' to satisfy his craving.

For Me

The costumes for my three characters were now abated but I had a minor problem – that of dressing me. I could not decide and had not the insight to decipher how I saw myself or how I would like the world to see me. Since Andy was in love with his

'Raven King' costume, I finally settled on two adventurous design ideas that were beautifully constructed by the lovely Badra.

Desiring to match my lover, I designed a 'Twin' costume that was based on a similar idea to Gabrielli's 'Happy and Sad' theme; 'Twins' was an over-sized costume which could easily accommodate two people when worn. It was black in front and white at the back. The sides were ombre shades of grey, graduating from black to white and vice versa. It is true that all colors merged to become black or white; 'Twins' was therefore representational of all beings connected as one and one as all. It was a Yin and Yang concept I didn't realize I had created at the time. Forty years had passed and I now realize this process was a part of an unconscious spiritual evolution: morphing from adolescent to adulthood.

The final costume for moi was a 'Black Virgin' outfit: a partial tribute to Queen Elizabeth I and a partial homage to Queen Isabella of Spain. Instead of the stereotypical ethereal white that was associated with virgins, black, to me, proved a challenging calamitous twist to an otherwise uncreative logical philosophy. The night of the Venetian Ball, I took on the persona of a 'Black Virgin' accompanied by my 'White Knight' in shining armor. Hand in arm; we descended the grand staircase into the Palazzo Rosa's opulent Sala da ballo (Ballroom).

25

Drama at the Sekham

"Thinking is easy, acting is difficult, and to put one's thoughts into action is the most difficult thing in the world."
Johann Wolfgang Von Goethe

February 2012

My regular correspondence with Arius had new developments in my quest to locate Andy. Through one of his contacts, some fresh information was unearthed. Arius wrote:

Hi Young,

I hope this email finds you well and my regards to Walter. You are in luck, as my friend David, who knew Andy, has some information which may be of interest to you. After Ottawa Andy returned to Germany to be with his mother, who was suffering from Lupus. After her death she left him her Vaduz property where he stayed for a number of years before settling in Quebec, Canada. David doesn't have any further information since their correspondence ceased in 1987. I will continue to keep you posted if I have news of your ex.

One of these days I'll make it to Maui to visit you and Walter. But for now I'm prodding along with my two beloved companions Pepsi and Cola (who are wonderful Siberian hounds). They keep me busy without moments of quiet dispersions. I continue to work diligently on the gay grassroots organization that we discussed in our on-going emails. If you have a chance to visit Frankfurt, I would love to meet you in person.

Be Well & Stay Healthy,
A.S.

1967 Trouble in the Sekham

The week and a half flew by as I kept busy supervising the construction of our Carnevale costumes, working closely with Badra and her team of machinists. A few days before we were to board the SAQR to Italy, a huge commotion was in session within the Sekham. Servants and Abds were running around the expansive property trying to locate a missing Mais. The Wazir was in a crass mood, cursing and swearing at his wives and the harem women that if they had been vigilant his daughter would not have gone missing. High and low they searched, but the teenager was nowhere to be found.

Neither did Tahu turn up for work. There were no forwarding messages left by either of them. Of course Naira was questioned relentlessly to the whereabouts of her sister, since there were very close and often confided in each other their deepest secrets. Yet the teenager swore she knew nothing of their mysterious disappearance. Although Thabit guessed his daughter knew more than she lead on, he could do nothing drastic except to question the distraught Naira insurmountably until the poor girl cried rivers of tears. Her father refused to release her from interrogation even though both mothers begged leniency of their angry husband.

The feisty Wazir swore he would not give up the search until Mais and Tahu were found. When that happened, she would bear her father's misbegotten wrath. Mais, of his three daughters, was the least he expected to run away unannounced. This act of defiance would surely bring forth a puritanical outcry from the Islamic community and the religious elders would definitely brand Thabit an irresponsible father who could not control his daughter's slouchy behavior. He would ultimately lose face and be alienated as a blemished nobleman within his religious community. This was not a viable reception for the Wazir. His successful career would be expendably doomed in the eyes of his insensitive peers. Under such heavy pressure, Mais must be found and punished at all cost; eventhough the dis-eased father secretly empathized with his daughter. He could not be alleged as a renegade to his Muslim faith. If this shameful act was made public, the religious elders would surely be in an uproar, demanding drastic action, for the poor girl to be publicly crucified. She would be branded a lascivious temptress of men – a sinful, shameless, woman unfit to be of servitude to a future husband and, at worst, unclean in the eyes of Allah, according to the country's strict religious laws.

An illicit love affair happening in Thabit's household would add further insult to injury, an unforgivable sin for the lovers. Mais would quite possibly be dragged into the streets and stoned to death. Though Tahu's conviction might be more lenient, this Arab would be forever drenched with the sin of coveting an unmarried woman and his guilt in witnessing his beloved stoned would more than likely sent him into an abyss of misery for the remainder of his life, thus destroying either of the lovers' only chance of happiness forever.

Hush Up

There was only one redeeming solution to this dilemma, even though the rational Wazir did not welcome the idea. A wedding could be organized as soon as possible if the couple were found. Unlike Mais, Tahu came neither from a wealthy nor aristocratic family. Under normal circumstances a union between two vastly different social classes would not prove an ideal marriage, especially when it came to the status of a Wazir's daughter. Traditional marriages were often arranged and betrothals were to strengthen family ties and improving social statues; Tahu's family would bring nothing to the Wazir's household if this marriage was consummated.

Therefore, the only solution the lovers could formulate was elopement. They had run away from their families, peers and religious dominance to start afresh; the drawback was to live a life of poverty and penniless existence. Disappearing where they could not be found, they went into hiding.

Aziz was equally as furious as his brother at Tahu for leaving no word or message and eloping with his niece. For the next few days, the Sekham was in a state of unsettled turmoil. Thabit laid down strict rules of conduct that this embarrassment could never be leaked out of the compound. The entire household entourage must keep silent about the incident until the patriarch found a solution to deal with the contemptuous situation.

A Marriage?

As with all problems there are always solutions; the one most sensible to Andy, Oscar, Devaj and me was for the lovers to marry and legalize their union. As much as we wished Mais and Tahu the very best, we as bystanders were helpless except to console the girl's parents, and we lent our compassionate ears in listening to their trials and tribulations without further flaming the fire of discontent.

My sensible teacher did wonders to soften the Wazir's anger, since he might also suffer Thabit's wrath if he did not tread with care. As Gabrielli and Sabiya were secret lovers, they would one day require the patriarch's blessing in granting them marriage. Therefore, the sensible Italian immersed himself in assisting his Arab partner in dissipating his wrath. Obsequiously, he advised that a swift wedding would be the logical solution for all parties involved. This would keep the elopement away from public knowledge. It was advisable to forgive the lovers so they could return to the Sekham. The ultimate defining moment was an elaborate wedding reception to welcome Tahu into the Sekham family. My teacher reasoned with his partner; if the Wazir's third daughter married into a lower caste family, it would not jeopardize the futures of the other two Sekham girls.

Wedding Preparations

After much servile persuasion, Naira finally confided to her father the whereabouts of her sister and boyfriend. Words were dispatched for their return. They had to promise solemnly to the appalled Thabit that they were in the wrong and beg his forgiveness. This they did, the day before we departed for Italy. A wedding celebration was planned in two months and the Wazir and the Habiibi enlisted the help of the foreign students where they needed assistance. Andy, Oscar, Devaj, Dominique, Anya and I were delighted that the dilemma was over and a forthcoming matrimony in sight. Our professor's positive premonition had toppled the contemptuous Wazir into accepting a metaphysical solution that best suited everyone involved. *"After all the happiness of two became the joy for all,"* said the relieved Professor Gabrielli.

Flying to Venice

The morning before we boarded the SAQR for Venice, our Carnevale outfits were pressed and hung in white garment bags, ready for the Abds to load into the golden Rolls Royce on its way to Abu Dhabi airport. The missing items to complete our outfits were the masks, which my professor suggested we have custom crafted in Venice.

I was glad that Oscar, now part of our triplet liaison, was accompanying us on the trip. He had been sneaking into the Maktub after Devaj retired to bed. Our lover could be found sleeping with my Valet and me four to five nights per week. Devaj didn't mind his guardian spending time with us; in fact, the Indian was delighted he have time for him without his Valet looking over his shoulders twenty-four seven. The boy needed space to do whatever he wanted to do without Oscar's presence. He had finally found solitude to pursue his own secret empire of seduction, of which we knew nothing until our return from Italy. Unlike me who felt loved and protected, preferring my lovers sleeping on either side of our King, Devaj had a vastly different, secret agenda. For the present I was simply grateful that Oscar was travelling with us on our *"Sacred Sex In Sacred Places"* mission.

Part Three

Italy – Venice, Rome, Vatican City.

26

The Count, the Professor & the Habiibi

"All strangers are relations to each other."
Arabian Proverb

1967 Venezia, Italy

I was at once excited and afraid as the SAQR flew our entourage to Italy. I was excited for the opportunity to meet the object of my affection after two months absence. At the same time, I was afraid at the thought of sparking another flurry of cupid's love in the presence of my lover Andy, who had been extremely patient and understanding throughout my childish infatuation with the Italian playboy.

Our first stop to Venezia was twofold. The first to introduce Habiibi Aziz to Count Mario, hopefully the two professional photographers would become friends and successfully collaborate on *"Sacred Sex In Sacred Places."* This project would benefit both parties in creativity as well as career advancement for the two when it was launched internationally.

The second was to locate a mask maker to craft our various masks for Mario's masquerade ball, which was scheduled in two and a half weeks. The mask maker would have ample time to complete our masks. Gabrielli affirmed that the mask maker would recommend the best solution when showed my costume sketches and the finished outfits, even-though I had no idea how Venetian masks were constructed. He said the artist would figure out the details for the characters we wanted to personify at the ball. True to his words, the artisan constructed our masks flawlessly and beautifully, and we wore them with confidence to the Count's fancy dress event.

My Valet & I

Once again we found ourselves located in a luxury suite within the Hotel Danieli, where Andy and I had stayed with Ubaid and Ramiz a few months ago. This time we were guests of Habiibi Aziz and our travelling companions were Gabrielli, Oscar and Devaj. Before our arrival Andy had written to the Count, inviting him to join us for dinner at the hotel's Restaurant Terrazza Danieli. A little before the appointed hour, my heart was thumping a mile a minute with anxious excitement, eager to see the man I secretly missed. Dressed in dinner attire, I paced up and down our suite while waiting for Andy to dress. Always sensitive to my needs and behavioral characteristics, my Valet said amusingly, *"Young, what's with you? Why the appertaining unsettled behavior? Are you dying with infatuation to see Count 'Casanova' again?"* Andy said laughingly.

His teasing threw me off guard, since there were elements of truth in his words. It took me several seconds to answer. *"Hurry up and get ready. We'll be late for dinner and we don't want to keep our group waiting."*

"You don't have to fuss. If we are not there, I'm sure Mario will approach our group to introduce himself."

Andy's remark was true. The Count was definitely more than capable in making himself known to our friends. We had met similarly when he approached my Valet after eyeing him from a distance. This would certainly be no exception to the rule, yet my specious heart continued banging like a voluminous drum. I had to close my eyes and breathe deeply, to calm my irrational thinking before I finally found solace within.

My guardian, seeing me in such a state of unease, held me adoringly. Kissing my cheeks he said, *"My sweet boy, your infatuation is destroying the very fiber of your being. Try balancing your energy through your breath work. Come, lay down by my side and I'll hold you."*

I did as was told, and with my soulmate's assistance, I finally regained my composure. We were ready to proceed to the dining room.

The Count & the Habiibi

As Andy envisioned, Mario was already seated and chatting animatedly with the rest of our entourage. He was sandwiched between Aziz and Gabrielli, speaking a mile a minute in Italian with my teacher. Both men behaved like long lost brothers, delighted to share Italian hospitality and a comprehensive servitude to their national and cultural identity. Gabrielli was overjoyed to be home in his native country, while the Count was delighted to meet new friends, especially the good-looking Aziz, Oscar and Devaj (who were potential conquests for this Italian playboy). I was also sure he would welcome the idea of bedding Gabrielli, if he could charm his way into my professor's pants.

Mario stood up to greet us as my Valet and I walked towards the dining table. Kissing me warmly on both cheeks, he whispered in my ears, *"I'm so happy you are in Venice. I miss you and Andy terribly."*

I returned his kisses affectionately. Being young and naïve, I took his charismatic words as if he meant exactly what he said. Over dinner the Count and Aziz bonded and were already discussing the best Venetian Basilicas they could use as back drops for their photography project.

"I'll get permission to film in Basilica di San Marco. I'm familiar with the church officials and I don't foresee any problems filming inside the cathedral."

"Great! How soon do you think we'll be granted permission to start?" Aziz enquired?

"I presume in a day or two. First thing tomorrow morning I'll make arrangements. Meanwhile, enjoy Venice; there are many holy sites you can visit while we wait for the Basilica's approval." Mario suggested, *"We'll scout for other suitable locations tomorrow. I'll be happy to be your tour guide."*

Basilica di San Marco

Two days later, we found ourselves setting up shop inside the grand cathedral. We were filming the interior of this massive monument. I, being detailed oriented, snapped the interesting wall murals and amazing ceiling frescos depicting Christ's life and saints. Although the object of our mission was to photograph the church's interior to create references for the set builders, I could not help but wonder what it would be like if we copulated inside this religious institution.

Mario invited our party for dinner at one of Venice's historical restaurants, Trattoria da Roma, after the shoot. As soon as we had ordered, the Count said with illuminated excitement, *"Let's drink to my new friends. I'm glad to be entwined with Aziz's photography project. I'm forthwith committed to making "Sacred Sex In Sacred Places" a successful venture for us.*

"I have been brainstorming with the Habiibi and Gabrielli on various approaches to launching this artistic endeavor. We have some ideas, and we'll share them with you guys soon."

As we clinked our crystal glasses, Mario pronounced, *"I'll be joining you guys to Rome or wherever we are travelling, to see this project through to fruition. Before we depart for the Capital, I'll organize a party at my palazzo to celebrate our collaboration."*

Gabrielli and Aziz were equally delighted that the meeting had progressed smoothly, much better than they had anticipated. If Mario was one hundred percent on board, we were certain that *"Sacred Sex In Sacred Places"* would be an astounding success. The Count seldom agreed to any project if he didn't believe it a viable proposition. The fact that he was well connected in Venetian society would definitely boost the credibility of this endeavor. We had no doubt that he would apply his social connections when it came time to launch this artistic exhibition.

The four foreign students, me included, were excited to be involved. Besides being the photographer's model, I had the opportunity to be a photographer's apprentice. What better way for me to learn, than on the job?

27

Vanquish The Jealous Heart

"Have you ever been in love? Horrible isn't it? It makes you so vulnerable. It opens your chest and it opens up your heart and it means that someone can get inside you and mess you up."
Neil Gaiman

1967 Basilica di Santa Maria della Salute

I had hoped for some alone time with The Count or with Andy's presence; unfortunately, we were constantly surrounded by our entourage. The following day after our photography session at Basilica di San Marco, Mario introduced us to several other holy sites, one of them the Basilica di Santa Maria della Salute. He, being the man about town, seemed to know every conceivable person who was of importance in Venice. Filming permissions were granted almost instantaneously without hassle. Like most ancient cathedrals, these imposing structures possessed an air of sanctified opulence and magical composition. Basilica di Santa Maria della Salute was one such example.

Infatuation

Mario, the busy bee, was going nonstop from one project to the next. He, a workaholic at heart, appeared ubiquitously everywhere. As he had promised, the Count devoted himself wholeheartedly to *"Sacred Sex In Sacred Places."* He was in our company the majority of the time. As the days passed, my hopes of catching the man alone or with Andy were getting slimmer than I had anticipated. My young and inexperienced mind had imagined a replay of our unforgettable Palazzo Rosa rendezvous. This playboy had imprinted me with a lasting infectious memory, and now my naiveté was wreaking havoc on my being. My infatuation was binding my imagination to heights of ecstatic fantasies. I had least expected our provocative replay to be channeled in a different direction.

At Palazzo Rosa

Our host had his chef prepare us a scrumptious meal the evening before we departed for Rome. It was our plan to film the Roman religious sites within a week, before returning to Venice for the Count's masquerade ball. Our masks would subsequently be completed, and they were delivered to us at Hotel Danelli in time for the festivities.

Mario had invited four other guests: two male models and two boys who were a few years older than me. As the evening progressed, our conversation turned from the day's photo shoot to playing card games after dessert. Although it was an all-male affair, it was never strange for my heterosexual professor to feel comfortable in the company of men, be they straight, bisexual or gay. Are Europeans more sexually liberated than their puritanical American cousins? I would never know.

Arabian Men

Although Aziz had a wife and children in Dubai, the Arab also had adolescent male lovers outside marriage. In the Quran, the prophet Mohammad promised his homosexual followers an endless homosexual pleasure with handsome pre-pubescent boys of perpetual freshness in Paradise (Quran verses: 52:24; 56:17; 76:19). In several ancient Arabic texts, the Nabi also affirm the followers of Islam that after committing plunder, loot, rape and murder in this life, they are "rewarded" by untouched virginal youths who are fresh like pearls. Since the beginning of Islam, pederasty has been permissible. Although homosexuality was and is still widely practiced in Islamic countries, only in extreme cases is sodomy punishable by death. During my four years of harem services, I felt love and acceptance of my homosexuality rather than hatred and prejudice in the six households I served. I quote a famous Arabian proverb: *"Boys for pleasure, women for procreation."*

Fun & Games

Mario was the first to initiate a game of strip poker. As the losers discarded pieces of clothing, the gathering began a rapid transformation from suggestive sensuality to active sexual magnetism. A few games later, some of us were down to our skivvies. Through the thin cotton fabrics, our erections were veritably obvious. The Count, standing next to his adolescent friend, Tino, began massaging the boy's shoulders, stimulating his excitement to full attention. Ugo, the boy's companion, was forthwith turned on watching his friend's hardness peeking out of his underwear. The sexual instigator had moved to kiss Tino's neck as he continued rubbing the boy's penile wetness, stirring him to tilt his bottom towards his aggressor. As we continued our poker game, we were glancing sideways to observe the unfolding erotica, all the while pretending nothing unusual was happening. Through the corners of our permissive eyes we witnessed The Count's hand sensually caressing the boy's scrotum. As with many experienced playboys, Mario was no exception to the art of sensuality and sexuality. He was now rubbing his skimpily covered erection against Tino's willing buttocks. The two items of clothing separating the man's hardness and the boy's slit were their moist underwear. Although the adolescent pretended to focus on his cards, his thoughts betrayed his actions as his body lovingly leaned against the Count's muscular physique. His hands were intimately gripping Tino's slender waist.

Our attempts to remain focused on our cards were feverishly diminishing with each ticking second. Gabrielli, the alpha male took charge to dismiss the game. Soon our palpable hands and mouths were on our sensual opponents who were standing next to us. A discarded heap of clothing lay scattered on the floor amidst a sea of entangled bodies, intertwined in pulsating positions on the carpeted floor. Sensual tongues like polished blades pried open voluptuous lips, darting into the inner recesses of our longing souls. Hungry mouths suckled bulbous lengths, savoring dripping emissions before proceeding to lap on globes of quivering balls. Our erections were in readiness to penetrate cruppers of youthful openings, our bodily heat turned full volume, sending shivers through our wrestling spines. The room was electrified with sublime vicissitudes of sexual postulations. We merged as a unified body casting us into the Aleph of timelessness. We were infinite Gods in motion.

The Angelic Hosts

Our angelic hosts sang moans of hosannas while some uttered groans of alleluias as we frolicked in the living room of Palazzo Rosa. Our shameless benedictions gave way to assimilated transcendent passion while joyful cries emigrated to murmuring salutations, all in praise of ecstatic jubilation on our final quest to sexual ecstasies. I was dominant at times, only to be muscled into submission, when love's dichotomy took flight to overturn my abating fancy.

Yet amidst this delirious sexuality, my jealous heart reared its ugly head, desiring the object of my infatuation to possess me. I did not want to share the Count with others. But I had to subdue this monstrosity, banishing the green eyed beast into the abyss of the underworld. The emerald intensity of this secret monster was diminishing the core of my very existence. It was relegating my being into dungeons of sorrows. I hated myself despite the joyful mask I wore. I surrendered the aching heart that was ripping me apart. This indescribable torment beckoned me to shatter into a thousand pieces. How could I pick up my broken rejections, mending that which was already lost?

Concentrating on my task at hand, my infatuation soon gave rise to an inner strength I never knew existed. I was able to turn the table around. I began to win this jealous battle of misshapen conflict. My sincere retribution was the heavenly sign I needed to transform my troubled cowardice into my spiritual awakening. Although the sojourn journey from love's recovery was not quick, it was by no means a rarefied success. I had managed to hold power over the emerald wizard, at least for now, impinging the fraudulent beast and relegating it back into its morbid lair of false intentions.

Thanks to my accompanying hosts of cute cherubim and handsome seraphim, the journey to self-realization and recovery was complete. Spews of sexual delights filled the Rosa's chamber with roars of thunderous releases, until each and every cherub and seraphs had had their fill of orgasmic ecstasies. Limp limbs in servile compositions bore witness to our synchronized amorousness, packaging our love into blissful fractions of sweet contentment before peaceful slumber plummeted our swirling hearts into a night of restful consolation. Tomorrow we commence our journey to the Capital.

End February 2012

My regular correspondence with Arius had brought much needed insights to our friendship. Although I was morally supportive of my friend's gay grassroots project, I was not ready to be intensely involved. In my email to A.S., I wrote:

Hi Arius,

Thank you for keeping me abreast of the organization's developments. I hope I will be an active participant one day. My blessings are with you. It is a delight to receive your news. Please continue to keep me in the loop of your various exciting projects.

I am grateful for your diligence in assisting me to locate Andy. I am a step closer to finding Andy with each of your emails.

Since writing A Harem Boy Saga, Book 1 – **"Initiation"**; I am currently working with a Hollywood script broker to revise the manuscript, to have it ready for publication, thus transforming my weekly blogs into a book. Although the process is slow and tedious, it is also an enjoyable journey. I will continue to keep you posted of my manuscript developments.

For now, I bid you Au revoir and Auf Wiedersehen.

Your dear friend,

Young.

28

Rome is Burning

"Love at first sight is possible, but it pays to take a second look."
Bernard Tristan Foong

1967 Villa Spallentti Trivelli

The eternal city of Rome was splendid and opulent. Needless to say, with Gabrielli's established family history and his far-reaching Roman connections, our entourage was invited to stay at the prestigious Villa Spallentti Trivelli, throughout the filming of *"Sacred Sex In Sacred Places."* Our host Piero was my teacher's school chum and the two had forged an everlasting friendship since their family bonds were tightly knit. Whenever Gabrielli was in town, he would lodge at his friend's villa. Therefore it came as no surprise that we were honorary guests at this historical estate. My professor had written to Piero of our Roman visit. Both men were approximately the same age and our hospitable host threw open his doors without reservations to entertain us. This palazzo had since been transformed into a luxury hotel, but in 1967 it held court to many rich and famous writers, poets and artists of the day.

Rome

Like Venice with an air of magical splendor, and Florence smelling of cultural antiquities, Rome, the eternal city, reeks of infectious opulence. Beneath its grand fiber flowed euphoric strains of sinister malice. Roman showmanship is beyond doubt the terra firma of Italian treasures, well represented by the city's massive architectural history. It has always given me chills when roaming the vestibules of these ancient corridors.

Maybe it's the heartless killings of Roman emperors from generations past or the dissipated ghosts of the humiliated; I am never able to understand the reasons for my uneasiness when in this Capital.

At the Coliseum

Our first stop was the Coliseum. Our group of eleven trooped into this gigantic monument, carting our photographic equipment, to begin our day's photo shoot. Through Gabrielli's government connections, filming permission had been granted and we set to work immediately. Mario had brought along both the male models, Luke and David, together with Tino and Ugo, with whom we had the Bacchanalian orgy a couple nights prior. I had an opportunity to talk with my professor when the models were on call.

"What do you think of the Coliseum? Isn't it impressive?" My teacher commented.

I answered argumentatively, "The structure is no doubt impressive but I feel uneasiness in this place."

"How so?"

"As much as the Amphitheatrum Flavium represents the glory days of ancient Rome, I detect the ghostly squeal of those that were brutally murdered at this very site. It is difficult for me to overcome the power struggle between those who sacrificed their lives in the hands of the gladiators and the wild beasts." I responded sadly.

My teacher answered tactfully, "Perhaps this is a good time to enlighten you with a brief lesson on ancient gladiatorial sports which my country is renowned.

"Fine examples to compare gladiators to are modern day boxers and wrestlers. Like most extreme combatant sports, the injury rates are high and casualties are bound to happen. In the past, I studied the history of gladiatorial sports. Although many gladiators were slaves, the winners often rose to great fame, accumulating freedom, glory and power along the way. This was a highly organized sport with numerous rules and regulations, much like international boxing and wrestling tournaments."

I interrupted my teacher, "What you say is indeed true, but the combatants were the property of their Masters and their sponsors. They were subjugated to fight against their will. They had to obey their owners, otherwise they would be put to hard labor or death. Modern day boxers and wrestlers are not slaves or criminals nor prisoners of war. They have a choice to fight or not to, unlike the gladiators."

"Young, you are correct; I'm only making a comparison between our present day extreme sports to that of ancient times. I do not approve nor disapprove of the gladiatorial, boxing or wrestling matches. I'm simply observing the fact that the general populace had not learned much from our ancestors. Maybe it is in our exacerbated human nature to delight in the sufferings of others?

"Personally I believe extreme sports should be terminated; more often than not, they cause internal injuries and sometimes death to the combatants; like the gladiatorial and bestiarii participants."

I nodded in agreement, acknowledging the facts my professor had just presented. As I was about to speak, Gabrielli was summoned by one of the photographers to assume the role of a faux gladiator. He was posing in next to nothing except a provocateur's helmet.

My Burning Heart

As I busied myself assisting Aziz, empathetic thoughts came flooding into my mind when Mario and Andy posed together. It was my unofficial role to grab the camera and snap away under my mentor's watchful guidance. Through the camera lens I couldn't help making comparisons between the object of my infatuation and my lover. My deep, bewildering thoughts were like wild fires burning a path through the heart of Rome. My still-small voice whispered discreetly into my ear as I clicked away at the handsome male specimens. An internal dialogue waged war within me when I aimed my camera at the duo.

"Are you so egotistical to think that you can win the heart of the Count?" snarled the voice, "Aren't you happy with the one who loves you unconditionally?"

I retaliated rapidly, "Mario is attractive, powerful, worldly, and a superb lover. Anybody in their right mind would be attracted to him. I'm no exception to the rule."

"Well you put your foot in your mouth, didn't you? You silly boy, you should listen to your intuition and realize that the handsome Italian belongs to the world and he's not for you to keep. Don't you see, you are just another in his line of conquest?"

I argued, "As much as I agree with your reasoning, I can't help falling in love with this charismatic man. Men always want to be a boy's first love and boys like to be a man's last romance." I quoted Oscar Wilde to myself.

The voice replied, "In that case you are heading towards disaster. I hate to see you suffer. But if you choose to travel down that path, I can only act as your reminder until you realize you are blinded from the truth."

"Thanks for the reminder. Now stop suffocating me with your idiotic chitter-chatter," I activated my wall of self-defense, when I knew full well I should be running the opposite direction rather than allowing my pride to lead me against a brick wall.

"Okay, okay!" Said the voice, "Rest assured; it's my job to remind you of the consequences. Act however you want. I'll be constantly nudging and guiding your omnipresent salvation's return, when your sensibilities are ready to abandon this dysfunctional journey."

My internal dialogue came to a grinding halt when Andy came over and sat by me. He was taking a break before resuming his modeling.

Chariots of Fire

Andy, noticing my melancholy mood, enquired, *"You look arbitrarily sad; what's the matter with you?"*

Not wanting to let down my defenses I smilingly replied, *"Nothing is bothering me. It must be my mind playing tricks on me. I can't help but surmise those that had been murdered and executed here are haunting this arena. In the name of glory and fame, innocent humans and animals were mindlessly slaughtered at this very spot where we stand.*

"Maybe the echoes of the un-departed are in the amphitheater? This place gives me the chills. I feel vengeful spirits clamoring for justice for their untimely deaths."

Concerned with my overactive absurdity, my Valet responded, *"It's been hundreds of years since the last gladiators and bestiaries took place. I'm sure the deceased have moved on to a peaceful realm. I think your imagination is running havoc."* Changing the topic, he said with bemusement, *"Do you know that another popular Roman sport is chariot racing?"*

"Do they also perform this at the Coliseum?" I asked.

"No, chariot races were traversed in large Circuses."

"You mean like a modern day circus?" My interest piqued, I inquired further.

"No, not like a modern day circus. It's a large oval-shaped forum similar in structure to the Coliseum. Have you seen the Charlton Heston movie, 'Ben Hur'? One of the scenes has a chariot race."

"Yes, I remember that movie. It's not as bloodthirsty as the gladiator combats," I replied.

*"These types of public entertainments remind me of modern day Football, Soccer or Stock car racing tournaments. Entire stadiums filled with unruly crowds jeering and cheering for their respective competing teams. There will always be serious injuries in competitive sports. Charioteers often die during the races when collision happens. Similar accidents apply to Football, Soccer and

Race Car drivers. Players bash into each other causing anticipatory head and bodily injuries. And I'm not adding hooliganism into the equation," continued my Valet.

"Why does the government not ban these types of dangerous sports?"

"Maybe we are quintessentially evil and enjoy seeing people getting hurt as long as we aren't the victims. It's these types of garish showmanship that we as a human race, have not the ability to mutate and learn from our past mistakes. The dictatorial mass media often obscure our sound analytical judgments and capabilities. They only promote that which are self-depleting." Andy said with a heavy sigh.

Wondering how our conversation transmuted from chariot racing to such a sentiment was beyond my comprehension. One thing for certain, it got me thinking; never be deceived by what is being seen at first sight. It pays to evaluate at a closer look the matter in hand.

29

The Holy City of God

"There are only two ways to live your life. One is as though nothing is a miracle. The other is as though everything is a miracle."

Albert Einstein

Early March 2012

Just as I was about to give up hope in getting a response from Aria (Andy's sister), an email arrived from Carol, my long lost friend for whom I had designed dolls' collections. Carol wrote:

Hello Young,

I hope you are well and enjoying Maui. We are experiencing a miserable winter in Germany. I wish I were in the tropics. I have some exciting news for you. I received a birthday card from Aria not so long ago, with her new email and postal addresses. Due to her husband's job transferal, her family moved from Gothenburg to Stockholm. Enclosed are her addresses, and I'm wishing you the best in locating Andy.

I haven't written to Aria but I'll forward your email to let her know that you are trying to connect with her brother. I'm sure she'll be delighted to hear from you. Best wishes to you and your partner.

All the best!
Carol.

1967 Vatican City

As our limousines drove into Vatican City I was giddily looking out of our Bentley's window, observing a group of marching Schweizergarde (Swiss Guards) in their colorful costumes, parading in front of the gated entrance. As our chauffeur presented the gate keeper with our official documents, we were waved into a large courtyard where VIP visitors were received. Standing by the open doorway were two men in clerical cassocks. They welcomed our entourage with wide grins and open arms. As they led us into the building, through a series of ornately arched corridors, a sense of grandeur befell me at every turn. Under the prient's instructions, several Schweizergardes had unloaded our photography equipment. They were carrying them to our destination. We had obtained permission to photograph the main sections of Saint Peter's Basilica before dawn, when these areas were temporary closed to the public. Notifications had been granted by the Vatican authorities. We were not to be disturbed during the duration of our filming.

Gabrielli and Piero's families were major financial donors to the Vatican's coffers. Formal documents had been dispatched to Pope Paul VI, the then acting pontiff; requesting a half day permission to conduct a photo-shoot at the Vatican's sacred premises. Permission was granted immediately and our party's receptive welcome into Vatican City was formalized.

Saint Peter's Basilica

Our initial filming destination was the Basilica's main foyer. Above us rose an enormous cupola, richly inlaid with gold mosaics depicting religious icons, saints, angels and of course Christ and his apostles. Our party and both accompanying priests had access to the entire premise. The clerics' roving eyes at our attractive entourage triggered Mario and Gabrielli to test the waters, to see if they could synthesize a visceral filming of the models in the buff. After much battering back and forth between the men, the Count promised a sizable donation would be deposited at the cathedral's offering box, if permission were granted on the spot. The holy fathers tottered indecisively over the Italians undignified requests. Mario's power of persuasion astounded us when both clergymen finally gave their nods of approval. The models could be photographed nude and in sexually compromising positions; subject to the priests pretending to be clueless during our filming of such sacrilegious acts within the Basilica's grandiose enclosures.

I later realized that the priests' erratic behaviors were mainly due to the fact that they secretly desired to see the models naked, but were unable to discern their personal homoerotic inclinations. Since Mario had offered a sizable monetary donation, they could apply this as an excuse for the benefit of the church. Therefore, they turned their impassive eyes to our insidious photography and labeling our work as artistic expressions instead of pornography. Although both men of God left us to our filming devices, our entourage could not help speculating if "the sins of our Fathers" were secretly masturbating behind darken corridors or in enclosed confessionals. Were they peeping at the copulating models within the walls of Basilica Papale di San Pietro in Vaticano (Italian meaning Papal Basilica of Saint Peter in the Vatican)?

Do religions offer their devotees double standards of guilty redemptions for sinful confessions? Or are sexual enjoyments our inherent birthright to embrace? Very often zealots found ways of curbing their sexual desires, decrying sexual acts as sinful. For centuries, strict religious moral codes were ordained by man to trap their flocks into believing that those activities held no truth. Is coitus a sacred act or an offensive placatory denouncement? If God had not intended connubialis intercourse (sexual intercourse in Latin) to be pleasurable, would 'HE' create such an enchantment just to shame the human race and lead it into temptations? These are debatable questions for which I continue to seek answers in my adult life.

A miracle did happen that morning at the Basilica Sancti Petri (Saint Peter's Basilica). If there are glimpses of truth in the idea that humans are made in the image of God, then we must be Gods and Goddesses in a way. Then it is no wonder 'money talks' and 'money travels a long way' when we desire miracles to manifest rapidly. Miracles did happen quickly that morning at the Holy City of God.

The Grottoes

The hour eagerly descended for the Basilica's upper section to reopen for public use, while we buried ourselves in the subterranean grottoes to continue our photo shoot. We models were posing naked next to saintly crypts and tombs of historical Popes. If the deceased Holy Sees had eyes to see, they would turn in their graves in fits of apocalyptic disorientation and very likely thunder their displeasure upon photographers and models alike. On the other hand they might be like the two priests, secretly reveling in the erotic invocations that were happening within the confines of their burial chambers, simultaneously delighting in our sensual reverie and also punishing themselves for their confounded guilty consciences from our wanton displays of sexual pleasures. I daresay with honesty, these are the thrilling munitions in the duality of Yin and Yang, of Good and Evil, of Light and Day, and the lists goes on.

30

The Fountains of Rome

"If I cannot brag of knowing something, then I brag of not knowing it, at any rate, brag."
Ralph Waldo Emerson

1967 The Romans

One of many things Mario and Gabrielli were good at was bragging! For this reason they were able to secure our artsy photo-shoot within the Vatican and at the fountains of Rome. Their-larger-than life charismatic personalities combined with their power of persuasion and handsome good looks proved to be great assets. Exercising their hypnotic charms, men, women and children affectionately did their bidding without question, and they could get things done with ease and grace. Maybe these are the reasons Italian men have garnered world-renowned reputations as impressionistic Playboys and notorious Casanovas.

The Fountains of Rome

After our Saint Peter's Basilica photo shoot, we were granted permission to film at the Trevi Fountain, by far the grandest and most impressive of all Roman fountains. Italian fountains are generally open to public but in this instance, at 2 A.M. in the morning, we obtained permission from the Italian government to conduct a private filming session. Again, thanks to Gabrielli's Roman connections; vehicles and pedestrian access were sealed off to this venue for the sole purpose of filming *"Sacred Sex In Sacred Places."* Both photographers had arranged special lighting for this shoot. Similar to filming a movie, the models were permitted to frolic naked. We posed and played as if we were acting in a full length feature film, while Mario and Aziz clicked away under the watchful eyes of several government security guards. They were placed in the vicinity to keep peace. We completed the four hour shoot without any problems.

Gabrielli

I had a chance to talk with my teacher, who was also taking a modeling break. As we stood naked drying ourselves with towels I commented, *"Sir, you remind me of Sean Connery in the James Bond movies."*

My professor replied laughingly, *"How so, young man?"*

"You are handsome, suave, and athletic, and you possess a larger-than-life personality, like a spy. Are all Italian men charismatic like Mario and yourself?"

My teacher burst out in roaring laughter. He replied, *"Young, you are funny! I've been told that we Italians are animated, vivacious with an excessive panache for living life. Our forebears are known for their eruptive high octane spirits and it's our inherent nature to embark on fun-loving adventures."*

"Is that why famous operas are written in Italian and by Italians, because of their passion for high drama?"

Gabrielli belted out in an unstoppable belly laugh. Andy, hearing the uproar, ventured over to join the amusement. *"What's so funny?"* My Valet inquired.

"This boy asks the funniest questions. His innocence is extremely amusing.

"Young, to answer your questions; no, I'm not a spy and yes, most dramatic operas are written by Italians."

Andy remarked zealously, *"That's why I love him; he has this childlike quality that I can't resist. He keeps me smiling most of the time when he's not being a pain in the butt."*

I took this excellent opportunity to consult Gabrielli, *"I've been told, if I throw a coin into a Roman fountain, my wish will be granted. Is this true?"*

Grinning amusingly my professor answered, *"That will depend on what you wish for?"*

"What's your wish, Sir?" I mirrored his question, which seemed to throw him off guard.

After a short pause he replied, *"I want to marry an obedient woman, much like my mother was to my dad. When the correct time arrives I will propose to this girl."*

"Who is this lucky female?" I asked inquisitively, although I had perceived who the woman in question might be. I did not let on my spying between Sabiya and him in the Sekham's olive garden.

"You'll be the first to know once I make the official announcement," answered Gabrielli slyly.

Andy pitched in tactfully, *"Young, don't be so imprudent and pry into your teacher's affairs. He has already mentioned that you'll be informed when the time is ripe."*

Defying my Valet's hint, I continued inquiring, *"If you marry, won't your future wife mind you having liaisons with men and boys?"*

My Valet, embarrassed by my forthright questioning, said, *"Young, this is none of your business. It is a private matter between your teacher and his betrothed."*

Turning to me, Gabrielli replied affectionately, *"It is okay for him to ask. I'm happy to enlighten my student with an example from the Roman poet Martial.*

"In one of his poems, he addressed his wife, who found him anally penetrating a boy. To her nagging observation that she too can provide him with similar pleasure, the poet responded with a catalog of mythological examples; illustrating the point that anal intercourse is more pleasurable with boys than with women. He concluded with a harsh dismissal: stop giving masculine names to my affairs; think of it this way, wife: you have two cunts."

My teacher continued, *"According to Martial, Jupiter is supposed to have preferred the anus of the boy Ganymede to that of* his wife Juno; which the poet claimed was the main reason Juno never ceased to hate the Trojans –because Ganymede was a Trojan."

Intrigued by this information, I queried, "Tell me more; this is an interesting educational topic."

"It's a Roman cultural tradition that we generally don't listen to our wives. There are many examples of wives getting jealous of boys in their husband's keep. This is part of Roman life. It is similar to Middle Eastern customs of keeping harem boys in Arab Households."

To my chagrin, Andy, Gabrielli, and I were summoned by both photographers to take our positions in the fountain for our modeling turn. I wanted to obtain more information on this intriguing topic.

Andy

While Andy and I were posing, I asked my lover, "Gabrielli's lesson is astonishing."

My Valet answered, "Pederasty traditions are well documented in a variety of cultures. I hardly need to mention ancient Greece and the early Dorian coming-of-age rites or the latter Classical obsession with young male beauty.

"For example in Athens, a boy could play the part of eromenos (the beloved) as long as he was beardless. After that, he would "switch sides" to become the erastes (the lover) of a younger eromenos."

Although my sex education Professor Andrew Henderson had touched on this subject, I was learning revealing information as I listened attentively to my guardian, "As much as the classical Greeks worshipped the boy, the eraste only penetrated the ermenos between his thighs (intercrural sex) while in a standing position, so he was not degraded to a woman's role by lying under the man. The Romans, on the other hand, enjoyed anal sex with boys."

"That's interesting," I interrupted.

My lover continued while we contorted in various sensual positions for our photographers, "This was possible because the Romans used slaves as their sexual partners, and free-born Romans were considered stuprum (taboo). A man could have one or more slave boys in his "stable" besides his wife. In most patriarchal cultures women had little say in this arrangement."

Mario

Before we knew it, the hours passed and we were done with the night's filming. While I helped Mario pack, he turned to me and suggested, "Young, it is good luck to throw a coin into the fountain and make a wish. All of us should do that before we leave."

As we followed Mario's lead I couldn't help wondering what his wish was.

It was already 5 A.M. and we were ready to drink strong lattes and cappuccinos to wake us from our exhausting photo-shoot. A sense of peaceful tranquility washed over me as we sat chatting in a nameless cafe nearby.

Sitting next to the Count I asked, "What was your wish when you threw the coin in the fountain?"

Mario replied smilingly, "My wish is to be like Alexander the Great; to love unceasingly and ferociously."

"Why be like Alexander the Great?" I asked fastidiously.

"He was the greatest lover of men, especially in his love for his long-lasting companion, Hephaestion. Not to mention Bagoas, the Persian eunuch of exceptional beauty. When he was in the very flower of boyhood, he and Alexander had an intimate relationship.

"Perhaps I am a romantic at heart and worship heroic love like that of Alexander for Hepaestion. The heroic warrior lay upon Hephaestion's deceased body for a day and a night after his death grieving, only to be dragged away by his friends. For another three days he remained mute, in tears and fasting. When he finally rose he sheared off his hair and ordered all ornaments in the city to be broken off the walls and the manes and tails of all horses sheared. He forbade joyous musical celebrations in cities, ordering every town within his empire to carry out mourning rituals. He then sent envoys to Ammon's oracle at the oasis of Siwah in Egypt to ask for divine *honors to be granted to his deceased lover. Hephaestion was then embalmed and his remains were taken to Babylon for cremation on a pyre. Alexander gave him an elaborate funeral rite."*

Mario continued when I noticed tears forming at the corners of his eyes. *"I try to imitate this kind of love throughout my life. Maybe I'm nostalgic for the halcyon classical life which Sir Lawrence Alma-Tadema painted so elegantly depicting Roman romanticism,"* sighed the photographer.

In distilling the history lessons I learned at the Trevi Fountain, I grasped a better understanding of both my Italian mentors and my Arab 'Masters.' They were from vastly different schools of thought, yet their cultural practices collided. They were phantasmagorically similar in more ways than I could imagine.

31

Love Among The Ruins

"All human actions have one or more of these seven causes: chance, nature, compulsions, habit, reason, passion and Desire."
Aristotle

Chance & Nature – Early March 2012

My unsure self was stalling, wondering if it was wise to contact Aria for Andy's information. In more ways than one, I was glad when the universe returned my earlier email to Aria as Mail Undelivered. I presumed my greeting card and letter to her postal Gothenburg address never reached its destination either, since she had moved to Stockholm. Chance had again presented itself and, like the nature of my Himalayan cat, Kali, my overpowering curiosity couldn't give up an opportunity to discover what happened to my beloved Andy (even-though I kept reminding myself to let sleeping dogs lie). I found myself contemplating to write or not to write. You guessed correctly – my alternate self-wrote.

Compulsions & Habit – 1967 At Café de Paris

Since it was my first time in the Eternal City I was eager to go exploring. Our entourage awoke hungry and ready to paint the town red, sleeping the entire morning and afternoon from exhaustion after our overnight photo-shoot at Trevi Fountain. Gabrielli suggested we watch the sunset at the prestigious suburbs of Palatine Hill, but first we proceeded to Café de Paris, a celebrity dining establishment on Via Veneto made famous by Federico Fellini in his classic 1960 movie *La Dolce Vita*.

Similar to Café de Flore in Paris, this eatery was filled with Rome's beautiful people. As soon as we entered, Gabrielli was greeting every other patron, as Mario had in Venice. By the time we sat and ordered, my jaw had dropped a hundred times over from celebrity gawking. Finally our food arrived (which took forever) and my starving child syndrome had worked its way down my grumbling stomach. I was ready to chomp down my last bite of spaghetti bolognese and my porcelain plate all in one mouthful.

As I was gobbling my food, Gabrielli announced, *"Let's take a walk up Palatine Hill after we finish dining. The gardens are beautiful during this time of day before it gets dark and seedy.*

Sitting next to my teacher I asked, *"What's the meaning of seedy?"*

Bursting out in laughter he turned to me and said, *"Oh Young, you make me laugh with your funny questions."*

Staring at him as if he had lost his mind, I said nothing. Andy, who was sitting on my other side, responded smilingly, *"Darling, seedy means things or people that are shady, disgusting and not particularly nice."*

"What is so seedy about Palatine Hill? I thought it was one of the most well-kept and wealthy suburbs in Rome?"

Gabrielli continued his laughter. Finally, he was sufficiently calm before answering my question, *"My innocent one, I don't think it is a good idea for you, to know or witness what goes on after dark among the Ruins. It is not for one so young to experience."*

By now my professor had perked my habitual curiosity, so I continued, *"That alone is reason for me to experience what kind of seedy happenings go on among the Ruins. I want to be worldly, like you."*

My comments sent the Italian into fits of uncontrollable sonorous merriment; he could no longer speak, let alone respond to my statement. I on the other hand watched in all seriousness as if the man had inhaled a spray of laughing mirth. I prayed he would not fall to the floor with hilarity while throwing up his food in the process. Finally the Italian wiped his boisterous tears from his eyes and spoke, *"Ok, let's do the walk and we'll see where it'll lead us. I'm not promising to show you the seedy aspect of my fabulous city,"* he continued speaking with gaiety.

The rest of our group also found the entire episode amusing before they changed the topic to a more serious one.

Reason & Passion – At Farnese Gardens

Strolling in the Farnese Gardens was a purifying experience. The setting sun metamorphosed into a hazy golden glow which was solely Italian. Since our mission in Rome was to photograph, we automatically brought our cameras along wherever we went. While enjoying the beautiful Farnese Gardens, passersby watched our entourage photographing each other. We were fully clothed, unlike the few days prior when we were naked at the basilicas and the fountains. This time we provided an illusory dignified facade to the public at large.

As we sat in an open cafe within the tranquil gardens, a sense of allay echoed over me; how did I end up in cosmopolitan Rome from my humble origins in Kuala Lumpur? And in the process, I had found a loving entourage who accepted me, transporting me into a blissful euphoric contention – at long last I had found my true family away from home. These people sitting by me and talking animatedly were my pacified brothers, more so than my own flesh and blood siblings were. While cradling my wistful ethereal thoughts, Oscar knelt beside me. *"Young, you are looking so dreamily pensive,"* my lover remarked.

Jolted back to reality, I replied happily, *"Because I love you and Andy very much."*

With tender concern, my handsome BB gave me a peck on my cheeks, winked and said, *"Andy and I are passionately in love with you too."* Getting up he gestured for me to follow.

We walked towards a secluded pond where Mario and my Valet stood waiting. The Count suggested excitedly, *"Strip, so I can take some pictures of you guys. This is a perfect location to capture some appealing photos of the loving trio."*

We did as he commanded while he snapped away before someone arrived to harass our party for posing in our birthday suits. Passionate shots were captured which now serve as unforgettable memories in my adult life.

Desire – Among the Ruins

Dusk fell over Palatine Hill while we were having fun. We had strolled pass the ruins of Circus Maximus and the remains of Septimius Severus Palace, both located in the southern end of this massive mount. Adjacent to the palace were the ruins of the emperor's baths.

Gabrielli explained as I kept in step beside him, *"Now is the perfect opportunity to give you a brief history of my city. From where you are standing, look towards the north-west section of this hill; you'll see Domus Flavia (the house of Livia). It is one of the best-preserved houses on Palatine Hill and dates back to the first century BC when it was Emperor Augustus and his wife, Livia's home. In ancient times the palace consisted of two wings: Domus Augustana and Domus Flavia. The remains of both wings are still visible.*

"But in the wee hours of the morning, this is a very dangerous place to roam."

"How dangerous is this place?" I asked.

"Remember at the cafe I mentioned that this area becomes pretty seedy after midnight?"

"Yes, I recall, and you laughed when I didn't know the meaning of seedy." I reminded my professor.

With a wide grin on his face he continued, *"A lot of men loiter among the ruins looking for sexual release and fulfillment;*

when the bars and clubs close at 2 A.M., this area will become a cruising ground for men who need sex."

"You mean they have sex in the open?" I badgered with great curiosity.

"Most of them hide behind the ruins or amount the trees and shrubberies to live out their sexual desires. One never knows who these guys are. They could be thugs, thieves or malevolent characters with a penchant for bullying and or beating up homosexuals. It's unsafe to walk these grounds in the middle of the night," advised my mentor.

"You see over there," he pointed to a different location on the hill. "The Domitian's palace, the largest of Rome's palaces for three centuries, was built in 81AD. It was constructed between two crests after the taller of the two; the Palatium was topped for use as the current heart of Palatine Hill.

"This is a notorious section of the mount. Mafia-type murders had been reported here in the past. So don't venture in there on your own; do you understand?"

I nodded and uttered a *"Yes Sir!"* to my teacher.

Exhausted, our entourage was ready for a light meal before heading back to Villa Spallentti Trivelli for a good night's rest, to commence another exciting day.

Early March 2012

My email message to Aria:

Hello Aria,

This may come as a surprise to you since we have not been in touch for many years. Carol gave me your contact email. I wish you and your family well. I'm not sure if you remember me? We met at your parent's home in Vaduz the Yuletide of 1966. I was the Asian boy with your brother Andy. We left abruptly on Boxing Day after your mother walked in on us while we were cuddling naked. She was stunned and shocked and dropped the breakfast trays she was carrying. Your father was furious and demanded Andy and I leave the house immediately. Do you recall the events of that fateful morning?

You probably already know that three years after that fateful day, Andy and I separated. Since then I had lost contact with your brother. Lately, I have been corresponding with Carol and she gave me your contact information. I am writing to inquire after you and your brothers' wellbeing. I hope to renew our friendship and any updates or ways of connecting with Andy will be most welcome.

Please stay in touch when you find time to correspond.

Best Wishes!

Young.

32

Shrouded in Mystery

"Life does not consist mainly, or even largely, of facts and happenings. It consists mainly of the storm of thought that is forever flowing through one's head."
Mark Twain

Early March 2012

One day I received an email from Arius. He wrote;
Hello Young,
How are you doing? Hope all is well on sunny Maui. I'm glad to announce I have some unexpected news for you. It is probably not what you are expecting, but this information may be of interest. Since putting the word out to locate Andy, my friend David met Oscar Jakobsson, who remembers you from the past.
*I immediately thought of Oscar, your other BB and lover, with whom you have also lost touch for all these years. Maybe he is the one and the same person mentioned in your "**Initiation**" blogs? David gave me Oscar's contact information, which I've enclosed in this email.*
I wish you the very best in connecting with Oscar. I'm sure there will be lots of reminiscing for the both of you.
Stay in touch, my friend, and I look forward to your news.
Regards,
A.S.

1967 Basilica Papale di San Paolo fuori le Mura

The following day was Sunday and, like obedient Catholics, Mario, Gabrielli, Tino and David decided to attend Mass at Papal Basilica of St Paul's Outside the Walls, one of Rome's four ancient basilicas. Since I had never been to a catholic religious service, I managed to drag Andy with me.

While Aziz, Oscar, Devaj, Luke and Ugo went shopping before our scheduled meeting at Castel Sant' Angelo after Mass, for further sightseeing and photography work.

A statue of the Apostle Paul stood in dictatorial guard in the center of the basilica's expansive courtyard. Riveting murals of the 12 apostles surrounded this opulent renaissance architectural marvel, especially within the huge golden mosaic dome. The cathedral was founded by Emperor Constantine and built over Saint Paul's burial site after his execution. His followers soon erected a sacred *cella memoriae* in honor of Christ's famous martyr on this lush ground.

Mass

As soon as we entered the building, intoxicating smells of frankincense permeated my nostrils with galvanizing euphoria, transporting me to my E.R.O.S. initiation and incantation ceremony. Like my school's non-denominational chapel service I had attended the morning prior to my initiation, the sermon at the basilica was also on the topic of LOVE. This engrossed me and I listened attentively to the holy message. Mario noticed my engagement and spoke to me after the service, *"You seemed overwhelmed by the sermon at Mass."*

"This is a beguiling experience, as it reminded me of my initiation ceremony at my boarding school chapel several months ago," I replied.

He teased me, saying *"Did the priest in your school put the moves on you?"*

Surprised by that question, I remarked curiously, *"What do you mean by putting the moves on me?"*

"Well, you know, him trying to solicit sex from you. Catholic priests are notorious for seducing adolescent boys, especially ones like you."

Shocked by Mario's information I continued, *"No, my school's Chaplin never tried putting the moves on me. I thought catholic priests made solemn celibacy vows to the church?"*

The Italian answered with a cheeky grin on his face, *"Don't be fooled by catholic dogmas and doctrines. Life is very different beneath their superficial pomp and circumstance."*

"Really? Tell me more."

The Count smiled devilishly and continued, *"I'll give you a little background to the central and irrefutable part of priestly celibacy which is generally believed derived from Jesus and the apostles' teachings, although some Fundamentalist Christians make a big Boo Haa of a biblical reference to Peter's mother-in-law (Mark 1:30), referencing that he had been married before. If this is the case, then the Catholic Church would be unable to regard him as the first pope.*

"In fact priestly celibacy is not an unchangeable dogma, but a disciplinary rule. The fact that Peter was married is no more contrary to the Catholic faith than that of the married pastor from the Masonite Catholic faith."

I was curious to learn more so I continued asking, *"Isn't celibacy unbiblical, since the Old Testament stated that God created man and woman in the creation story of Adam and Eve so they could bear children to continue the family tree?"*

"It is claimed that every man must obey the biblical injunction to "Be fruitful and multiply" (Gen. 1:28); even Paul commands that "each man should have his own wife and each woman her own husband" (1 Cor. 7:2). It has been argued that celibacy somehow "causes," or at least correlates with higher incidence of illicit sexual behavior or perversion." Mario commented with determination, as if making a vital point in his argument.

"Didn't Jesus and Paul practice celibacy?" I teetered.

"Although Paul endorsed celibacy for those capable of it, he also wrote, 'To the unmarried and the widows I say that it is well for them to remain single as I am. But if they cannot exercise self-control, they should marry. For it is better to marry than to be aflame with passion' (Corinthians 7:8-9).

"Because of the 'temptation to immorality,' (7:2) Paul gave the teaching about man and woman having a spouse and giving each other their 'conjugal rights' (7:3). He specifically clarified, 'I say this by way of concession, not of command. I wish that all were as I myself am. But each has his own special gift from God, one of one kind and one of another,' (7:6-7,)" continued The Count.

I asked with parlance, "Why are you so beguiled by this analogy?"

"Even-though I am born catholic, there are various liturgies that I strongly disagree with and one of them is the topic of priestly celibacy. I know several priests that live double lives, pretending to be celibate but having secret liaisons behind locked doors. You'll understand further when you attend my carnival ball." The Italian conflated as he continued enlightening me on the subject.

"In the bible, Paul went on to make a case for preferring celibacy to marriage: 'Are you free from a wife? Do not seek marriage...those who marry will have worldly troubles, and I would spare you that...The unmarried man is anxious about the affairs of the Lord, how to please the Lord; but the married man is anxious about worldly affairs, how to please his wife, and his interests are divided. And the unmarried woman or girl is anxious about the affairs of the Lord, how to be holy in body and spirit; but the married woman is anxious about worldly affairs, how to please her husband' (7:27-34). Paul's conclusion: He who marries 'does well; and he who refrains from marriage will do better' (7:38).

His teachings are so contradictory!" The photographer announced.

"What has celibacy to do with priests soliciting sex from young boys?" I asked smugly.

"Young, many men go into the priesthood because they are latent homosexuals and have difficulties accepting their sexuality. Most believe that by taking a vow of celibacy they can somehow avoid dealing with their own sexuality, that Jesus and God will lead them away from sexual temptations. This to me is utter nonsense.

Instead, these vows serve to encourage sexual perversion. But the church authorities often cover up the priests' affliction by pushing the issue undercover, hoping it will disappear without taking the initiative to deal with the problem. To me this is an irony I have difficulty accepting.

"I knew I loved men as soon as I reached puberty and am not afraid to accept my sexual preference. I live an honest and truthful life. I don't make a secret about my sexual preferences, although there are those that disapprove of my unorthodox way of living. But I don't give a damn what they think."

"Aren't you afraid they will persecute you?" I heralded my concern.

"Well no one has thrown stones at me. I'm firm in my beliefs." The man spoke with a strong stance. "Besides, Rome has a pagan history of pederasty. I'm sure you've been taught that Romans and Greeks have similar pederasty traditions."

By the time we arrived at Castel Sant'Angelo the other half of our entourage was already waiting by the 'angels' bridge. The time had arrived for us to visit Hadrian's Mausoleum.

33

A Love Story

"I think I would rather possess eyes that know no sight, ears that know no sound, hands that know no touch than a heart that knows no love."
Bernard Tristan Foong

1967 Gli angeli di Roma

The impressive bridge leading to Castel Sant' Angelo became the principal crossing point for pilgrims to St. Peter's Basilica. In 1668, Pope Clement IX commissioned ten stone angels to line its balustrades, thereby transforming the Castle of the Holy Angel into the most theatrical monument of Baroque design. Over the centuries the angels on the bridge became icons for millions of pilgrims, but the most exquisite, the only two carved by Bernini himself, never took their designated places. Copies by lesser artists were installed instead. This information started Gabrielli's history lesson of the day for Devaj and me, as we walked across the bridge to Hadrian's Mausoleum.

"Why were copies installed instead of Bernini's originals?" Devaj asked.

"Some say the Pope couldn't bear the thought of exposing such beautiful statues to the elements while others contend he wanted to move the pair of angels — one carrying the crown of thorns and the other the mocking inscription I.N.R.I. (Jesus, King of the Jews) to his own palace.

"Or perhaps, Bernini, as a way of promoting his not-so-talented offspring, claimed that they were the work of his son Paolo Valentino and kept the "lost" angels in his studio opposite the church of Sant'

Andrea delle Fratte (St. Andrew of the Thickets), so called because it was once literally out in the sticks.

"But in 1729, Bernini's nephew donated the angels to the church, which was partly designed by Bernini's former student and eventual rival Francesco Borromini. The angelic pair remains in the church, their beauty undiminished by fire, earth, water or air, to each side of the front altar. I think of these heavenly messengers when the bells toll from Sant' Andrea ring out the Angelus." My teacher remarked.

As we were admiring these amazingly crafted messengers of God, he continued, "The master artist and architect Gian Lorenzo Bernini did the all- male angel drawings with grieving faces and graceful bodies. They're brilliantly positioned to be observed and appreciated from every direction. Each of the angels carried a symbol of Christ's passion and death, such as the whip that scourged him and the nails used to crucify him."

"Why are the angels lining the bridge?" I asked.

"My dear boy, a virulent plague was ravishing Rome in 590 and Pope Gregory the Great entreated God's mercy. The archangel Michael, fulfilling the original meaning of angelus as a messenger from God, appeared in a vision sheathing his sword over the fortress, a signal of the plague's end. The grateful pontiff christened Castel Sant' Angelo in his name and had an imposing statue of Michael mounted on top."

As we proceeded in the direction of the archangel, my teacher continued, "Here stands one of the most famous angels in Rome, atop the Castel Sant' Angelo. This mammoth structure on the banks of the Tiber was originally built as a mausoleum by the emperor Hadrian in the year 123. From its ramparts, Romans fought back the assaults of the Visigoths in 410 and the Ostrogoths in 537."

Hadrian's Mausoleum

We proceeded into the mausoleum museum that housed a permanent display of Hadrian's antiquities and artifacts.

Mario, Andy, and Oscar joined Gabrielli, Devaj, and me as we walked round the displays and my teacher continued our history lesson. The rest of our entourage had wandered off on their own before they joined us again at the end of our tour.

Mario was the first to speak as we admired a life-size marble statue of the Roman emperor. He said, *"I really admire the love Hadrian showered upon Antinous. Their relationship was a perfection of Greek Love."*

Devaj asked, *"I didn't know that Hadrian was gay?"*

"Of course he was. It's one of the greatest love stories ever told," Mario answered before proceeding, *"We learn that when we are kids in school. It's a well-documented fact that Hadrian was devastated when Antinous drowned in the Nile while they were touring Egypt."*

"Pray do tell us more," I said.

Mario said smilingly, *"Where do I begin?"*

"Start from the very beginning," I replied.

Gabrielli chimed in quickly, *"Let me tell them, since I am Roman and Roman history is best told by a citizen of the Empire."*

We all responded simultaneously, *"Okay!"*

"Publius Aelius Hadrianus was born in 24 January 76 A.D. and died on 10 July 138 A.D. He is commonly known as Hadrian, and after his apotheosis, Divus Hadrianus, who was Roman Emperor from 117 to 138. He is best-known for building Hadrian's Wall, which marked the northern limit of Roman territory in Britain. In Rome, he built the Pantheon and the Temple of Venus and Roma. He was also a humanist and was philhellene in all his tastes. He is named as the third of the so-called Five Good Emperors."

"Very good, professor!" Mario said in a congratulatory tone before the professor continued the lesson.

"Hadrian was born to an ethnically Italian family in Italica, near Seville. His parents died when the boy was ten. He then became a ward of both his father's cousin Trajan, who became Emperor in 98 C.E., and his father's dear friend Publius Acilius Attianus, who later became Trajan's Praetorian Prefect.

"Although the love-hate relationship between Hadrian and Trajan is open to speculation, it is often said that the only thing the two truly had in common was a love of boys. It is possible that they were lovers. It has long been alleged that many of the troubles between the two men were caused by the boys they kept."

Mario cheered Gabrielli as we came to view a bust of the gay emperor. Pointing to the figurine, my teacher explained, "Hadrian was schooled in various subjects particular to young Roman aristocrats of the day. He was extremely fond of Greek literature and was nicknamed Graeculus ("Greekling").

"His predecessor, Trajan, was a maternal cousin of Hadrian's father who never officially designated an heir; but according to his wife, Pompeia Plotina, Trajan named Hadrian emperor before his death. Trajan's wife and his friend Licinius Sura were well-disposed towards Hadrian. He may well have owed his succession to them, as they put in a good word to the dying emperor."

Mario couldn't help adding before the professor ended his sentence, "Two years after his guardian became Emperor, Hadrian was wed to the young great-niece of his guardian, Sabina, who was approximately thirteen and fairly young by Roman terms of marriage.

"There was never much fondness between Sabina and Hadrian, but rather hostility. They were married purely for political reasons, since Sabina was the Emperor's closest unmarried female relative. In retaliation to the lack of emotion, Sabina took steps to insure that Hadrian would never have a child by her."

Gabrielli added, "Hadrian used the words, 'moody and difficult' when describing Sabina. He declared that if he were a private citizen, free to do his own will, he would divorce her. Rumors abounded that he tried poisoning her."

Mario continued, "During his reign, Hadrian traveled to nearly every province of the empire. An ardent admirer of Greece, he sought to make Athens the cultural capital of the empire and ordered the construction of many opulent temples in the city. This was where he met Antinous, a Greek boy who became his lover, underlining his philhellenism. This led to the creation of one of the most popular cults of ancient times. Antinous was an adolescent when they met. Similar in age to Devaj and you," he nodded towards my direction as if playing the role of Hadrian in the process.

Hadrian & Antinous

As we continued looking at the exhibits, Andy announced, "It states here that Antinous was born in the town of Bithynion-Claudiopolis, in the Greek province of Bithynia on the northwest coast of Asia Minor. It is now north-west Turkey. He was probably born on 27th November, although officially the year of his birth is unknown."

He continued reading the wall placard, "At the time of his death, he was described as 'ephebe' and 'meirkakion,' the two words meant to convey a boy in his late teens or a young man of around twenty.

"His parentage is unknown. It is thought that his parents may have originally been mentioned in the epitaph on the obelisk that Hadrian erected for the boy after his death, but the section where such mention is thought to have been contained is agonizingly chipped off the stone. What a bummer this information is lost; I like to know more about Antinous's life," commented Andy.

Gabrielli chirped, "Little is known as to how Antinous came to be in the house of Hadrian. It is thought that he was taken from Claudiopolis during one of Hadrian's tours of the provinces, when he was around eleven or twelve. Whether he was taken by force or went willingly is open to speculation.

"He became the Emperor's favorite, which seems to preclude his ever being a slave since Hadrian was known to accept social boundaries. The fact that many busts were made of an Antinous aged around thirteen would indicate that he was a member of the Emperor's circle soon after leaving home. It is speculated that he was taken to Rome as a page and perhaps entered into the imperial paedagogium."

I asked with curiosity, "What is the imperial paedagogium?"

"The paedagogium's official role was that of a polishing school designed to train the boys to become palace or civil servants but may have, in part, served as a harem." Mario conveyed as he came to stand by my side.

Gabrielli continued, *"It is impossible to say when Hadrian became enamored of Antinous; it is thought to have been sometime between the Emperor's return to Italy in 125. Antinous accompanied him as his favorite on his next trip to Greece."*

Without prior warning Mario suddenly pinned me against the wall, hands above my head, French kissing me in front of everyone. Stunned by his action, I didn't know how to react. I surrendered to the Italian's passionate assault. I was surprised but stimulated by his actions. This unannounced act toppled me into a cascading tailspin just as I was learning to get over my infatuation for the Count. My heart was thumping fast while I did my best to remain composed.

Onlookers quipped in disbelief before the Count's probing tongue parted my enthralling mouth. My head was spinning in a nauseated flurry from this frothy affection; I held tightly to the man in case I fainted.

A moment passed and I regained my senses. The Count spoke, *"The relationship between Hadrian and Antinous would be looked down on today but in ancient Greece and Rome, pederasty, a sexual relationship between an older man and an adolescent boy was common and an accepted part of society."*

He spoke loudly and eloquently to make certain that those gathered around could hear him, *"In case you don't understand the word pederasty; it derives from the Greek word paiderastia which translates to 'love of boys'. Pederasty has existed in a variety of customs and practices within different cultures, like I just demonstrated to you; love comes in a variety of shapes, forms and sizes."*

Andy noticed my disposition, rushed over and wrapped his arms round me. This provided Mario the perfect opportunity to use my Valet and me as an example for his monumental demonstration, *"While relationships in ancient Greece involved boys from 12 to about 17 or 18, in Renaissance Italy, boys were typically between 14 and 19."* He presented us to the cheering crowd as if we were in a forum.

Cheered on by the growing crowd, Gabrielli joined forces with Mario. My teacher said, *"In antiquity, pederasty was seen as an educational institution for the inculcation of moral and cultural values by the older man to the younger, as well as a form of sexual expression. It gained representation in history from the Archaic period onwards in Ancient Greece."*

Both men had created an imaginary platform, as if speaking in a forum at an ancient amphitheater. *"According to Plato, in ancient Greece, pederasty was a relationship and a bond, be it sexual or chaste, between an adult man and an adolescent boy outside his immediate family.*

"Most Greek men engaged in sexual relations with both women and boys, though exceptions to the rule were known; some avoided relations with women and others rejected relations with boys. In Rome relations with boys took a more informal and less civic path, with older men taking advantage of their dominant social status to extract sexual favors from their social inferiors. They carried on illicit relationships with freeborn boys." My teacher spoke heroically.

Mario added animatedly, *"It was obvious and proper in most circles that spiritual love should have a physical component. Hence, few thought anything wrong or even odd about the system of pederasty. Much poetry and art was dedicated to this practice, and even men who never took eromenoi and who seemed to have actually preferred the attentions of women often wrote verses praising boys so that they would be accepted by their peers."*

While both Italians continued their harebrained thoroughfare with the crowd, my lover gently and effectively propelled me out of the limelight before we snuck away from the maddening crowd. Andy and I left my professor and the

Count to their explosive and controversial collaboration. This is the nature of Italian vivacity.

34

The Room of Mysteries

"Our humanity is a poor thing, except for the divinity that stirs within us."
Francis Bacon

Mid-March 2012

Arius certainly had unexpected news for me when he gave me Oscar's contact information. I had never intended to relive my teenage years, which had brought an abundance of joy and also a load of heartache during and after my Harem services. Men I loved and had been in love with during those young years were neatly packaged into a lock box, banished to the recesses of my mind; I never intended to reopen that which had hurt irrevocably after Oscar and Andy's departure. In writing my memoirs I had reopened my Pandora's Box. They forced me to face the demons that haunted me after returning to reality from my fantasy-bubbled life, which came to a crashing halt when Andy and I terminated our four-year loving relationship. He went his merry way to New Zealand in pursuit of an engineering career and I stayed in London to follow my fashion ambition.

When Oscar announced he was leaving to pursue his medical studies at the University of Vienna, specializing in Plastic and Reconstructive Surgery after his Sekham service, I was sad that our triplet relationship was coming to an end. After his departure, Andy consoled and comforted me, guiding me to regain an emotionally stable footing. My Valet loved me unconditionally and had hoped I would follow him to Christchurch, New Zealand when he left to pursue his engineering studies. I did not.

Now the possibilities of connecting with my ex-lovers loomed large and I had to make a decision; do I contact them or not? *"Dear God!"* I prayed. *"Please provide me with insights to make the correct decision."*

1967 The Vatican Museums

Since the majority of our basilica photography sessions were conducted after church closing hours, I found myself back at the Vatican a couple of days before our return to Venice to attend Mario's masquerade ball. Thanks to Gabrielli and the Count's connections, together with a sizable financial donation, the Vatican Museums were now open for our private use. Most chambers within this city-state are ornately decorated, and the Musei Vaticani was no exception to the rule. As our entourage *oohed* and *aahed* at the impressive artworks, Mario and Gabrielli chatted with a cardinal and a chorister. They were both our official tour guides but unofficially doubled as naked boy salivators. They watched with great interest during the thrilling fake love-making scenarios that the models were simulating.

Cardinal Javier and Chorister Balrucci were introduced to Aziz and the models before they took us on a private tour of the newly restored papal rooms. We approached the *"Room of the Mysteries,"* situated on the first floor of the Pontifical Palace. It was located in the wing facing the south side of the Belvedere Courtyard which was built during the pontificate of Nicholas V (1447-1455). This was the first venue of our photo-shoot.

Sala Dei Misteri Vaticano

Mario, who was walking beside me, suddenly burst out in exclamation, *"These series of rooms made up the Borgia Apartments when Pope Alexander VI Borgia was the head of the church!"*

Cardinal Javier responded, "Yes indeed, these rooms were the Borgia Apartments, the pontiff's private chambers."

Mario announced loudly without any consideration, "This is where Rodrigo Lanzol Borgia (Pope Alexander VI) conducted his adulteries, rapes and incestuous relationships with his daughter, Lucrezia and his numerous mistresses."

Stunned by the comment, the cardinal quickly changed the topic, pretending he did not hear the Count's announcement.

Javier commented quickly, "These chambers were painted by Bernardino di Betto, better known as il Pintoricchio. He was a contemporary of Michelangelo and Raphael. From 1492 to 1495, Pinturicchio painted a series of Renaissance murals using precious materials. Some art experts commented that his work is more impressive than the Sistine Chapel. Aren't they beautiful?"

For reasons unknown to us, Mario continued to speak loudly, "When Rodrigo became Pope; the Vatican's already costly parties grew wilder and more expensive. As vice-chancellor of the Roman Church, he had amassed enormous wealth and lived like a Renaissance prince.

"It is documented when guests approached the papal palace; they were greeted by spectacles of living statues of naked, gilded young men and women in erotic poses.

"Flags bearing the Borgia arms portrayed a red bull, rampant on a field of gold, flew at every themed fete. One fete in particular known as the 'Ballet of the Chestnuts' was held on October 30, 1501. After the banquet and the dishes were cleared, the city's most beautiful whores danced with the guests; first clothed then naked. The exotic dancing commenced before the erotic 'ballet' began, with the Pope and two of his children in the best seats."

Intrigued by Mario's awkward commentaries, Oscar asked, "What's the Ballet of the Chestnuts?"

Embarrassed by the Count's erratic announcements of the Vatican's immoral disreputable history, the cardinal and the chorister walked rapidly ahead with Aziz and a couple of the models, leaving Mario, Gabrielli and the rest of our entourage trailing behind, listening attentively to our photographer's proclamations.

My teacher, ushered by Mario, added his spicy version to the Borgia's scandalous stories, *"Candelabras set up on the floor were scattered with chestnuts for the crawling courtesans to pick up before serious sexual intercourse began. Guests ran out to the floor stark naked, either mounting or being mounted by the prostitutes. The Bacchanalian orgy took place in front of everyone present, while servants kept score of each man's orgasms.*

"The Pope was said to greatly admire virility and measured a man's machismo by his ejaculatory capacity. After the guests were exhausted, His Holiness distributed prizes such as cloaks, boots, caps, and fine silken tunics to the winners who made love with the courtesans the greatest number of times."

David exclaimed, *"How sacrilegiously scandalous!"*

"That's not the end of the story, there's more," Gabrielli continued with vigorous excitement. *"His daughter, Lucrezia, had just turned seventeen and was at the height of her beauty. Here the tale darkens; The Pope was her lover. While Romans had scarcely absorbed the news that the father lusted for his daughter, they learned that Lucrezia was also deeply involved in a triangular entanglement with her two handsome brothers.*

"Although she enjoyed coupling with both brothers, they were jealous of each other. Each wanted their sister for himself.

"On the morning of June 15, 1497, Juan Borgia's (the younger of the two brothers) corpse was found floating in the Tiber, mutilated by nine savage dagger wounds."

I vociferated in amazement, *"How diabolical!"*

Mario continued lustfully, *"Borgia's enjoyment of the flesh was enhanced when the woman beneath him was married, particularly if he had presided at her wedding.*

"Breaking commandments excited Rodrigo, yet he was partial to the seventh. As priest he married Rosa, his mistress, to two men. She may have actually slept with her husbands sometimes, since Borgia

always kept a stable of women. She was allowed an occasional night off, to indulge her own sexual preferences, but her duties lay in his eminence's bed.

"At the age of fifty-nine, Rodrigo yearned for a more nubile partner, though his parting with Rosa was affectionate. He gave her a little parting gift and made her brother a cardinal."

My teacher and Mario were both animatedly reenacting the Borgia tales.

Gabrielli added, "Cesare, the Pope's eldest son was born so there might be one man vile enough to carry out the designs of his father. He practiced butchery in order to keep alive his thirst for blood."

Mario completed what the professor was relating, "One day, he went so far as to have the square of St Peter enclosed by a palisade, into which he ordered some prisoners. Men, women and children were bound hand and foot. He mounted on a fiery charger and commenced a horrible attack upon them.

"Some he shot and others he cut down with his sword before trampling them under his horse's feet. In less than an hour, he wheeled around alone in a puddle of blood among the dead bodies of his victims, while His Holiness and Madam Lucrezia enjoyed the horrific scene from a balcony."

I cried, "How gross!"

"Do you want to know how the Pope died?" Mario said metaphorically.

"Yes!" We replied in unison.

"Rumor has it that Rodrigo would appoint a cardinal after accepting a bribe. He would then poison the newly-made prince before reopening the bid for his replacement. His favorite poison is believed to be cantarella, made of white arsenic. This was the poison he was thought to have drunk by mistake, which he had intended for Cardinal Adrian Corneto, who switched the glasses.

"Borgia's face slowly turned mulberry colored and his skin began to peel off. The fat on his belly turned to liquid and he bled from both ends."

"Yuck! How vile and disgusting!" I blubbered out.

The Count continued compulsively, "The deformed blackened corpse was prodigiously swelling and exhaling an infectious smell, and his lips and nose were covered with brown drivel. His mouth opened widely, his tongue, inflated by poison, fell out upon his chin; therefore, no fanatic or devotee dared to kiss his feet or hands, as custom would have required of a dead pontiff."

"Say no more! This is absolutely loathsome and wretched!" I voiced squeamishly, aghast by the Count's gruesome descriptions of the dead pontiff.

I was thankful to the lighting crew when they called us to our modeling stances. Another adventurous photo-shoot was about to begin, undoubtedly under the tantalized eyes of the cardinal and the chorister.

35

Under The Blessed Knife

"Knowledge is like climbing a mountain. The higher you reach the more you can see and appreciate."
Bernard Tristan Foong

1967 Basilica Papale di Santa Maria Maggiore

During our week in Rome we visited the four ancient basilicas begun by Emperor Constantine, when he made Christianity the empire's religion. We had already photographed Saint Peter's and St. Paul's outside the Walls. We were now assembled outside the main entrance of Basilica Santa Maria Maggiore, waiting for our official guides to lead us inside this religious institution. Among the Patriarchal Basilicas of Rome, St. Mary Major is the only cathedral to have kept its original structure; though it has been enhanced over the years. My visit to the Liberian Basilica (as it is also called in honor of Pope Liberius) not only enriched my soul but also my mind as we progressed with our photo shoot.

Our Lady of Snows

Legend has it that a devout fourth-century Roman Christian aristocrat known as John had a profound dream. He and his wife could bear no children and were fearful that a lack of an heir would put an end to their family's prominence in the government of the city. Praying for a child without success, John's wife said, *"Let us ask the Blessed Virgin to nominate an heir."* And so they did, and their prayer was answered dramatically.

In August 352, Mount Esquiline, one of the Seven Hills in Rome, was covered with a rectangular area of snow. In the middle of the hot summer, snowfall was indeed a miracle, yet it had fallen in a specific pattern in one place. People crowded to see the patch of snow which persisted despite the heat. John and the Pontiff had simultaneously dreamt that 'Our Lady' desired a church to be built on the premise and the shape and size of the snowfall indicated the structure's layout. The Holy Father so moved by his dream decided to visit the mysterious snowfall. Upon arrival he discovered John and his wife kneeling in prayer to The Virgin at the holy site.

As soon as the plot for the building had been staked out, the snow melted. John met the cost of completing the building in 354 AD and dedicated the structure as Basilica Liberiana. Seventy years, later it was rebuilt on a grander scale with silver decorations and ornaments added by Pope Sixtus III. From then forward the church was known as Basilica Sixti and the Church of Santa Maria Maggiore (St. Mary Major).

The Borghese Chapel

Two kindly monsignors guided our entourage through the basilica's grand façade. This massive building was covered with impressive mosaic murals and frescoes. The ornate Borghese Chapel created by Pope Paul V Borghese (1605-1621) was the first stop of the photo shoot. Also known as Pauline Chapel, this opulent structure was designed by Flaminio Ponzio between the years 1606 and 1612. This refined monument featured precious marbles highlighted by gilded cornices, bronze and stucco angels radiating light in joyous poses, and a majestic altar made of an intense blue stone reflected the grandiosity that was indicative of Baroque taste.

Mario and Aziz decided to set up shop under the cupola of The Assumption of Mary, painted by the famous Ludovico Cardi otherwise known as Il Cigoli. With the moon underneath The Virgin's feet crushing the serpent while the heavens opened to rejoicing angels, we began the shoot fully clothed. As the models discarded their clothing in mid-session, they resembled the myriad of angelic spirits blowing their horns, playing their trumpets and scattering flowers as the ones depicted on the dome were.

By the end of the filming, we were posing naked like jay birds below the clouds of The Blessed Mary, who in turn was ascending towards the Heavens where the Apostles gazed at the triumphant Mother of God holding a royal scepter in her hand. Like Galileo looking through his telescope, Mario, our beloved photographer clicked away at his copulating subjects as he saw through his camera lens. He began his story telling to our group of tantalizing models.

The Liberian Musical Chapel

"They have one of the most outstanding boy choirs sing at this chapel every Sunday," Mario uttered while pointing his camera at us.

Andy, a keen music aficionado, asked, *"Really! What's the name of the choir?"*

"The Liberian Musical Chapel," Monsignor Grego replied as he stood by the sidelines watching the shoot. He began relating the history of the not so humble origins of the Musical Chapel.

He continued, *"Alessandro Scarlatti was the one who made the Basilica of St. Mary Major famous, leaving his mark in the two years he worked here as our choir director and sacred music composer."*

Before he could continue, the controversial Count Mario added, *"Wasn't Cardinal Borghese's favourite pathic a prima donna castrato who dined every evening with his protector?"*

The Count's outrageous remark left the monsignor speechless. He stopped short, not knowing how to respond to the remark. The photographer smilingly continued, knowing that he had gained the upper hand, *"Long live the knife, the blessed knife!"*

Castrati

This was reason enough to back Grego into a corner, providing Mario fuel to continue, *"Top castrati had careers like modern rock stars, touring the European opera houses from Madrid to Moscow commanding fabulous fees. They were true divas of their time; famous for their tantrums, their insufferable vanity, their emotional obsessions, their extravagant excesses, and their bitchy in-feuding and, not surprisingly, their sexual prowess."*

Now the two monsignors were slowly moving away from our photographer's presence, afraid that they would be asked to comment on this hot topic.

"Hysterical female admirers deluged them with love letters, fainting in the audience while clutching wax figurines of their favorite performers. "Long live the knife, the blessed knife!" screamed ecstatic female fans at opera houses as the craze for Italian castrati reached its peak in the 18th century; a cry that supposedly echoed in the bedrooms of Europe's most fashionable women."

Mario's campy comments sent us laughing as we posed seductively for the camera. He continued, *"The brainwave to create castrati first occurred two centuries before Pope Paul V Borghese. Previous popes had banned women singing in churches or on stage.*

"The voices of castrati were revered for their unnatural combination of pitch and power, with the high notes of a pre-pubescent boy wafting from the lungs of an adult. The result was magically ethereal and strangely disembodied. But it was the sudden popularity of Italian opera throughout 1600s Europe that created the international surge in demand for castrati."

Andy asked, *"Why would any boy want to be castrated?"*

"Often, Italian boys with promising voices would be abducted to back-street barber-surgeons and drugged with opium before being placed in a hot bath, where the expert would snip the ducts leading to

the testicles that would wither over time. It is estimated that by the early 1700s around 4,000 boys a year were operated on.

"The Santa Maria Nova hospital in Florence ran a production line under one Antonio Santarelli, gelding eight boys at once." The Count answered.

"How terribly disgusting!" I cried, "I, for one, wouldn't want to become a castrato just to become a famous rock star."

Mario continued, "It seems high-society European women loved them for the obvious benefit of built-in contraception. This made castrati ideal targets for discreet affairs. Before long, popular songs and pamphlets suggested that castration actually enhanced a man's sexual performance as the lack of sensation ensured extra endurance. Stories spread of castrati being considerate lovers, whose attention was entirely focused on the woman.

"As one groupie eagerly put it, the best of the singers enjoyed "a spirit in no wise dulled, and a growth of hair that differs not from other men."

By now, Gabrielli had joined the conversation, "This may seem to anticipate the safe, sexless allure of 1950s teen idols like Frankie Avalon. But congress with castrati was not at all physically impossible, although effects of castration on physical development were notoriously erratic, as the Ottoman eunuchs in the Seraglio of Constantinople knew. Much depended on the timing of the operation: Boys pruned before the age of ten or so often grew up with feminine features such as smooth, hairless bodies, incipient breasts, "infantile penises," and a complete lack of sex drive.

"Where did you obtain all these information?" Oscar enquired.

"I read the autobiography written by the castrato Filippo Balatri. He joked that he had never married because his wife, "after loving me for a little would have started screaming at me." But boys castrated after age ten, as puberty encroached, could continue to develop physically and often sustain erections. The operation was performed as late as age twelve."

Mario spoke laughingly while his shutters clicked away, *"It was rumoured that Farinelli, the most handsome castrato of all, visited London in 1734; a poem written by an anonymous female admirer derided local men as 'Bragging Boasters' whose enthusiasm 'expires too fast while F-----lli stands it to the last.'"*

"It has also been reported that English women seemed particularly susceptible to Italian eunuchs. Another castrato, Consolino, made clever use of his delicate feminine features in London. He would arrive at trysts disguised in a dress, and then conduct a torrid affair right under the husband's nose.

Gabrielli, Mario's accomplice chimed in again, *"Yet another, the beautiful, 15-year-old Irish heiress Dorothy Maunsell, eloped with castrato Giusto Tenducci in 1766. He was hunted down and thrown into prison by her enraged father. Marriage with castrati was normally forbidden by the Church, but two singers in Germany did acquire special legal dispensation to remain in wedlock."*

"Here comes the juiciest part," announced the triumphant Count, *"Male opera fans, meanwhile, sought out castrati for their androgynous qualities. Travelers report how coquettish young castrati in Rome would tie their plump bosoms in alluring brassieres and offer 'to serve...equally well as a woman or as a man.'"*

Gabrielli amused by the conversation added, *"Even Casanova was tempted, and he is reported to have written, 'Rome forces every man to become a pederast,' in his memoirs. His most confusing moment came when he met a particularly lovely teenage castrato named Bellino at an inn. Casanova, bewitched by the youth's beauty, went so far as to offer a gold doubloon to see the boy's genitals.*

*"In an improbable twist, when Casanova grabbed Bellino in a fit of passion, he discovered a false penis: it turned out that the castrato was a girl, whom historians have identified as Teresa Lanti. She had taken up the disguise to circumvent the ban on female singers in Italy. The pair became lovers, but Casanova dumped her in Venice; after she bore a son that may or may not have been his, Lanti 'came

out' as a female and went on to become a successful singer in more progressive opera houses of Europe where women were allowed on stage."

By the end of our photo session, none of the two monsignors could be located; only after our photographic equipment was packed and models fully clothed, did they reappear out of the blue. Instead of the bubbling selves we had first met, they had suddenly fallen silent as if the wrath of God had struck them mute. They led our entourage into the Chapel of the Most Blessed Sacrament, commonly known as Michelangelo's Sistine Chapel. The models again stripped bare, simulating sexual positions under the directions of our professional photographers. This time the monsignors watched vigilantly from the balcony above, without doubt promulgating their private sexual voyeuristic fantasies, as we continued our provocative poses around the sacred relics honoring the divine Mother.

36

Christo Salvatori –
"Christ the Savior"

"Love is composed of a single soul inhabiting two bodies."
Aristotle

Third Week of March 2012

My curiosity got the better of me and I wrote to Oscar:
Dear Oscar,
It's been a long time since we connected, if my memory serves me correctly, far too long. My friend Arius gave me your email. I am writing to you after more than 40 years of absence. I've heard through the grapevine that you are a successful cosmetic surgeon. The last time we corresponded was in 1970 when you were studying in Vienna. Have you moved to greener pastures since graduating medical school?

I have been living in Hawaii since 1996 after travelling and residing in different cities around the globe. I settled on Maui with my life partner of 16 years, Walter Bissett. He is an enlightened man, much like Andy when the three of us were together. Walter is a successful realtor. Our relationship is based on unconditional love, similar to that we shared in 1967. I have not been in contact with Andy since our separation in 1970. As you may or may not know, he went to university in Christchurch, New Zealand. I stayed in London for 10 years before moving to Hong Kong to teach at the Hong Kong Polytechnic University.

After Daltonbury Hall, I was accepted into Belfast College of Art, Northern Ireland for my year of foundation art studies before I returned to London. For the following three years I was at Harrow College of Art and Technology. I graduated with a diploma in fashion design before entering the Royal College of Art and Design. In 1977, with a Master degree in Fashion Design, I went to work for Liberty's of London. The rest is history.

Where are you living, my dear ex "Big Brother"? I have often thought of you over the years; wondering how you are doing. I'll be delighted to receive your email. Hopefully we can reconnect. For now I send you and your family blessings across the oceans.

A Hawaii greeting; Aloha!

Young (your ex "Little Brother").

1967 Papal Archbasilica of St. John Lateran

The final of the four oldest Roman Basilicas that Gabrielli had gained access for us to photograph was none other than St. John Lateran's Archbasilica. It claims the title of ecumenical mother church among Roman Catholics. St. John Lateran housed a monastery. Greeting our entourage the evening of our arrival was Abbot Beppo and two of his fellow monks. They were already stationed at the steps of the mother church entrance with hands extended; waiting to shake both our Italian spoke persons, Gabrielli and Mario. Like old friends they hugged one another and exchanged hearty cheek kisses.

As we followed our regimented guides into St. John Lateran, Christendom's earliest basilica, Beppo gave us an introductory tour to the history of this grand establishment. He began, *"Constantine the Great, our first Christian Emperor, ordered that this would be the Popes' own cathedral and official residence.*

"As you can see, standing before the basilica's ponderous eighteenth-century façade, towering against the midnight blue Roman sky is a seven-meter high statue of Christ, flanked by saints and doctors of the Church, triumphantly displaying the Cross of Redemption. It was to Jesus our Savior that Constantine dedicated this original church, confirming Christ's superiority over the Capital's pagan gods and assuring the worldwide expansion of the Christian religion."

Eager to inform his visitors of the cathedral's opulent grandeur, the Abbot proudly proclaimed, *"The interior retains the original Constantinian arrangement: a large rectangular hall with impressive nave, flanked by double aisles before terminating in an apse. The Emperor had conceived of an edifice to rival the monumental public meeting halls of Rome, the imperial city and this basilica has provided the model for the great majority of Roman churches, from the earliest to the most recent."*

While Beppo's loud voice explained, Mario fell several paces behind. Sandwiched between Andy, Oscar, and me, he began his own revolutionary commentary of this ancient place of worship. As we passed numerous religious icons, sacred statues and holy images of Christ the Savior, the Count started, *"Did you guys know that Jesus was a best man at a 'Gay Wedding' ceremony?"*

The three models trailing behind us burst into hilarity before Andy shushed at them to keep their voices down. Mario continued his theoretical explanation, *"Before the current bible came into existence, it is documented and proven that certain Biblical figures had homosexual relations, despite Biblical injunctions against sexual relationships between members of the same sex.*

"Examples are Ruth and her mother-in-law Naomi, Daniel and the court official Ashpenaz and, most famously, David and King Saul's son Jonathan. I'm sure some of you may have heard or read about those people in the bible's Old Testament.

"Adding to that, there are discussions about the significance of an Ethiopian eunuch as being the first gentile conversion. The inclusion of a eunuch represents sexual minority in the context of the time."

Adelphopoiesis

While Mario was speaking, David added excitedly, *"There are Christians that consider Christ made the commandments to "love God* and one's neighbor," and also to "love one's neighbor as oneself" touchstones of the moral law. These imply a radical equality and by this principle of equality, the Law of Moses is to be adjusted or abrogated.

"Jesus also exemplified this principle in his teaching on divorce. It is said that Christ instituted a virtue ethic, whereby the worth of one's action is to be adjudged by one's interior disposition. Because of these reasons, to condemn homosexuality is to fall into a pre-Christian 'Pharisaical' legalism."

Gabrielli and Luke had formed a separate group and were listening attentively to David's perpendicular explanation, while Andy, Oscar and I paid undivided attention to Mario's explanations. Aziz and the rest of our entourage had since proceeded ahead with the abbot and the monks.

Since our entourage had split into three parties, I frittered between Mario and David. Both provided interesting and unconventional explanations of biblical history, which I found fascinating.

The Count was now on a controversial topic that Andy and I found riveting. "Rites of so-called 'same-sex union' were found in western and eastern churches ancient prayer-books. The rites of adelphopoiesis (Greek for the making of brothers) unions were "spiritual" and not "carnal", according to the church's explanation, but arguably these should also be regarded as sexual unions similar to marriage."

The Count continued, "Scholars have dissenting views of this interpretation and believe that they were rites of becoming adopted brothers or 'blood brothers.' Some evidence comes from two saints: Saint Sergius and Bacchus (at St. Catherine's on Mount Sinai). Drawings depicting Jesus as a 'pronubus' (modern parallel to a best man) at the wedding feast of Emperor Basil I to his male partner are also discovered."

Brother-Making

Andy was all ears, listening to the Italian's speech. It suddenly dawned on me that the reason my Valet was engrossed in this topic; he had thoughts of marrying me when we had a conversation at the Kosk's Peacock Chamber. I had hurriedly run to Ramiz's class when my lover was about to propose. At the time, I had no clue of my lover's intention. Now I was keen to gain further insights about adelphopoiesis.

While Mario was about to continue, Gabrielli barged into the conversation, *"A mass 'Gay Wedding' occurred a couple of centuries ago, here in this very Basilica of St John Lateran, the seat of the Pope as Bishop of Rome!"*

As soon as my teacher finished, Mario said grinningly, *"I had knowledge of this event, but the current church authorities are desperately trying to downplay this information.*

"You see, the Orthodox Church regards this ceremony as purely spiritual, indicating brotherhood and aptly described as 'brother-making' or 'making of brothers.' This is an 'anachronistically literal' translation but I propose 'same-sex union' as the preferable rendering.

"'Sex,' for instance, while pointing to a seemingly 'objective' characteristic of the participants involved in the rite, draws attention to the physical condition or biological sex of the 'brothers'; whereas the rites for adelphopoiesis explicitly highlight the spiritual nature of the union over a physical one. But I differ in my point of view," the Count chortled.

David's group was now moving in unison to ours and the model reciprocated, *"Homosexuality is not a sin, if it is a loving, monogamous relationship, according to Christ's teachings.*

"St. Sergius and St. Bacchus are acknowledged saints by the Holy Roman Catholic Church in the modern era. Their joint saint day is October 7th. They were a well-documented homosexual couple, praised by contemporaries and by future generations. An icon exists of them at St. Catherine's on Mount Sinai, depicting their 'wedding' and Jesus as their best man. And they are by far not the only homosexual couple in the church with a public acceptance."

Andy, who was well-versed in Greek and Latin literature and philosophy added, *"Plato's philosophy accepted homosexuality as a valid form of love which was culturally sound."*

"The early church was heavily influenced by Plato and Greco-Roman culture. Although the Romans emulated Greek culture and they endorsed homosexuality in certain situations, it focused on the negatives of effeminacy, seduction and prostitution among those who engaged in homosexual activities."

"The complexity of the Roman response introduced heterogeneous standards into their culture, which would have been incorporated into the early Christian tradition. The combined evidence from Plato and classical civilization indicates broad acceptance of homosexuality around the Mediterranean in biblical times." Gabrielli responded.

Pronubus

My Valet, with exaggerated hand gestures, said, *"Plato's take on relationships is that those that are truly about love, founded in possession of wisdom and virtue are worthwhile because they achieve something. They are achievements brought about by a successful application of standards and possess good in whatever those standards measure.*

"For this reason, homosexuals must be accepted with respect, compassion and sensitivity. As heterosexuals are called to fulfill God's calling, so are homosexuals.

"A Father of the church once said to me," Andy reiterated, 'It is harder for homosexuals as they have more challenges to overcome in their distribution of the ministry, but God made them as they are for a purpose.' His Holiness remarked, 'Homosexuals are called to fulfill God's will in their lives and, if they are Christians, to unite to the sacrifice of the Lord's cross.'"

Oscar remarked, *"This is proof that the church is inconsistent, at the very least. This is well worth it on its own terms. It shows that the theological conservatives are dishonest, ignorant, or downright willing to use fabrications."*

Luke quickly dispensed his opinion, *"Theological conservatives are sometimes dishonest, or sometimes suffering from self-delusion or cognitive dissonance.*

"I, for one, apply 'theological conservative' more widely and precisely than most, looking not just at the content of beliefs, but the methods used to form them. Anyone who tries to justify a progressive position by appealing to a hidden tradition is a conservative in my book, as they're attempting to conserve instead of change. Yes, the churches are inconsistent. Thankfully so, or they'd still be supporting slavery and a God-given orders to obey the state no matter what. The difficult thing is getting them to acknowledge their inconsistencies."

By now both monks had arrived to inform us that Aziz had settled on the location to begin our shoot. We trotted behind the church 'brothers' and in no time we were ready to commence modeling for *"Sacred Sex In Sacred Places"* once again.

37

Osiris-Dionysus = God-Christ

"Knowledge is proud that it knows so much; wisdom is humble that it knows no more."
William Cowper

1967 Venezia

Our two weeks' roam in Rome flew by as quickly as the SAQR returned us to Venice. Delighted to be in the canal city we had a of couple days to catch our breath before the masquerade ball at Palazzo Rosa. While busy photographing in Roma, the Count's efficient staff had made necessary preparations, ensuring the success of the Sfera Mascherata di San Valentino (Valentine Masquerade Ball) went according to their master's plan.

The morning of our return, Aziz, Oscar, and Devaj went shopping while Gabrielli, Andy, and I had a relaxing brunch at Hotel Danieli before proceeding to Burano to visit my teacher's lace-designer friend, Maurizia. As we stepped out of our vaporetti (Venetian motorboat) onto dry land, we were greeted by buildings of sassy pinks, turquoise blues, sunflower yellows and hues of terracotta oranges. Judging from the sleepy village atmosphere of this charming island, I surmised the inhabitants must live a blissful existence. Lazy dogs were more plentiful than active people.

Lace

Maurizia, a slim, tall and elegant woman in her late 20s with long nimble fingers, welcomed us happily. Being the head designer of her growing enterprise, she was busy supervising the workshop ladies. After formal introductions, I stood mesmerized watching the women at work. Their intricate lattice work drew me closer to inspect. Maurizia, seeing me observe with keen interest, spoke in heavily accented Italian English explaining, *"There are a minimum of five steps to the creation of a piece of lace, which are normally made by five different women. I have assigned (indicating to a female close to where I was standing) the step which she is good at even if she knew all the various stitches. This will ensure profitability in her work since they are pieceworkers.*

"These ladies (gesturing to several others working in a corner) are responsible for the neckline. This is the step in which the lace design is fixed on the fabric. Paper layers acting as woof is the process that comes before rendering the 'ghipur' or 'punto Burano' (the stitch of Burano) on the entire drawing.

"These other lace-makers (pointing to another group of women located near the workshop entrance) carry out the 'sbarri,' the 'punto rete' which is the relief emphasizing a trim size. Finally the lace is pinched from the paper cutting where all seams and extra yarns are accurately removed by tweezers."

The Legend of Burano Lace

I asked, *"Why is Burano famous for lace making?"*

The proprietress replied smilingly, *"Legend has it that an ancient betrothed fisherman, while fishing outside the lagoon in the east sea, held up to a siren who tried to entice him by her canto. Because of his faithfulness he received a gift from the sirens' queen, who thumped the side of his boat with her tail, creating white foams from which a wedding veil emerged.*

Returning home on the day of marriage, the fisherman gave the wedding veil to his fiancée, who was envied and admired by the island's young ladies. Whereupon the town's women begin to imitate crafting the lace like the wedding veil; employing needle-and-thread that was thinner than usual, hoping to create a more beautiful lace veil for their own wedding."

I replied, "Legends are well and good, but I like to know the true reason."

"Well, young man, in that case I will disclose the truth about Burano lace to you. In the first years of '900, laces were made by limited number of women. In the 16th century many adolescent girls found work in 'Burano's conterie' and in small Venetian sartorial labs, where they were paid more money. Lace making became popular, thus developing into the industry it is today."

For now satisfied with her commentaries, we moved to her living quarters for beverages to enjoy a brief conversation before bidding *"Ciao Bella"* to our hostess until the following evening at the ball.

Osiris-Dionysus to God-Christ

Before 5 P.M. on the day of the Sfera Mascherata di San Valentino at Palazzo Rosa, Aziz arranged to show our entourage the proof sheets that he and I had snapped during our Roman whirlwind. As he passed the sheets around the group, Andy erupted in exclamation, *"These pictures are amazing! You are an excellent photographer, Aziz!"*

The Arab nodded with an appreciative grin, said, *"I too am pleased with the results. I can't wait to see Mario's pictures. I believe between the two of us...(suddenly remembering I also had a hand in taking some of the photos) and Young, we did a pretty good job, don't you think?"* He was addressing his question to no one in particular at our table.

Gabrielli laughed irresistibly while flipping through the proofs, *"I love the pictures of our hosts of naked boys copulating with Jesus icons as backdrops.*

"While on the subject of Jesus of Nazareth, I may as well give Vaj and Young a lesson on the similarities of Christ the Savior, Osiris and Dionysus. This I hope will enlighten both of my students and anyone else who may find my research information useful.

"Do you boys realize that there are many similarities between God, Jesus Christ and the ancient pagan religion of Osiris and Dionysus?" My teacher inquired.

Before Andy could respond, I spoke, *"No I don't."*

My Valet added before Gabrielli could continue, "I have some knowledge of scholastic comparisons and was beginning to wonder whether the Devil has perfected the art of diabolical mimicry or there is a mystery to be solved."

"Now that we are on the topic, let us review the evidence, shall we?" My Italian professor suggested. "For starters, Jesus the savior of mankind, God made man, the Son of God equal with the Father; so too were Osiris and Dionysus.

"Secondly, Jesus was believed to be born of a mortal virgin who after death ascended to heaven and is honored as a divine being; so too are Osiris and Dionysus.

"That brings me to my third comparison; Jesus was said to be born in a cave on 25 December, so were Osiris and Dionysus.

"Point 4; the birth of Jesus was prophesied by a star; so too were the births of Osiris and Dionysus.

"Point 5; Jesus was born in Bethlehem, which was shaded by a grove sacred to Osiris and Dionysus.

"There are more to come; Jesus was visited by the wise men, which, in the Osiris and Dionysus legends, were followed by three Magi. The Magi brought Jesus gifts of gold, frankincense and myrrh, which a sixth-century BCE Pagan scholar wrote; was the way to worship God.

"Jesus was baptized, a ritual practiced for centuries in the Mysteries. The holy man who baptized Jesus with water miraculously shares the same name as a Pagan god of water, who was also born on the summer solstice and celebrated as a Pagan water festival.

"Then Jesus offered his followers elemental baptisms of water, air and fire, as did the Pagan Mysteries."

Oscar jumped in with additional information before my teacher could continue, "Jesus was portrayed as a quiet man with long hair and a beard, and so were Osiris and Dionysus.

They bantered back and forth. Andy was next to comment, "Jesus turned water into wine at a marriage on the same day that Osiris and Dionysus were previously believed to have turned water into wine at a marriage. Jesus went on to heal the sick, exorcise demons, provide miraculous meals, help fishermen make miraculous catches of fish and calm the water for his disciples; all these marvels had previously been performed by Pagan sages. Am I correct?" My Valet was preening as if he was on his way to winning the grand quiz price.

My teacher finally managed to chime in, "Like the sages of the Mysteries, Jesus was a wandering wonder-worker who was not honored in his home town and was accused of licentious behavior, like the followers of Osiris and Dionysus. To add insult to injury, Jesus was not at first recognized as a divinity by his disciples, but then was transfigured before their eyes in his glory, just like Osiris and Dionysus were alleged to have been."

Before anyone interrupted he continued, "Jesus was surrounded by twelve disciples; so were Osiris and Dionysus. The savior rode triumphantly into town on a donkey while crowds waved branches, as did Osiris and Dionysus."

This was turning into a frantic game of impromptu relevance. I joined in with little to no knowledge of what or who Osiris and Dionysus did or did not do. All I cared was to participate in this fun quiz, so I jumped in, said, "Jesus was a just man unjustly accused of heresy and for starting a new religion; so were Osiris and Dionysus." I didn't really know if my assessments were correct.

Professor Gabrielli turned to me, giving me a thumb's up before I continued, "Jesus attacked hypocrites, stood up to tyranny and willingly went to his death predicting he would rise again in three days and so did the Pagan sages."

"Jesus was betrayed for thirty pieces of silver, a motif found in the story of Socrates," Andy added.

Waiting for my chance, I chirped in quickly, "Jesus is equated with bread and wine and his disciples symbolically eat bread and drink wine to commune with him, as do the followers of Osiris and Dionysus. Adding to that Christ was crucified, as were Osiris and Dionysus."

Oscar overtaking me, commented, "Jesus died as a sacrifice to redeem the sins of the world and his corpse was wrapped in linen and anointed with myrrh, similar to the corpses of Osiris and Dionysus.

"Wait, there is more! After his death Jesus descended to hell and resurrected on the third day before his disciples; then ascended into heaven, where he was enthroned by God and waits to reappear at the end of time as a divine judge; just like in the Osiris and Dionysus myths."

Andy followed suit, "Jesus died and resurrected exactly on the dates that the death and resurrection of Osiris and Dionysus were celebrated. The Savior's empty tomb was visited by three women followers who saw an empty cave; so were the Osiris and Dionysus stories."

The last words were spoken by Gabrielli, "Through sharing in his passion, Jesus offered his disciples the chance to be reborn, as did Osiris and Dionysus."

Aziz, the silent observer of our amusing debate, finally put an end to our conversation by providing us room for thoughts. He advised, "Discounting the diabolical mimicry argument, as you sane people must, how are we to explain these extraordinary similarities between Pagan myths and the story of Jesus?"

We looked at the Arab in a state of wonderment, pondering without any responses. We parted ways only to reassemble at 4 P.M., dressed in fancy masquerade costumes and elaborate masks. We boarded the hotel's speedboats ferrying us towards Palazzo Rosa in time for the evening's grand event.

38

Holy Father "John VIII" alias "Pope Joan"

"For most of history, anonymous was a woman."
Virginia Woolf

End March 2012

One morning as I was checking my emails after my daily meditation, a reply arrived from a Mr. Oscar Jakobsson. He bore a similar name to my ex-'big brother' and lover. At once anxious, curious, and afraid to read its contents, I waited, leaving the unopened message sitting in my laptop. I went about my daily chores. A nagging feeling left my stomach churning throughout the day. I was curious to find out its contents, yet I deliberately avoided opening the message. I needed to be in a right frame of mind to reconnect with this ex-lover. I was at a loss. It had been 43 years since I saw Oscar. I was an adolescent and he 19. We had moved forward with our lives and I had fallen in and out of several relationships, until Walter came into my life. I'm happy in my current relationship. I wasn't sure if I was ready to reconnect with an ex-lover for whom I continued to have un-finish emotional feelings. My inner voice was sending warning signals to tread with caution and exercise self-control rather than to rejuvenate the prime of our lives. For now, I was only confident to travel those paths in the remembrance of things past, when writing my memoirs.

1967 Sfera Mascherata di San Valentino

(Valentine Masquerade Ball)

The Danieli speedboats jetted us towards the Lido Excelsior Hotel. From the hotel pier, invited guests boarded phantasy gondolas specially charted to deliver partygoers to Palazzo Rosa. Gondoliers, dressed in black cloaks and white beaked masks, rowed the flamboyantly attired revelers towards their destination, while they serenaded each floating vessel with love arias. Our gondola slowly made the journey towards the dock of Count Mario's ancestral home. Numerous black-cloaked white-masked security guards were stationed by the palazzo's pier. They assisted guests from their boats, leading them towards the decorative floral entrance. Rows of fairy lanterns lit the large renaissance tents, creating an air of sophistication such as my young eyes had ever seen. I was in awe by this monumental display the Count had furbished on this night of love and romance. Nothing was left to chance, every path on our opulent journey was paved with well-trodden details for the enjoyment of his wealthy socialites and sophisticated invitees. Like any respected hierarchy of worldly pathos, Count Mario Conti events were no less a la conquete de chasse syduction. The man who counted himself as a classy playboy of the western world had outdone himself at this uber-spectacular. No expenses were too decadent for this Italian "Casanova" as we cavorted at the Sfera Mascherata di San Valentino, Venezia.

Il Gran Ballo (The Grand Ball)

I followed the two costumed footmen up the steps as each guest was officially announced at the ballroom entrance. The interior, decorated with garlands of sweet gardenias entwined with many shades of white, pink, red roses and geraniums transported me to A Midsummer Night's Dream where Puck was bound to appear before the night was over. Elaborate wall hangings twisted with sprinkles of lilies of the valley, interwoven with hues of cascading Madonna lilies, spumed euphoric sensuality in anticipation for the exalted sexuality that was soon to regale this majestic palace. An array of floor-to-wall candelabras merged with a menagerie of wax-candled Murano glass chandeliers, hung unashamedly on the high mural ceiling, transforming the spacious salon into an indemnified secularist world fit for Rossini's Othello.

A white-tie twelve-piece string orchestra played movie, opera and dance music late into the Venetian night, tantalizing revelers onto the floor with the beat of lingering erotic Tangos. They thumped exuberant Quicksteps to embracing romantic Waltzes. Weaving amongst each other for space in this joyful ephemeral contentious repository, guests were present to dispense la chasse au bouheur until daybreak, when all good things must come to an end. Hardcore partiers would carouse into the nights ahead until bodily exhaustion bid them rest, yet their youthful spirits cajoled them to the next soiree in this city that didn't sleep.

Pope Joan

While I was busy watching the parade of fantasy costumes floating before my eyes, someone tapped me on my shoulder. It was none other than 'Mr. Happy & Sad' (Gabrielli). He said, *"Young, I'd like you to meet a dear friend of mine."*

Turning around, I was confronted by an inordinately disguised male impersonator of a pope. Although her elaborate mask concealed her face extraordinary well, her amusing feminine voice gave her identity away. She greeted me, *"Nice to meet you, Young. Your teacher told me you're artistically gifted and incredibly inquisitive. Do you know who I am?"*

Loss for words, I looked at her searchingly before responding, *"A female Pope."*

Both she and my teacher burst out laughing when the Raven King came to join us. He bent down to kiss Her

Holiness hand, *"It's a pleasure to meet you, Holy Father John VIII, or should I address you as Most Holy Mother?"*

"Ahh, you know who I am. I must go into hiding before the angry mob kills me," she said laughingly.

The Raven King curtsied with regale gusto, *"Your Holiness, have no fear. I am a man of honor and will not expose your Most Holy Mother."* He stressed the words "most holy mother" as he spoke.

As they briefly entertained themselves, Pope Joan noticed my befuddlement. Turning to me, she said, *"The Raven King is very charming and witty. You are lucky to have him as your chaperone and lover."*

"He is indeed a delightful Valet. I love him very much and he teaches me many things."

"Then you must question him about Pope Joan. Otherwise I'll be delighted to tell you all about myself," replied Her Holiness.

"Why don't we elucidate this young man," answered Mr. Happy & Sad. *"As his professor, it is my duty to do so, don't you think, Holy Father/ Mother?"*

As we moved away to the quieter terrace lounge, the female Pope asked, *"Do you know of Pope Joan?"*

"I didn't know women could be elected as popes?" I was desperately trying to remember whether my Daltonbury Hall professors had ever taught me that there was a female pope. None came to mind.

"Let me tell you a little about my background, although this is based on a highly contentious story. In the ninth century, a baby girl was born in Germany to English parents who had moved to Europe as Christian missionaries. According to legend, she grew to be an unusually intelligent young female. Frustrated by a lack of opportunity for women, she disguised herself as a boy in order to enter a Benedictine monastery; she called herself Brother John Anglicus."

"Didn't John Anglicus study in Greece," commented Andy, *"Before travelling to Rome, where 'the monk' so impressed the*

Vatican with her abilities, she soon became a cardinal and was eventually elected pontiff in 853, after the death of Pope Leo IV?"

"You're right, Raven King. She supposedly ruled as head of the Church for nearly three years before her deception was uncovered," Happy & Sad continued. "One account insists that she was riding a horse near the Colosseum when she suddenly went into labor. The crowd shocked and angered to find that the Holy Father was in fact a Holy Mother, either stoned her to death or tied her to a horse and dragged her through the streets of Rome."

Pope Joan heralded, "The Catholic Church has long argued that I should not be mentioned in any contemporary records and the tale is a fantasy, cooked by scheming opposing Protestants. But proponents of the story point out those papal records are almost non-existent in the 10th and 11th centuries. Even male popes are barely documented."

Happy & Sad conflated, "Although they pointed to one particularly extraordinary artifact – as evidence that you existed, there is a wooden chair with a hole in the seat which they claimed, was used for 600 years to establish the gender of would-be popes in the wake of the Pope Joan scandal.

"Papal candidates were made to sit on the 'sella stercoraria' while a deacon prodded their genitalia from underneath to be sure of their manhood."

Pope Joan went on, "My absence from contemporary church records is only to be expected. The Roman clergymen of the day, appalled by the great deception visited upon them, would have gone to great lengths to bury all written reports of this embarrassing episode."

"The Dark Ages were really the dark ages," commented The Raven King.

"There is absolutely no certainty about who the popes of the ninth century were. Instead, we have to rely on medieval chronicles, written hundreds of years later. Therefore, it is perfectly feasible that I existed.

"We also know that some women bound their breasts and cut their hair short in order to pass as men. After all, a monk's baggy cowl is well suited to covering a woman's body." Her Holiness responded.

My teacher shrugged his shoulders and said, "That is categorically not true. There are plenty of pre-Reformation Catholic texts which mention Pope Joan. They were written by bishops, archbishops, and even a secretary to a pope. They accept that she existed. The Catholic Church, embarrassed by the story, crudely decided to erase it from their records. Of course, the official histories of the popes make no mention of Pope Joan, and many historians dismiss the story as a fable."

My Valet indicated with a refreshing disposition, "The sede stercoraria and other toilet-like chairs were also used in the consecration of Pope Pascal II in 1099. In fact, these artifacts are on display in the Vatican Museums and at the Musee di Louvre.

"The reason for the configuration of the chair is widely disputed. It has been speculated that they were originally Roman bidets or imperial birthing stools. Because of their age and imperial links, they were used in ceremonies by popes' intent on highlighting their own imperial claims, like they did with their Latin title of *Pontifex Maximus*."

Intrigued by this unusual topic, I listened with pricked ears throughout the entire conversation.

Gabrielli spoke next, "As a consequence, certain traditions stated that popes throughout the medieval period were required to undergo a procedure wherein they sat on the 'sede stercoraria' and a cardinal would be assigned the task of putting his hand up the hole to check whether the pope had testicles. At times, they also performed a visual examination. Still, this procedure is not taken seriously by most historians, since there is no documented instance.

"It is probably a scurrilous legend, based on the existence of two ancient stone chairs with holes in the seats which dated from ancient Roman times. These may have been used because of their ancient imperial origins, though their original purpose is obscure."

Alexis, alias Pope Joan, cited Alain Boureau, "He quotes the humanist Jacopo d'Angelo de Scarparia, who visited Rome in 1406 for the enthronement of Gregory XII. The pope sat briefly on two 'pierced chairs' at the Lateran: '...the vulgar tell the insane fable that he is touched to verify that he is indeed a man,' a sign that this corollary of the Pope Joan legend is still current in the Roman street.

"Medieval Popes, from the 13th century onward, avoided the direct route between the Lateran and St Peter's, as Martin of Opava claimed. There is no evidence that this practice dated back any earlier. The origin of the practice is uncertain, but it is quite likely that it was maintained because of widespread belief in the Joan legend, and was thought genuinely to date back to that period."

Raven King continued, "Although some medieval writers referred to the female Pope as "John VIII," a genuine Pope John VIII did reign between 872 and 882. Due to the lack of Dark Ages records, confusion often reigns in the evaluation of these events. A problem sometimes connected to the Pope Joan legend is the fact that there is no Pope John XX listed. Rumors have circulated that this reflects a renumbering of the Popes to exclude Joan from history."

Her Holy Mother commented, "However, I am deeply saddened that while riding on horseback during one of "My" official parades, I gave birth, thus exposing "My" gender. In most versions, I died shortly after, either being killed by an angry mob or from natural causes. My memory is then shunned by "My" successors.

"What a pity! I think a female pope would most likely do a much better job than a Holy Father. The Catholic Church will be a better place with a matriarchal rather than a patriarchal reign, don't you agree?"

Mr. Happy & Sad, together with The Raven King, agreed unanimously as I, The Black Virgin Queen sat dumbfounded, trying my best to decipher the abundance of information fed to me in such a short span of time.

As the fun and merriment rolled on into the night, the true bacchanalian jubilation did not begin until the clock struck midnight.

39

The Call of the Wild

"Life is a zoo in a jungle."
Peter de Vries

1967 The Announcements

As the Sfera Mascherata di San Valentino (Valentine's Masquerade Ball) continued, a number of ballroom guests were dissipating by the hour. Many proceeded up the grand staircase for a different kind of party. But when the grandfather clock chimed midnight, the 12-piece string orchestra abruptly ceased to play and the musicians began proceeding to the upper floors. Wondering where they were going, I asked my Valet, *"What is happening? Shall we follow them above stairs?"*

Before the Raven King could respond, a masked trumpeter standing in the middle of the ballroom blew his horn demanding the revelers to be silent. Untying ribbon scrolls with three other masked tuxedo guards, they each held an edict in gloved hands before proclaiming their announcements in four different languages. The first was in Italian followed by French, then German, and lastly, English.

"Onorevoli Colleghi, benvenuti Sfera Mascherata di San Valentino di Conte Mario Conti. Intrattenimento della serata 'Amore A Venezia' è presto per iniziare. Folleggiare, godere e libere voi stessi di una notte bagord lasciva," announced the handsome trumpeter, before stepping aside to make room for his French compatriot to take position.

"Les dames et les Gentilshommes, accueillez à Count Mario la Boule de Valentin Masquerade de Conti. L'amusement du soir 'l'Amour à Venise' est bientôt de commencer. Espiègle, appréciez et hearkenen vous-mêmes à une nuit de débauche impudique,"

bellowed the bonny French guard while the good-looking German prepared to take center stage.

He repeated in his native tongue, "*Damen und Herren, herzlich willkommen in den Maskerade-Ball von Valentinsgruss von Graf Mario Conti. Der unterhaltung des Abends 'Liebe in Venedig' soll bald beginnen. Herumtollen, genießen Sie und harkened selbst zu einer Nacht der mutwillig Liederlichkeit.*" He roared his pronouncement for the benefit of the Count's German speaking guests.

The attractive Englishman vociferated his proclamation, "*Ladies & Gentlemen, welcome to Count Mario Conti's Valentine Masquerade Ball. The evening's entertainment 'Love in Venice' is soon to begin. Frolic, enjoy and hearken yourselves to a night of wanton debauchery.*" Guests were already scoffing and chasing the announcers off stage, ready for a night of bacchanalian excess.

The Lion & the Dominatrix

The announcers began pushing three cages to the center of the dance floor. Growling noises emanated from behind the luscious velvet coverings draped across these large confinements, concealing their hidden treasures. With a signal from the Count, the trumpeter blew his horn again. Off came the drapes, revealing three ferocious naked human animals and a scantily clad man, pathetically struggling behind his roped bondage. Their elaborately crafted masks were the only items concealing their true identities.

Pounding his fist on the golden cage was a human lion, roaring intensely to the rowdy, jeering crowd. The naked beast shook the fence for release. A dominatrix carrying a long leather whip in her black, rubberized hands stepped to the front of the cage door. Dressed in a skimpy rubber corset and a revealing thong, she cracked her whip loudly to quiet the deafening beast. Defying his mistress' commands, the beast stuck out his hands, snatching at the whip before catching its tip and pulling it towards the cage. The animal and trainer became enmeshed in a tug of war. Planting her spiky high-heeled boots on the floor for anchorage, she pulled relentlessly at her whip. The growling Lion proved stronger, and soon she came face to face with the wild beast. Reaching out his muscular hands, he caught the scantily clad female before planting a lingering kiss on her ruby red lips. She unwillingly surrendered as he forced his masculine tongue into her orifice. With her lithe body pressed firmly against the barrier, the lion used his free hand to open the gate. The ferocious beast held firmly onto the dominatrix to prevent her deceitful escape.

The cage door flew open, and out jumped the roaring beast. She steadied herself while cracking her whip on his naked buttocks. Lunging towards his controller, the beast pinned her to the floor, straddling her before planting his pearly fangs into the side of her neck, sucking his prey as if drawing blood. The audience clapped and cheered as if witnessing a gladiatoress in combat with a savage brute. The Lion's throbbing penis was clearly visible against his mistress's G-string as the couple rolled around the dance floor, desperately trying to subjugate each other. Pinning her wrists above her head, the beast penetrated her moistness in a single stroke, causing her to moan in waves of ecstasy before she reluctantly relinquished herself to the animal she was trying to tame. Tilting her hips to receive his unrestrained pounding, she enjoyed the animalistic dance. Waves of orgasm traversed her capitulating body. Her sublime submissiveness aroused his raw animal instinct to tactile heights of pre-ejaculatory stimulation. His bouncing buttocks intimated his imminent climax. No longer able to stave off his insistent emissions he erupted jets of oozing intoxicants into her luscious sex.

The Bengal & White Tigers

While the lion and the dominatrix were in combat, a ferocious human Bengal and its equally virulent White were trapped in the adjacent silver cage. The mesomorphically built pair clawed at their herculean Master who lashed his whip at the solid iron palings. The Master ruled the naked beasts with an iron fist. His bulging muscles were covered only by a skimpy leather jock. Unlocking the cage, the Bengal pounced at his tamer, missing him by mere inches. His fellow White followed suit as they thundered at the cheering spectators. Crack! The whip sounded as both tigers lunged at their tamer once again, this time throwing him to the floor. The Bengal sank his luscious tongue into his Master's seductive mouth, while the White tore at his leather jock, ripping it to shreds. His bulbous genitals were exposed to the frenzied crowd. Cupping the prey's dangling testicles in his powerful palms, the tiger rubbed them as if they were delicacies to be devoured. The brawny man wriggled relentlessly, struggling for release, but both sinewy animals had planted their weight on top of the herculean, pinning him beneath their athletic musculature.

The Bengal straddled his Master's hairy chest as his throbbing erection swayed above the captive's face. His sturdy thighs imprisoned the victim's head. The White, in synchronicity, forced the man spread-eagle, burying his face into his intoxicating crotch, inhaling his muskiness. He engulfed the Master's length into his hungry mouth, tasting his oozing emissions from his bulbous head. The prey, in ecstasy and agony, managed to free his hand to snatch the horse whip. A mighty crack sounded and the whip's tail landed on White's smooth buttocks, compelling the animal to howl loudly. Refusing to release his hold on his enticing meal, the beast continued suckling the organ in total disregard of the walloping he was receiving on his rear.

Snatching a pair of handcuffs from the floor, the Bengal pulled his tamer's hands above his head, cuffing his prey to the iron railings. Trapped by both animals, the study captive wiggled desperately in a fake attempt to liberate himself. The tiger landed a slap on the man's face to quiet him. Instead he let out a distressing ululation – a call of the wild. Taking this opportunity, the Bengal stuffed his throbbing shaft into his prey, subduing him. The animal's protuberant onslaught forced his victim to relinquish his oral orifice. Leaning the captive against the cage, the animals manipulated their Master with ease. White straddled the tamer's groin, bouncing rapturously on his stiffness, gliding effortlessly in and out of his lubricated opening. He showed no signs of slowing, until the last drop of steamy semen was milked into the animal's inviting passage. Only then was the beast satisfied, stroking himself to the rhythmic motion of his own orgasmic submission. For now, he was rapaciously galloping to the compliant groans of his captive fan. Riding furiously at times, and at others sensually, slowly, and tantalizingly, White was in complete control of his sexual destiny.

The Bengal was busy plunging his protruding manhood down the acquiescent receiver, who was thoroughly basking in his tumescent feed. The previously formidable Master stared bewilderingly into the eyes of the beast, in awe of the brutal strength of this domineering feline that he envisioned he could control. Laying passively the prey surrendered himself to the climaxing Bengal, who wasted no time in depositing his seed. The howling beast beat upon his chest to the deafening accolades of the rambunctious spectators.

The Cougar, the Panther & the Masochist

A female snow cougar and her counterpart the black panther appeared between the lion taming the dominatrix and the sexually enticing threesome. These voracious felines were roaming the ballroom periphery, waiting for their opportunity to claw at the drapes of the bronze cage. Seizing the right moment, they sprang into action, ripping the fabric off of the solid enclosure with their sharp talons. Lying helplessly in a corner was a bound, gagged masochist. The naked cougar tore open the imposing lock, while the nude, spiky-heeled Panther dragged the slave onto the dance floor, exposing him to the vociferous throng. She whipped the man's naked buttocks viciously with a riding crop and a paddle. Desperately wiggling to avoid the cruel lashes inflicted upon his posterior, he struggled perilously only to be held in place by the unforgiving Panther. The cougar's aggressive heels pressed against his muscular chest forcing the Masochist into submission, while her companion unzipped the captive's leather thong, exposing an aroused phallus to the mocking multitude.

Unable to struggle free he surrendered to the domination of the felines, conceding to their beastly wishes. He endured the continued agony of the cracking wallops on his backside, savoring every demeaning physical lash he could endure. Tears streamed down his eyes from this public humiliation, yet he obediently conformed to his predators' emphatic demands. His swollen erection was a significant sign that he was reveling in the attention of his current vassalage. Longing for ravenous fustigation, the cougar untied his gag as he begged in remorseful penance.

The unrelenting Panther smacked the whimpering wretch before thrusting an elongated dildo into her prey. The sudden shock sent the slave into a series of jolting spasms. He ejaculated onto his punisher's 6-inch stilettos. Wham! Another blow landed on the victim's fiery buttocks, sending him into bouts of torturous orgasms. Under such severe conditions his hardness remained undeterred. He yearned for an encore assault. Both beasts accommodated the slave with dynamic aplomb.

Strapping a large vibrator to her hips, the cougar mounted the panther. She straddled the masochist in clear view of the vexatious assemblage. Riding both priapic organs, she moaned rhapsodically to her assailing animal pleasure. Waves of orgasmic contractions washed over her perspiring body.

Changing partners, the females rode wantonly on their engorged prey until physical exhaustion vanquished their pulsating animalism. Their carnal ring of Dionysian transgression was met with uninhibited jubilation.

The Exotic Erotic Cirque

Without moving a single muscle, I sat mesmerized in my seat. At that tender age, I had never observed anything like it. This fervent performance was thirty years before Cirque De Soleil's human circus made its mark in our popular culture. It was also precisely thirty-two years prior to the last movie Stanley Kubrick directed, "Eyes Wide Shut." The exotic erotic cirque was already playing at Sfera Mascherata di San Valentino di Conte Mario Conti, and I had the opportunity to witness this spectacular extravaganza first hand.

At 2:00 A.M., the night was young. My partners in crime, exploring the upstairs, were The Raven King and The Twins (Oscar and Devaj).

40

Tie Me

"Tie me up, tie me down, tie me front, tie me back, tie me left, tie me right, bind me eyes, gag me mouth, now, I'm fucking yours to keep."

Bernard Tristan Foong
Song Lyrics (copyright)

April 1st 2012

I finally plucked up the courage to open Oscar's email after several days of leaving his message sitting in my computer unopened. He wrote:

Hi Young,

It's been far too long since we connected. It is wonderful to know you are well and living on Maui with your life partner, Walter. I am also in a long term relationship with Scott since 1993. We live in Munich and have adopted 2 children, Sarah, 6 and James, 8. They are a handful and require constant attention, but we are happy to have them in our lives.

I sold my medical practice last year and am currently a retired stay-at-home dad. It has been difficult for us to travel frequently since the children and our dogs, Turtle and Rabbit came into our lives. As you can tell by their names, Turtle is super slow and Rabbit is hyper fast, but the children love them.

I have often thought of you and Andy, wondering what you guys are up to. I heard you are writing your memoirs, and will love to read the books when they are published. Keep me posted when available.

1967 Valentine's Masquerade Ball

After an enticing erotic performance in the grand ballroom, the Raven King, the Twins, and I proceeded upstairs to the musician's footsteps. Several mask guards greeted guests at the top of the stairs, before guiding us to an adjoining room to change out of our costumes, which were carefully stored away. A cloakroom assistant directed us to a changing area, where we disrobed. Naked as a jay-bird, each partier was given a number, written in black marker on our ankles as identification for our eventual clothing collection. Two options were provided to the upstairs revelers: either to wear our mask at all times or be blind-folded securely before exploration of the premises was permitted.

Andy and Devaj opted to don their masks while Oscar's and my eyes were bound tightly by two pieces of black kerchiefs. Under no circumstances were we to peek behind our blindfolds, unless we decided to exchange the kerchiefs for our masks. No one was permitted to know the true identity of the participants as we explored the mysteries of each polygamous chamber. My lover the Raven King led me towards a chamber nearest the closet room while Devaj guided Oscar to a bedroom along the long corridor.

Tie Me Up, Tie Me Down

Fearlessly trusting my protector as *"my eyes,"* knowing that no harm would befall me, my face completely covered except for the breathing holes, I was at once afflicted with a sense of unheralded expectations. Not knowing what would transpire next, I trustingly surrendered to my guide as we proceeded in search of the unknown. A heightened sense of mystery played pervasively across my active imagination while erotic scenes of hedonistic seduction loomed large. Sounds of live flute music joined with soft groaning and moaning noises emanated rapaciously around me. I longed to sneak a peek out of the darkness, but my trusting obedience prevented me from doing so. Several longing hands caressed my youthful body as my Valet led me to an empty seat on top of a large mattress. Afraid to let go of *"my eyes,"* I held firmly to the Raven King. His closeness assured my safety as he stood above, straddling my face. An overwhelming sense of peace washed over my being as he gently rubbed his growing manhood against my eye fabric. Reaching behind to grab his firm buttocks I felt the tautness as his bulbous length beat playfully against my tantalizing mouth.

Contrary to my expectation, an unknown pair of hands spread my legs apart before sensual tongues lapped and licked at my organ and cod. Before long, esurient mouths were delightfully feeding on my straining erection. These ravenous sensations steered my tilting hips towards their devouring mouths, while I enjoyed my lover's delicacy pumping hungrily into my throat. Relinquishing my being to this virtuous moment of sweet serenity, my fingers explored the depths of my guardian's crack while savoring his passionate kisses as his loving tongue slid effortlessly into my accepting oral orifice. Wetting a couple of my fingers, I pushed into my lover's carnal opening as he stood pressed against my face. His bobbing cock grew with each probing insertion. A mouth next to mine replaced my suckling motion while another pried open my unquerulous lips, demanding undivided attention for his amorous kisses. Losing control to this unseen inebriant sensuality, I fed my saccharine love to the relishing oral orifices that were voraciously devouring the ejaculating nectar from my fountain of youth. Drops that landed on my naked belly were eagerly consumed and shared in passionate French kisses by those lying beside me.

Turning my mouth towards the Raven King, he shot into my receiving orifice, pushing my head against his engorged berth as jets of intoxicating liquid streamed into my willing throat. His rustic masculinity penetrated every fiber of my soul. I was at once impishly revitalized by this onslaught of tasty bucolic nourishment until Andy guided us to a different chamber for further sexual consolations. This time I saw from behind my carnival mask.

Tie Me Front, Tie Me Back

A strange sensation washed over me as I watched from behind my painted mask. Before, while under the blindfold I was at once vulnerable to a whirling sense of helplessness, trusting in the mercy of my sexual aficionados that they would obey the rules of this unsighted game. Now in complete control, I was an alpha male seeking servitude of willing omegas to satisfy my sexual deprivation, and many would willingly perform within the guise of this candlelit room.

Andy, my partner in love and crime, guided us to a corner where several blindfolded men lay servicing their muscular virtuosos, as the tops manipulated their receptive partners every which way to the musical strings of a group of naked quartet playing Ravel's Bolero. As the distant musical sound started softly, so did the slow, sensual foreplay, as if the participants were synchronizing their passions to each rhythmic note. Only when the bass crescendos of the tops finally exploded into and onto the moaning pitches of their receptive bottoms did their sublime ecstasies subside, only to rebuild when the passive released their masturbatory ejaculations, after which the musical voices cease to exist. Through it all, the quartet played an assortment of classical sonatas unceasingly, serenading the endless streams of shuffling guests entering and leaving these love chambers.

Better Safe than Sorry

All photography upstairs was forbidden except for the Count's private video monitors, which were discreetly hidden in unobtrusive areas within the various chambers. I wanted to whip out my automatic to snap away, but my possessions remained with the cloak room attendants until I was ready to part the confines of these sexual domains. Strict security was installed, since millions of dollars were at stake in the unfortunate event that jewel thieves manage to make in-roads into the palazzo's heavily guarded estate. The Count would then have much to answer to, therefore his organizers made sure nothing was left to chance. Better be safe than sorry, so they advised.

Tie Me Left, Tie Me Right

Each room had taken on its own identity and as my protector and I entered the perfumed Camera Rosa (Rose Chamber). An air of romantic seduction permeated this erotic confine while heterosexuals and bisexuals were in various stages of passionate lovemaking. Although I was unable to decipher to whom these bodies belonged because of their masks and blindfolds, there were a couple of nude torsos I had no problem identifying, since I had bedded these masculine musculatures prior to this evening's Dionysian debauchery.

Two hairy torsos in particular were those of Aziz and Gabrielli, the former of dark brown skin and the latter of lighter tone. Their beards and after-five shadows gave clues to a Middle Eastern and an Italian national, and even-though their eyes were concealed I knew the photographer and my professor instinctively.

Aziz's hands cupped two voluptuous breasts belonging to a slender woman as she parted her moist vulva to the mounting Arab with ecstatic cries of irresistible desires; she rode his pulsating length as each penetrating stroke plunged deeper and harder into the core of her being. Riding with wild abandon, the horsewoman wriggled and bounced to the musical rhythm of a Mozart minuet, played expertly by a naked serenading violinist as the trio collaborated in a transcendental symphony of polygamous union.

Bind My Eyes, Gag My Mouth

As he stood at an impressive height of 6 feet 2 inches, the professor's raging member swayed above the bouncing female before her delectable lips wrapped around all nine inches. Holding her head firmly, Mr. Happy & Sad fed his deliciousness into her suckling mouth, at times gagging and choking his captive fan with evanescent remission and at others plunging devilishly into her willing orifice. Yin and yang, hell and heaven were operating simultaneously in this erogenous act of sexual intercourse.

The two men jerked in unison as they climaxed simultaneously to the finale of the musical minuet. They seeded the wolverine with gustoes of dripping manliness inside her receiving orifices, lending validity to her multiple heights of orgasmic consummation before the trio descended into a sodden pelage of perspiration. Yet the men's virile masculinity remained undeterred as they moved on to their next carnal adventure. As to the lady in question, she was none other than Maurizia, the lace designer I meet a day ago.

I'm F**king Yours to Keep

The last I saw Mario was a few hours ago when he stood on the balcony, signaling the trumpeter to announce the commencement of the Exotic Erotic Circus. Since then he had disappeared from view. As Andy and I explored the last and final room it was beyond doubt that the Casanova of all Casanovas, our one and distinguished host Count Mario Conti, would hold court in the center of this humongous room. Without doubt, he would be surrounded by a host of angelic seraphim and cherubim at the ready to service his royal highness, willingly indulging in his fantastical sensual whims and sexually loving demands. Wearing a golden crown and a Zeus mask, he stood naked while his blindfolded angels took turns worshipping his bulbous life force. Its protrusion pointed skywards, offering to those who cared to suckle its length from every conceivable angle, be it front, sides, back, above and under; his God-ship was perfectly idolized by his angelic throng.

A pair of muscular hands spread Zeus' taut, muscular buttocks apart offering the holy orifice to nibbling tongues, kissing lips and licking mouths in rapturous velocity in case a boy missed his turn while another fought to claim entry. The playboy was in 7th heaven, playing his role to perfection as he readied himself access to the numerous buttocks placed in line for his sexual pleasures.

If not for my authoritative guardian, I would have joined the queue to partake in this gustatory indulgence which was so sexually enticing; calling my leaking libido to attention for another round of Bacchanalian debauchery. Instead, we were joined by one half of the naked Twins (Oscar) while his other half (Devaj) went exploring in the heterosexual chambers.

Several guys cornered us, ready to commence our personal fun and games, as I enviously watched the Count pleasuring his concubines through the peek holes of my Virgin mask. Before the green-eyed monster could appear, Andy's and Oscar's alluring mouths were already caressing me. Needless to say without any opposing resistance I gave in to my seducers. We were young, and so was the night.

April 1st 2012

...I miss the happy times we spent together, which I thought would never end. Here we are, reminiscing of the good ole days, and I'm missing you more than ever. It was a vastly different world then and didn't we have fun! Well dearest boy, you are forever etched in my mind and will always be the Young I know so well.

Let's stay tuned.

Love,

Oscar.

Part Four

The United Arab Emirates, Abu Dhabi,

The SEKHAM Household.

Italy, Rome.

France, Paris.

41

Sunnat of Rasulullah Sallallahu Alayhi Wasallam

"Once in a while, right in the middle of an ordinary life, love gives us a fairy tale. Or does it?"
Bernard Tristan Foong

First Week of April 2012

Surprises arrive when I least expect them. A day after I received Oscar's response and left his message unopened in my computer, an email from a woman I had forgotten I had written to prior April Fool's Day also turned up. Finally, on the 1st of April, I plucked up the courage to read Aria's message but I did not reply immediately. Instead I contemplated for several days before responding.

I left Aria's message unopened until I was intellectually ready to read its contents. The reasons for not opening her email was manifold; my active imagination had been whirling with many *"what ifs"* and I had to mentally prepare myself before returning to face the emotional demons I had long banished into the recesses of my mind. It had been terribly difficult after Andy and I separated in 1970, sending me to a near nervous breakdown which took me some years to recover. Opening Andy sister's message meant opening the lid to a can of worms that I had cleverly hidden for 40 years. Now I'm forced to face my inner devils head on.

The problem is that my feelings for Andy had never dissipated. Unconsciously I had been looking for *"The Andy"* in all my past relationships until Walter came into my life. He has, in more ways than one, borne remarkable similarities to my ex-lover, the man I had consciously relinquished 40 years ago.

The *"what ifs"* that were bombarding my brain had to be brought under control and I did this through daily meditations. Like ghosts, or, better yet, like vampires, the *"what ifs"* continued haunting me, waiting for opportunities to suck me dry, except it wasn't blood they were after but my emotional uncertainties.

"What if" Aria's email contained devastating news of Andy?

"What if" my ex-lover is now a cripple or an invalid?

"What if" he is suffering from a terminal illness?

"What if" my ex-guardian had wiped me out of his memory after we split?

Worst of all, *"what if"* the man is dead?

These were devastating pieces of news I was afraid to find out, but these ugly thoughts would not leave me alone, so I did what I had to do. Throwing caution to the wind, I opened Aria's email.

1967 The Sekham

Our whirlwind Italian photography tour finished the day after Mario's grand masquerade ball. Back at the Sekham, a different kind of celebration was in preparation. Like a dysfunctional family Thabit, the patriarch was up in arms, threatening his household with the wrath of Allah two weeks ago when he found Mais and Tahu had eloped. Now a joyous wedding jubilation was meticulously organized by the one and the same, who had granted approval to their civil and religious union. The Wazir had miraculously redeemed his family from any social disgrace that might have befallen if the elopement had been made public to his overly religious peers and judgmental business acquaintances.

Of course, the wedding must be a grand affair, the talk of the Arab community for a long time after. Mais wasn't the patriarch's eldest daughter – she was the 3rd in line; nonetheless, the Wazir splashed out on an elaborate wedding reception so as not to lose face as a community leader, since the groom's family was neither socially nor financially compatible with the bride's. Thabit's generous act provided enough reason to publicly validate this marriage, at least on the surface, to accept Tahu's family, the poor in-laws.

Muslim Marriages

While the Sekham women were busy preparing for the upcoming festivities, Gabrielli resumed regular tutorials with the household students. One morning during class with only Anya, Devaj and me present, our teacher decided to enlighten us on the topic of traditional Muslim marriages, especially that of the United Arab Emirates.

He began, *"Marriages in the Islamic world are generally propagated by the elders of the prospective bride. The initiation of the proposal from the groom may be instigated by him to the father of the bride or through his parents."*

My professor continued, *"Usually the womenfolk keep an eye out for available and eligible brides. The groom's sister or mother would look for an alliance as per his preference. After viewing potential candidates, they would then inform the prospective groom or the father of the groom, who would then contact the family members of the potential bride to be."*

Speaking in a softer tone, as if he was divulging a secret, he said, *"In the case of Tahu, he has personally initiated the scouting and mating; therefore the above mentioned procedure was deemed obsolete but under proverbial scrutiny, he had to ask the Wazir's permission for his daughter's hand. This, I will say with* honesty, was superficially performed in front of both the bride and groom's families as a sign of respect as per tradition."

I listened attentively as my teacher continued, "If the girl's family has no objection to the man's proposal, she may or may not be let in front of him to have a prior look. Normally, the man's consent is shown by the gifts which he will give to his prospective bride. In Tahu's case he already knew the bride intimately; yet, he had to perform this duty as a sign of respect to Mais.

"The bride has every right to refuse if she does not want to go ahead with this marriage alliance. But in this particular case, Tahu's parents provided the best they could afford since this was performed as a flatulent token. And with secret financial assistance from their soon-to-be in-laws, his parents were able to present a substantial dowry for their son to obtain Mais' marriage permission." I was surprised that our teacher told us the latter with honesty. Since the three of us were not of Arabian origin, I presume he had no obligations to anyone but to tell the truth.

"On a more favorable note, after this procedure the elders would sit down to sort out the preliminaries of the marriage conditions, regarding the amount to be paid to the bride and to other tentative clauses. If the negotiations are agreeable, then three days before the wedding the bride will be exclusively prepared."

I couldn't help asking, "What does the bride have to do to prepare?"

Gabrielli answered, "She is cleansed and anointed with all kinds of scented oils and perfumes on her body. Her hands are drawn with flamboyant henna designs the night before the wedding ceremony. Her trousseau will often consist of extensive jewelries, perfumes, and lavish silk materials together with a variety of other necessary items presented her by the groom. Throughout the entire preparation, the bride's sisters and female relatives will sing and dance to celebrate this soon-to-be union."

Muslim Marriage Requirements

Anya raised her hand to ask, *"How will the family know if the boy is interested in a potential bride?"*

"Usually when a boy becomes of marriageable age, the relatives try to discern his opinion about marriage. If he declines to give an opinion, his feelings will be determined through his friends. If the girl in whom he has an interest becomes known, then the parents of the boy will look at the general condition, such as the piety of both the girl and her family. If these are favorable to an Islamic code of life, then the marriage will most likely be accomplished," replied the Italian professor.

"I have difficulties understanding arranged marriages," Devaj responded, *"Because one day when I am of marriageable age, my parents are going to arrange a prim and proper Indian girl for me to marry. I don't think I'd like that to happen but I also don't wish to defy my parents' wishes. What's your advice for me, professor?"* Devaj asked with a sad ring to his question.

Consent

"One of the primary and fundamental factors of a happy and successful marriage is that it is contracted with mutual consent and agreement. If the boy or girl have not given their consent and are tied in marriage by force, the seeds of dispute and dissension are sown in their marriage. Such a marriage is neither lawful in the sight of Allah nor conducive to the happiness and pleasure of the married couple.

"My advice to you, Vaj; it is necessary and vital that the couple to be married be consulted and their willing consent obtained before their marriage. This is, to Muslims, the law of the Shariat, which is most appropriate and reasonable in respecting the person's dignity and the honor of the woman. It is the best way to preserve and develop happy and peaceful relationships in a family.

"Both Tahu and Mais had unmistakably given their consent to the marriage, since the bride is already with child." Gabrielli added.

Kafa'at

Although I was born in a Muslim country I had very little knowledge of Islamic matrimonial contracts. Gabrielli's information was therefore interesting in and of itself, and I was curious to understand the conjugal traditions of an Islamic country.

I raised my hand to speak, "This is a very interesting topic, since Islam is Malaysia's official religion. Yet, I know nothing about Muhammad's teachings or Muslim traditions. Tell us more."

My teacher said smilingly, "After the Islamic law has been taken into consideration the question of compatibility and suitability between a man and a woman, before contracting their marriage, the Shariat commands and approves Kafa'at (equality) between both parties. A man and woman who are equal to each other in regards of their morals, education, religious inclination, family ways and connections plus cultural aspects of living are more likely to develop relationships of affection, kindness and love according to the Shariat.

"However this may be taken as a mark of distinction for some families and disgrace for others. It is simply that there should be maximum coordination, conformity and similarity of habits, and qualities and socio-economic system between the partners, so that they may live together and maintain their relationship cordially and peacefully."

Devaj pronounced firmly, "Therefore, viewing each other is another requirement of a positive marriage, for it helps in the development of love and affection between the couple."

Our professor acknowledged, "The Prophet Muhammad said, "When one of you seeks to marry a woman and if he is able to have a look at the one he desires to marry, let him do so." It stipulates that the man must see the woman, but many Muslim scholars and jurists agree that a woman has similar rights to see the man.

"In regards to Tahu and Mais, this was no problem since they had seen and bedded each other many times prior to their forthcoming betrothal."

Proposal and Nikah

"I've heard of the word Nikah mentioned by the Household women. What does it mean?" Anya quipped.

The learned Italian continued, *"If a proposal is intended, then one should make wudhu (ablution) and perform four Rakaats of Nafl Namaaz. The first two should be for Salaatul Hajaat (seeking Allah's help) and the other two for Salaatul Istikhaarah (seeking Allah's guidance). As far as proposing, there are no special or prescribed methods since this is only an agreement between the parents of the betrothed.*

"The agreement can be concluded by verbal discussions, through correspondence, or through other means. The acceptance of a proposal is an agreement and a promise and should be upheld and accomplished, much like a gentleman's word of honor.

"Shortly thereafter, the date of the Nikah, which Westerners call engagement, will be set. The sooner the better – it is more advantageous for the couple and their respective families. In setting the date one should desist from wrong customs, which are often prevalent, the Nikah should be performed in accordance with the beliefs of the friends and relatives. Special care and precautions are taken that one proposal should not be made upon another, since Nikah is a Sunnat."

Sunnat Allah

"I've heard my Malaysian Muslim friends mentioning the term Sunnat of Rasulullah Sallallahu Alayhi Wasallam. What does it mean?" I asked with curiosity.

"You must understand, Young: to get married is a Sunnat of Rasulullah Sallallahu Alayhi Wasallam. If a person practices on a

Sunnat, he will be richly rewarded, according to the Quran. And it also states that by Nikah a person saves himself from committing lustful sins thus his thoughts are kept under control. According to a hadith, a married man receives more reward for his Ibadaht (worship) in comparison to an unmarried man, and an intention can be made that one will receive more reward. It also states that a married man will also be blessed with pious children. Through Nikah, the children born will be additions to the Ummat of the Prophet."

My teacher went on, "As far as the legal view of marriage in Islam, men and women are completely equal partners. Both parties take equal responsibilities to provide physical, emotional, psychological and spiritual happiness to each other, but men generally have the added responsibility to provide for the financial needs of the wife."

Devaj raised his hand again to question, "Can Muslim couples divorce? If so, what are the laws regarding this issue?"

"If the husband initiates divorce, he is obliged by religious law to pay some maintenance expenses. This prescribed alimony belongs to the wife by right. However, when the woman initiates the divorce, she does not pay any compensation to the husband as part of any requirement of religious law; she need at most return part of what she received from her husband as dower, if such payment contributes to an amicable settlement.

"A man can divorce his wife on his own while a woman needs to go through court or introduce a clause into the marriage giving her the right to divorce her husband," explained our educator.

He continued, "The Quran states: 'And (wives) shall have rights similar to those (the husbands have) over them, in accordance with justice, (except that) husbands' rights are a degree greater. Husbands are guardians (qawwamun) of wives because God has favored some more than others and because they (i.e. husbands generally) spend out of their wealth.' (4:34)

"The degree by which husbands' rights are greater should therefore be understood as the degree by which the husband is freer *than the wife to break the marriage bond. This, however, is not a particularly important decree, since as stated earlier the wife can get out of the marriage bond whenever she wants to without giving any reason. It is only that she has to follow a more indirect approach."*

Before Gabrielli could confer further, Vaj chimed in, *"In my country of birth, the husbands often become the decision makers, usually without consulting the wife or wives. Is it the same here?"*

"To some degree: the second Koranic statement refers to the greater responsibility of husbands to be protectors and providers of women, and the greater power they have to make decisions. The fact that husband's rights are somewhat greater does not affect the claim that Islamic men and women have equal rights, since men's greater rights within the marriage do not mean that men also enjoy greater rights outside that relationship. That's because within the marriage relationship, men's greater rights are completely justified by their greater responsibility." Our teacher clarified.

"When members of a society have equal rights, it is never precluded that members of that society cannot freely enter into terminable arrangements in which some take greater responsibility and therefore also have greater rights. Equality of rights can only be asserted on the assumption of equality of responsibility. This principle sometimes works in favor of women. For example, as mothers, women give much more to children than men do as fathers; so, Islam recognizes greater rights of mothers over children than of fathers, except where economic considerations demand otherwise. This then forms the basis of a Muslim marriage contract." This ended our lesson on traditional Muslim marriages.

42

Are Marriages Made In Heaven?

*"Bachelors know more about women than married men:
If they didn't, they'd be married too."*
H. L. Mencken

First Week of April 2012

Aria wrote:

It is nice to hear from you. I received a message from Carol a month ago but was too busy with family and work to write to you until now. Your email arrived when I was on the phone with Andy and I read your message to him. There was a long silence at the other end before his shaky voice returned, sounding distraught, as if he was sobbing. My brother went through a difficult period after you separated. He missed you terribly and thought of returning to England to be with you. He was close to being a nervous wreck, often contacting me in devastating states of misery. Plunging full steam into his engineering studies eventually healed his wounds. He did well at the University of Canterbury, where he met Toby a few years later. They separated when Andy moved to Canada after graduation.

My brother often talked about you and wished he had stayed in London. I know the two of you were very close in school and you were his first true love. From personal experience, our first love lasts longest and can be the most difficult to release. I count myself fortunate that my husband of 37 years, Jay, is my first love. We have 3 children; Jamie, 27, our eldest is a pharmacist in Stockholm; Charles, 24, his brother, will be graduating from law school in a few months and last but not least Angelique, 20, is a computer science major at the Ecole Polytechnique Federale de Lausanne. We moved to Stockholm when

Jay got transferred by his bank so we could be in closer proximity to Jamie. I'm assisting and keeping busy with several nonprofit charities now that the children have left home.

I've enclosed Andy's contact information. Maybe the two of you can reconnect.

1967 Child Marriage

The same day, after Gabrielli's morning lesson on Muslim Marriages, Andy and I were summoned to the Wazir's chambers. Jasim, already seated comfortably on the settee, was waiting our arrival while his father spoke on the phone. We sat waiting for the patriarch to finish his call while the manservant brought us beverages. Our host greeted us with the traditional Arabian nose rubs as soon as he replaced the receiver. Sitting next to his son, he started, *"I haven't had a chance to ask how your photography trip went. I have to designate assistants to prepare Mais wedding arrangements over and above my busy business schedules. Now this young fellow (directing his gaze at Jasim) is also preparing his betrothal to Ria."*

Surprised by what I heard, I turned to Andy for a response before Thabit continued, *"Jasim is getting married a month after Mais' wedding. I'd like to ask a favor from you."*

Andy replied, *"We will be glad to be of service and will do the utmost to assist in any way possible. Please let us know what you'd like us to do?"*

Gladdened by my Valet's response, he said, *"There are several things with which the two of you can assist. I've informed Gabrielli, Aziz, Sayid and Jasim to chaperone their sisters and my wives to Rome to purchase Mais and Ria's wedding trousseau. Since Young has an eye for fashion and I don't, I'd like you to accompany the women in their trousseau selection.*

"And when in Rome, you can also outfit this young man. He is marrying his 10-year-old cousin, Ria (Ula's, Thabit's second wife brother's eldest daughter). She and Milawa, her mother will also be

travelling with the entourage to select her daughter's wedding trousseau."

Andy inquired, "Would you like me to make appointments with the Italian couture houses? I'm sure our friend Count Mario Conti can assist, since he is well-connected in the fashion industry."

"That will not be necessary. I have informed our country's cultural attaché to make arrangements. But if the Count can assist, that will be splendid," the Wazir answered.

"When do we travel?"

"This weekend, you'll be gone for three days."

I couldn't resist asking, "Which couturier are we visiting, Sir?"

Looking puzzled, the Arab replied. "Sabiya mentioned a designer named Valentino or Valentino Garavani? Since I'm not a fashion aficionado, I'm leaving the logistics to you and the household women. Gabrielli will be my representative in any business dealings with the attaché and the couture houses, since he is Roman and speaks Italian.

"How was the photo shoot? Did Aziz obtain the necessary pictures required for the American set builders?" Thabit inquired, "Now that Tahu is part of our family and is a good business administrator, he'll be fully involved in Aziz's photography projects and will travel with you on future photo-shoots."

"Will Tahu be going to Rome with us?" I queried.

"No, he'll be here organizing his upcoming wedding," the patriarch attested.

Throughout our meeting, Jasim sat without uttering a word. His father did the talking as he twiddled his thumbs. I was curious to find out what the adolescent thought of his eminent arranged marriage. An opportunity arose as we flew towards Roma on the SAQR. Just back to the Sekham for less than a week and I'm off to the Eternal City again, I was thinking. This time, I was on a different assignment, one that I embraced with great aplomb; fashion is my eternal love.

Before we left the Waziz's chamber, he handed Andy a couple of envelopes containing two checks, each for the amount of US$25,000.00. He said, *"Accept these gifts as my token of appreciation in assisting my brother and my daughter and son's upcoming wedding arrangements. A note of caution; make sure no one knows about Mais and Tahu's prenuptial liaisons. Do you understand?"*

My Valet and I nodded before replying, *"Rest assured our gentlemen's agreement is tightly sealed. Thank you for your generosity Sir!"* We bowed, leaving father and son to their private discussions.

Conversation with Andy

As soon as we closed the doors behind us, I questioned Andy, *"How can Jasim get married when he has just reached puberty and his bride-to-be is ten? He doesn't know anything about sex or the responsibilities of being a husband!"*

He did not answer but kept walking silently. As we turned into a courtyard we bumped into Gabrielli. Greeting my professor, my guardian spoke, *"Have you been informed that we are leaving for Rome this Friday?"*

"Of course I have! Nothing in this household transpires without my knowledge," replied the Italian. *"I'm currently making arrangements with the cultural attaché to set up a Haute Couture appointment with Valentino. Sabiya insists that her sister have the couturier design her wedding wardrobe."*

Jumping with monumental excitement that another grand fashion experience was in store, I kept my cool, appearing more adult than my years would suggest. Yet I couldn't help blurting the question I had asked my Valet to my professor, *"How can Jasim get married at auch a young age? Does he have any knowledge of sex or husbandly duties?"*

"I see that Thabit had decided to proceed ahead with the boy's wedding after my attempts to dissuade him from doing so," my teacher sighed. *"It's an age-old Arab custom, which is difficult to break. When he asked my opinion, I told him it was not a good idea*

for Jasim to marry so young, since he just begun puberty. His reasoning was that the boy should follow in his father's footsteps because he married Zeba (Thabit's first wife) at age 13 when she was 11. They did not consummate their union until he was 16 and she 14. During the early years after their marriage, they did not see each other until his 16th birthday. Zeba lived in the female harem with her female in-laws in the same compound as her husband, but under separate roofs."

"Then why marry at 13 when he doesn't get to see or spend time with his wife?" I questioned.

Gabrielli replied soberly, "Because the 52-year-old Prophet married Aisha when she was 6. Although Muhammad didn't consummate the marriage until she was 9 and he 54 according to Quran documentations, Muslims use this as an excuse to marry off their daughters to keep them in the control of men. First, they're under the obligations of filial piety to their fathers and then total obedience to their husband. That's my opinion on the issue."

Andy asked, "Was the union consensual between Aisha and the Prophet?"

"That's a debatable topic. According to the hadith, Aisha professed that they had a strong bond and his favorite wife. She was an active witness in numerous historical events and contributed to the growth, development and understanding of the Islamic faith. Being a role model to a significant number of women, she also served as a consultant to Muhammad's prayer and practices, introducing herself into the world of Arabic politics.

"According to the Sunni point of view, after Muhammad's death, Aisha readily involved herself in spreading his messages. She was present throughout the reigns of the first four caliphs, her father Abu Bakr being the first caliph to succeed Muhammad. He was later succeeded by Umar, the second caliph. During the reign of Uthman the third caliph, Aisha rebelled because she did not approve of his practices. She became readily involved in the Battle of the Camel, riding her camel while giving speeches. Although she lost the battle, her involvement shone through in her determination to continue spreading the Prophet's message," my teacher said.

"You must understand that most females here marry to strengthen family ties rather than for love. As you already witnessed in the households you serve, majority of males and females live separate lives after marriage. Therefore it is no surprise that Jasim is betrothed to his first cousin, since both families are incredibly wealthy, religious, and socially connected in the business world.

"Ria's mother is the 2nd wife of the Prince's uncle. Therefore, Jasim's status will automatically rise to become a royal cousin after his matrimony to Ria, and Thabit's family will join the aristocracy merely through an act of marriage."

My Valet and I nodded our understanding the reasons for Jasim's marriage. I also came to the realization that I would have much to gain if I cozied up to the Prince, which was what I did when I saw P at Mais and Jasim's wedding receptions. Besides being a good-looking man, he was also an excellent lover and wittily intelligent. Without Andy's encouragements to be pleasant to his Royal Highness, I decided to do my own bidding as I progressed in the fine art of human relationship maneuvering.

First Week of April 2012

...I've also forwarded your contact information to Andy and leave you guys to reconnect. I'm sure you'll have lots to catch up. My brother will love to hear from you.

All the best and stay in touch,
Aria.

43

Which Coin Will The Fountain Bless?

"A man marries to have a home, some to further their social and aristocratic standing, but also because they don't want to be bothered with sex and all that sort of thing."
W. Somerset Maugham

1967 On The SAQR

All my bags were packed I was ready to go back to Rome on the SAQR with an entourage of Sekham men, boys and women. The idiosyncrasy was that the group of women automatically gravitated towards the rear section of the luxurious plane, enclosing themselves in a private chamber while the males sat in the spacious living areas scattered throughout the jet. An hour in flight, I found the perfect opportunity to corner the two brothers, Sayid and Jasim, sitting by themselves looking out the window away from the rest of the male entourage. I sat on the vacant seat next to them.

"Are you looking forward to Rome?" I began.

Sayid answered excitedly, *"Yeah! I've been to Rome with my father when he was on a business trip and I had a fun time. This is my brother's first visit."*

"Are you excited?" I asked Jasim.

The usually bubbly prankster pondered. He'd seemed lost since the day his father announced his up-coming betrothal to Andy and me. Seconds passed before he spoke in broken English, *"Yes I suppose so. I'm not sure what to expect in Rome."*

His brother chimed in, *"I've been giving him advice on marriage."*

His smugness came as no surprise, as I guessed he must be married to a wealthy cousin to strengthen his family connections. So I asked nonchalantly, *"What advice have you given your brother?"*

Sayid replied with a smirk on his face, *"I told him he'll be receiving lots of presents in the two weeks leading up to his wedding day."*

"That's wonderful," I replied. *"What are you expecting to get?"*

"When I married three years ago, I received many gifts and an abundance of gold items that my father is keeping safe for me. The best part of my wedding was getting gazillion new toys and games to play," answered the teenager.

Trying to redirect my question inconspicuously, I asked, *"Do you spend time with your wife?"*

"We've been together a few times, but I find her boring. She is not interested in the games I like to play. I expect her to be fun, but all she wants to do is play with dolls and study the Quran, which I do daily in school. I don't need to read the holy book every minute of the day. Besides, praying five times a day is more than sufficient for me. I want to play sports, games and have fun with my guy friends."

I continued, *"Don't you care about your wife and what she'd like to do?"*

"She does her female things in the women's quarters, which do not interest me. I tried having sex with her but she doesn't like it and doesn't know how to pleasure me, so I gave up. I'll rather have sex with you guys or with Anya and Dominique, which is much better than with Nawal."

"Don't you have to produce children with her eventually?"

The adolescent mustered a lame answer, *"Maybe in a few years she'll be better at sex. Otherwise I'll just impregnate her for the sake of my parents to continue the family linage. I don't have to spend my entire life with her. I can continue having fun or marry several wives who know how to please me."*

Throughout our conversation Jasim remained silent while his brother continued to jibber-jabber about his wife's ineptitude. "Don't you care about Nawal's happiness?" I enquired.

Sounding remarkably positive, he answered without doubt, "I'm sure she is happy in the women's harem. She should be; she's going shopping in Rome as we speak. That's what makes women happy.

"In a couple of years I'll be going to study in Australia; then I'll be free to do whatever I want to do. My family will not be there to watch over me. Nawal is certainly not coming with me. She'll be staying in the Sekham with the harem women."

"What about her education?"

"She'll continue attending Islamic school in Abu Dhabi. The women in my family will look after her. Besides, she can't go anywhere when she's with child. She will have to look after my babies and be a mother. That's her job as my wife," concluded Sayid.

Directing my question to Jasim, I asked, "What's your opinion on your upcoming marriage to Ria?"

Speaking in less-than-perfect English, he said, "I want see her sex organ look like? I've never seen girl without clothes. I like put my finger into sex to feel it like and taste juice?"

His brother responded laughingly, "This one likes to rub the head of his penis to taste the leakage from the slit. I'm teaching him some techniques on masturbation, but so far he hasn't shot anything yet."

After a short pause, Sayid continued, "When I'm horny, I stick my cock in his ass and cum inside him. He likes it."

Looking out the window, Jasim looked belittled and embarrassed but said nothing. I felt sorry for the boy and my heart went out to him. I said, "You don't have to be shy; Andy, Oscar, Devaj and I are here to assist if you want to learn about sex. We'll be happy to educate you. Whenever you require our company, don't be embarrassed to call on us. I'm sure when the time is ripe your father will have Dominque and Anya give you an education too. We'll be glad to be of assistance anytime."

I detected a culpable smile on his innocent face when he replied, *"I come see you and Andy soon."* Just then Andy, Oscar and Vaj came to join us and our conversation turned to shopping in Rome.

Contemplation

Needless to say, our view from Hotel d'Inghilterra was spectacular. Saint Peter's Basilica's imposing cupola loomed large straight ahead from our French window. Looking down the balcony, I could see Minis, Fiats and Vespa scooters zooming past, reminding me of the 1953 blockbuster movie *Roman Holiday* starring Audrey Hepburn and Gregory Peck. A sense of euphoric contemplation fell over me.

I felt like the royal princess, played so eloquently by Ms. Hepburn, escaping the boredom of her kingdom in search of excitement before falling in love along her journey of self-discovery with a newspaper reporter played by Gregory Peck. I had escaped the treachery of a domineering father, and, in the process, found love away from home, manifested in persons of Uncle James, Oscar, the Arab Household members and, of course, my beloved Valet and lover, Andy. Much like the reporter who loved the princess unconditionally, Andy, my prince charming, also loved his young "prince" (moi) unconditionally. The only difference: we were chauffeured in fancy Rolls Royces and Bentleys with an entourage of wealthy and elite Arabians instead of riding around Rome on a Vespa. Like Ms. Hepburn, Mr. Peck and Eddie Albert played roles as a princess, news reporter, and photographer; my Valet, Oscar and I were also playing temporary roles as male courtesans, except we were for real while they were on film.

Three Coins in a Fountain

Andy, wrapping his muscular arms around my waist, jolted me to reality. We leaned and kissed each other lovingly, and I surrendered to our intimacy before knocks on the door separated us. Oscar and Vaj were standing on the opposite side when my Valet invited them in.

"It's such a beautiful evening; let's go exploring before tomorrow takes us by storm," Oscar announced.

"Are you guys ready for a stroll?" inquired Vaj.

"Let's go; I'm as ready as can be."

In the elevator, we bumped into Gabrielli, Aziz, and his nephews, who, like us, had similar ideas to go for a walk. We trooped off round the neighborhood. It was Jasim's first time in the Eternal City, and his immense excitement rubbed off on us when we came upon Trevi Fountain after descending some ways down the Spanish Steps. Gabrielli our Roman guide suggested we each make a wish by throwing a coin in the fountain.

Jasim, being the youngest, was the first to make his wish. With his back turned, he flipped a coin over his head, landing the silver onto the tail of a merman before it rolled down into the splashing water. Sayid's coin landed smack in the middle of the water. Since my previous wish in the same fountain had manifested, when my turn arrived I mumbled a silent prayer for my young friends. I hoped they would find happiness and love in their respective marriages.

Despite my good intentions, an admonitory sadness befell me as I reflected on our conversation on the SAQR. I thought of Jasim's up-coming marriage to Ria and Sayid's betrothal to Nawal; I couldn't help but wonder which one of us had inherited the true price of wealth. Will my adolescent pals find happiness and love like I have with Oscar and Andy? Can the world of wealth, power and social accolades bring inner peace? Or can money buy love? Last but not least, between

Jasim, Sayid, and me – which coin will the fountain ultimately bless?

44

From Grey to Pink

"For me, this summer will be pure gray, 50 Shades of Grey. To me, this is the big statement for this summer. Then we have 101 shades of Arabian pink, from 'Initiation' Pink to 'Unbridled' Pink. To me, these are fashion statements for all seasons."
Bernard Tristan Foong

Second Week of April 2012

Mixed feelings rose when I read Aria's email. On one hand, I was relieved to know Andy was well and alive, but on the other I was afraid. I had not connected with my ex-lover, and the prospect of reconnecting with him was closing in by the minute. I wouldn't know how to react if and when he wrote. It had been extremely painful for us after our separation. I had plunged into the deep end trying to find the love we shared. For more than a year and half, I lived a double life through a series of licentious sexual encounters, often visiting underground sex clubs; it brought nothing but further depression. I was desperately trying to find the kind of unconditional stability, mentorship, and companionship my 'big brother' had so lovingly provided. I, being stubborn, faced a myriad of difficulties without my soulmate's guiding presence. Not admitting defeat, I told myself that if I could survive alone in a major metropolis, I could survive anywhere in the world. As much as I hated this hellacious experience, it also strengthened my courage in the face of adversity. My single-mindedness to succeed in my chosen career saved me from sinking into progressive deterioration.

Now, a possible reconnection with Andy would open years of concealed wounds that I might not be able to reconcile. The best solution I knew was to sleep on my fears and meditate on the problem until an answer arrived without active participation on my part.

1967 At Valentino Garavani

Early next morning, Mario joined us for breakfast before two limousines drove us to 24 Via Gregoriana, Valentino Garavani's atelier. A separate Rolls Royce ferried Gabrielli, Oscar, Devaj, and the three Arab males menswear shopping. Like at the Parisian couture Ateliers, our entourage was received with great enthusiasm as we proceeded to the third floor for Val's haute fashion presentation. Instead of day dresses, the designer presented a mini evening and bridal wear collection for the Sekham ladies' purview. After the private showing, the head venduse sat with the women and me, discussing the styles we selected to add, alter or take in to ensure that the designs were suitable for Mais' wedding trousseau. Naira, Sabiya and I thought a soft vanilla pink would look fabulous on the bride's skin tone, though the designer suggested a pastel sugar candy pink. Abu Dhabi being hot and sunny, Thabit's wives advised a magenta color for one of the reception dresses, with which I agreed full heartedly. After battering back and forth for several hours, an unanimous decision was reached; a blush bluish pink gown and a magenta colored reception dress were the order of the day while an ethereal snowflakes ivory pink for her wedding ensemble. Mais wanted an all-pink wedding, and that was what she got.

Zeba and Ula insisted that gold be incorporated into her ivory-colored wedding dress. As much as Mais wanted a pure white ensemble, she was outnumbered by the women's votes. Personally, I agreed with the women that ivory and gold was a much better color choice for a gala wedding than brilliant white. Secretly, I was glad the women won the color vote of the day.

Mario, a friend of the designer and his business and life partner Giancarlo Giammetti, acted as our professional fashion consultant, while our accompanying cultural attaché spoke Italian to the two venduses, who were servicing the ladies.

Seeing my curiosity to explore the atelier, the Count pulled me aside and said, *"I know you are interested to see the workroom, right?"*

"That would be nice. I like to learn the design and manufacturing aspect of high fashion."

Overhearing my dialogue with the Count, Signor Giammetti said with a strong Italian-English accent, *"Young man, the business of fashion is equally important. A great design talent requires an excellent business mind behind the company. Fashion, like all businesses, is teamwork. Just as we have gathered an excellent team of pattern makers, seamstresses, craftsmen and women to complete an exquisite collection, we also have an excellent team of able staff in our various departments from marketing, promotion, and publicity to the hospitality service personnel; all these are crucial in order for our enterprise to run smoothly."*

Mario and Giancarlo's conversation switched from Italian to English as we conversed. The fashion photographer asked, *"Possono Giovani hanno un tour del l'atelier? Egli è affascinato da vedere come abiti sono abiti haute couture sono costruiti (Can Young have a tour of the premise? He is fascinated to see how haute couture gowns are constructed)?"*

"I'll be glad to show the young man. Come with me while they (he indicated Valentino, the attaché and the women) are busy discussing styles and models to order."

Andy, Mario, and I followed Valentino's business partner to the workshop. Similar to the Parisian ateliers, I was able to catch a glimpse of the workings of a haute couture sample room, affirming my determination to be a fashion designer after graduating from boarding school.

Little did I realize while we were touring the premise, Sabiya was secretly gathering fashion information for her own betrothal to none other than Gabrielli, my professor.

At Sorelle Fontana

Mario, the fashion go-to man about town, recommended we pay the Fontana sisters a visit. *"They are couturiers to the Stars and they run Rome's oldest fashion house, the glamorous Sorelle Fontana story reads like a fairy tale,"* The Count announced before proceeding to give our entourage a brief history of the designers' trio.

"It is a story of three young women who made their way from a tiny town near Parma to Rome and then America, whose beautiful designs became highly sought after by Hollywood stars and the Italian aristocracy.

"The three sisters, Zoe, Micol, and Giovanna, from Traversetolo, were taught dressmaking by their talented mother, Amabile. In 1907, they inherited their grandmother's atelier and gained popularity with their feminine clothes before opening an atelier in fashionable Parma.

"Before long, God bless Zoe's restless soul, she wanted to move their design house but found it difficult to decide between Rome and Milan. Her instinct took her to Rome, the city of the Italian aristocracy. Her sisters and mother joined her at the start of the Second World War, opening their new atelier in the Eternal City."

I asked before Mario could continue, *"Why move to Rome when there is a war going on?"*

The Count reiterated an article in 'The Scotsman' by John Davidson, in which Micol said, *"We could still hear bombs going off on the beaches when we moved into our first atelier. But that didn't matter. It was our dream to own an atelier."*

"Young, when we get to their fashion house you'll see that their glamorous clothes are often based on Christian Dior's 'New Look,'

which gained favor with Italian aristocracy in the late 40s. One of their famous clients is the Russian e'migre'; Principessa Irene Galitzene loved wearing their designs.

"Why open in Rome and not Paris, since Paris is the fashion capital of the world?" I queried.

"Even though Paris is the principal center of fashion, some Italian designers decided to rebel against the monopoly. They believed their informal and sexier styles will appeal to American buyers, so they made plans to attract the major store buyers. Marchese Giorgini, a dear friend of mine, and several other Italian designers (including Sorelle Fontana) invited eight American buyers and several leading fashion journalists to their fashion presentations. In the beginning, their designs were greeted with silence – Micol told me about it sometime later. But they did love the designs, and the sisters received substantial orders from this showing.

"Before long, Hollywood stars making movies here started showing up at Sorelle Fontana's atelier. Now their clothes are worn by people like Ava Gardner and Anita Ekberg in Fellini's film, La Dolce Vita, where she frolicked in a Roman fountain. Hers was the perfect dress for the film portraying our jet setting lifestyle," the Count said, preening with pride before adding, "Their other famous clients included Linda Christian's wedding dress when she married Tyrone Power in "Made in Italy", and the American president's daughter, Margaret Truman's wedding outfit. The trio also dressed the young and gracious Audrey Hepburn in "Roman Holiday." My friends Princess Grace, Jacqueline Kennedy and Elizabeth Taylor wore Sorelle Fontana to perfection."

"They must be excellent bridal wear designers," I chirped.

"Yes! The sisters are famous for their exquisite wedding ensembles, evening wear, and full-skirted cocktail dresses. They didn't just achieve their dream in opening an atelier; they've become synonymous with glamour and elegance. That's why I wanted the ladies to meet them," Mario advised with a series of exaggerated hand gestures before we arrived at Atelier Sorelle Fontana, overlooking Piazza di Spagna.

Flabbergasted with Sorelle Fontana's designs, Naira ordered five evening dresses to wear to her sister's and brother's wedding. She became a Fontana haute couture fan the minute she set foot in their showroom to view the sister's private haute couture collections.

At Giovanna Caracciolo Ginetti

The last of our three stops for the day was Carosa, Giovanna Caracciolo Ginetti the princess-seamstress atelier. During the golden age of couture, this atelier was one of the most important places in a noblewoman's life. Fashion represented many things, and the right dress could make or break your appearance in society. A noblewoman needed to trust the seamstress and her taste as well as her sense of occasion when choosing a dress. When they walked into Atelier Carosa, it was much simpler, as Giovanna Caracciolo Ginetti, the head designer, was one of them.

Born in Rome in 1910, to the historical Italian noble family, Princess Giovanna Caracciolo Ginetti was not an average noblewoman. She had selected to market her innate elegance and experience through socializing at the highest echelons of society and providing service to other noblewomen.

After formal introductions at Carosa, our entourage was ushered into the fashion show salon for a private haute couture viewing. While the presentation was in session, Mario, seated next to me began an earnest private biographical commentary while the head venduse introduced each outfit to her audience. Knowing I was interested in every aspect of fashion, the Count whispered as I watched, mesmerized at each passing model. Each ensemble was more beautiful than the next.

"In 1947, Caracciolo and her friend, Barbara Angelini Desalles, set up Atelier Carosa. Very soon, many Italian and international nobility became her clients. Her fashion, to me, is an intricately detailed visitation of her two great loves: Balenciaga and Roman Baroque," Mario detailed.

"Her aristocratic elegance and taste are supported by her eye for talent. They looked to the Domes of Saint Peter's as inspiration for their collection proportions and volumes; Roman fashion came to life and Carosa is currently enjoying great success."

I had difficulty concentrating on the Count's commentary as a menagerie of ethereal pastel-colored gowns sent me into a state of euphoric ecstasy. Each garment filled me with awe before the fashion show finale dress shook me back to reality. Only then did I realize the venduse was already taking Ria's measurements in a private chamber, ready for fabric, color and style selection for her custom-made petite wedding dress. Ria, being ten years of age, also wanted many shades pink, pinker, and pinkest for her Big Day.

By the end of the day, I had more than enough shades of pink coming in and out of my six senses. I was happy to be back in the mundane world of white, beige, cream, gray and black.

The best fashion lesson I learned during my visit to the Italian couturiers was the geodesy of team work. Spick-and-span the three ateliers functioned because every team member performed his or her integral task with precision, professionalism and love. As much as a designer makes a fashion company, without a robust team of artisans and craftspeople, good designs will be wasted with shoddy construction and a disconsolate attention to details. Over the years, I had the good graces to learn from many grand masters that great designs equate extraordinary teamwork.

45

The Butterfly Experience

*"I embrace emerging experience. I participate in discovery.
I am a butterfly. I am not a butterfly collector.
I want the experience of the butterfly."*

William Stafford

Second Week of April 2012

Dear Oscar,

I'm delighted to hear from you after more than 42 years' absence. I am happy to know that you are in a loving relationship with Scott and the kids. I look forward to meeting them one day. Walter and I are happily "married" although we haven't officially tied the knot. We met through a personal ad while I was on a scholarship program at the University of Hawaii, pursuing my 2nd Master Degree in Theatre Costuming. Three months into my studies, I found myself on the beautiful island of Maui, living with the man I had known a few months earlier.

No one can or will ever replace the love Andy, you, and I shared, but life goes on and we have to flow with it. I completed my postgraduate fashion design at the Royal College of Art, London in 1977; I then worked for Liberty of London for a few years before venturing into designing my own bridal wear collections for several major London department stores. In 1979, the Hong Kong Polytechnic now a university invited me to teach fashion design at their clothing and textile institute.

Andy and I separated in 1970. He left for New Zealand to pursue engineering while I stayed in London to complete my fashion studies. Those early years of our separation were extremely difficult for the both of us. As you are well aware, we were very close at boarding school. After your departure to Vienna, Andy and I were inseparable. He asked me to join him permanently in Christchurch, but I was determined to enroll in a London fashion school. We corresponded for a couple of years before mutually deciding that it was best to severe ties and start afresh.

Writing my memoirs brought back many wonderful memories. The universe does have ways of making us deal with issues that we had kept under wraps these many years. I'm sure when my books are published you'll have the opportunity to read my memoirs, but for now I am enjoying the writing process. Connecting with you again is certainly an unexpected bonus through my current journey of self-discovery.

Do send me pictures of your lovely family, **especially** Turtle and Rabbit. We have a beautiful "daughter," Kali Durga, a fluffy Himalayan who is as adorable as Husni – remember my white Persian kitty? Their personalities are very similar. They are all about giving unconditional love and more love.

1967 At Pino Lancetti L'Atelier

The weekend flew by as quickly as our arrival on the SAQR. We were already on our way to see Signor Pino Lancetti, the Italian "artist-couturier," before I had time to catch my breath. The designer best known for his printed fabrics inspired by well-known artists such as Picasso and Kandinsky, and was among the first in Italy to draw inspiration from Chinese folk clothing. In 1963, his famous military style dress collection, heavily influenced by Modigliani's female portraits, was sought after by international society ladies.

Our entourage arrived at his second-story showroom on Rome's Via Condotti, where he welcomed his international clientele with much flair and fanfare. Impressive artworks covered the walls of his salon, creating a museum-quality space which I was sure would make any Florentine proud. In my young years, I had never seen such an impressive art collection opulently displayed in a fashion atelier. As soon as we were comfortably accommodated, several models casually paraded around the salon, mingling with the audience as if at a cocktail reception. Pino ran his own garment commentary as each model sashayed by our entourage, describing in detail the origin of each creation. A particular dress covered with an array of butterflies caught my attention as the model passed, and I reached out to feel the texture of the embroidered inserts so delicately crafted on sheer satin and chiffon. Intrigued by my observation, the designer commented in heavily accented Italian English, *"Aren't the embroideries beautiful? I was inspired by a Chinese Ming dynasty Qípáo when I designed this ensemble."*

Before he could continue, I said, *"My mother wore qípáos at formal functions. She has a cheongsam with a thousand brocade butterflies embroidered on a red satin fabric."*

"You know Chinese traditional dress well; I thought you are Arabian?"

Andy sitting next to me chimed in quickly before I could divulge too much information regarding our presence in an Arab household, *"We are British students on an exchange program learning Arabian cultures. We are here to assist our hostesses on their bridal shopping spree. Young loves fashion and wants to study fashion design when he leaves school."*

"In that case, all of you must attend our next Sala Bianca fashion presentation in Florence. It is a major fashion event to showcase the best of Italian fashions," exclaimed Signor Pino.

Without thinking, I responded excitedly, *"That would be splendid! I'd love to attend?"*

"Several Roman designers and I are showing at this function, I'll make sure VIP invitations for our upcoming autumn show are dispatched to the Sekham household."

By the time we finished at Signor Lancetti's Atelier, the ladies and I had secured invitations to Florence Sala Bianca fashion presentation, which were mailed to the Sekham after our return to Abu Dhabi.

At Emilio Federico Schubert Atelier

The last of the couture houses was none other than the atelier where fashion came to life and hard work was of the order of the day. Emilio Federico Schubert was born in Naples, in 1904, to an eccentric tailoring couple. As any other craftsman, hard graft and passion characterized this designer. His father was a noble Saxon, and his mother a famous Spanish flamenco dancer. The designer moved to Rome in the early 1930s to become a painter without much success. With an interesting aesthetic background an eye for beautiful women and their fashions, he soon began sketching hats and dresses for society ladies. Naturally gifted with flair and an aptitude of self-publicity, he garnered a reputation as a connoisseur of style and elegance. Soon, the Duchess Ratti, niece of Achille Ratti (Pope Pius IX) encouraged him to open his own atelier and, with her patronage, Schubert opened his first atelier in 1938 with his wife.

Mario greeted the flamboyant designer as if they were the best of friends, patting each other on the shoulders and kissed cheek to cheek as if they were long lost lovers. He then introduced our entourage to his designer friend. I had never seen a man with so much jewelry on his fingers and wrists. Donning a fur stole and makeup, he greeted the Sekham ladies ostentatiously, which astonished the women into fits of girlish giggles. Signor Schubert was the first designer I've met who behaved like an eccentric and flamboyant diva.

Before the fashion presentation started, the designer's PR lady, dressed head to toe in Emilio Federico Schubert couture, announced, *"We are honored with your presence at Atelier Emilio Federico Schubert. Before we begin the fashion show, I would like to introduce our distinguished designer.*

"Signor Schubert's creativity and opulent fashions have made our atelier singular amongst celebrities and princesses. He is known as the tailor of the Dolce Vita, and we count Signora Gina

Lollobrigida, Sofia Loren, Brigitte Bardot, Linda Christian, Joan Crawford, The Duchess of Windsor, Soraya, and, last but not least, Signora Evita Perón among our loyal clients.

"Our atelier has also provided costumes for films such as Carlo Lastricati and Vittorio De Sica's Anna di Brooklyn (Fast and Sexy, 1958) starring the famous Signora Gina Lollobrigida. Signor Schubert has also dressed her in her other movies; Pane, Amore e fantasia, La Provinciale, and La Romana. Please give our designer a big hand." While she and the audience clapped, Emilo took a bow of acknowledgement.

As the music began, his fashions unfolded with an array of eclectic fabrics, each outfit was as flamboyant and opulent as the man who designed the clothes. Intricate beading, embroideries and plush prints abounded with lavish embellishments sparkling like the crystal chandeliers hanging on his grand salon ceiling.

Before long, my thoughts drifted to the persona of this ostentatious designer, relieved that there was salvation for effeminate boys and that we could be accepted and excel in our chosen careers. If this married man could dress to the nines, wear makeup publicly and gain celebrity status, I too could achieve fame through my god-gifted talent, if I carried myself with confidence like Signor Schubert. The influence Emilo had on me proved to be the turning point in my fashion ambition. Besides desiring to be a fashion designer, I also longed to reach international recognition like the designers I had met in Paris and Rome. But my inner voice reminded me not to fall prey to the trappings of being an egotistical celebrity when fame became mine. As much as Signor Emilo's over-the-top eccentricity was amusing, I had also made up my mind not to imitate the man's demeanor. Though I was unaware at the time, I was leaving behind my childhood effeminacy and coming into my own boyish adulthood.

While the Sekham ladies were busy discussing their wardrobe with their allocated venduses, Signor Schubert came over to Mario, Andy and me and said, "*I hope you like my designs. This season, my collection is inspired by the Ming Dynasty court costumes."* Before any of us could respond, he turned towards me and continued, *"Are you from China, young man?"*

Before I had a chance to speak Mario answered in Italian on my behalf, *"Questi ragazzi vengono dall'Inghilterra e che accompagnano loro amici mediorientale su un romp dello shopping a Roma (These boys are from England and are accompanying their Middle Eastern friends on a shopping romp in Rome)."*

"Wonderful! Did Mario show you much of our city? I would be delighted to show you our Roman nightlife," he replied.

Detecting the man coming onto us, with his eyes glued unblinkingly on my Valet, Andy answered, *"Thank you for your kind offer, but we are returning to Abu Dhabi tomorrow morning. Count Mario showed us your beautiful city the last time we were here."*

"Very good. I'm sure you are in good hands. You will have to come to Florence for the Sala Bianca fashion event. I'll love to see you boys again," he gave Mario a wicked wink before joining the ladies to discuss their couture outfits.

Conversation with Mario

The Count began as soon as the designer left our company, *"Emilo's talent and character gained celebrity status to match that of his clients since I started photographing his clothes. His Neapolitan creativity, accompanied by the din of his jewels and trinkets, is often heard in this city's exclusive venues.*

"His constant presence near throngs of beautiful models made him a favorite amongst the paparazzi. He loved the image of a classic opulent woman as much as women loved to look like he imagined them. His exuberant fashion comes to life in large, floor-length tulle skirts embellished to the hilt with cascading crystals. And he is a butterfly collector when it comes to handsome men."

Scratching my head I asked, *"I thought he was married and in business with his wife? Doesn't his wife mind him chasing after handsome men?"*

Mario laughingly replied, *"He is married alright, but that doesn't mean he can't go catching 'butterflies' for fun. Just like Aziz or Gabrielli."*

"But my professor isn't married?"

Laughing harder the Count answered, *"Let me tell you a little insider secret. Being seen with entourages of impeccably dressed female models is a facade to cover his homosexuality and to further his public persona. Emilo loves dressing in female clothing in private. Only close friends know of his passion. I know because we move in the same social circles. Recently he narcissistically released his own perfume, which he aptly named Schu-Schu."*

Andy burst forth with a question, *"Is Signor Schubert a transvestite?"*

Not understanding what a transvestite was, I asked, *"What's a transvestite?"*

Without addressing my question, Mario continued amusing himself with laughter said, *"His fame also brought him to the Italian silver screen, where he portrayed himself on TV and in a movie. That said, behind his dichotomous heritage he's really an icon of Neapolitan baroque fashion.*

"Personally, I prefer the experience of a butterfly, doing the things I love to do and loving those I love to love instead of catching the fleeting and encasing them in glass jars like the Victorians. I will always be a free spirit and not be encumbered by society's imposing rules and so-called 'proper' social etiquettes. I don't impose judgments on what others do or how they behave. I'm comfortable in my own skin and I don't care what people think of me."

On that note, he changed the topic, asking Andy, *"Are you boys able to join me in Florence for the Sala Bianca fashion presentations?"*

I answered quickly, *"Yes, we will!"* I didn't want to miss an opportunity of a lifetime to attend a major fashion event.

My beloved Andy ruffled my hair said smilingly, *"Especially for you, my boy, we will go."*

Second Week of April 2012

...Similar to the way we loved each other. I do miss our time together in Italy. It's been great fun. Did you keep in contact with Andy after your departure from the Sekham? There is so much to catch up on, I don't know where to begin.

For now I'll say Ciao to my ex- "Grande Fratello" ("Big Brother") Oscar!

Love,
Young.

46

I Hope Your Troubles Are Few

"I've had an exciting time; I married for love and got a lot of money along with it."
Rose Kennedy

1967 At The Sekham

The minute we returned to the Sekham, the harem ladies went to work on Mais, the bride. Like any traditional Arabian bride, she went into hibernation for thirty days instead of the usual forty. Three of those had been spent shopping for her wedding trousseau in Rome, while she spent the remainder in the privacy of the female quarters surrounded by the Sekham women and her female companions. Tahu, the groom, was not allowed access to his fiancé until the day of the wedding ceremony. Curious to understand the reason why Mais had not joined our group tutorials with Professor Gabrielli, I cornered Sabiya to enquire after class.

"How is Mais, is she not well? I haven't seen her at our group tutorials," I asked, concerned.

"She is fine, busy preparing for her upcoming wedding. It's our tradition to keep her in our company so she is properly prepped before her Big Day," Sabiya replied.

Naira came over to join her sister when she saw us talking said, "Mais is undergoing a month-long spa treatment."

"What sort of spa treatment takes a month to prepare?" I asked inquisitively.

Sabiya answered, *"For a start, we cook her the best nutritional food while our spa beautician cleanses her with conditioning oils and creams before anointing her with perfumed amber and jasmine."*

"Her hands and feet will then be Laylat Al Henna," Naira added.

"What's Laylat Al Henna?"

Both sisters giggled incessantly before replying simultaneously, *"A Henna Night."*

Sabiya continued happily, *"It's a celebratory ladies' night before the bride is given away to the groom. We have lots of fun singing, dancing and generally making a joyful noise with our girlfriends, female relatives and family members. We also get to have our hands and feet decorated with henna and apply Al Athmed kohl eyeliner for our eyes to look brighter and larger."*

"Oh! You mean a Hen's Night, like in a western style wedding? What's Al Athmed kohl eyeliner?!" I exclaimed.

"Yes, it's kind of like a Hen's Night except we celebrate for a couple of weeks instead of an evening.

"Al Athmed kohl is a special eyeliner made from the Al Athmed black stone, found only in our country and used only during festive occasions. Making the eyeliner is a complicated distillation process, which our womenfolk do. Our spa therapies heat the stone until it disintegrates, then process the paste in water, Arabian coffee, and henna before leaving it for several weeks. Then, the dried paste is ground into a fine powder ready for our use," Naira explained.

A Joyful Noise

Sure enough, 2 weeks before the wedding, the sound of felicitous noises took precedence, reflecting the jubilation that was to unfold. The dholki and khliji (drumming) played continuously as the wedding parties and their families congregated to sing and dance, celebrating the propitious union. The women performed their version of dholki while the men did their own khaliji adaptations, choreographed brilliantly by the mothers of both bridal parties. Tahu's and Mais' relatives and friends sang and danced vigorously to celebrate the couple's soon to be union.

Lavish tributary gifts arrived in abundance to congratulate the Sekham household in honor of Thabit's daughter's matrimony. In reality, it was a political and conducive gesture to be in the Wazir's good graces in the event that a favor from His Honorable would be requested by the giver in the future. This proved dexterous, as the saying goes *"I'll scratch your back if you'll scratch mine."* It is a standard exchange in the world of religious, political, business and social hierarchy.

To start a new life it was also customary for the bride and groom to discard their old clothing and purchase fresh wardrobes, which was precisely what Mais, Ria and Jasim did in Rome.

The Meher

The Meher is a formal statement specifying the monetary amount that the groom will give his wife. Similar to a prenuptial agreement, it was also a dowry to obtain the bride's hand in marriage. In the case of poor Tahu, the Meher was secretly arranged, and Tahu received a monthly stipend from his soon-to-be father-in-law, only to be redirected to Mais as the groom's dowry. Her fiancé could not afford to keep Mais in the style she was accustomed to in her father's household. This was a surface gesture to stop malicious tongues from wagging behind the Wazir's back if done with circumspect discretion.

Traditionally, the Meher also serves as a blueprint for the groom to plan his wife's financial upkeep throughout their marriage. In this instance, it played to the advantage of Tahu since he was now the secret recipient of Thabit's generosity. The groom also ensured his wife's protection throughout their marriage and guaranteed the bride a stipulated monthly stipend once the Meher was signed. As it was customary for the groom to present his betrothed a ring as a pre-wedding gift, this too was surreptitiously arranged by the Wazir, unbeknownst to Mais, who was under the impression that the present came directly from Tahu's hard-earned savings. To me, this bamboozle was definitely not a healthy beginning to a positive marriage. But who was I to judge, since I was only a temporary observer within the Sekham household?

My friend's Meher was held at the Al Ain Palace Hotel, the newest and grandest resort establishment in 1967 Abu Dhabi. It was a moderate-sized ceremony where the couple's marriage was solemnized before a religious Sheikh (an Islamic magistrate) together with two females and a male witness (who happened to be Ula, Mais' biological mother, Naira, her half-sister and Aziz, the bride's uncle).

Separate seating was organized for the Sekham ladies away from the groom's immediate male relatives and friends. Away from his fiancé, Tahu, accompanied by his male entourage, celebrated his Meher by singing traditional Arabian songs. It was only after the feast that the couple was escorted to be amid relatives and friends.

The main celebration was then held at the same hotel two weeks later.

Educating Jasim

While the Sekham was busy preparing for Mais' grand wedding, Jasim was also preparing for his upcoming betrothal and sex education by the Islamic clerics and by me, Devaj, and my BBs. After our conversation aboard the SAQR, the boy cornered me after class one day, asking timidly, *"You said on the plane that Andy, Oscar, Devaj, and you will be able to teach me about sex?"* He whispered the word "sex" almost inaudibly.

"Sure, Jasim, we will be more than happy to teach you a few tricks. Come to the Maktub this evening before dinner and we'll have a chat. This will give me a chance to speak to Andy, Oscar, and Vaj before you arrive." I advised.

"That's wonderful! I'll be there at 5 pm." With those last words he ran off excitedly, no doubt informing his friends of his imminent sex education.

After ingeminating my conversation with Jasim to both my BBs and Devaj, they agreed to sit with the boy, to find out how much he knew about sex before proceeding with possible practical lessons.

Sure enough, at 5 P.M. sharp, Jasim, the adolescent soon-to-be husband of Ria, came knocking at the Maktub. Just like I saw him at his father's chambers a couple of weeks ago, he was nervously twiddling his thumbs. When we invited him in for a casual conversation, he sat between me and Devaj on the spacious settee before Andy broke the ice, asked, *"Jasim, are you excited about your forthcoming wedding? Young told us your brother was giving you advice on your impending marriage to Ria. You can be honest and tell us the truth; we are here to assist you."*

The shy boy said nothing while he continued twirling his thumbs. Oscar chirped in to ease the boy's jitteriness, *"We are your friends and here to help. We can't help if don't tell us what you'd like to know."*

I added, *"On the plane, your brother was making fun of you. We don't do that when you are in our company and we're here to help you be comfortable with your sexuality. You don't have to be shy to confide in us,"* I tried to encourage the adolescent out of his protective shell.

Finally the boy muttered in broken English, *"Sayid treat me not nice. When he want sex he push me around to get me to do what he want."*

Vaj asked curiously, *"What did he do to you?"*

Jasim said reluctantly, *"He catches me when I run and push me down to put his thing in my mouth. I try to escape but he pull my hair and force me to suck it. I try running but he always catches me."*

Andy asked, *"Did you tell him not to do that, or retaliate?"*

Obviously not understanding the word retaliate, he kept silent. I said, *"Did you fight back?"*

"I try but I'm smaller so he catches me all the time. I see the four of you and you don't do that to each other. I wish my brother is like you and treat me nice."

"Of course we will be respectful of your wishes and not be like your brother. We want you be comfortable with us."

Jasim's gelidity was showing signs of dissipation as our conversation progressed. We continued his education through a series of respectful approaches, mostly by lending the young man an understanding and compassionate ear. Soon, his sexual fears evaporated, making way for his journey to unbridled sensual sexuality. That evening was the beginning of our friendship with this sensitive adolescent. He soon became a regular fixture at the Maktub and the Sirocco, when he needed lessons on human relationships.

Mid-April 2012

A strange premonition fell over me that Tuesday when I woke from my slumber. In the middle of the night, a discombobulating dream had woken me. A beautiful white crane flying above a cloudless winter sky was circling around the middle of a large field, where I stood. The crane landed near me, beckoning my presence. The moment my hand touched its feathery wings, the bird rubbed his head on my palms as if communicating to me that all was well as the impending storm clouds bellowed above the darkening sky. Stretching out its gigantic wings, the crane shielded us both from the falling raindrops. A thunderous lightning woke me to the present. Lying in the dark, I tried deciphering the prognosticated message, yet no celestial illumination came to my wondering mind.

After a routine breakfast, I sat down to check my incoming emails. My heart missed several beats as I starred unflinchingly at an email from my long lost ex-lover, protector, Valet and trusted friend. Goosebumps formed on my shielded skin while my body went into involuntary concatenate convulsion. Terrified, I sat frozen for several minutes, not daring to read its contents. For no apparent reason, tears of joy and sorrow began forming in the corners of my eyes, throwing me into a state of utter confusion. Pulling away from the computer, I sat hypnotized on my veranda's chaise lounge, desperately trying to calm myself from this recalcitrant ambivalence. Years of hurt and despair exploded to the vanguard, issues kept neatly and tidily locked in my recesses were ripped open by the invisible impending storm. The inception of my dream was simply too terrifying to perceive what was to happen next.

47

The Wedding

"It is only shallow people who do not judge by appearances. The true mystery of the world is the visible, not the invisible."
Oscar Wilde

Mid April 2012

As I had done with Oscar's email, I did not open Andy's message while butterflies churned in my stomach until I was emotionally and mentally ready to read its contents.

Dearest Young,

It has been more than 40 years since we communicated. When Aria mentioned that she received your email inquiring after me, I was held speechless for a while. Throughout the years you've been on my mind, but I wasn't sure if it was appropriate to locate you. After our separation, my emotional life went on a roller coaster ride. I could not get you out of my head for several years until I met **Toby**, *my ex, who helped ease my sense of loss – yet, your image continued to haunt my existence often. After* **Toby** *I've been through several relationships, but they were nothing like those four years we shared. I know it is sentimental of me to drag out our past, but you continue to be on my mind. I have moved forward with my life, and I'm sure you have too. Although I have stored our past into distant memories, there were occasions when your sweetness came rushing head on, like a euphoric air du printemp.*

I hope you are well in health, spirit and life. I don't know how to begin reconnecting, as it's been so long since we parted. Are you happily 'married'? If so, I am delighted to know you are in safe hands. I'm sure your beloved takes loving care of you. **Albert,** *my lover for the past 8 years, died 17 months ago after a long battle with AIDs-related illnesses. Mourning for his loss threw me to near* depression for several months. But I'm blessed that I'm healthy and back in full swing regaining my life. As you are well aware, we Bahriji boys are very resilient to life's many challenges. :)

For now I'm enjoying my company and rowing several days a week. The sport is immensely meditative, clearing my mind to face new challenges. Being close to nature, away from the maddening crowd, also helps ease me through the grieving process. I moved to Casterton, Victoria, Australia after Albert's death. I'm semiretired from engineering, although I continue working on a few consultancy jobs for a couple of major companies. Life is good. Now tell me about you...

1967 At The Wedding

Mais' Big Day arrived, and she was up at the crack of dawn in preparation for her 10 A.M. departure to the Al Ain Palace Hotel. Her two weeks of pre-wedding preparations had gone well after the couple's Meher. Adorned in haute couture Valentino and wearing a dupata (a kind Middle Eastern wedding veil), she appeared a little after 10, followed by her singing and dancing female entourage. The Sekham was thrown into undaunted dormiration while dohki music played unceasingly and the bridal party making a havoc of joyful noices. Thabit's vintage Rolls Royce sat waiting at the entrance, ready to transport the bride and her immediate family to the Al Ain Palace Hotel, where they received a host of VIP guests upon arrival.

Our 4 males and 2 female foreign students, including me, followed behind in a caravan of fancy vehicles heading towards the wedding ceremonial destination. Tahu and his male entourage were already making joyful noises outside the hotel while waiting for the bride's party to arrive. Two huge reception halls, decorated with an abundance of pink tulle and floral arrangements, welcomed the guests. A large ballroom was devoted solely to the men, while the females were housed in the adjoining grand hall. Andy, Oscar, Devaj, and I joined the male members while Dominique and Anya accompanied the females. While the majority of our Arab friends wore traditional headdresses and ceremonial thobes, we were dressed in our western-style Sunday best. The groom, in a pristine white thobe under a golden overcoat, welcomed well-wishers, thanking them for their illustrious presences and their munificent gifts.

Male Celebrations

While the Sekham's men kept busy greeting guests, Tahu was getting ready to make his grand entrance into the gilded hall with his male entourage, led by a group of traditional Khaliji musicians. I spotted the prince as soon as I entered the grand salon. He was busy chatting with several of the Wazir's guests before taking his honorary place at the head table. Andy, tapping me on my shoulder, said, *"There's someone we know. Look over there,"* pointing his finger towards several seats away from the Prince. My Valet directed his gaze to none other than the Hadrah, the patriarch of the Kosk Household.

"We must go over to say hello," my guardian advised.

As we progressed towards the Hadrah, the Prince noticed my presence. Giving me a friendly nod, he smiled, indicating that he'd like to have a word with me after our acknowledgement of Hadrah Hakim. Andy extended his hand to greet our ex-host when he stood to give us the traditional Arabian nose rub greeting. After polite exchanges, Hakim said, *"How are you boys doing? I'm so happy to see the two of you."*

Andy did a little bow and replied, *"We are well, Sir and we are equally delighted and honored to be in your presence."*

Turning to me, he inquired, *"Are you enjoying your time at the Sekham? Are the brothers treating you well?"*

"Thank you for your concern, Sir. We are doing splendidly and learning much at our present household," I answered.

"You look well, Sir," my Valet said.

"I'm very well. Thank you," replied the Hadrah before being cornered by several guests who came to pay homage to the patriarch. Turning to us he said, *"Remember, boys, my offer for the use of the Simorgh and Khayya'm still stand. We'll catch up later."* On that note, he was off chatting with his acquaintances.

His Highness the Prince

I said to Andy, *"I think the Prince wants to speak to me,"* indicating the direction where His Highness was stationed.

"Let's pay our respect," my Valet advised.

The Prince stood as we approached. As per tradition, he was surrounded with an army of males. We bowed to kiss his hand as a gesture of respect. To my surprise he held onto my hand, lifted it to his lips, and kissed it. Taken aback by this sudden twist of etiquette, I was lost for words. Looking at my Valet for guidance, he nodded as if to say, *"It's alright. Go with the flow and don't pull your hand away."* I did as was instructed before P whispered into my ear, out of earshot from his entourage.

"Meet me after the ceremony, I want to see you."

With that gentle command, he pulled away, resuming his proper social etiquette as guests arrived to pay him respect. As soon as we found our seats, Andy asked, *"What did he say to you?"*

"Who?" I answered as if I didn't know whom my Valet was referring.

"You know who. Don't play the naive coy boy with me; own up and tell me what he said when he leaned over!"

"He wants to see me after the wedding ceremony," I answered truthfully.

"Where are you meeting him?"

"I don't know, he didn't specify."

Nikah

Just then, the grand entrance door flew open and the wedding procession began to emerge. First in line came the Khaliji drummers, followed by a couple of dancing women with candelabras on their heads. I was surprised to discover that Mais had already changed into a Sorelle Fontana wedding dress. Tahu, in black tuxedo held his fiancé's hand firmly, and following behind was a line of female relatives and friends from either sides of the couple's families. Turning to Gabrielli, I asked, *"You mentioned in class that the bride and groom celebrated their wedding separately with the females in one hall and the men in another. Why are they coming into the men's salon together?"*

My teacher answered, *"They are here to sign the Nikah."*

"What's a Nikah?"

"It's a marriage contract, witnessed by both families and friends," the Italian replied.

As the group proceeded towards the stage, the Sheikh who had two weeks earlier conducted the couple's Meher was at the ready to initiate the Nikah. The drumming stopped as abruptly as they had started while the Fatihah (the first chapter of the Quran) and Durud (a Blessing) were read aloud by the Islamic magistrate. The bride, covered by her dupata, stood modestly next to the groom as wedding rings were exchanged, attended by Jasim, Mais' adolescent brother, whose wedding was to recrudesce at the same venue a month after his sister's lavish ceremony.

The Valima (Wedding Reception)

Immediately after Nikah, the bridal party with the womenfolk left the men's hall, leaving the men to dig in to a scrumptious buffet consisting of a huge variety of ambrosial dishes. Al-Kabsa, Saleeg, Burghul, Arabic Mezze, Chicken

Shawarma and Falafel were replenished many times over by uniformed servers. The list of enticing entrees seemed endless, not to mention an entire table full of nectarous deserts, offering wedding guests the chance to satiate their taste buds. Of course there was Arabian coffee, sweet tea and alcoholic beverages were derigure at any grand occasion, and this was no exception to the rule. Being a worldly entrepreneur, the Wazir manipulated the power of visible appearances to full advantage. After all, the lifestyles of the rich and powerful are all about showmanship, and he made sure his daughter's wedding was the event of the year. *"One up from the Jones,"* as the saying goes.

Party, Party, Party

After an appetizing meal, the men were ready to party, and party they did. So did the women in the adjoining hall as music, singing, dancing and laughter were heard in competition with the men. Tahu reemerged after a fresh change of clothing and so did Mais when she rejoined the women's party. It was indeed an unusual custom that males would party in one room and the females in another, but, as with any long-held Middle Eastern tradition, I was not one to reason or judge its purpose, but rather to experience the country's rich cultural heritage.

The men sang and danced, amusing themselves. Before long I noticed P sitting alone while his cronies were busy having a good time. I proceeded over to His Highness to inquire, *"Are you enjoying yourself Sir?"*

He replied smilingly, *"I'm not great at this type of function, but I've got to attend out of respect for my subordinates. I'll rather be with you and your Valet, enjoying your private company."*

Surprised by his remark, I stumbled, not knowing how to respond, when Andy came to my rescue. *"Is your Highness having fun?"* my guardian asked politely.

"No, I was telling Young that I'd rather be in the private company with you boys. Let's get out of here. Now that I've made my official appearance, we can sneak away and have some real fun!"

Before Andy or I could respond, the Emcee announced that the groom was now proceeding to the women's hall to be officially introduced to the female clan. Since Tahu was busy being the bridegroom, I had offered my service to be Aziz's photography assistant, which meant my presence was currently required to document the proceedings in the adjoining hall. Unsettled that I could not accommodate the Prince's request to sneak away, Andy made a polite excuse for us, saying that we would make it up to His Highness as soon as the ceremony was over.

"*Meet me at the hotel lobby in three hours,*" announced the chafed Prince.

"*Yes, Your Highness!*" My Valet spoke on my behalf before we departed to assist my host in documenting the groom's grand entrance into the women's hall.

Dressed in an Emilio Federico Schubert turquoise blue-and-gold gown, the bride accompanied her new husband for their walk down the red carpet, towards the floridly decorated stage where two reddish-golden velvet chairs were placed next to each other. As the bride and groom passed their flamboyantly dressed guests, the women *ooh*ed and *ahh*ed at the groom's handsomeness and the bride's beauty while the smiling couple took their seats. Guests approached to pay their congratulatory respect to the matrimonial couple. Aziz and I snapped away as each guest proceeded forward for his or her photo-op with the happy couple. This procedure reminded me of pictures I had seen of children and adults posing with their favorite cartoon characters in Disneyland.

Mehendi

An hour and half passed before the bridal party left the women's hall. They changed outfits before proceeding to a quieter suite specially set up for the Mehendi ceremony. It was a solemn affair where the groom presented Arabian coffee, tea and alcoholic beverages to his family members and to his new in-laws' household members. This ceremony took place on the first night of the three-day wedding celebration. It's a customary ritual to bring the two families closer together and has also been rumored to calm the pace for the bridal couple to start afresh their new life together. The womenfolk wore brilliant shalwar kameez clothing while Mais, the bride wore a vivid red Ghaagra, (a long skirt covered in gold) and a Valentino Garavani designer version of a traditional Zaboun, completing the look with a matching gold embroidered Yashmak.

Finally, the wedding couple departed the Al Ain Palace Hotel amidst rambunctious hooting and cheering conveyances from revelers and guests alike, while partiers continued their festive soiree into the wee hours the following morning. Although exhausted from assisting Aziz, I still had an important task to perform, and that was to keep my appointment with His Highness, the Prince.

48

"Gaiety is often the reckless ripple over depths of despair."
Edwin Hubbel Chapin

Third Week Of April 2012

...Young, there is so much we need to catch up on, now that we have reconnected. Let's stay in touch on a regular basis and we'll take time to be reacquainted. I'd love to hear everything about you after our separation.
Warm Regards and Love Blessings!
Andy.

1967 In The Batmobile

Andy and I packed into P's 1966 Batmobile with me sitting on my Valet's lap. The vehicle sped away as soon as we were buckled in. The prince zoomed down the deserted Abu Dhabi streets, running red lights in the city owned by his family. I broke out in a cold sweat as the speedometer leapt to 120 miles and continued to rise. Andy's perspiring hands held me tightly while I leaned against his muscular chest for assurance. I could also feel my protector's heart racing against my back as he pleaded despondently for P to slow, to no avail. The Arab was convinced that his Batmobile was "everything-proof" and that no harm would come to us even if we crashed into a sand dune. Off we flew at 2.00 A.M., towards Abu Dhabi airport. Andy and I had no idea where we were heading. All we had was blind trust that the reckless driver would get us there in one piece.

The Al-Fayoum

We finally arrived at a private airfield heading towards a huge hangar. With a click of a button from the Batmobile's dash, the hangar doors slid open as our vehicle came to a screeching halt. P honked loudly until several attendants came rushing towards the entrance; they had been rudely awakened by the bright lights and their employer's incessant honking. The enormous hangar doors opened, revealing a fancy emerald jet, its nose pointing in our direction. P's arrival had set off a commotion. Ground personnel, pilots and two stewards busied themselves firing up the plane for departure. We had no idea where we were heading until P dispatched his instructions to the pilots. I was fascinated by P's commanding power and equally in awe of the glimmering flying machine. My jaw dropped as I was mesmerized by the action buzzing around me. I was at a loss for words. Andy held out his hand to me as we exited the Batmobile before proceeding towards the red carpet and into the Al-Fayoum (P's private Jet).

Love in The Al-Fayoum

The minute we stepped inside this spacious aircraft I was transported into an odyssey of anticipation. The ivory interior was accented with luxurious green leather settees, loveseats and comfortable armchairs lined both sides of this sleek flying machine. Rose wood paneling accented by gold beams framed the windows. In the middle of the end chamber, paneled off from the rest of the interior, sat a king-size bed. Sound-proof insulation added impenetrable privacy for the occupants within.

As the plane gilded out of the hangar onto the runway, the prince at the cockpit gave the pilots instructions to our destination. His two burly bodyguards, already belted in and ready for departure, sat discreetly outside the cockpit, while the stewards offered the prince, Andy, and me beverages. A few minutes later we were airborne on our way to Paris. I had no clue why we were heading to Paris except that His Highness had instructed the pilots to do so. P, turning my head towards him, planted a lingering kiss on my lips. He rapaciously devoured my mouth with passionate French kisses in front of everyone. Surprised and flustered by his sybaritic spiritedness, I turned a shade of red. Glancing at my Valet for advice, he gave me a mischievous wink, telling me to ease into the rhythmic flow of my sensual encounter with His Highness.

Paying no notice to the prince's actions, his bodyguards and attendants went about their business as if nothing extraordinary had transpired. Holding my hand, P led me and Andy towards the bedchamber. Perched on a comfortable seat, my Valet concomitantly observed P and my every move. The prince wasted no time pushing me onto the king and tearing hurriedly at my clothes as if he could not wait to see me naked. He had been drinking at the wedding to loosen his inhibitions, yet he was sufficiently sober to be in control.

His seductive eyes never left mine as he unbuttoned my dress shirt. He urgently unbuckled my belt and unzipped my pants to reveal a pair of white undergarments, the only piece of clothing separating my nakedness and His Highness's muscular physique. The man's eucalyptus scent drifted up my nostrils, sending me into shivers of unbridled curiosity. Goosebumps were coursing through my body in a state of uncertain expectation. Fascinated by P's erratic behavior, I did not know how to react in front of my superior. His every move captivated me. Going with the flow, as per my guardian's instruction, was my only choice. I surrendered to his alpha masculinity. In my young life, I had never encountered a man as mercurial as His Highness. I desired to understand this naked aristocrat who was bewitching me with his recklessness; I was hypnotized by his unpredictability. Little did I guess that P had started spinning a charismatic spider's web, holding me spellbound to his every wish. My journey as his captive boy toy had begun.

Andy sat watching as if witnessing an X-rated movie. My protector made sure His Highness abided by E.R.O.S. guidelines, although no affirmative verbal exchanges were necessary. My Valet laid siege as the unobtrusive silent observer. He was getting aroused by the unfolding visuals of his irresolute charge under the caressing hands of this masterful male. I was deliriously excited by this attractive rogue who was now my magnetic inamorato. My enjoyment, combined with P's sensual expertise, sent me lusting for him. I was ready for his hardness and ready to subjugate myself to his athletic sexual desires. Like a devouring spider luring his prey, P was slowly enticing me into his imperative world of risqué decadence.

Kissing, lapping, and licking, he suckled my boyish, sinewy physique, leaving no parts unexplored. Tilting my firm buttocks to his jabbing tongue, he savored my parting orifice with expert precision. Squirming to such tantalizing simulations, I moaned loudly, only to be silenced by his powerful masculine palms. Cupping my whimpering ecstasies, he attempted to quiet my swelling crescendos. I desired his length, yet he kept it at bay, teasing, luring me further into his unscrupulous web of physiological manipulation. He was playing his game of dangerous liaisons. I had not been taught these rules at the Bahriji, nor by any of my 'big brothers.' Like a game of chess, I was left to maneuver this perfidious mind game as if I were grown, in person and in spirit. For now, P's tantalization was driving me to desirous insanity. I wanted him and he made me beg for the object of my affection.

Swinging his protuberant erection in front of my face, he slapped it against my cheeks, demanding oral attention, yet he refused to feed my hunger. He wanted me to beg before he satisfied me. Suddenly, my sexual concentration dissipated with a blow on my cheeks, turning my face a shade of red from

P's forceful hand. My protector caught the aggressor's hand before another blow rained down my buttocks. Without a word my savior twisted His Highness's wrists to his back, constricting his arm movements while I devoured the alluring attraction dangling in front of my face. I fed nymphomaniacally on my "Master's" bulbous protrusion while he tried freeing his hands from his captor's assertive restraint. Andy, spotting a pair of golden handcuffs by the bedside table, bound P's wrists to his back while his swollen rod basked within the sweetness of my mouth. Turning his captive's head to the side, my protector pried open the Arab's mouth and their sensual tongues intertwined into a passionate purgatory kiss. While unfastening Andy's trousers, I inhaled deeply, engulfing their throbbing hardness simultaneously. I was relishing in my gustatory feasts until their orgasmic convulsions covered my face in dripping rivulets of rapture. Before long, I too was drenched in my own rhapsodic releases. Yet, we were unexhausted. We continued our delirious sadomasochistic play until the pilots announced our imminent descent towards Roissy. We showered, dressed and were ready for our next thrilling adventure; Breakfast at La Tour Eiffel.

49

"Prince Alberts" & "Cock Rings"

"Sex was like Disneyland to him: an allotment of organized wonders and legal mischief."
Martin Amis

1967 La Tour Eiffel

P's Ferrari was already waiting for us at Roissey's tarmac as soon as the Al-Fayoum touched down the runway. We zoomed towards La Tour Eiffel with the prince hot at the wheels. Remembering the last time I was at The Eiffel Tower, when I had acrophobia going up the rocking staircase, my palms were again perspiring while chills quavered through my body at the imminent prospects of ascending this wobbling structure. But I wanted to be brave for Andy and was determined to overcome this phobia. When we arrived, I was surprise to find not a single soul in sight except the restaurant's welcoming staff and the elevator operator, standing at the ready to bid us welcome. That morning, the place was deserted and the wind was not as strong as I had previously imagined. The restaurant's maître d'hôtel stood at attention inviting us into the eatery. There were no customers except P, Andy, and me. His Highness had reserved the entire Eiffel Restaurant. We had the whole venue to ourselves.

The view from the top took my breath away. When P extended his hand to lead me towards the ledge, he said beguilingly, *"Come, let me show you Paris."* My heart was already thumping a mile a minute from fear.

I looked to Andy for a response, and my chaperone replied on my behalf, *"Young is afraid of heights. The last time we were here, he dared not step out of the elevator."*

My Valet could not finish his sentence before P vociferated, *"Nonsense! I will hold him and make sure he doesn't fall."* He extended his hand to mine to guide me out of my seat.

Andy jumped up immediately, pulling my chair back. Besides being a well-mannered gentleman, he was also providing an opportunity for himself to be at my side as we proceeded towards the railings. P clasped my hand as my heart pounded furiously. I was at once excited by the prospect of seeing Paris from the Eiffel's edge and terrified by my acrophobia. True to his words, His Highness held my hand tightly as he stood behind me by the rails. Not daring to look down, I stared straight ahead into the distance. Paris seen at a height was certainly more romantic than observed from the ground. Leaning close, P planted a lingering kiss on my neck, pressing me against the ledge. I was petrified. Although he was holding my waist firmly, an attack of nausea befell me. A sudden relief washed over me when I felt Andy's hand clutching my wrist, pulling me towards him. Leaning against his muscular chest, tears of assurance trickled down my eyes as he shielded my trepidation from our mischievous host. My protector stroked my hair lovingly and calmed my terror.

"See, he's not afraid!" Commented His Highness as if I had overcome my acrophobia, not realizing I was already traumatized. If he did, he pretended not to notice.

I did not reply. Neither did my protector as the prince continued, *"Look at the beauty of Paris."* He pointed his finger to nowhere in particular, as he turned my face to see the view. Andy had wrapped his arms around my waist to make sure I was securely guarded before replying, *"It sure is. Let's return to our table, the waiters have brought our food."* It was my guardian's way of directing me back to safety without insulting the prince.

A Prince Albert

During breakfast, Andy inquired, *"When did your Highness have a Prince Albert piercing?"*

Not knowing what a Prince Albert piercing was I asked, *"Who's Prince Albert Piercing?"*

Both men laughed before His Highness responded, *"A year ago.*

"I like the feel of it, as it creates greater friction when I'm fucking."

Surprised by such forwardness, I shook my Valet's hand, urging him to enlighten me, *"What is a Prince Albert piercing?"*

The men continued laughing when P answered, *"Boy oh boy! Didn't you feel the titillating sensation when I was inside you?"*

I was beginning to get the idea, replied, *"Oh! You mean the silver ring around the head of your penis?"*

"Yes boy! That's call a Reverse Prince Albert," advised His Highness.

Curious to understand further I asked, *"Why is it called a Reverse Prince Albert?"*

Andy said smilingly, *"There are many theories about the history of the Prince Albert piercing, but very few are true. Rumor has it that it was a "Dressing Ring," used to pull the penis into a man's tight-fitting trousers during the Victorian era. It is said that Prince Albert wore it to keep his foreskin from retracting and stay 'fresh smelling' so as not to offend his queen, Victoria."*

The Prince added lightheartedly, *"When I was studying at Eaton, some of my classmates wore Prince Albert Wands.*

"In school we had a discussion on Beau Brummel, who started the craze for ultra-tight men's trousers. The pants were so tight, the penis needed to be held to one side or the other, so as not to create an unsightly bulge. To accomplish this, some men had their penis pierced, to allow their member to be held by a hook to the inside of

their trousers. Thus this piercing, as you just mentioned, became known as a "Dressing Ring". Tailors would ask a gentleman if he dressed to the left or the right.

"When I visit my London bespoke tailors, they continue to ask me whether I dress to the left or right, simply because I wear a Prince Albert."

Cock Rings

Fascinated by the topic I questioned further, *"What's the function of the rings that are around your penis and scrotum?*

His Highness laughingly resumed, *"The cock rings keep my erection harder and longer. You do like the feel of it, don't you? You obviously enjoyed the sensation since you begged fervently for it."*

I was embarrassed by such conspicuous sexual discussion over breakfast and within such proximity to the listening waiters. On the contrary, P seemed vitalized by our descant, especially in front of his subordinates. Andy on the other hand was using our open discussion as an abecedarian opportunity to educate me in genitalia adornments and piercings.

My Valet excogitated, *"Young, cock rings are rings placed around the penis and/or around the scrotum to slow the flow of blood from the erect penile tissue, thus maintaining an erection for a longer period during the act of lovemaking. These jewelries are often made of stainless steel, titanium, or gold."*

I asked my mentor explicably, *"Why, then, do you not wear a Prince Albert and/or cock rings?"*

The two men thought my question amusing. *"My sweet darling, you are such a sexy boy. I don't need to wear either of those because I'm extremely turned on by you and I don't require extra stimulation to excite me further,"* Andy explained.

Without thinking I burbled out, *"Are you implying that His Highness is not as stimulated by me like you are?"*

The moment I asked that question, I knew I had put my foot in my mouth. The men looked at me as if I'd suddenly grown two horns on my head and had transformed into the devil. Andy diverted my question quickly, responded, *"Quite the contrary, His Highness had on the jewelries for you to adore and admire their prowess. By the look on your face during our sexual soiree you seemed to crave more. That's why he wanted to demonstrate how excellent a lover he is to you. Am I correct Sir?"* He turned to the Prince for his approval. His Highness nodded in agreement, knowing full well that that was not the main reason why he wore cock rings and a Prince Albert. P, delighted by my Valet's favorable answer, suggested, *"After breakfast, let's head over to 26 Place Vendome."*

That happened to be The House of Boucheron.

50

Hey Big Spender

"The most precious jewels are not made of stone, but of flesh."
Robert Ludlum

End April 2012

A week had passed and I finally plucked up the courage to reply to my ex-lover.

Dear Andy,

It is good to hear from you. I agree it's been too long since we connected. My condolences; I'm deeply saddened to hear of your partner's passing. It is difficult for those who are left behind, grieving, when a person we love departs to the next realm. I'm sure you are coping splendidly, though; knowing the nature of my beloved friend, you'll be back living a full life in no time.

I went through extreme consternation the two years after our separation. Your presence has always been my strength during trials. In order for me to grow in spirit and propriety, I concluded that it was best to cope with my personal difficulties alone. Still, my overwhelming urges to contact you were decisively irresistible. During our time together, you taught me valuable spiritual lessons to withstand calamity and your masterful mentorship opened my eyes to truthful honesty (both to myself and to others), which I had often omitted through my delusional ordeal. Yet my journey of self-recovery was not easy. I am still unsure if our reconnection is a good idea, even though my abience told me no but my urge impelled me otherwise. I'm afraid to reopen the hurtful can of worms which I had kept hidden for so long. Being truthfully honest with you, my dearest lover, I'm scared of your presence.

I was desperately trying to relive the love we shared after you left. I began visiting underground gay sex clubs in the hope of finding another like you. Instead I spiraled into disillusionment. I used sex as a pervasive tool to drown my sorrowful loneliness, which drove me deeper into abysmal miseries. I knew I had to leave London and salvation arrived with my acceptance into The Belfast College of Art and Technology, to pursue my Foundation Art Studies. I plunged myself passionately into my college projects in war-torn Belfast, where the IRA (Irish Republican Army) were in conflict with the British Army. There wasn't much a nightlife to divert my attention, and I had the perfect opportunity to devote time to my numerous artistic pursuits. Being a workaholic, I channeled my pervasive vexations into my eternal love: fashion design.

A year later I was accepted into London Harrow College of Art and Technology, Fashion Department to commence my 3 years of Diploma studies in Fashion Design. In the Fall of 1975, the prestigious Royal College of Art and Design accepted my application to continue my postgraduate fashion studies…

1967 The House of Boucheron

Two of P's bodyguards were already stationed outside the House of Boucheron, when we sped to the entrance in his Ferrari Spyder. As soon as we entered the opulent establishment, the manager was waiting to welcome the 'Big Spender' who often dropped thousands of Francs in a single visit. This time was no exception. After formal introductions, the manager and a senior sales executive attended to the prince. I took the opportunity to look at the exquisitely detailed jewelry on display in the glass cases. Andy, seated next to the prince, was providing His Highness a second opinion on the items being shown.

Hypnotized by such a glittering array of precious sparklers, I remained spellbound until Andy summoned me into a private antechamber where His Highness, the manager and the sales executive were located. I was surprised to find

P's pants on the floor and his genitalia exposed, while the manager was fitting several rings onto the prince's penis. His white gloved hands held His Highness' phallus like a priceless jewel. The expression on the Arab's face was less than satisfied; he wanted to be sure that his custom made cock-ring designs would fit snugly on his erect manhood.

A Blow Job

I had no idea why I was being beckoned into the chamber until my Valet spoke, *"Young, will you do His Highness a favor?"*

Without second thoughts I answered, *"Sure! What will you like me to do, Sir?"*

Andy replied seriously, *"Will you give His Highness a blowjob?"*

Shocked by such a request, I was speechless until my guardian led me by the hand and bid me kneel in front of the prince, while the manager and the executive watched in amazement. As much as I loved to suck on P's cock, I never envisioned performing such a private act in public. Yet my extroverted attributes found this proposition very tantalizing. It was by far the most unusual request I had ever received from anyone, let alone a prince. Ignoring the overhead halogen lights, I set to work using my Bahriji-taught skills to pleasure my host. Before long, he was groaning in synchronicity to the soothing piped music that was playing in the background. Since I was enjoying this voyeuristic attention, I wasn't prepared to stop and neither was the prince ready to end his exhilarating oral stimulation.

Andy, the sensible one, finally uttered, *"Thank you Young! You've done well. Measurements can now be taken satisfactorily."*

On that note, the dumbfounded manager and the sales executive, hands shaking, zoomed in, staggering to measure the erect phallus to ascertain the circumference.

"Voila! Merci Monsieur. We now have the exact measurements we require," the manager announced politely as if it was an everyday occurrence for a client to bring a personal fluffier for a cock ring measurement.

On the other hand, the stupefied senior executive was left speechless, bewildered by what he had just witnessed, only to be jarred back to reality by his superior requesting his presence in the outer chamber. It was a move to provide His Highness, Andy, and me our privacy to finish what I had started. A few minutes later, the three of us emerged. Judging what had happened from P's happy visage, Andy's satisfactory countenance and me licking my lips, savoring the luscious residuum, the manager and the executive went about serving us nervously.

Gold Sculptures

I was admiring several pieces of sculpture that were displayed on a couple of pedestals. The cutting-edge simplicity in shape, form and design piqued my interest before Andy came over to explain, *"These sculptures are sculpted by Dame Barbara Hepworth."*

"They are beautiful. Are all her creations so elegantly simple?" I inquired.

The prince, noticing my interest in the artworks, commented, *"Do you like them?"*

"Yes, I like their unencumbered sophistication," I answered.

"I like them too, because they suggest a certain sexual je ne sais quoi. Maybe it's the hollow in the middle that reminds me of your enticing orifices." The prince commented loudly within earshot of the sales executive, who was now staring at me unblinkingly.

Embarrassed by his comment, I turned a couple shades of red. I quickly turned my gaze away from the art, moving rapidly to an ornate jewelry display case that was located in another section of the Maison. Andy putting his arms around my shoulders remarked, *"Don't take P's obiter dictum seriously.*

He likes to antagonize you, because you are so genteel and an easy target to razz. He doesn't mean it maliciously; that's the way he is."

"I'm not perturbed by his remarks. I don't take his teasing seriously," I replied. "But there are certain things I don't understand about him."

Just then, the manager arrived, informing us that our presences were required by His Highness.

Cologne

The prince was dabbing on a sample of cologne which he'd had the House specially formulated for him. He asked, "*Young, do you like the smell?*" He offered his neck for me to take a whiff. As I bent over, His Highness suddenly turned his head and planted a lingering kiss on my unexpecting mouth, in front of the manager and his sales associate. I tried pulling away but he held me tightly, as if empirically determine to exhibit his prowess over me. Knowing full well I had been embarrassed twice, he was pushing his consilience yet again. Stunned by his action, I didn't know how to react. Left with no choice, I went with the flow, playing to the wishes of this despotic aristocrat. From the corner of my eyes, I saw the staff's expression of disbelief as His Highness continued his act of proliferation. Andy watched for a bit before breaking the ice, saying, "*I like the smell of the scent your Highness, and I'm sure Young will agree with me.*"

Releasing his hold His Highness replied, "*What do you think, Young*"?

Regaining my sense of propriety I answered, "*The scent you created is extremely captivating, Sir!*"

"*What do you think I should name it*"? He turned to me for my opinion.

Caught off guard, I glanced across the counter and noticed the name Jaipur staring at me; from a label describing a piece of flamboyant necklace on display. I said, "*You should name the fragrance Jaipur. The scent reminds me of your princely heritage and your regal aristocratic deportment."* I had meant the last segment of my sentence as a sarcastic remark.

"*I like Jaipur, and Jaipur it will be.*" Obviously, my sarcasm flew over his princely head.

Relieved by my callidity, my Valet congratulated me with a cryptic nod of approval. P asked, as I was adjusting my clothes, "*Are there any items you like in the shop? I'll buy it for you.*"

Astonished by his offer, I replied, "*Oh no, nothing, Sir! You don't have to buy me anything. I'm glad to be of assistance.*"

Andy added, "*Young is correct. We are at your disposal whenever our services are required.*"

The prince smiled charismatically before returning to his purchases. By the time we left Boucheron, my guardian was at the ready to persuade His Highness to return us to the Sekham. Andy was positive that the Sekham Household would be searching for us, since we were Thabit's responsibility if we disappeared, and we had been gone for more than 18 hours.

End April 2012

...*It seemed not so long ago I graduated, but time flew and here we are, reconnecting after a long absence. You are living in one end of the world and I in the middle of the Pacific Ocean. I find it riveting that our ambitions have taken us to many locales. But my love for you has never waned or quivered. It was stored within the abeyance of my mind, unable to confide in anything except my remembrance of you; through the many photographs we took during our E.R.O.S. days.*

At times, my E.R.O.S. pledge of allegiance and oath of confidentiality wore thin, yet your gentlemanly word of honor rings loud in my mind, reminding me to be silent until the correct moment requires the truth be told. For now, my dear Andy, I await your news and I'm glad we reconnected.

Best Wishes and look after your good self.

Young.

51

Money Can't Buy Me Love

"Love and kindness are never wasted. They always make a difference. They bless the one who receives them, and they bless you, the giver."
Barbara de Angelis

1967 At The Sekham Household

The moment we arrived at the Sekham, Oscar came knocking at the Maktub, inquiring, *"The Wazir, Gabrielli, and Aziz are worried, asking Vaj and me if we knew where the two of you had disappeared to,"* Oscar said, in a concerned voice. *"You guys are to report to Thabit's chambers and explain yourselves."*

Our lover continued, excitedly, *"The last time Vaj and I saw you, you were at the Al Ain Palace Hotel lobby, waiting for the prince. That's what I told Thabit. Where did you go?"*

Before Andy could reply, a manservant informed us that we were required by the Wazir immediately. Without hesitation, my Valet guided me by the arm towards our host's chambers.

As soon as we closed the chamber door, our Master wasted no time and spoke authoritatively, *"We were searching for the two of you. You guys vanished without informing anyone where you were going, causing us great anxiety. You are my responsibility when at my house. This is not acceptable behavior!"*

My Valet responded, apologetically, *"We are terribly sorry to have caused you and your household such anxiety. Our heartfelt apologies, Sir."*

"Where were you?"

"His Highness, the Prince, requested our presence after the wedding ceremony. We had no idea he was whisking us to Paris. I did not have the opportunity to inform you or anyone at the Sekham. Had I known, I would have told you, Sir. We are terribly sorry to have caused you unnecessary worries." Andy apologized again, emphatically.

Thabit's demeanor transformed from aggravation to befuddlement when he spoke again, "So! It was the prince who abducted you. That tricksy hellion! I should have guessed."

Bemused by the knowledge, our host advised, "I will not be surprised if he requests your services in his Household when you have completed your time at the Sekham. Aziz and I were hoping to keep the two of you for another term, in order for Young to complete "Sacred Sex In Sacred Places," but it appears that won't be the case, now that His Highness has shown interest in the both of you."

"His Highness hasn't indicated that he will require our services at his Household," I answered in a befogged tone.

Amused by my naiveté, the Wazir commented, "You know very little about the Prince's attributes. As charming and personable as His Highness is, he is a descendant of one of the wealthiest families in the Emirates, and whatever he sets his eyes on, he gets. My advice to you is, play your cards right and you'll not be hurt. P was my classmate in school; we grew up together, and I know him and his family well."

"Thank You for your advice, Sir." My Valet said with gratitude.

"Be careful."

Before we left the Wazir's chamber he announced, "Aziz will be calling you for a meeting. We have received word that the Vegas and Hollywood sets are close to completion. My brother and Tahu will arrange the departure date to the United States. They will handle the logistics and advise you on what to do.

"I'm glad you're back from your whirlwind flight of fancy with His Highness. Come to my chamber tomorrow evening at 10.00 P.M.." With that summons, he dismissed us.

Questions & Answers

As we proceeded to the Maktub, I couldn't help replaying the conversation my Valet and I had on our return flight from Paris, in the Al Fayoum. After much persuasion, His Highness finally relented and flew Andy and me back to Abu Dhabi. He stayed in Paris for more fun and shopping, insisting, at first, that we accompany him. My clever guardian managed to convince P to release us, at least until our next meeting, which would be at Jasim and Ria's wedding celebration. Life was back to normal (or, rather, what was considered normal) at the Sekham Household at least for now.

On the plane I had the opportunity to ask Andy the question I did not finish asking, when we were interrupted in the House of Boucheron. I began, *"I have numerous questions about the prince."*

"What do you not understand, my love?"

"Why is he so irrational"? I cocked my head as I asked.

My guardian replied, *"Often, boys from affluent families are pampered and spoiled by their parents; the prince is no exception to the rule. Servants provide overly solicitous attention and run their errands. With a snap of their fingers, their desires are met, making them inexplicably antagonistic, on occasions.*

"In the case of His Highness, I believe his nature may go deeper than his apparent mischievousness. I think it is his way of releasing his inner frustrations that his high station in life does not allow him to pursue his ambition."

I continued my queries, *"What frustrations can he possibly have? He has everything money can buy."* My remark triggered a skeptical laughter from Andy. He continued, *"Young, there are many things money cannot buy. In the majority of cases, money can purchase a temporary fix. But once that fleeting satisfaction leaves, the negative feelings once again become pervasive."*

"What can money not buy?" I asked.

"Inner peace, a sense of achievement, and, most important of all, love. Young man, you mustn't confuse love with sex. Sex can be bought, but true love has to come from the heart," my Valet said softly.

"Is that the reason His Highness enjoys our company"?

"Why, my love?"

"Is it because of our unconditional love for him? The love you taught me to embrace when we were back at The Hanging Gardens of Babylon? Remember, you read me excerpts from The Art of Loving by Erich Fromm.

"You said, 'if the wall between two strangers suddenly breaks, and we feel close, as one, then this moment of oneness is the most exhilarating and most exciting experience in life.' Maybe that's why he is drawn to us, since we ask nothing of him?" I questioned.

"Maybe you're correct, my boy, maybe."

"One of the first things you have to learn is that love is an art, just like living is an art; if we want to learn how to love, we must proceed in a similar manner to learning any other art form. Maybe here lies the answer to the question of why people in our culture rarely try to learn this art, in spite of their obvious failures, in spite of their deep-seated craving for love. Almost everything else is considered to be more important than love: success, prestige, money, power. It is rare that people focus on cultivating the art of loving.

"Therefore, my dearest boy, we must try to live up to the standards of our beliefs. One day, our behaviors will be acknowledged and they will be a light to those with whom we come in contact. For now, we perform our assigned tasks. You understand?"

"Yes! I understand," I said, gazing at my lover adoringly.

Gabrielli's Announcement

Aziz, the photographer, was glad to see my Valet and me the following day, when we were called to his studio. Tahu's status had risen overnight from that of a photographer's assistant to a junior business partnership, through marriage.

He was already developing an air of superiority when speaking to us. Aziz had hired another assistant to do the menial tasks, which Tahu had previously done.

Our meeting consisted of Gabrielli, Aziz, Tahu, Bahir (the new assistant), Oscar, Devaj, Andy, Dominique, Anya and me. Gabrielli spoke on behalf of the Wazir, *"Before I begin, we'd like to welcome back Andy and Young."*

He continued, *"We have received news from the builders that the sets will be completed in a few days. We'll be flying to America to continue shooting "Sacred Sex In Sacred Places." Las Vegas will be our first stop before proceeding to the City of Angels. Count Mario will be joining us on location."*

My teacher paused for questions before continuing, *"We'll be boarding the SAQR at 1:00 P.M. on Thursday. Please be ready a half hour prior to departure and wait at the Sekham's main entrance. Your personal Abds will collect your luggage from your suite an hour before we are scheduled for Abu Dhabi airport."*

Andy inquired, *"Will there be other models joining us on this shoot?"*

"Yes, the Count will bring several of his models. You'll be meeting them in Las Vegas at the hotel where we'll be staying," answered my professor.

As excited as I was with the upcoming adventure, I couldn't help but wonder why the Wazir wanted to see Andy and me the following evening.

Early May 2012

Andy's E-mail reply caught me by surprise as I was starting the daily writing of my memoirs. He wrote:

Dear Young,

I am saddened to hear that our separation caused you so much pain. I would have come running if I knew. Like you, I was equally unsettled. I missed you significantly. Your childlike phantasm continues to haunt me wherever I go. At times, memories of you have thrown me into unfathomable melancholy and at times into paralytic states, from which I have been unable to rise to perform the simplest of task. My daily rowing saved me from falling into depression during those early days of our parting. The natural beauty of New Zealand nurtured me, helping me to recover. No one in my life has had this effect on me. We must have been inseparable in our past lives and our alienation in this life has ripped a gaping perforation through my heart.

I've had several long term relationships since we parted ways, yet they could never fill the emptiness within. During our four years together I was complete. This may come as a surprise to you, after our years of severance, but you continue to remain in my mihrab during my daily meditation. I like to believe that we are victors and not victims of this world. Therefore, my dearest friend, we have reconnected; let's continue to stay in touch. I trust the Universe will guide us in everything we do.

I'm happy to hear from you.
Loving you always,
Andy.

52

Worship The Creator

"I love you when you bow in your mosque, kneel in your temple, pray in your church. For you and I are sons of one religion, and it is the Spirit."
Khalil Gibran

1967 In The Wazir's Chambers

At 10.00 P.M. the following evening, Andy and I met Thabit in his chambers. The Wazir wasted no time in getting us settled before speaking, *"Tahu, Sayid and his brother Jasim are going to Mecca for Hajj, after you return from America. I will like the both of you, Oscar and Devaj to accompany them. This will be an opportunity for Young and Vaj to learn about us Muslims, once in a lifetime pilgrimage to the Holy City."*

Although my Malaysian Muslim classmates had told me about Hajj, I had never considered the significance of this Muslim rite. The experience had now presented itself, and I was excited to learn more about this pilgrimage. Andy answered on our behalf, *"We will be delighted to accompany your children and Tahu to Mecca, Sir."*

"That's excellent!" Our host exclaimed.

He continued, *"I believe my boys have been seeing the two of you for male sexual education. You have my blessings. Teach them well and keep me posted on their progress."*

"We will do our best to be their mentors and we'll inform you of their developments," my Valet responded.

The Wazir, Andy & Me

"Now, I have a personal favor to ask of you. You two love birds, perform your sexual dance! The Prince mentioned that you're a great couple to watch. Perform!" Our host commanded.

I looked at Andy for a response. Without uttering a word, my guardian leaned across me and slid his tongue into my mouth for a lingering French kiss. My lover's alpha masculinity never failed to titillate my libido. My penis stirred as his hands began unbuttoning my djellaba before reaching in to play with my sensitive nipples, arousing them to erection.

In the heat of our passionate sensuality, my thobe was lifted above my thighs. With a single yank, my briefs slid off my hips, exposing my throbbing erection. A stimulating mouth engulfed its pulsating length, while Andy's tongue continued to explore every crevice of my yearning mouth. Chilling thrills rushed over my skin as a pair of mature hands caressed my indulgent body. The probing hands cupped my buttocks, lifting my groin towards the warmth of a yearning mouth. Enjoying the sweet sensations traversing my being, I closed my eyes, savoring every moment of this loving sexuality. I tilted my pelvis, granting my Master oral access to my throbbing hardness. His pulsating organ ground against my inner thighs, sending shivers of electric currents through my spine. Kneeling between my legs, the Arab savored every inch of my perkiness as I wiggled my toes, involuntarily on his dangling scrotum, in reciprocation.

The scent of Musk permeated my nostrils as I glanced down at my handsome host, whose face was bobbing up and down in my crotch. I continued kissing my saucy Valet, gripping his manly nipples as I invited his curling tongue to delve deeper into my longing mouth.

My guardian pushed me onto the bed, lifted my legs into the air, and burrowed his tongue into my tunnel. His aggressiveness as he jabbed and licked my orifice, sent shudders through my spine. Surrendering willingly and openly to his oral incursion, I moaned, *"Don't stop!"* Thabit watched, mesmerized, stroking his stiffness, readying himself for the right moment.

In a single stroke my lover entered my core; his fortitude triggered fluttering convulsions. Andy's unwavering velocity, pushing all of himself inside my spasming slit, consumed me. My Master's length thrust into the back of my throat. I inhaled his masculine muskiness with delectation. Both men took turns pleasuring me, as I pleasured them. I did not want this passionate evening to end.

We did not leave Thabit's chambers until the morning sun peeped through the gauzy veils of the lacey damask curtains. Cuddled between the Wazir's hairy chest, and my protector's musculature, a peaceful contentment befell me. Closing my sleepy eyes, I inhaled my Master's scent while savoring my lover's length, still buried in my being after a delirious night of wanton indulgence. I did not desire this gratifying synesthesia to end. Andy turned me towards him and planted a delectable kiss in my mouth. Without stirring to wake our host, we quietly crept out of his chambers and back to the Maktub from whence we came.

Hajj

I had the opportunity to ask Professor Gabrielli the significance of Hajj, after our regular tutorials. *"Professor, can you explain the purpose of Hajj? Wazir Thabit has asked Andy and me to accompany Sayid, Jasim, and Tahu to Mecca."*

"I'm glad you asked, Young. Throughout history, people have been drawn to a particular place for commercial, cultural, political, and spiritual purposes. Nothing can compare to the Hajj; it is a sacred pilgrimage established by Abraham, the father of the Prophets. Allah commanded him: 'Declare to the people the Hajj. They will come on foot and on every lean camel. They will come from every remote path,'" Gabrielli quoted from the Sūrah al-Hajj: 27.

I continued questioning, "*In Malaya, my Muslim friends tell me they have to go to Mecca at least once in their lifetime. Why is that?*"

"*You have to understand, Young; Allah made the Hajj an obligation. People were magnetized to Mecca from every corner of the world. When humanity is gathered as one, and called to worship its Creator, that is a very powerful force which can shift the energy of the world. According to the Sūrah Āl `Imrān: 97, Allah said, 'And upon humanity is the pilgrimage to the House, whoever among them is able to undertake the journey.'*"

Muslims & Catholics

"*Is it similar to the way that Catholics go to service and prayer at Saint Peter's Square during Easter?*" I asked.

My professor replied, "*I suppose there are similarities. In the case of Muslims, it is Allah calling his people, and their hearts respond to His call. Therefore, for faithful Muslims, the result is an awe-inspiring gathering of faith. It was Abraham who proclaimed the Hajj, and today, the people who assemble in Mecca follow the rites as taught by Prophet Muhammad, whom Muslims believe to be Allah's final messenger to humanity.*

"*In the Quran, the Prophet Muhammad said, 'Whoever performs the Hajj without engaging in any obscenity or wickedness, will return as sinless as the day his mother gave birth to him' (Sahīh al-Bukhārī.)*"

Gabrielli continued, "*In the case of faithful Catholics assembling for Mass and prayer at Saint Peter's Square, it is not God who summons them, rather it is the Pope, God's official spokesperson. Saint Peter was said to have received the keys to the Kingdom of Heaven; he was an Apostle as well as the first Pope. Catholics from around the world congregate at Saint Peter's Basilica for Mass. They gather to celebrate the risen Christ, according to the gospel of Matthew 16:18-19. Therefore there are differences between the two gatherings.*"

I continued, questioning, "*Don't Muslims and Christians pray to a similar God? If they pray to one God, the same God, there must be similarities?*"

"Good question, young man. Let me explain further; the Hajj is an event of great spiritual, moral, and worldly significance. It is an opportunity for purification and strengthening of relationship with Allah. It is also an act of formal worship and devotion with prescribed rites. Carrying out these rites with a huge crowd of fellow Muslims affirms and reinforces the virtues of patience, good conduct, and love in their relationships with fellow pilgrims.

"Similarly, Catholics who gather at Saint Peter's are there to strengthen their relationship with God and their fellow man, through Christ. They also have prescribed formal worship and devotional practices such as the participation in the Eucharist. Similarly to Muslims, Catholics advocate the practice of patience, good conduct, and love in their relationships with others."

My teacher explained further, "Prophet Muhammad stressed the values of patience, compassion, and clemency, especially during the Hajj. He urged pilgrims to act in a composed manner, 'Be calm and steady, because righteousness is never attained through gruffness and haste' (al-Muwatta.)

"The prophet also added that pilgrims should not shout, jostle or shove each other as they strive to observe their Hajj rites. Mercy and love for fellow pilgrims are prerequisites; dignity and good manners should be maintained at all times. The prophet also said, 'What purpose is there in donning humble garments and forsaking material comforts, if my followers are conducting themselves selfishly and arrogantly? How can they espouse the jamrahs as a rite of worship and obedience to Allah, when they are kicking and shoving others?'"

I asked, "Isn't it common courtesy to behave in a civilized manner? Why do Muslims require their prophet to tell them to behave decently?"

My professor answered, "For you, me and to most, common courtesies are taught to us by our elders, parents and mentors. As Islam's prophet, Muhammad established the Hajj for his followers to unite together through faith, love, and the collective worship of Allah. He posted these questions to Muslims, 'How then is this realized by pilgrims who cause disorder, defy the policies set in place to ensure the safe conduct of the people, while shoving aside anyone who stands in their way? They will surely know that Allah sees what they do. Can they think that He is pleased with their behavior?' These questions remind Muslims to act in a civilized fashion."

Gabrielli quoted from the Quran (Sūrah al-Baqarah: 177,) "'It is not righteousness that you turn your faces towards the east or the west; but it is righteousness to believe in Allah and the Last Day, the angels, the scriptures, and the messengers. To love Allah is to practice regular charity for your kin, the orphans, the needy, the wayfarer, those who ask, for the ransom of slaves, and to be steadfast in prayer; thus fulfilling the contracts which you, as Muslims have made. Be firm and patient, in suffering and adversity in times of strife. Such are the God-fearing people of truth.'"

"Isn't Muhammad's teaching similar to that of Jesus?" I queried, curiously.

"Yes, both sages taught similar philosophies. Muhammad reminded Muslims to remember that the Hajj is performed for Allah, while the Pope reminded Catholics to remember Easter, Jesus' resurrection, to guide mankind back to Godliness. Both were created for devotees to worship the Creator, to glorify His name, and to uphold that which He made sacred. And, indeed, the most sacred thing is human life," advised the Italian.

Our discussion came to an end when Andy came to collect me after class. He informed me that gifts had arrived at the Maktub and I should make haste to see who they were from.

53

The Wonder in Everything I See

"Men never remember, but boys never forget."
Bernard Tristan Foong

Early May 2012

In response to Andy's Email, I wrote:

Hi Andy,

I'm glad to know you are doing well, and I trust that you are coping with the loss of Albert. Without doubt, your daily meditations and rowing exercises will do wonders for your healing process. We have both been through rough periods after our separation. We grew stronger in body and spirit through these experiences. Although we have matured, you are still the person I'll always love and cherish. I'm sure there are many men who would be thrilled to have the opportunity to be in a relationship with you. Your charismatic personality traits and stunning good looks ensure that you will come out on top, every time! If I were single, I'd be the first in line to solicit a relationship with you, you handsome man! Are you currently dating anyone?

My life partner Walter, is the person who spearheaded my search for you. He's enamored with the way I describe you as God in human form. The two of you have very similar personalities; that's the reason I love you both very, very much. This, my friend, is the undeniable truth. I am extremely grateful for the years we shared and I look forward to meeting again. For now I am grateful for our long distance friendship…

1967 In The Maktub

A bouquet of blood red Calla Lilies for me and a bouquet of vanilla Calla Lilies for Andy greeted us in the Maktub. As I drew closer, I noticed exquisite rings around the center of each stem of my bouquet. In total, there were twelve rings, several encrusted in precious stones. Each was joined by a tiny clasp, which formed a necklace. Individually, they were rings for different parts of the anatomy. I was flabbergasted by such extravagant gifts. Enclosed within a golden Boucheron case was an inscription that read:

A gift for a beautiful boy:

One emerald ring to adorn your perky boyhood, another to embellish that buoyant organ. Two gold rings for both of your nimbly earlobes, another pair to clasp those perky nipples. Three gold rings for sensual probing fingers, a trio for twinkling toes wriggling in sexual delight.

Love & Kisses!

P

I was speechless when I saw Andy's gift. Around the stalks of the bouquet of white Calla Lilies were entwined a pair of emerald covered handcuffs. The card to Andy read:

A present for a Master:

Punish me when I'm bad; cuff me when I'm naughty. Your obedient slave,

Prince.

We looked at each other with bewilderment, not knowing how to respond to such unconventional gifts. Finally, my guardian broke the silence, and said, "We must write our respective thank-you cards to His Highness."

"How shall I respond?" I asked.

"Write what comes to you naturally," Andy advised.

I could not help but inquire of my Valet, *"Is P like Ramiz? Is he into sadomasochism?"*

"I didn't know he is a sadomasochist until I read the note.

"Unlike Ramiz, whose sadomasochism was due to canings by his father at an early age, P felt the need to be dominated occasionally because everyone kowtowed to his wishes all the time. At times he needed his every velleity to be denied. Being submissive was a rare opportunity for him.

"Young, as we venture to different Harem Households, you will notice that people enjoy different kinds of role play. Although our sex education professors have provided us with the basics, you will learn that every individual has his own unique preferences. We have to use our intuition to best maneuver through these personalities. It's like a mine field that you and I have to decipher in order to determine the best steps to take." My Valet replied.

"So, you are here to guide me through mine fields?"

"Yes! Along the way, these experiences will help you grow in person and in spirit. That's the reason why we are members of the Enlightened Royal Oracle Society. We are royal oracles called to enlighten royal households through our impeccable services. Always remember this, my boy." My guardian added.

There were many questions to which I wanted answers, so I continued asking Andy, *"Doesn't P's father disapprove of his son's homosexuality?"*

"Quite the contrary. As you already know, when an adolescent boy hasn't sprouted facial or body hair, they are considered a bacha bereesh (beardless boy) and men can perform bacha bazi (Persian meaning 'boy play' or 'playing with boys') with them without taboo. But when a boy becomes a man, he is to revert to a "heterosexual" life, marry, have a family of wives, and procreate. Although the men can have bacha bereesh on the side, homosexuality is altogether frowned upon.

"Therefore, a gay relationship for the Prince, other than with a bacha bereesh, will not be accepted in the Islamic society."

"Is that why he's into sadomasochism? As a form of punishment against himself, for the 'sins' he commits when having sex with you, since you are no longer a beardless boy?"

My Valet thought for a while before replying, "That may be one of the reasons. You must understand, Young, sometimes religion, when taken to the extreme, can play havoc with a person's mind. P may be punishing himself for enjoying sex with a man. Sadomasochism may be a form of repentance to Allah, a self-inflicted punishment like the ones the Penitents perform."

"I don't feel guilty or sinful when I have sex with you or other men I like. Why is that?" I questioned.

"My darling boy, that is because we are not brought up with the notion that sex with men is a sinful act. That is one of the reasons E.R.O.S. educated us not to be afraid of our sexuality, but rather to embrace who we are with openness, honesty, and truth. So, we are not encumbered with religious dogmas and doctrines. We are not indoctrinated by religious zealots, who use their authority and power to control the minds of their believers. The Enlightened Royal Oracle Society (E.R.O.S.) frees us from religious doctrines and dogmas and allows us to grow into strong and balanced adults."

"I thought the teachings of all the great sages such as Jesus, Muhammad, Buddha, Krishna, etc., taught mankind humanity and to live as decent human beings? How can some believers become twisted, believing that hurting themselves will heal them of their sins?" I asked.

Carefully selecting his words, my mentor replied, "It is, indeed, true that the teachings of the world's great sages encourage mankind to love one another. Often, organized religions warp ideologies and misinterpret truths in order to control their believers, especially when the followers are not sufficiently educated and rely on their religious leaders to know how they should behave. This is where problems arise.

"That's when religious wars start. While God teaches love and peace, power-grabbing zealots teach otherwise in order to further their own ambitions. Often, they exercise their perceived right to control the less fortunate."

"Are you telling me that organized religion is not a good thing?" I queried.

"That is something that you, as an intelligent person, will have to decipher. My advice to you, Young, is to listen to your heart. You have the knowledge within you to guide you, so you will know what is right and wrong. When you listen carefully to what your inner voice tells you, you will know what to do. You don't need any religious zealots, or me, for that matter, to advise you on what is the correct path to take.

"Don't be taken in by the teachings of false prophets," advised my enlightened protector.

"You are such an excellent mentor. What will I do without you?" I exclaimed.

"You, my dearest boy, will do just fine without me. I will always be close to your heart." My lover answered.

"Don't leave me!" I cried.

"Silly boy, I'm not leaving you anytime soon. I'm your Valet and will remain so throughout your time in the various Households. So don't be sad, and don't start crying. I'm here with you now, aren't I? You sentimental boy," consoled my protector.

Little did I know then that it was me who would leave my mentor, and not the other way around.

Early May 2012

...And for all the heartfelt lessons you taught me during our years in the Households.

"If I held in my hand every grain of sand since time first began to be. Still I could never count, measure the amount of all the things you are to me. If I could paint the sky, hang it out to dry. I wouldn't want the sky to be. Oh such a grand design an everlasting sign, of all the things you are to me. You are the sun that comes on summer winds. You are the falling years that autumn brings. You are the wonder, the mystery in everything I see. The things you are to me. Sometimes I wake at night, suddenly take fright. You might be just fantasy, but then you reach for me and once again I see, all the things you are to me.

"You are the sun that comes on summer winds. You are the falling years that autumn brings. You are the wonder, the mystery in everything I see. The things you are to me. All the things you are, to me." (The Things You Are To Me by Elaine Page).

Love,

Young.

54

A New Generation

"I believe that one defines oneself by reinvention. To not be like your parents. To not be like your friends. To be yourself. To cut yourself out of stone."
Henry Rollins

1967 Preparation for Las Vegas

Before I knew it, our Abds were packing our bags. We were on our way to America. Aziz was in a quirky mood before we left. Being the perfectionist, he drove us crazy making sure that all his photographic equipment was properly packed. Even Tahu, generally the calm and rational junior partner, was thrown into a disconcerted fit in his efforts to ensure that nothing would be left behind. Bahir, the photographer's new assistant, was wedged in between his boss and the junior partner, resulting his own heightened anxiety as he tried to accommodate the wishes of both men.

My heart reached out to the young apprentice. Andy and I found him sitting alone in the photography studio. His hands covered his face, as if he were about to burst into tears. Reaching out to the wreck of a man, Andy asked, *"Bahir, what's the matter? Why are you so sad?"*

The young Arab did not speak. Instead, he continued to cover his distraught face, shielding it from view. Andy continued, *"I know Aziz can be demanding at times because he's so particular about having everything organized. He wants this photo session to come off without a hitch, especially when so much time, money and effort have been invested into 'Sacred Sex In Sacred Places.' Don't take Aziz's and Tahu's agitated demands personally. They don't mean to be nasty to you; they are just uptight."*

Finally, Bahir spoke, *"I know they don't mean it in a nasty way. Sometimes I get too overwhelmed by everything that needs to get done before we leave. I'll be fine; it's just the pressure of working with a perfectionist."*

Without thinking, I piped, *"Perfectionists are a pain in the ass!"*

Andy looked at me as if I'd said something terribly wrong, but my statement seemed to have cheered Bahir a little. He replied smilingly, *"All said and done, I do enjoy working with perfectionists. I learn from their attention to detail, and from their work ethic."*

After comforting the photographer's assistant, Andy and I returned to our suite to pack for our trip. While packing, my Valet counseled, *"Young, it is not a nice thing to say that perfectionists are a pain in the ass, especially in front of Aziz's assistant."*

"Isn't what I say true?"

"Don't forget my boy, whatever you say is a reflection of yourself. How would you feel if someone told you that you are a pain in the ass because you are a perfectionist?" My mentor queried.

"No! I would not like it if they were serious in their criticism. But, if it is said as a joke, I would take it lightly."

"Mark my words young man: if you don't have anything positive to say about someone, it is best to say nothing at all. Life is like a boomerang; whatever you dispense will return to you," advised my guardian.

Nodding my head, I gave my Valet a kiss to thank him for his words of wisdom.

Family Dynamics

The following day, our three-car convoy, loaded with people, photographic equipment and supplies, was en route to Abu Dhabi airport. We were once again on board the SAQR, flying to Las Vegas. Andy, Oscar and I started a conversation while Vaj was off chatting with Dominique and Anya. I couldn't refrain from asking my Valet, "*Have you spoken with your parents since we left their house a few months ago?*"

Andy looked out the window as if he didn't hear my question. After a few seconds of silence, he finally replied, "*I've heard from my mother. She said that they are both doing well. She sends you her regards.*"

"*Have you spoken to, or heard from your dad?*"

Andy fell silent again, before Oscar chimed in, "*Have you communicated with your parents, Young?*"

"*My parents hardly ever write or call. I'd love to receive news from my mother, although it doesn't matter if I don't hear from my dad. My relationship with him isn't all that great. With my family, no news is good news.*"

"*What's between you and your father*"? Oscar asked.

"*He can't come to terms with me being gay and he's always trying to change me into a person I am not, and never will be. Does your dad know you are gay?*"

The BB answered, "*I've never openly discussed my sexuality with my parents. I presume they don't know, although whenever I'm home they try to find out if I'm dating anyone. It's a case of 'don't ask, don't tell' with my parents.*"

"*Does it bother you if you don't come out to them*"?

"*As much as I'd like to be honest, I don't think folks of their generation can understand what we are going through.*"

Andy finally spoke, "*You are correct; most parents do not understand the sexual issues we deal with. They don't have a clue what we are going through. I had a major falling out with my dad when he discovered Young and me sleeping together. He freaked out and ordered us out of his house. I haven't heard from him since that fateful day.*

"*Mum is more understanding, but her letters are still very intimidating. She tries to persuade me to repent from my sinful ways, which to me is a bunch of baloney.*"

Oscar asked, "*How do you deal with those remarks?*"

"*I either change the subject or ignore her altogether. As I was advising Young, it is no good trying to argue with them. That will only deepen the estrangement. I'm my own man. I certainly am aware of and comfortable with what I'm doing."

"Well said, Andy. I wish I could be like you and stand up to my parents. If I invited you and Young to my parent's home and they find us in bed together, I wonder how they would react."

I chirped, "I guess they will throw all of us out, just like Andy's father did. I'm sure my dad would do the same."

"Your Uncle James didn't mind. In fact, he embraced our freedom, and wished us well," Oscar quipped.

"Oscar, Uncle James is a rare breed. Don't forget, he is an E.R.O.S. member and has been through training and experiences similar to ours. You can't use Uncle James as the average 'father' example," Andy added. "He's an exception to the rule."

"That's why I often fantasize that Uncle James is my stepfather. I imagine us having a wonderful father and son relationship. He is such an enlightened man; I love him very much. I can tell him everything," I sighed.

Andy and Oscar commented together, "He's your surrogate dad. Since he is your official guardian, he's your dad away from home. Young, you are truly blessed to have a 'father' like Uncle James. We all love him a lot!"

I nodded in agreement although I had never thought of Uncle James as my father away from home, which of course he was.

Mid May 2012

Andy wrote in his Email reply:

Dear Young,

You are still the boy I grew to love and cherish forty-four years ago. The lyrics you sent, to "The Things You Are To Me" brought back many fond memories of our time together. You, young man, do have a way with words. In more ways than one, you always touched the core of my heart with your innocence and childlike approach to life.

Walter is a lucky man to have you in his life. I wish I were in his shoes, you little 'faerie' boy, stirring up an emotional storm within me which I had kept hidden for so long. Now that our parents are deceased, we can be free from the emotional baggage imposed upon us.

You had mentioned briefly that you are writing your memoirs. I hope you are not revealing anything that we pledged to never reveal. My advice to you is to stay clear of those subjects. It is not advisable to tamper with the school or the Society, especially when you swore an oath, a gentlemanly honor of confidentiality to never reveal any of our membership secrets. If the word gets out, the paparazzi will have a field day digging for whatever dirt they can find. I hate to see you being sued by any parties involved. I'm speaking to you as a trusted friend, confidant, and ex- lover. Tread with caution, Young! You are old enough to decide for yourself. I'm sure you don't need your ex-Valet to tell you what to do.

Please send my regards to Walter and maybe we'll have a chance to meet one day, soon. Let's continue our regular correspondence.

My love always!

Andy.

Part Five

United States – Nevada, Las Vegas, Arizona, Grand Canyon, California, Los Angeles.

55

Viva Las Vegas

"Things are in their essence what we choose to make them. A thing is, according to the mode in which one looks at it."
Oscar Wilde

1967 Las Vegas

Waiting for us at the Las Vegas McCarran airport were two crisply tailored, broad shouldered, wonderfully proportioned 1967 Cadillac Eldorados, "El Conquistadors." I had never seen such long cars in my young life. Gabrielli, Aziz, Andy, Oscar and I were ushered into the back seat of the candy-apple red open-top vehicle, while Dominique, Anya, Vaj, Tahu, and Bahir led the convoy in the golden road machine. A large van filled with our photography equipment and luggage followed behind. We were on our way to The Aladdin Resort, where we stayed for three days.

The sun cast brilliant hues of orange over the distant Grand Canyon. The desert landscape resembled the Middle East, except for the oversize neon signs, billboards and wide boulevards. Everything in Las Vegas was super-sized, including the huge, flashing Aladdin's lamp, beckoning tourists to enter the hotel. I could not help but think that everything in this city seemed so fake.

I asked Andy, *"Does size matter in America?"*

My Valet gave me a strange look before replying, *"I suppose size does matter. To Americans!"*

Gabrielli laughed out loud, said, *"Young, my amusing friend, of course size matters to Americans. The larger, bigger, and more imposing, the better. That's how Americans live. Can't you tell by the expansiveness of the city's layout?"*

Oscar added, *"It is so hot and dry here, just like Abu Dhabi. I'm dying of thirst!"*

Gabrielli pulled at a hidden drawer by the side of the Cadillac, and out popped an array of alcoholic beverages and a miniature ice cooler. He said, *"Let's celebrate Sin City!"* With that, he popped the cork of a champagne bottle, passing Andy, Aziz, and Oscar a glass each. Turning to me, my teacher said, *"You, young man, are getting a glass of water with a slice of lemon."*

All of us held up our glasses and toasted to Las Vegas and to our upcoming successful photo shoot.

The Aladdin

In 1966, Milton Prell, who had owned the Sahara Hotel, purchased The Aladdin Resort for $16 million. Prell envisioned a theme-based hotel and a large casino, based on the ancient Persian legend of a boy named Aladdin whose oil lamp contained a wish-granting genie.

Our entourage arrived a couple of days before an event at the hotel which went down in rock n' roll history. Elvis would wed the innocent and beautiful Priscilla at The Aladdin, in front of 100 friends and an armada of paparazzi. All we knew about the following day was that we had our work cut out in the wilderness.

The Aladdin looked like a cross between a United Arab Emirates' mosque and a Sheik's palatial home, except everything looked fake, lacking the spirit of the actual places. Although I did not utter a word, Andy already knew what was going through my mind. He said, *"Young, I know what you are thinking. That's the same way I feel about this place."*

We both giggled, but said nothing. Two bellboys, dressed in red and gold vests, black satin blouson pants, gold neck chains and custom jewelry bangles, opened the car doors to help us out. One wore a red Arabian hat and the other a white turban, reminiscent of the *"Thieves of Baghdad"* from a *Thousand and One Nights*. They had fake daggers strapped to their belts.

Mario was already having drinks at the bar when we checked in at the reception desk. The Count, being himself, arrived ahead of time. He had solicited one of the cute bellboys to join us on the photo-shoot. Obviously, he'd had his eyes on him the moment he arrived at The Aladdin. The boy, Timothy, was more than delighted to accommodate the Count. He was flabbergasted at the opportunity to be the photographer's model during our time in Las Vegas. Tim's friend George was also invited to join us on our photo shoot. They both knew that healthy tips would come their way if they complied with the wishes of the hotel's wealthy clients.

I was, of course, happy to see the "apple of my eye" again. He looked suave and full of confidence. The Count was every gay boy's and every heterosexual girl's, dream lover.

Las Vegas

Over dinner at The Aladdin's gourmet restaurant, Mario, the man of the moment, said, *"Do you know that Howard Hughes is staying at the Desert Inn?"*

"Howard Hughes, who is he?" I exclaimed.

"He's the famous eccentric aeronautical engineer. HOWARD HUGHES!" exclaimed Andy. *"He is the wealthiest man in the United States."* he added incredulously.

The Count continued, *"It's rumored that, since his arrival, he has never left his suite."*

Aziz asked, *"How do you know?"*

"Ahh! I know more than you think!" announced the preening Count. *"It's my business to know all that's happening around me, especially on a shoot."*

Andy was intrigued by this information and continued, *"What's he doing in Vegas?"*

"He, my friend is rumored to be buying Vegas, big time."

"Really? What's he buying"? I asked.

"His people are negotiating deals on the Castaways, the Silver Slipper, the Frontier, and the Landmark. He has already bought the Sands for a reported $14.6 million, and offered twice that for the Stardust," explained the Count.

Oscar added, "He'll soon own Las Vegas."

"That's what concerns the powers that be. Other Investors are worried that Hughes is creating a monopoly. Their links with organized crime are threatened." The Italian continued.

Gabrielli joined in the questioning, "What else do you know about what is happening in Sin City?"

"In a couple of days, a very famous Hollywood couple is getting married in this hotel."

"Who?" We all shrieked simultaneously.

"As long as you keep it confidential, I'll tell you." We all agreed.

"Elvis Presley and Priscilla Wagner," Mario exclaimed excitedly. "I have solicited a press pass to photograph the couple on their wedding night."

"How did you do that? Can I go?" I inquired.

"Have you forgotten that I'm a famous photographer for Vogue Italia?"

Mario thought for a second before responding, "That means I'll have to get Andy in, too. Can't promise you anything, but I'll do my best to conjure something up."

"Why don't you rub your magic lamp – or do you want me to?" I quipped. We all laughed at the implied meaning.

"You guys better catch a good night's rest. We have a long day of shooting tomorrow. I want you to be well-rested and look your best."

Mid May 2012

Dearest Andy,

After all these years, you have not changed. You'll always be the Valet I've grown to love and adore. When I read your email, I can hear the sound of your voice as it was so long ago. Although we are miles apart, I continue to feel you close to my heart.

After our separation, I looked for a 'big brother' and lover like you and failed miserably, until Walter came into my life. He inquires about you persistently. I think he is hoping for a triplet relationship, similar to the one we shared with Oscar. He thinks highly of you. Walter is very similar to you, in that you both know that you are gods who could do no wrong. In the majority of cases, that is how I remember you. Of course we both have our shortcomings, as humans do. The wonderful times we shared definitely overshadowed the negative moments.

I fear that having two alpha males in the same house will be a disaster because you'll both be competing for power and lording your masculinity over me. That's scary! LOL!

That said, my partner and I discuss you frequently. The difference between you two is that he fully supports the writing of my memoirs while you, my friend, have made it clear that writing about my adolescent life experiences isn't a good idea. I respect both your differing opinions, but this is something I will have to decide on my own. I sincerely believe that now is the moment to tell my story and I will tell it without hurting or exposing anyone unnecessarily. I've changed the names of the schools, the society, and, of course, the people that played an important role in my young life.

Do you remember when we were in Las Vegas working on "Sacred Sex In Sacred Places"? The Count told us that Howard Hughes was in town and you dragged me along for an audience with the tycoon? You desperately wanted an apprenticeship in his aerodynamics engineering company. I remember the episode well. That experience is definitely worth documenting in my memoirs.

We will have many opportunities to reminisce, but for now I am simply happy that we are communicating regularly. Tell me more about yourself in your next correspondence.

I love you and miss you. Wishing you all the best!
Young.

56

Let Your Spirit Soar

"Nature is at work. Character and destiny are her handiwork. She gives us love and hate, jealousy and reverence. All that is ours is the power to choose which impulse we shall follow."
David Seabury

Third Week of May 2012

Dearest Young,

I remember Las Vegas well. I regret losing my temper and taking it out on you because I didn't get to meet my aeronautical engineering idol, Howard Hughes. I was extremely frustrated. He was close, yet so far away. Looking back, I now realize that I would never have garnered an audience with the reclusive Mr. Hughes, no matter how hard I might have tried. At the time, I thought I had a chance to obtain an apprenticeship in his company. I wanted to learn from the man who seemed to know it all.

Now, I understand that the universe had a greater plan for me, and that I was not supposed to meet the tycoon. I would have lost you earlier than I did if I had obtained a position as his apprentice. When you decided to stay in London, I was devastated! I couldn't bear the thought of losing you. You were my first love; I longed to be with you. I left for New Zealand in haste, deeply saddened by your decision to not join me. Being miles apart, I thought I could start afresh and the distance would eliminate my hurt and heartaches. Unfortunately, you continued to haunt my consciousness. I flung myself into my engineering studies, working every conceivable project I could lay my hands on. Yet you loomed large during my quiet moments. Images of you followed me everywhere, until I met Toby.

As much as I loved Toby, he was not you and never would be. I had unconsciously fallen into a relationship through default, using Toby as your replacement. Although our sexual rapport was excellent, our relationship did not touch the soul-to-soul level I shared with you. At twenty-two, there were many things I did not understand about love. I thought I knew it all. I plunged full steam ahead, and, soon after we met, I found myself sharing a home with Toby. Our lives together came crashing down a year later. I concluded that there wasn't anyone who could replace you in my heart. It was best for Toby and me to separate. He realized that I could not provide the love he so desired. You, Young, are the boy I've been trying to replace, all these years. You are an ever-present apparition who never leaves me. Images of you continue to follow me everywhere I go. You are my shadow...

1967 Timothy

The set designer and a couple of their representatives met us at The Aladdin early the next morning. They guided our convoy of models and assistants towards the wilderness, where the sets were already installed. We were ready to commence the day's shoot. Aziz, Mario and Gabrielli had helicoptered ahead to the venue. By the time our jeeps arrived at the parking lot, horses and donkeys were waiting for us. We proceeded away from civilization and trekked into the mountainous desert on horseback, loaded with photographic equipment.

In the jeep, Timothy sat next to Andy and me and his lascivious predilection of my lover soon became obvious. My immediate thought was that he was being friendly, but as the journey progressed, Tim was licentiously vying for my lover's attention. He made every effort to strike up a conversation with Andy. Several times, he purposely leaned his body against my lover when our vehicle took sharp turns. My Valet had to brush him off. He made attempts to let the teenager know he was in a relationship. But the subtle protests didn't deter him from pursuing my Valet.

In the beginning, Andy and I thought Tim's solicitation amusing, but as we journeyed ahead, the teenager became obnoxious in his ardor. Not taking 'NO' for an answer, he continued his pursuit of my lover. He was, obviously, embarking on a fantasy journey of seduction, until my Valet requested a change of seats with me at a rest stop. Although my lover knew he would be photographed in intimate positions with Timothy, it was clear to him that he would be play acting, for the camera. But for Timothy, it was a case of lubricious affliction. The boy had fallen head over heels for my lover. He, being immature, could not differentiate between play acting and infatuation. He desperately wanted Andy to return his affection. He threw himself at my lover whenever the opportunity arose. He seemed to want Andy to fall in love with him right then and there. This was reason enough for my lover to avoid his advances.

The Shaman

Finally we arrived on location, after an hour's hike. Before me was one of the most luscious waterfalls I've ever seen. We couldn't help stripping naked, jumping into this secluded aquamarine pool with its natural cascading waterfall tumbling over our heads. The beauty of Havasu Falls was simply too breathtaking to ignore. We were one with nature; Mother Earth called to us with outstretched hands.

The American Indian tribal shaman, Opai, blessed the sacred ground before we began the photo shoot. Gabrielli had specifically summoned this Havasupai shaman to perform a sacred ritual, so that our sexual energies were positively charged. My teacher wanted to ensure that sacred sex performed in this sacred place would be a magical experience for all parties involved.

The Circle of Life

The shaman had asked us to hold hands and form a circle in the pristine pool while he stood in the middle reciting an American Indian sacred chant. He then proceeded around the circle, pouring water over our heads. I was immediately transported back to the Daltonbury Hall chapel, during my E.R.O.S. initiation ceremony. This time, Andy stood naked next to me. He reminded me of a demi-god from a Greek legend as he stood there with his eyes closed. Observing Oscar in the nude, standing opposite me, I had a celestial epiphany. The sacredness of the Havasu Falls, combined with the shamanic chants and trances induced an experience of Gaia herself. Oscar, my BB, appeared to have sprouted a gigantic pair of white wings on his back. He had taken on the persona of the angel I had envisioned in my dream, the night before my initiation into the Enlightened Royal Oracle Society.

Suddenly, I saw my life unfolding in slow motion as the shamanic ceremony progressed. All at once, I was in a different plane, yet my feet were planted solidly on the floor of the crystal clear aquamarine pool. Everything around me stood still for several seconds; it seemed like hours. Watching my reflection in the pristine water, I witnessed my imminent separation from the man I loved. At that moment, we stood at a crossroad of our lives. Tears streamed down our cheeks, as our hearts, beating in unison, were ripped apart. He and I would never be whole until we were reunited in this or another life.

I did not wish to continue this heartbreaking scene. I shook violently, terrified of the vision I had just witnessed. Tears welled in my eyes. My Valet did not know what had consumed me. He comforted me in his arms, begging me not to cry as I stood shivering in the warmth of the morning sun. Andy thought I might have hypothermia. He had never seen me tremble uncontrollably and shudder, as if in a trance. He ushered me out to dry land. My guardian wiped me dry and laid me gently on the ground in the sunshine.

Opai instinctively sensed that I had had an out-of-body experience, much like an American Indian boy on a vision quest. He asked me to close my eyes. He performed a healing ritual above my trembling body. I heard a soothing chant echoing, along with the piercing cry of a condor, above. By the time he finished his healing rite, I had calmed considerably. Both my lovers sat on either side of me, holding my hands until I was well enough to resume participating in the shoot.

Andy asked, *"What's the matter Young? What came over you during the sacred ceremony?"*

I said nothing. I had no desire to tell my Valet that our future wasn't as rosy as we thought it would be. I did not want to inform my beloved of our separation, which I had witnessed a few moments ago. I had no desire to create unnecessary anguish between either of us, so I uttered a mindless reply, *"Nothing! It must be the excitement of being in America and my lack of sleep. Don't worry; I'll be alright after a little rest."*

Unfortunately, that vision continued to linger over the next two weeks. I dared not confide my melancholy to anyone, especially not to Andy or Oscar. Normally, they were the two people to whom I could divulge my secrets. Instead, I kept my pensiveness hidden, putting on a happy face as if I didn't have a care in the world. Unbeknownst to me, my inner turmoil was simmering, until one fateful day I erupted like Mount Vesuvius. My toxic volcanic ashes burst forth, burning everything in sight, as if spontaneous combustion had occurred.

Third Week of May 2012

...I wasn't sure if I should contact you after our separation. Long distance communications in the 70's weren't as facile as they are now. My daily rowing helped to alleviate my stress during those

early years of our breakup. Over time, Mother Nature healed my aching heart. Do you remember Opai, the American Indian shaman we met at Havasu Falls? He came to your aid when you were nauseated and performed a healing ritual over you.

He said, "Fly like the condors, swim like the dolphins and slither like the serpents. The creatures of the air, water and earth will guide you back to your rightful place. Release, and let your spirit soar."

My dear Young, I love you and always will. Distance will never keep us apart. I am always with you in spirit. Be well, stay safe, for you and for me. Please send my regards to Walter, whom you claim is a reflection of my "godlike archetype."

Love,
Andy.

57

Cat Fight & the Kokopelli

"We are not human beings having a spiritual experience. We are spiritual beings having a human experience."
Pierre Teilhard de Chardin

1967 Grand Canyon

The day's photo shoot began with Aziz and Mario pairing us with different models. The heat of the desert sun and the sacred sexual energies swirling around the area proved to be deliriously intoxicating. The gay boys performed with zeal, even when paired with the two female models. We "looked" excited, but looks can be deceiving! Aziz and Mario were excellent photographers; they captured a thousand and one lies, camouflaging our actual sexual orientations. To this day, it continues to amaze me that even the most convincing images may be "manufactured."

Cat Fight

I was paired with George and Oscar for the first shoot. We posed around the waterfall and in the creek before moving to the outdoor sets constructed especially for this shoot. My out-of-body experience had left me disoriented. Timothy once again solicited the attention of my lover while I was modeling. Andy, being polite and non-confrontational, did his best to conduct a civil conversation with the teenager. My seething displeasure at Timothy's shameless enticement made me fume with anger. Had my unsettling epiphany brought on this intense emotional hatred, or was it a subconscious reflection of my inner self with which I could not yet come to terms? Whatever it was, I was ready to pick a fight with this impervious teenager, even though he was a few years older.

As soon as the photographers released me of my duties, I went over to Tim, who was busy making small talk with my lover. I said sternly, *"Tim! Will you stop seducing my lover? Can't you tell he's only interested in being your platonic friend? Stop pestering him!"*

The young man continued talking with Andy and ignored my remark. He pretended he did not hear what I said, which further provoked my resentment. I thundered, *"Did you hear what I said?"*

He ignored me. This made me utterly furious. I do not know what came over me. I shoved him onto the floor, and pounced at him like a wild cat. Before he could get up, I was on top of him, seizing a tuft of his hair. I pounded his face vigorously on the sand while punching his body with my other hand. The boy was completely taken by surprise, not knowing what had hit him. Andy was aghast by my unusual behavior and did not know how to react for several seconds. Tim was shouting, *"Help! Get this mad person away from me!"*

By now, the film crew had heard the commotion and came running towards us. Tim was struggling and managed to turn around. I had straddled the boy and was slapping and punching his naked body while he tried desperately to claw at me, without much success. Andy was trying his best to separate us, but I stubbornly refused to be dragged away. My Valet yelled in disbelief, *"Young! Stop this madness at once! What's wrong with you! Get off him!"*

Tim managed to break free and was lunging at me for revenge. Before he could throw a punch at me, Gabrielli caught hold of him forcefully and held him back. Andy had pulled me away from my adversary, preventing us from beating each other up. My rage was erupting like Mount Vesuvius. I did not want to stop the fight. Breaking free from my lover, I plowed head on against the teenager's abdomen, throwing him onto the ground again. He shouted, *"You crazy bitch! Get your hands off me!"* I did not. Instead, I bit hard at his nipple, which was protruding, right in my face. He screamed bloody murder, *"Owww! You sadistic cunt! Get away from me, you son of a bitch!"* I bit him again while holding his head to the ground. This time, he yanked himself free as he continued swearing at me.

Oscar and Andy caught my arms, preventing further attacks. Mario and Tahu shielded Timothy. They guided the boy as far away from me as possible while my lovers, Oscar and Andy, dragged me into the waterfall, hoping that the onslaught of cascading coolness would calm my fury. The downpour of chilling water brought me to my senses, instantly calming my nerves. Before long, I found myself sitting by the water's edge with my lovers on each side, guarding me in case I made a mad rush to confront the terrorized teenager again.

The Kokopelli

Andy said, *"Let's go for a little hike to get away from the shoot. Taking a little break will do you a world of good."*

The grandeur of the canyons was breathtaking and hiking with both my lovers calmed me tremendously. Standing on top of the majestic mountain, Oscar took some snap shots of us as my Valet gave me a brief history of the sacred site to take my mind off what had transpired earlier. He stated, *"Do you know why Gabrielli chose this place for the photoshoot?"*

I answered nonchalantly, *"Because of its majestic beauty and grandeur?"*

Oscar and Andy smiled at my simplistic comment before my Valet explained, *"American Indian legend has it that a supernatural deity, a fertility God known as the Kokopelli, was worshipped by the Indian tribes, most notably by the Hopi and the Zuni."*

Oscar added, "He is usually depicted as a dancing hunchback, a flute playing minstrel. He wears antlers and horns on his head. He also possesses a large phallus."

"Now I understand the reason behind the mask and headdress you wore when Aziz and Mario were filming you and Dominique this morning." I said, excitedly.

Andy smiled and continued, "Yes, you're right, young man. Aren't you clever to figure that out! You see, Kokopelli is associated with fertility, dance and spreading love. He is also a trickster who brings change and a successful harvest. He is known for defying rules and conventional behavior, which is similar to our group's credo. This is why the photographers embrace him, and this sacred spot."

Oscar chimed in, "Kokopelli's hunchback represents the sack of seeds he carries for the harvest. His beautiful rainbow colors complement his rejoicing songs and dances. His musical flute changes winter to spring. The antlers and horns reflect his potency. Last, but not least, his large phallus...well you know what that means."

"I've seen rainbow kokopellis sold at the gift shops in Las Vegas. They are very colorful," I said cheerfully.

Andy resumed, "The 'Rainbow Kokopelli' is a Yei deity who commands the rainbow. He appears to those who are spiritually harmonious. You, my boy, definitely need the blessing of the 'Rainbow Kokopelli,' after your atrocious behavior. I better get you a 'Rainbow Kokopelli' when we return to Vegas."

Oscar chirped, "Kokopelli is often depicted with animal companions such as rams and deer. Other creatures he's associated with are snakes, lizards and insects. I'd better get you a kokopelli doll as an amulet, to keep you out of vicious cat fights."

Both my lovers laughed at the memory of my audacity. My Valet continued, "Native American Indians are deeply spiritual; they communicate through dreams, signs, and symbols such as the Yei symbol (Yeii). A majority of their symbols are geometric portrayals of celestial bodies, natural phenomena, animal designs, and totems."

Before my guardian could continue, I asked, "What does the Yei symbol signify?"

Oscar spoke, "The meaning of the Yei symbol represents the Navajo Yei Spirit, who mediates between humans and the Great Spirit."

"Yei comes from the word Yeibicheii, meaning the Holy People. Navajo Yei (Yeii) spirits, or deities, are believed to control elements such as the rain, snow, wind, and sun. They also control the night and day. Navajo deities are either beneficial or harmful to the Earth People, depending on their mood or impulse, and on how they are approached. The Yei is also believed to be associated with the rainbow goddess." Andy remarked.

Our conversation was abruptly ended when Bahir called for us to resume our modeling duties.

58

To Get & Beget

"The natural man has only two primal passions, to get and beget."
William Osier

End of May 2012

    Hi Andy,

    I guess we were too arrogant to admit we missed each other after our separation. There were moments when I felt lost and did not know which direction to turn, because my Valet wasn't there to guide me. I descended into an abyss, looking for love in all the wrong places. I was too inexperienced to understand the spiritual love we shared. I mistook sex for love. A major mistake! I was lonely and I missed your presence. To fill the void, I visited the London underground sex club dungeons and back rooms. These places offered me nothing, except a temporary sexual fix that became a habit and an addiction. Nine months passed before I finally picked up the broken pieces of my life.

    Lucky to be accepted into the Belfast College of Art and Design, I took this opportunity to start fresh. I left London in the autumn of 1971 for Ireland. My departure proved to be my saving grace.

    There was nothing to do in the evenings in war-torn Belfast. I plunged myself into my art studies, which I enjoyed tremendously. You'll never guess what transpired in Belfast that year.

    KiWi, my first lover from Kuala Lumpur, studying at a boarding school in the outskirts of Belfast, appeared at my hostel one evening. I have no idea how he tracked me down or knew that I was in the city. Thinking it was the maid coming to turn down my bed, I was shocked to discover KiWi standing outside the door. He forced his way in without uttering a word. I had not seen the man for the past five years and had no wish to see him again. He locked the door behind him and shoved me roughly onto the bed, demanding to have sex with me. He pointed a pocket knife at my face, threatening disfiguration if I did not comply. Forcing my head on his groin, he commanded me to give him a blowjob. I was left with no choice – I agreed to his threats. I begged him to lay down his dangerous weapon before I gave in to his sexual peremptory. Before long he was moaning and groaning ecstatically while I sucked his cock. I made sure he did not strike a blow at my face with his blade.

KiWi was not a violent man by nature. He was a half-closeted homosexual who had difficulty dealing with the sexual demons that he could neither control physically nor mentally – especially when his intense, efficacious sexual desires reared their ugly head for release. I was an easy target for him to subjugate, like in the old days when he and his gang bullied me at The Methodist Boys' School. This repressed man only wanted to use me as a device to fill a sexual void in his life. He possessed neither sensual nor sexual skills. There was no love in his dictatorial approach.

He disappeared as quickly as he had arrived. There were no goodbyes or thank yous. I was relieved to be rid of the guy, thinking that I would never see him again. I was wrong: he returned several times that year. He found me when I tried to avoid him, until I left for London the following year without providing a forwarding address to the hostel staff. That was the last I saw of KiWi, until many years later when I bumped into him in Kuala Lumpur. That, Andy, was another devastating episode which I will reveal to you another time…

1967 Tropicana, Las Vegas

On our return journey to Las Vegas, Mario asked, *"Anyone interested in joining me to the Follies Bergere in the Tropicana this evening?"*

I immediately jumped in, not wanting to miss an exciting evening out in Sin City. If I went, Andy, my Valet, would surely follow. Before long Mario had gathered a group of revealers, me included. The two Italians in our entourage arranged the same limousines to drive us to our destination. This time Andy, Oscar, Devaj, Mario, Aziz, and I traveled in the gold vehicle while Dominique, Anya, Gabrielli, George, and the infamous Timothy went in the red Cadillac.

After our catfight that morning, the teenager stayed as far away from me as possible in the event that I may strike again. Gabrielli, my teacher, gave me a good talking-to and demanded that I apologize to the boy. Although I did not mean what I said, I reluctantly uttered a simple *"Sorry I hit you,"* to my adversary, under the insistence of Mario and Andy, who wanted to keep peace with our entourage. Tim did not speak to me under any circumstances, but continued to flirt with my lover when he thought I wasn't looking.

Little did I realize that the knavish Tahu had taken some snapshots of our catfight earlier that day until Aziz showed me the pictures some time later. The photographer was going to incorporate a couple of them in his *"Sacred Sex In Sacred Places"* photography exhibition. He named them "Cat Fight One and Two" in the behind-the-scenes series.

I was hoping to see Kismat and a few of her lady-boy friends at the Las Vegas Follies Bergere. Nirob, her Nubian boyfriend, had mentioned that she may be performing in Vegas. It was a black-tie event and our entourage looked stunning in our tuxedos and evening gowns. Before the show started, I spotted Nirob sitting several tables away from mine. He was with a group of men who looked familiar, but I could not recall where I had seen these faces. Turning to Andy I said, *"Look who's here!"*

"Who?" my Valet asked. Looking in the direction I was pointing, he exclaimed, *"It's Nirob! Let's go over to greet him. He must be here for Kismat."*

Before my lover could continue, Mario (sitting next to me) announced, *"There's Frank, Dean and Sammy!"* pointing towards Nirob's table.

"Who are Frank, Dean and Sammy"? I asked in puzzlement.

Mario laughed at my ignorance before promulgating to our party. *"Frank Sinatra, Dean Martin and Sammy Davis Jr.! I must go over to say hi."*

Andy chirped, *"Young and I will come with you. Nirob, our friend, is at their table."*

Nirob stood as we approached. He was surprised to see us, extending his hand to shake ours before introducing us to the Rat Pack (which consisted of Frank Sinatra, Dean Martin, Sammy Davis Jr., and none other than the famous actor Peter Lawford).

Nirob was the first to speak, *"What brings you guys to Vegas?"*

Mario interposed before my Valet could answer, *"We are doing a photo shoot here. I'm Mario Conti, and I photograph for Vogue Italia. Your friends,"* he directed his glances at Andy and me, *"Are part of our modeling entourage. I'm delighted to meet you."*

I did not know what to say amidst such celebrities, so I kept quiet while the men spoke. Andy inquired, *"You must be here for Kismat?"* directing his question to our Nubian friend.

"Yes! I'm also here to celebrate Dean's birthday today. Have a glass of champagne with us." The men toasted the 'King of Cool' while I sipped my Perrier water. Mario, being the charmer and socialite, had very quickly gotten himself acquainted with the Rat Pack and was chatting with the guys, as if they had been friends for years. Before we returned to our table, the Count had convinced Nirob to join us in our next day's shoot. He was delighted to oblige, since he had nothing planned and Kismat would be at rehearsals all day. The Nubian became our new model recruit.

Follies Bergere, Las Vegas

As soon as the curtains rose, I spotted the voluptuous lady-boy Kismat among the sea of sonsie chorus girls. The leggy she-boy was one of the star performers in the show. Needless to say, her provocative presence bewitched many in the audience, especially the men (whom I was sure would be delighted to spend an enticing evening with this exotic creature). She was a connoisseur in the art of titillation and plied her trade with remarkable aplomb.

The show was as luxurious as the showgirls themselves, who were decked from head to toes in furs, feathers, rhinestones and sparkles. They were the epitome of opulence from start to finish. This time around, Gabrielli, Mario, Aziz, Andy, and I went backstage to congratulate the dancers. I could tell Gabrielli already had eyes for Kismat, the most luscious half-naked femme fatale in the changing room. My professor's roving eyes were already undressing the rest of the showgirl, although neither Andy nor I mentioned that she was a lady-boy. We decided that it was best to keep our mouths shut and let the horny Italian discover the truth for himself. After all, it would be none of our business if anything should happen between the showgirl and my teacher.

Aziz, on the other hand, like Ubaid, was chatting up a storm with a pretty chorus girl, a friend of Kismat whom I suspected also to possess both male and female sexual organs. By the time we returned to our table to join the rest of our entourage, the second part of the show was about to begin.

Siegfried & Roy

A special act was incorporated to celebrate the Follies Bergere centennial celebration that evening. Neither Mario nor any one of us had any idea who Siegfried & Roy were. These two whiz kids had just returned from performing at the Paris

Lido and were doing a magic act with a tiger, a cheetah and a female assistant dressed in a cheetah outfit. It was a short presentation, but it lifted the house to standing ovation.

Mario, the photographer of the moment, was enraptured by the two magicians. He announced that theirs was the best magic act he had seen, and wanted to do a feature shoot with them before we left Vegas for Los Angeles. I found myself backstage again, this time face-to-face with the two gay magicians, who were cuddling the tiger and the cheetah as if they were their beloved children. The animals, out of their cages and free of their leashes, looked sweet and adorable. I couldn't help but stick out my hand to pat the tiger. Before their owners could give me any warning, the tiger's thunderous roar sent me scrambling to my lover for cover. I was frightened shitless, hoping I wouldn't be mauled by this dangerous beast. Roy quickly held onto the tiger in case the animal decided to pounce on me.

He said, *"Young man, you must be careful not to stick your hand out at them. If they are not familiar with you, they'll think you are doing them harm. We raised them, so they know who we are. They are still in the process of being trained and tamed."*

Siegfried added, *"I'm terribly sorry, they don't mean you harm. Are you alright? Do be careful when you handle wild animals. They can turn vicious when you least expect them to."*

Andy replied on my behalf, *"He's OK. Young's exuberance can get him into trouble at times. This boy should be more careful. Hopefully he's learned his lesson."*

Before we said our farewells to the boys, Mario had secured a photo shoot the following afternoon at their residence. He wanted pictures of Siegfried and Roy with their animals for an article in an Italian entertainment magazine. He also wanted erotic pictures of the models posing with the animals. This was a challenging act in and of itself, especially now that I was afraid to be near these ferocious beasts.

59

Communing with Animals

"Animals are reliable, many full of love, true in their affections, predictable in their actions, grateful and loyal. Difficult standards for people to live up to."
Alfred A. Momtapert

End of May 2012

The continuation of my email to Andy:

...*I was delighted to return to London after war-ravaged Belfast. The students in our college had to evacuate several times due to IRA bomb threats. I must have subconsciously selected to be in Northern Ireland because of my unsettling inner upheavals. Much like the riots that went on in the city in 1971, I was unconsciously fighting my inner demons within myself. I needed that year to overcome my sexual additions and to immerse myself in my fashion studies. By the following year, I had compiled an impressive fashion design portfolio for application with various London Art and Design colleges. Foundation students generally required two years to complete their studies. I graduated from the Belfast College of Art with flying colors within a year. By the autumn of 1972, I was accepted into the prestigious Harrow School of Art and Technology.*

Around that period, my father's business was waning and my family had financial difficulty sponsoring my graduate studies. Unbeknownst to my family, I had earned sufficient money during my Harem services to comfortably put myself through college. I lied to my parents and told them I was working part-time in London to make ends meet so I could finance my fashion education. They believed my tall tale. For the next three years I put my heart and soul into my fashion projects. I would occasionally work as a waiter at the famous Rainbow Room in Biba, which is now defunct. Working at this dinner dance club was a convenient way of meeting beautiful and trendy patrons, who often visit this capricious establishment. I did it more for my personal amusement than for pay. I did meet many interesting and flamboyant people, and dated a few of the patrons. I was having a fun time, when my family was under the impression that I was a struggling student, trying to make "ends meet" in the English metropolis.

You continued to haunt me in the quiet of the night, no matter how hard I try shaking the image of you out of my head. I missed you, Andy. I have never stopped loving you. You were constantly on my mind, until I met a 22-year-old Oxford graduate who became my lover for six years. I will leave the segment of my relationship with Jorge for another time.

I'm delighted we reconnected and we have this opportunity to catch up on things. I love you and always will.

Young.

1967 The Sands, Las Vegas

Our entourage was divided into two groups. Aziz continued his photo-shoot in the Grand Canyon location, while Mario took the morning to prepare for his two important photo sessions: a half day with Siegfried & Roy and the following evening at Elvis and Priscilla Presley's wedding reception. Gabrielli, Dominique, Anya, Timothy, Devaj, Oscar and Bahir followed Aziz into the wilderness, while Nirob, George, Andy, Tahu and I went with Mario to the magicians' residence. We were free to conduct our own business in the morning.

Andy pursued me to accompany him to the Sands immediately after breakfast. He wanted an audience with Howard Hughes, who was staying at the Sands.

My Valet inquired of the Sands' receptionist, *"Ma'am, I'm delivering a personal message to Mr. Howard Hughes. Can you tell me which room he's at?"*

The receptionist replied, *"I'm sorry sir, we were given strict instructions not to disturb Mr. Hughes under any circumstances. Would you like us to forward a message to him?"*

"I need to see him in person. It's an important document I have to hand to him personally," Andy quickly answered.

"Oh! Can you please wait for a moment while I consult my manager?"

As soon as the receptionist disappeared behind the counter, a burly gentleman in black wearing a narrow gray tie addressed Andy, *"What business do you have with Mr. Hughes?"*

"My father is a close friend of Mr. Hughes and entrusted me to deliver a personal package to him." I was surprised at Andy's statement, since he had mentioned he did not know the tycoon. He was trying his luck to gain access to meet the man. This was obviously a lie, and I had never known my Valet to lie.

The man replied, *"Come with me, son."*

Without waiting for the receptionist to return, we followed the man in black. Taking us through a series of corridors and up an elevator, we finally arrived at the penthouse suite. Guarding the entrance was another man in black. The only difference between the two bodyguards was the color of their ties. The burgundy tie guard knocked on the door. There was no answer. He knocked again. Again, there was no answer. After waiting for a few minutes, a husky voice bellowed from the suite, *"What is it? What do you want?"*

The man with the gray tie responded, *"There's a gentleman here to see you, sir. His name is Andy Finckenstein. He says he has a personal package to deliver to you from his father."*

There was a long silence before the cacophonous voice answered annoyingly, *"Ask him to slide the package under the door and leave me alone!"*

I could see Andy's disappointment. He had no choice but to do as the voice instructed. He slid the large brown envelope he had carefully prepared, containing his resume and an introductory letter, through the door's slit. My Valet replied with chagrin, *"Have a good day, sir. I hope to receive a response from your good self before I leave Vegas in a few days. My father would like very much for me to meet you."*

No response came from behind the locked door. We thanked the men in black and the receptionist before heading out of the Sands. Although my Valet was deeply saddened, he did not show any despondence. The only contrite comment he gave me was, *"I was so close and yet so far. I know I shouldn't have lied to Mr. Hughes about my father being his friend. You know, Young, there will always be better prospects around the corner. Seek and I shall find."*

I uttered, *"This is why I admire you, Andy. I'm learning from the best teacher, YOU!"*

Andy never received any response from the eccentric recluse.

Siegfried & Roy's Residence

By the time we arrived at the magicians' residence, they were ready to be photographed by the distinguished Vogue Italia photographer. Tahu assisted with the lighting while Mario worked his camera magic. Siegfried and Roy were experienced and natural in front of the lens. They posed and played with their beloved tiger and cheetah in and out of the swimming pool. Two cheetah cubs had recently been acquired by the duo, and these baby sucklings were as adorable as they come. When Mario was photographing our hosts and their animals, Nirob, Andy, and I were getting better acquainted with the bellboy, George, who was also a model. Sitting in the spacious living room, Nirob inquired, *"How did you end up working at The Aladdin?"*

"My girlfriend and I moved from Chicago eighteen months ago. I wanted to get away from the cold and she wanted to be a dancer. Vegas offered us the warm weather and career opportunities Lili desired. So, here we are," replied the twenty-year-old.

Andy asked, *"What are your long term goals?"*

The young man seemed taken aback by this simple question. He shook his head and said, *"I'm happy with my life. I've got a steady job, I work as a male escort on the side, and I get to hang out with my friends. Smoke some dope and have lots of sex. I can't ask for anything better."*

I couldn't help but ask, *"Don't you have an ambition you want to achieve?"*

He laughed and said, *"I'm happy to be away from my dysfunctional family. I don't get along with my dad, my mum drinks like a fish, my eldest sister ran away from home when she was seventeen, and my youngest brother joined the Mormon Church in Utah. He says he is destined to be a prophet.*

"I'm happy here and I'm earning good money, doing what I enjoy."

It was strange to talk with a young person who didn't have any long-term direction in life. In my adolescent experience, all the students I had been acquainted with at Daltonbury Hall and the Bahriji had career goals. Here, sitting next to me was a young man, the first I'd met, who didn't have any ambition in life. I had no idea how to react to his answer, so I kept quiet.

Nirob, seeing my puzzled look, continued questioning George, *"Is this the life you want? Having a good time, smoking 'grass', doing LSD, drinking, partying and having plenty of sex?"*

"It sounds good to me," he replied nonchalantly as he casually put his hand on my Valet's lap, next to him. Before the conversation could develop further, George was French kissing my lover. His roving hand stroked the fabric that was concealing Andy's loin. My teacher and I sat observing, mesmerized by the unfolding sensuality. I was getting turned on, watching these two handsome men caressing each other.

I unzipped my trousers and began rubbing my erection. Pre-ejaculatory fluid leaked from its bulbous head. My lover motioned for me to join in the fun, which I obliged without hesitation.

The first person to disrobe was the Nubian. He posed in front of the group, showing off his muscular body. He was tempting us with his engorged, circumcised organ that pointed skywards and waiting for attention. My animal instinct urged me to engulf its enticing length in my yearning throat. My mouth, like a young bird needing feed, was on my black friend. He was enthralled to regurgitate nourishment into my pining orifice. Before I knew what had transpired, the three men had formed a circle around me. I took turns devouring their throbbing manhood. One at a time, I was savoring every drop of oozing fluid from their manly slits. Their masculinity intoxicated me. I desired this pleasurable sexuality to last. Before I got to the third participant, four newcomers had joined the circle. I was in "seventh heaven," rotating round and round the circle of life, feeding on each (and sometimes two) pulsating vitals with vigor and accreditation.

Mario, our virile leader, was the first to shoot on my face, followed by Tahu and the magician. Andy lifted me up on my knees and kissed my luscious lips, lapping at the releases staining my baby face. He shared these credulous wholesome deliveries in George's lusting mouth.

Nirob had leaned the other magician against the edge of the leather couch. He was passionately easing his tumescent rod into his bottom. Soon, my teacher was pumping the man furiously while he moaned in sexual ecstasy.

Beside the frantic couple, George, with his legs spread, was preparing to receive my lover's cock into his orifice, which was slick with saliva and lubricated with oral semen. My Valet slid into the compliant orifice with ease, and trembles coursed through the young man as he received the solid inches into the core of his being. Their frenzied enthusiasm ignited my libido. I was ready for Mario's second cumming. My volitional desires granted the playboy unlimited excess deep within my derriere. I was on the floor, my buttocks tilted; I was basking gloriously from this blue-blooded Italian's erotic lovemaking. The Count never failed to satisfy my sexual appetite. This expert carnal provocateur left me lusting for more. It was no small feat that males and females gravitated towards this seductive Casanova, wherever his charismatic presence was seen and felt.

Our other host was already pounding the handsome photographer's assistant. He had lifted Tahu against the wall, his legs supported on the magician's shoulders. The Arab was groaning in rhythmic synchronicity to the rest of our passive recipients, who were simultaneously vocalizing our high-pitched swan songs before final orgasmic climaxes reached their personal ultimate crescendos.

The exhilarating smell of sex permeated the love chamber. I, invigorated to the point of no return, shook involuntarily, shooting my seed onto the highly-polished rosewood floor. Mario filled my sex to overflowing capacity with his seminal releases. Before I had a chance to turn around, Andy had mounted me from behind. His heavy breathing from the vigorous onslaught threw him into a frenzy. Holding tightly onto my slender waist, he unleashed his semen, burying his sacred ishq (love, in Arabic) deep into my willing soul. I gave myself fully to my lover. In return he did the same to me.

I had one final task to fulfill. George's bouncing phallus was bobbing in my face. I engulfed the bulbous shaft into my mouth, stimulating the man to his tantalizing climax. Pushing my face into his groin, he liberated his intoxicating fountain of youth into my craving orifice. I drank every drop of his delicious spill.

Andy and I shared George's orgasm before the model joined in our three-way kiss. We continued our love dance and changed partners until the even sun lowered its lazy head behind the distant Canyon blue. Mario was more than pleased with his photo-shoot. He was ecstatic, since he got more than he bargained for.

Our erotic love dance must have beckoned Siegfried and Roy's dangerous carnivores to the call of the wild. These ferocious animals behaved as if they were affectionate pussycats, extending their heads for us to pat as we posed provocatively against their warm, amiable bodies. Their lovey-dovey precociousness was as playful as any tamed domestic felines. Is it true to say that, *"Animals are reliable, many full of love, true in their affections, predictable in their actions, grateful and loyal"*? Are these difficult standards for people to live up to?

60

Wise Men Say, "Only Fools Rush In"

"Covetous friends are like wolves in sheep's clothing."
Bernard Tristan Foong

1967 Grand Canyon

The morning after our Siegfried and Roy's photo-shoot, I found myself at a different location in the Grand Crayon. Our entourage had flown via helicopter to Canyon de Chelly, a sacred dwelling place of the Ancient Pueblo peoples, or Anasazi. They are a part of the Navajo tribe who lived in the Chelly cliff dwellings, now known as "The White House Ruins".

Our entourage assembled in a circle. Gabrielli introduced Hastiin, the tribal chieftain, to our group. The leader welcomed us with a sacred chant. He blessed the photo session, which would soon commence in this sacred site. As soon as the chieftain had finished his spiritual veneration, a scantily clad male dancer in feathered wings and an elaborate headdress appeared. He began dancing to the sound of drumming. His performance was to summon deities to bless the unions of our sexual acts; before, during and after the photography session.

If malevolent forces were to interfere with our photo shoot, it would be attributed to evil beings disturbing the union of our sexual sacredness. In that case, magical witchcraft would be performed by the medicine man to dissipate the ominous devilry.

In my case, I was about to practice my own sorcery to ward off Timothy, who was now after my other lover, Oscar.

Andy had successfully discouraged his advances. This boy coveted my relationship with my two lovers, even-though neither was interested in him.

Timothy

"Sacred Sex In Sacred Places" went according to the photographers plan, until the three-way liaison between Oscar, Dominique and Tim. During their penetration scenes, the teenager was obsessed with my 'big brother's' well-endowed equipment. He desired a replay of their simulated love making, in private. He devised a devious plan to lure Oscar away from the group when the photographers called me for some sensual action with Devaj.

"Come with me, I want to show you a secret site." The boy said to my BB.

Oscar, being the genuine person that he was, thought Timothy had found a good location for our photo-shoot. He asked Tahu to accompany them. Tim led them away to a deserted creek before disappearing ahead, when they turned a corner. The men chased after him but could not find the boy, who was hiding in a ravine some distance away. He was hoping Oscar would come looking for him alone. Little did he realize that a poisonous rattlesnake was lurking a few feet from where he laid in wait. Both boy and snake were waiting for the right moment to pounce on their respective preys.

Oscar and Tahu waited for several minutes, hoping the teenager would return to look for them. He did not. My responsible BB decided to go searching for the boy while Tahu waited, in case Tim reappeared when Oscar was gone.

The Valet called to Timothy but heard no reply, except the echoing sound of his own voice. Out from a corner, Tim sprang at his prey, knocking the BB to the ground. A loud rattling sound was heard and before they came to their senses, the serpent had coiled around Timothy's leg. The boy let out an excruciating scream, sending his cries bouncing off the canyon walls. For a brief moment, the glaring sunshine blinded Oscar's eyes. Not realizing what had happened, the Valet was stunned to see the boy rolling on the ground in pain. He was holding his left ankle in agony. Standing next to the wriggling serpent was Hastiin, the tribal chieftain. He had miraculously appeared to strike down the snake with his staff. Bending down, he bled a vial of venom from the dying snake before applying the potion to the teenager's injured ankle. He then applied herbal leaves and a white gauze to bandage the wound while reciting a healing chant.

The chieftain spoke, "*You, young man have bad intentions and the malevolent spirits have sent the snake as a warning to you.*"

Tim was too shocked to reply, so he kept quiet as Hastiin continued, "*The Great Spirit has power over all things including animals, stones, trees and clouds. They are watching you.*"

Finally, Tim regained his breath and uttered, "What did I do to deserve this"?

The Indian shook his head before replying, "*You covet your neighbor's lover. The serpent's bite is a warning. It is an immoral act against your fellow neighbor to seduce another person's lover when they are not interested in you.*

"*I am called to warn you to discontinue your coveting behavior; otherwise worse tragedies will befall you, if you do not take heed.*"

Neither Tim nor Oscar knew how to respond to the sage's cautionary words. Before they fully regained their senses, Tahu, Gabrielli and Andy had arrived on the scene. They assisted the boys to their feet. Hastiin disappeared as magically as he had appeared. My Valet and teacher helped the hobbling teenager back to our shoot location before a helicopter flew the model to an emergency ward in a Las Vegas hospital.

Unfortunate for Tim, he was unable to join us for the rest of our Canyon and Vegas shoot. Our entourage visited him in hospital, brought him flowers and wished him a speedy recovery before we departed for Los Angeles a few days later.

I was glad I did not have to practice my own form of witchery on Timothy. The Great Spirit had mysteriously taken care of the issue for me without me having to take action.

Oscar related the tale of Timothy and the rattlesnake to us that evening, when Andy, Oscar, Devaj and I were assisting Mario. The Italian was busy photographing the celebrity event of 1967; Elvis Presley and Priscilla Wagner's wedding, at the Las Vegas Aladdin.

First Week Of June 2012

Arius' email read:

Hello Young,

I haven't heard from you for a while. How's life treating you? Did you locate Andy?

I've been keeping busy with my Gay grassroots hotline organization and have received a number of enquiries from teenagers having issues with their parents and peers. As I had forseen, cases such as these seem to be rather common with young gays and their traditional parents. Most of the stories I've heard are very similar to our experiences when we were growing up. Most parents have difficulties coming to terms with their children's alternative sexual preferences. In the majority of cases, they think their GLBT kids can be cured of their 'malice'. In my opinion, the parents don't know any better or their religious indoctrination had made them prejudiced against GLBT people.

*I am looking forward to reading **Initiation** (your book). When will it be available on the market? I'm sure to recommend that my callers read your fascinating memoirs. I enjoy reading your blogs and I look forward to seeing your story in print. The erotic pictures you've posted are certainly titillating and provocative.*

I wish I had the courage to tell my story as openly and honestly as you. Unfortunately I'm not blessed with the abundance of past photographic records, written diaries, journals and opportunities you experienced during your young years.

It is rare to know someone who is unafraid of his sexuality. Your story has a pure and innocent adolescent voice which I find delightful. I admire your courage and wish you great success with your memoirs. Your written words will serve as an enlightening roadmap for sissy boys to stand up to be themselves and be proud of their uniqueness.

Have you found a publisher for **Initiation** or are you planning to self-publish? It is much easier to self-publish than to wait for a publisher. I strongly suggest you get your word out to the world. I have faith that it will flourish and take on a life of its own. Sound marketing and strong promotions are key elements to reaching a wide audience in this day and age. With the social networking media rage, it will not be long before 'the cat gets out of the bag' and your memoirs to take flight.

Are you writing a sequel to **Initiation**? I would love to read more of your memoirs, when you are ready to share your rich experiences with the world. I'll be delighted to be of assistance in any way possible.

Your ardent admirer,
Arius.

61

I Asked God...

"I asked God for a minute and he gave me a day. I asked God for a flower and he gave me a bouquet. I asked God for love and he gave me that too. I asked God for an angel and he gave me himself. YOU!"

Bernard Tristan Foong

First Week Of June 2012

Andy wrote in his email:

Hi Young,

I wish I had been there to protect you from KiWi. I'm glad you were unharmed. I should have returned to England to spend my life with you. Both of us have gone through difficulties after our separation, and I needed you more than ever. When reading your email messages, flashbacks of our wonderful times together seemed like they happened only yesterday. I feel closer to you now than ever. I'm intrigued to know more of what happened after your return to London from Belfast. Tell me everything.

You are still the boy I knew; sweet natured, pure of heart and gentle of spirit. These are the unique traits that I love about you. Although I have had many relationships, you remain in the recesses of my mind when I meet adolescents that vaguely remind me of you. You are definitely one-of-a-kind; there is no doubt about it.

The cute, sexy noises you make during our lovemaking sessions never fail to stimulate me to multiple orgasms. When I am with other men, it is you I fantasize about in my mind's eye. I fell for Toby and a few others because, subconsciously, they reminded me of you. Unfortunately none of them lived up to the love we shared. These relationships fell apart quickly. I had finally given up looking, when Albert showed up in my life. He was vastly different from my past relationships. We bonded on a different level; he became my mentor. He was 74 when he passed. I felt as if I had lost an understanding father, a dad I didn't have.

Our fathers were not the kind of people we could open our hearts to. We were never able to reconcile after he threw you and me out of his house in Vaduz. He eventually discovered the triplet relationship my brother, Ari was secretly conducting with Sabrina and Yann. He could not come to terms with his alternative lifestyle either, even though Aria did her best to persuade him to love and accept us back into the fold. He never did. He would rather cut off ties with his two sons than to admit his narrow-mindedness. On his deathbed, he told my mother that his greatest regret was that he never took the opportunity to make peace with Ari and me. I had forgiven him, but he, being a stubborn man, didn't want to have anything to do with us. He died an unhappy man.

Ari and I attended his funeral. It was a compassionate gesture to comfort our mother rather than to honor the dead man. Mother had long ago come to terms with our alternative lifestyles. She got on splendidly with Sabrina and Yann, treating them like her extended family. I introduced her to my lovers, but I believe she likes you the best because she would occasionally inquire whether I had been in touch with you. She never took the trouble to ask about the well-being of my other lovers...

1967 At The Aladdin

Although Elvis Presley and Pricilla Wagner had invited a hundred guests to their wedding reception at the Bagdad Theatre, a host of paparazzi turned out en mass to photograph this celebrity event. Mario, representing Vogue Italia, had Andy, Oscar, Devaj and me help him as his photography assistants. By 8 A.M. that morning, the Nevada Supreme Court Justices, David Zenoff entered the Theatre to conduct the marriage ceremony for "The King of Rock." All stops were pulled for this elaborate wedding. Sure enough, Mario snapped away like the pro that he was as the place buzzed with activities.

1967 was also the year that Thomas John Woodward made his first appearance in Las Vegas. He was better known as Tom Jones. A friend of the wedding couple, he sang a rendition of *"Pussycat, pussycat I love you"* to roaring cheers and catcalls from the invitees. Some excited females threw their bras, knickers, panties and room keys on to the stage, hoping that the singer would magically appear at their boudoirs. This gig was one of many successful events where his career "took off," so to speak. Before long he was playing at the Flamingo Hotel and making headlines at Caesars Palace, where our entourage had the opportunity to stay for the next couple of nights.

Mario and Aziz managed to convince Gabrielli, our *"Sacred Sex In Sacred Places"* financial officer, that we should experience the one-year-old Caesars Palace. Both photographers did not want to miss the opportunity to witness a once-in-a-lifetime daredevil motorcycle jump across the Caesars Palace fountain. From their bedroom windows, they could acquire a perfect view of the famous Evel Knievel zooming over the fountain on his Harley Davidson. Not only did his landing fail miserably, the stuntman spent the next forty days in a coma with thirty broken bones. Mario and Aziz had captured it all on film, and our entourage lived to tell our own versions of this tall tale.

Oscar's Concerns

While Devaj was called to assist Mario at the wedding ceremony, Andy, Oscar and I had a chance to catch our breath at the hotel coffee shop. We sat enjoying our beverages before we were summoned to our respective photographic duties again. I asked Oscar casually, *"Are you enjoying pairing with Anya? The two of you seemed very chummy during your simulated lovemaking scene."*

My lover replied, *"She's like my 'little sister' and she tells me everything. She needed an older 'big brother' to confide her problems to."*

"Why can't she talk to Dominique, her 'big sister'?" I asked.

"Sometimes it is better for an adolescent girl to talk with a man than to another female. Men are generally more logical in their responses than women."

"What secrets does she have that she cannot confide to her chaperone?" I continued inquisitively. "What's she hiding?"

Andy reprimanded me for my inquisitive questioning. *"Young, don't be so nosy. If Anya trusted Oscar, it's none of your business to go schnozzling."*

Oscar, amused, shook his head before answering, *"I may as well tell the two of you, since we promised to be honest with each other. I know you will keep this confidential.*

"Since Nirob joined our entourage, Anya has been head-over-heels infatuated with the Nubian. She's in love and says Nirob feels the same about her."

I couldn't help exclaiming, "But Nirob is already attached to Kismat! Doesn't she mind?"

"Doesn't who mind, Anya or Kismat?" my BB said laughingly.

"Are they having a triplet relationship like we are?"

My remark sent both my lovers laughing uncontrollably, as if they had just heard the funniest joke. Oscar continued, *"That's why Anya dare not confide her feelings to Dominique. She's afraid her 'big sister' will reprimand her for her emotional desires."*

Andy turned, advised, *"Oscar, since Anya trusts your opinions and she discusses this freely with you; maybe it is wise for you to explain the pros and cons to her. She can make her own choice."*

"It is really Dominique who should be explaining the consequences to her. Not me." Oscar replied.

"If you want, I can have a private word with Dominique. She can have a heart-to-heart talk with her charge."

"That will be great, Andy. I appreciate that very much."

Just then, Devaj came to join us. It was my turn to assist the photographer, Mario – the man I was infatuated with. I too was experiencing emotional pandemonium, like Anya. Except in my case, I confessed neither to Andy nor Oscar. I kept the secret to myself.

First Week Of June 2012

...In some aspect, Toby was like you. He had a good heart and we shared a lot of laughter together, but he also possessed a streak of unpleasant bitchiness. Unfortunately he wasn't Bahriji-trained and gentlemens' words of honor meant nothing to him. That was an issue I had difficulty with. That said, Toby is in the past. You, my boy, are here and now. You are always in my heart.

Now that we have reconnected, I hope the next chapter in our relationship will be deeper and wiser. I remember the prayer you recited one night after our lovemaking:

"I asked God for a minute and he gave me a day. I asked God for a flower and he gave me a bouquet. I asked God for love and he gave me that too. I asked God for an angel and he gave me himself. YOU!"

Love,
Andy.

62

Myth Is More Potent Than History

"I believe that imagination is stronger than knowledge. That myth is more potent than history. That dreams are more powerful than facts. That hope always triumphs over experience. That laughter is the only cure for grief. And I believe that love is stronger than death."
Robert Fulghum

1967 Outing

As a token of appreciation for the hard work we had put in for the past five days of the photo-shoot, Mario and Gabrielli suggested we take a little vacation to enjoy the city and the Grand Canyon before departing for Los Angeles. We welcomed our break with loud vociferation and merriment. Aziz announced that 'management' had organized a canyon hike and a rafting experience for our entourage.

Tahu promulgated before we readied ourselves for the outing, *"Guys and gals, make sure you pack sufficient drinking water, sunscreen for protection and wear a hat. The sun is very strong. You may get burned."*

Antelope Canyon

Two tribal guides; Askook (snake) and Huritt (handsome) were waiting for us at the entrance when our mules, donkeys and horses arrived at Antelope Canyon. Before we journeyed into the unknown, the pair recited a chant of prayer and briefed us on the history and legends of this "8th Wonder of the World".

Huritt advised, *"There are two sections to this unique Canyon. Upper Antelope Canyon is also known as The Crack. Our tribe calls it Tsé bighánílíní, which means 'the place where water runs through rocks.'*

"Lower Antelope Canyon or The Corkscrew, also known as Hazdistazí means 'spiral rock arches.' Both are located within the LeChee Chapter of our Navajo Nation."

Askook warned, *"Be careful when you're in the caves and rocks. Do not venture anywhere alone; have companions with you at all times. There have been cases of visitors who disappeared and were never found.*

"Legends have it that there are underground tunnels and channels which are sinkholes into another dimension.

"During the monsoon season, the canyon can be flooded instantanously. Rain does not have to fall on or near Antelope Canyon for flash floods to whip through the terrain. Rain falling many miles 'upstream' can funnel into the canyon's cavities without any prior warning."

I raised my hand before either one of them could continue. *"How do we get out of the place if the floods appear?"*

The men grinned amusingly, *"You'll have to trail behind one of us. We'll lead you to an escape route. A magical wooden ladder will appear when we call on the 'Spider-Woman' for help."*

"Who and where can we find the Spider-Woman?" I questioned with great curiosity.

Our group burst into laughter as if I had asked a silly question. Mr. Handsome replied, *"Spider-Woman" is an important heroine in our mythology. She is the mythical being who weaves the clouds so that rain may fall. She is a deity who will guide her believers out of perilous situations.*

"Our great hero, Tiyo was guided by the Spider-Woman to learn the ceremonies that we Hopis perform at our annual Snake Dance (to produce rain when we suffer from drought).

"Tiyo also met the Sun and the Great Snake (Go-to-ya), as well as Mu-i-yin-wuh (a divinity of the underworld who makes all the germs of life). They taught him the great mysteries of the world. After many fantastical adventures, he was lifted out of the underworld. He was seated in a ho-a-pah, a kind of wicker pannier, with two beautiful maidens of the snake kiva. It was Spider-Woman who deposited him back to his home. There, he married one of the maidens and founded the Snake Clan.

"His brother married the other maiden and founded the Snake-Antelope Clan. Each year, members of our two clans perform the Snake Dance ceremony so we can have rain in our desert landscape. We are the descendants of Tiyo and his brother."

I couldn't help but ask, "Are the both of you cousins?"

More laughter ensured before Mr. Snake replied, "We are more than cousins. We are "blood" brothers. I am from the snake family and he," Snake pointed to Mr. Handsome, 'He's from the antelope clan. We are descended from the union of Tiyo and his brother with the two sisters; daughters of the snake mother. Tiyo is the paternal Ancestor of the Snake Clan, and his brother of the Antelope Clan."

I chirped before Askook could enlighten us further, "I'm a 'Snake.' I am born in the year of the water snake in Chinese horoscope. Does that make us 'blood' brothers too?"

Our group was laughing hysterically. Andy chimed in, "Young, stop interrupting our guides. Let them continue with their explanations."

Mr. Snake was laughing so hard, Handsome had to continue on his behalf. "I'm sure Askook's clan will be more than delighted to initiate you into their midst, you witty boy! Before he does that, let me continue explaining the origins of our Snake Dance.

"Although the ritual is known as a Snake Dance; it really isn't a dance, in the strictest sense of the word. It is a prayer for rain, and of thanksgiving for the blessings of harvest. It is definitely not an act of snake worship.

"Tiyo sailed down the Colorado River in a sealed hollow pinion log that he fashioned into a boat. He passed through "shipapu" journeying to the underworld. Nine days prior to the Snake Dance ceremony, our clans sing sixteen dramatic songs in the secrecy of the underground ceremonial kivas before the open-air public dance is initiated. This is performed in honor of Tiyo."

I couldn't help blabbering again, "When is the Snake Dance held?"

Askook answered, "Not for a while yet, young man. It happens during the month of August. You and your friends will have to return to celebrate with us. The celebration lasts sixteen days."

As it was getting late, our two guides decided to separate our entourage into two groups: one party was led by Askook and the other by Huritt. Mario, Nirob, Tahu, Dominique, Anya, Andy and I went with Mr. "Handsome" to explore *The Corkscrew* while the others followed Askook into *The Crack*.

Early June 2012

I waited a few days before responding to Arius's email. I wrote:

Hi A.S.,

Thank you for your recent email and your enquiries.

I did connect with Andy and we are corresponding regularly. Thank you for your efforts in helping to locate my ex-lover. My ex-'big brother' is well and was delighted to hear from me. He is currently living in a coastal town in Southern Australia. Unfortunately, his partner of eight years, Albert, died nine months ago from AIDS-related illnesses. He is mourning for the lost. I'm sure time will heal the wound. I believe that he is moving forward in a positive direction without Albert. We are catching up on our past and I'm sure we'll continue to do so for a while yet. After all, we haven't connected for more than 42 years; there are many things for us to reminisce.

In regards to your numerous questions, I'll do my best to answer them:

* Yes, I'm publishing Book 1 of the A Harem Boy Saga; **"Initiation,"** and if no problem arises, the book will be available in major bookstores and online retail outlets by early January 2013. This will be my belated personal birthday gift – to see the first edition published.

I am currently working diligently with the publisher on the provocative book cover design, and the interior page layout. I am also including some black and white photographs in the book. **"Initiation"** will also be available as a eBook. There will be a few colored pictures in this electronic format.

* Yes, to your other question; I'm halfway through the sequel to **"Initiation."** The 2nd book will document my experiences in my 2nd Arab Household. It will also detail my many erotic travels to exotic locales with the two professional photographers, Aziz and Mario, for "Sacred Sex In Sacred Places". This sensual memoir was a further development of my educational and sexual growth while in service at the Sekham Household. I'm sure it'll be a titillating read for many.

I'm toiling with the title for Book 2 of the A Harem Boy Saga. **"Unbridled"** is high on my list of possible titles. By the time I finish writing the manuscript, this title may change. For now, **"Unbridled"** is my number one choice.

In total there will be five books in the A Harem Boy Saga series. The first three will be dedicated to my harem services; the fourth is a love story between Andy and me. The final work will be life after Andy to present day – my years of searching for the soul mate whom I had discarded due to my intractable and stubborn impertinence. I lived to regret my mistake.

On a different note; I'm delighted to hear that you are keeping busy and enjoying your new found passion in assisting troubled GLBT youths through your Gay grassroots organization. Thank you for offering to recommend **"Initiation"** to your callers. I'm dedicating this book to Sissy Boys the world over, for their courage to stand up for their rights and not be intimidated and bullied. Faith will prevail and there is always light at the end.

Please continue to keep in touch. I'm always happy to hear from you, Arius.

Be safe, be happy and enjoy life to the full.

Love,

Young.

63

"Love is like a sudden storm; it blows me along with you."
Bernard Tristan Foong

Early June 2012

In respond to my ex-lover's email, I wrote:

Dearest Andy,

It's so long ago; I don't know where or how to start relating what happened when I returned to London after Belfast. I was simply delighted to be back in London, away from war torn N. Ireland. Of course Uncle James welcomed me with open arms. I stayed at his luxurious townhouse for the next few months until I began at Harrow College of Art and Technology. I did not see James the week I arrived; he was hard at work in Hong Kong.

Being in Belfast was like spending a year in prison. There was no nightlife and certainly no social life to speak of. I was very much a loner most of the week, except Sundays. I started going to the Belfast Methodist Church. As much as I didn't care for the church's doctrines and dogmas, I went because there was nothing else to do especially on the day where most businesses were shut. College was closed and I couldn't return to the fashion department to work on my design projects. There were no gay establishments to venture to nor were there any gay social activities available; when the Catholics and Protestants were busy raging a rampant civil war against each other. I followed my mother's footsteps and went to church.

Before long, I was looped into teaching Sunday School and to church outings. More often than not with my young charges which I had delectable platonic relationships. I found precocious children interesting to talk with. They reminded me of me when I was their age; innocent, pure of heart, gentle of spirit and eager to learn the ways of the world. These were traits that had thrown me far off the beaten track since we parted ways. I enjoyed their youthful company more than I did with the church elders.

One day the pastor invited me to join the church's youth group. I reluctantly agreed because Pastor Rick thought it would help me tremendously if I socialize with people closer my own age. Unfortunately, I could not confide to Pastor Rick I am a gay man and in 1970, homosexuality was not out in the open as it is now. I kept my secrets to myself. I did not have a confidant, a 'big brother' or Valet I could exchange my Harem, Bahriji and E.R.O.S. experiences with. I'm surprised I didn't turn into a nervous wreck and suffered a nervous breakdown that year I was in Belfast. My saving graces were my fashion projects and my positive rapport with the Sunday School kids. These adolescents were the ones that kept me sane.

One particular effeminate boy, Bernard, reminded me when I was his age. He is gay and like me he had difficulties divulging his sexual orientation to his parents and peers. I became his surrogate 'big brother'. Since I had splendid training as a 'big brother' and as a Valet, I was able to help Bernard when he had problems with his conservative parents. His mother came from a traditional 1950s parenting background and did little to support the boy's sexual orientation. I became Bernard's confidant. My heart reached out to help the boy when bullies were threatening to beat him because of his effeminate behavior. Thanks to my Daltonbury Hall and Bahriji education, I was able to confront the bullies on the boy's behalf, saving the adolescent for the tyranny of these vicious hooligans. In the process I taught Bernard to stand up for himself, defensive tricks we sissy boys use to protect ourselves from ruffians. Bernard was very sad to see me leave Belfast. My departure was as heart wrenching as our separation. I hated leaving my protégé, which I grown to love and cherish…

1967 In The Corkscrew

As our entourage journeyed into Antelope Canyon, we were at once in awe with the beauty and the splendor of these unusual rock formations. I for one was overwhelmed by the majesty of the place. Beams of light filtered through potholes high above us. It was as if I had just descended into another dimension. Andy took this opportunity to talk with Dominique about Anya and Nirob's relationship. I did not want to disturb their privacy so I fell some steps behind our group.

Emotional sensation stirred my inner being as I stood watching the light display which was illuminating the ground through an open pothole above the rocks. Mesmerized by such magnificence I notice a tiny fluttering of wings. It was a monarch butterfly circling around the beam of light. Before I could blink my eyes, there were half a dozen of these flapping insects, only to be joined by more of the same; except their wings were not smooth and rounded but jagged and irregular. I had never seen butterflies like these before. I was beginning to wonder if my eyes were playing tricks, yet they looked real and they gesticulated me to follow. Their breath taking beauty was a sight to behold. I did not know I had entered a catacomb until an unusual exteroceptive vision greeted my eyes. There were spider webs everywhere but no spiders were visible.

A Prognostication

Time had stood still and visions of my inevitable separation with my lover once again appeared as vividly as the other day at Havasupai Falls. This time around I felt my heart torn from my chest. I couldn't breathe, and the pain was excruciating. I was terrified. My heart's pumping vessels were strewn all over the canyon floor. In a state of panic I stooped to mend the shattered corpus but the pain was too intense. I crushed to the floor from my agonizing calamity. No one heard my cry for help.

Similar to my earlier out of body experience, I saw myself rolling in dirt unable to rise. Andy was nowhere to be found. I was alone, alone to suffer the throes of my personal crucifixion which I knew was of my owe doing. My physique convulsed rapidly before plummeting into unconsciousness.

When I awoke I was in a different dimension. An open doorway invited me to pass but I had difficulty seeing the other side. The light's intensity blinded my eyes. Singing angelic voices were beckoning me to cross over the threshold into this ethereal magical realm. I wanted to enter but a voice restricted my movements. The voice like Andy's said enticingly, *"Come back, return to me. Don't leave. I'm here with you. Don't go!"*

Suddenly like a light switch being turned off, darkness enveloped my entire being. The brightness was gone. I had blacked out. I had no idea what happened next.

When I came around, I was perched above a distant rock. Looking down into the sinkhole I saw my lover performing mouth to mouth resuscitation to my unconscious body. I desperately wanted to revive but I also desired to venture to the other dimension. The brightness had returned, beckoning me entry. The light shone fervidly into my tormented soul, healing the gaping hole where my heart was.

I heard the flapping of gigantic wings and the angel I had envisioned in my dreams descended through the sinkhole, heading towards my woeful body. Holding my face in his hands he planted a loving kiss on my thirsty lips. His rejuvenating Gaia's breathe streamed into the core of my existence sending waves of orgasmic intoxicants coursing through my body. My heart began pumping again, this time it was beating in sync with my earthly rhythmic duress.

Revival

I finally opened my eyes; I was lying on the ground. Andy's mouth was on mine and tears rolling down his handsome face. He was rocking me back and forth in his arms as if caressing a baby who has just departed his earthly home; he was desperately bringing me to life. He cried softly into my ears, *"Don't leave me. I don't want you to go."*

In a daze, I did not know how to respond or what had transpired? I starred unblinking at my savior. A few minutes passed before I plucked up the courage and uttered, *"What happened to me? Why am I lying on the floor?"*

My Valet did not answer. He picked me up with both arms and carried me to a flat rock, laying my head on his lap while our party looked on in bedazzlement. Huritt had wanted to get me to the hospital when Andy was in the process of resuscitating me.

A few minutes later, I was well enough to rise to a sitting position. Mario and Nirob were planning to carry me to a waiting emergency helicopter. I refused to leave, informing them that I am alright if I laid and rested for a while. I insisted they go on with their exploration and I will wait for their return. Reluctantly they complied to my wishes, leaving my Valet as my body guard in case I collapsed again.

My breathing had stabilized, Andy asked, *"What happened to you? As soon as my back is turned, you blacked out! I can't leave you out of my sight."*

I did not reply, instead I closed my eyes and laid my head on his lap; wondering if I should obligate to my lover what I attested during my out of body experience.

I whispered, *"The sublimity of this sacred site must have caused a spiritual empyreal euphoria to my person. I have no idea what happened to me? I felt nauseated and the next thing I knew, you were performing resuscitation on my mouth."*

Although my confession was true, I omitted telling my 'big brother' the scene I witnessed when I blacked out. I did not dare tell Andy of our imminent separation and the pain that we would suffer because of the choices we made. Now was not an appropriate moment, to presage such a heart wrenching prognostication when we were together and in love. I wanted our rubicund bliss to last forever. Besides, the vision I saw may never come to pass. Little did I realize that snake born folks are psychic prone and often times have clairvoyant powers to see into the future?

Andy pressed for details. He asked, *"What did you see before you passed out?"*

An Omen

Before I could answer, Askook's group had returned and the news of my fainting had already spread to their group. Mr. Snake came to sit by my side. He queried, *"I've been a guide to Antelope Canyon for several years and I have witnessed a handful of people passing out. Most have life altering experiences after their fall. Tell me boy, what happened? What prompted you to faint?"*

I had little choice but to relate my vision of seeing the fluttering monarch butterflies leading me into a cave covered with spider webs with no spiders. I did not tell the guide about the angel or my out-of-body experiences. These I kept to myself.

Askook responded, *"Young, you are blessed. Our deity, the Spider Women has given you a sign. We must get out of this place as soon as we can."*

I asked, *"What kind of sign? What are you talking about?"*

He was already off garnering Huritt's party before he had a chance to answer my question. Before long our entourage was together and our guides convoked us to follow them quickly. Leading us to a narrow passageway, they told us to climb a precarious wooden ladder that seemed to have magically appeared on the side of the canyon wall. We did as instructed. Just as the last person was a few steps up the ladder, I heard a series of rumbling noises. Mr. Snake commanded urgently, *"Hurry up, we must get out of this pothole onto high grounds. A flood is heading our direction!"*

To Safety

We scrambled towards the skylight as quickly as our legs could carry us. Aziz was the first person out, not wanting to miss this perfect opportunity he already had his camera at the ready, photographing each one of us as we climbed to safety. Mr. Handsome was the final person to emerge. He uttered, *"Thank You, young man! You saved our lives!"*

Confused by his gratitude, I asked, *"What did I do to deserve your gratitude?"*

"Look into the pothole and you'll know the truth," was his reply.

I peeked down but saw nothing. A few minutes passed, nothing happened. As I was about to question my guide again, roaring sounds came through the tunnels where we had just emerge, followed by titanic gushes of tyrannous water as if a dam had been broken abruptly. I turned towards Huritt, speechless.

By the time our entourage gathered at the venue where we had left our donkeys, mules and horses; all of us were chattering nonstop of our narrow escape. Both our guides came to me, extended their hands to shake mine. Huritt was the first to speak, *"Now, do you understand the significance of your vision?"*

Spider Woman

I answered, *"Kind of but not fully. How did you know we had to leave of the caves immediately because I saw butterflies?"*

"You didn't just see butterflies; Spider Woman arrived in time to give us ample warning to bequeath the tunnels!"

Scratching my head I continued questioning, "I didn't see any Spider Woman; all I saw were beautiful fluttering butterflies that lead me into a cave covered with spider webs."

Askook said with appreciation, "Spider Woman manifested in the form of spider butterflies. She took you into a cave of spider webs to protect you from harm. It is her yarning way of informing us to get out of the premise as soon as possible. You are a blessed one."

"What if I didn't wake up from my coma to relate what I saw? You wouldn't have known that a flood was on its way?"

"We would have because we would have departed with you to the hospital. We would all have reached safety before the floods arrived. But you did wake in time to relate your vision." Mr. Snake continued jokingly, "You certainly deserve to be initiated in the Snake-Antelope kiva. You can be our 'blood' brothers."

"Really! Are you serious?" I replied excitedly.

Our guides laughed at my exuberance as we rode out of Antelope Canyon.

Early June 2012

...Bernard and I had developed a bond similar to the love we shared. Andy, you are an excellent teacher, you taught me well. I in turn had passed on the knowledge acquired from you to the next generation. I hope the brief period I spent with Bernard had made him stronger in person and in spirit.

Although I did keep in touch with him for a while but with life's many demands, we soon lost touch. In my next email I will tell you more. It is getting late and Walter is calling me to bed. I'll have to say Goodnight. As you say in German, Gute Nacht.

My love for you will never wane.

Young.

64

Guess Who's Coming To Dinner

"Christian virtues unite men. Racism and sexism separates them."
Sargent Shirver

Early June 2012

Arius responded to my reply almost immediately. He wrote:

Hi Young,

I'm delighted to know that you'll soon be a published author. As you know, I have been following your blogs after you forwarded me the password and username. I find your memoirs fascinating and compelling. I am interested to conduct a case study of your life. During our earlier correspondence I mentioned that I am a retired psychiatrist and I continue to be intrigued by people who had riveting experiences. Throughout my years as an active psychiatrist, I had conducted many researches on the power of the human spirit. Reasons some people have nervous breakdowns while others in similar situations had managed to turn unscathed; going on to live active healthy lives.

Your memoirs captivated my attention to thinking of our current duplicitous educational system; the methods that schools are teaching young adults, to the growing number of suicidal and shooting cases in learning institutions. If I may, I'll like to request your permission to administer a human behavioral study on your adolescent life. This is a simple study which entails me asking you questions through our regular correspondence so I can better understand what's going through your mind when you were inducted into the Enlightened Royal Oracle Society and subsequently your services in the various Arab Households.

Although I am familiar with the ancient Greco Roman pederasty ideology, I am beginning to excogitate if there are valuable merits, to this form of mentorship between an erastês and an erômenos. In your memoirs you mentioned that your secondary school education derived from this ancient practice. Obviously your positive experiences had made you a balanced and well-rounded man of the world. Let me know your thoughts if you are interested in this research?

I'll continue reading your weekly blogs and wish you the very best in the soon to be published **Initiation**, the 1st of your five books memoir.

My spirits are uplifted when reading your correspondence. Keep them coming, my friend.

All the best!

Dr. A.S.

1967 Colorado River

On our last couple of days at the Grand Canyon, Gabrielli and Mario suggested we spend a night camping in the wilderness, after our whitewater rafting expedition. That morning as we travelled by river boat to board the two floating rafts down the winding Colorado River, the perfect opportunity presented itself for me to talk with both my lovers. As we sat enjoying the sprawling cliffs and extraordinary rock formations, I turned to ask Andy, *"Did you get a chance to speak with Dominique?"*

Andy replied, *"About what?"*

Oscar who was listening to our conversation, said, *"I think this inquisitive boy wants to know if you spoke with Dominique about Anya and Nirob's relationship."*

"I know why he's being inquisitive. I was teasing him, pretending I didn't know what he was asking about."

"Well?" I questioned.

Andy took his time to respond. Oscar and I were all ears waiting for our lover to speak. "*I did have a lengthy discussion with Dominique. She already suspected that Anya is infatuated with the Nubian. She has no problems with their relationship but she does have some concerns she reiterated. We are figuring how best to handle possible racial prejudices if it becomes an issue.*"

"What racial prejudices?" I questioned.

"Young, although we are inducted into an enlightened clandestine society and living in the free world; social prejudices continue to exist within the human race. Although the majority of young people our generation is open minded and accepting of different races and cultures; the older generations continue to struggle with the way we conduct our lives.

"One of the concerns Dominique has with Nirob is that he is a man of color. Anya may face difficulties within her wealthy elite society if she falls madly in love for the Nubian. If their relationship develops further where Anya and her beau decide to marry, there will be faced with major obstacles with her parents and their peers." My Valet reiterated with sadness in his voice.

Oscar declared, "This is 1967. The world is changing and so are society's attitudes towards interracial love and marriages. I'm sure Anya can make her own decisions as to whom she chooses to love."

"You are correct, Oscar. I'm sure Nirob and Anya have every right to be in love and marry whomever they chose. Dominique and my concern are with Anya's position in her wealthy and well-connected family. Her conservative parents will think otherwise."

I added, "Nirob is a wealthy entrepreneur. If their relationship develops into a mutual consensual marriage, Nirob will surely look after his wife. Don't you agree?"

Just then Mario and Gabrielli came to sit by us. Mario overheard the end of my pronouncement, asked, "Who will Nirob look after if they marry?"

The three of us looked embarrassed that we were caught gossiping about our friend's sexual liaison, went silent for a few seconds. Andy was the one who spoke on our behalf, "Since the both of you overheard part of our conversation, I may as well ask your opinion about Anya and Nirob? Maybe, the both of you being older and wiser can shade some light on this controversial topic. Dominique and I are trying to decipher how best to advise Anya regarding their infatuation of each other."

The men replied almost simultaneously, "We already guess what's happening between pretty Anya and our colored friend."

Mario continued, "I'm not blind when looking through my camera lens. The rapport between them is too passionate and intense when performing in front of the camera.

"While we are shooting our controversial pictures in Las Vegas, Hollywood is making a controversial movie about interracial love. This movie will impart a whole new way of preconceived ideas of interracial love and marriages."

"What movie is that?" I queried with curiosity.

"Aah young man! You are always quick to jump to questions. That's a great way to learn. Seek and ye shall find."

Gabrielli answered for Mario, "I believe the motion picture he is referring to will be released in December. The trailers are already showing in cinemas around the world."

"Tell us, what's the name of the picture?" I chimed impatiently.

"Guess Who's Coming To Dinner," came Mario's reply.

Oscar chirped, "I've read an article in a magazine about this film. It's suppose to be a 'must-see' movie of the year."

Before Oscar could continue Mario intervened, "When we get to Hollywood in the next couple of days, we'll pay a visit to Columbia Pictures to get further scoops on this motion picture. Being a Vogue Italia photographer has its perks, I can use my status to gain entry to photograph the stars and conduct interviews with the producers, directors and of course the actors and actresses."

Gabrielli added, *"The three of you will be able to conduct your own research and form your own opinions to advise Anya. Andy, you can pass this information to Dominique as well. I'm sure she'll be relieved to have some idea of what to say to her young charge."*

We had already arrived at the rafting dock to board the floating vessels that were waiting to take us, on a wet and exhilarating fun filled journey.

Early June 2012

Andy's reply arrived a couple of days after I emailed him. His message read:

Dearest Young,

I'm delighted to hear from you. I googled your profile and came across your "Life Of A Harem Boy" blog. I noticed you have omitted the actual names of relevant people and places. I'm glad you thought out the details. Just like the Young I know so well. As much as I'm not in favor of you writing about the clandestine society, I also admire your honesty in telling our positive experiences during our E.R.O.S., Bahriji and the Arab Households years. Those were wonderful times we shared and I missed them tremendously.

Most importantly, I missed you; the love we shared was sublime. As much as I love Albert and appreciate our precious moments together, our relationship was vastly different from the love you and I shared. The sensual, sexual and spiritual rapport we had was simply too empyrean. Since our separation I have not been able to find another to enjoy this amorous passion.

My regular rowing kept me from falling into depression. I am actively involved in a rowing club near my home and our group travel to different places on rowing expeditions; frequently to Asia and parts of Australia, New Zealand and Tasmania. This assertive exercise assisted my wellbeing enormously during the early months of Albert's passing. Being at one with nature is a staggeringly positive way to heal the aching heart and connecting with a group of likeminded compatriots eased my pain, during those long lonely evenings without my life partner.

I have long given up those bacchanalian years of debauchery and one night stands. I prefer friends and companions I can talk intimately with. Several of my friends had asked me to give online dating a try but I'm hesitant. I believe that the appropriate time will arrive for the right person to manifest, without any desperate attempts on my part to go cruising for a warm body to share my bed. Maybe, the universe has bought us together for a reason after such a lengthy absence. I firmly believe that our reunion is not by coincidence but by universal design. I suppose the best way to find out is to live and let live and the rest will take care of itself.

Thank you for your compliments. I'm happy I had the opportunity to pass on my mentorship skills to someone like you, and in turn you are able to help others.

Do you remember that one of "E.R.O.S." dictums is for its members to pass the mentorship baton to the next generation of initiates? I'm gratified that I've done my part to honor this adage. That said I'm looking forward to hearing more about Bernard. How did he cope after you returned to London? Did his parents approve of your mentorship to their son?

I'm looking forward to your next correspondence. Please send my regards to your significant other. Are the both of you married? Maybe, I will have a fortuitous blessing to court you again (joking). Please tell Walter not to take offence to this comment. I will never imperil both your relationships. I am happy when you are happy. Remember the passages I quoted you from The Art of Loving by Erich Fromm when we were young and so in love? Well, my sweet Eros, until I hear from you. Stay happy and love unceasingly.

Your ex-Valet and lover,
Andy.

65

To The Place Where I Belong

"Every kid needs a mentor. Everybody needs a mentor."
Donavan Bailey

Second Week Of June 2012

I agreed to be Dr. Arius' case study. In my reply to the psychiatrist, I wrote:

Good Day Dr. A.

I'm surprised and flattered that you consider me an appropriate candidate to conduct a case study on my unique E.R.O.S., Bahriji, elite Arab Household, and secondary school experiences. As much as I am delighted to agree to your proposed challenge and to answer your questionnaires to the best of my abilities, I also have questions for you for which I would like answers before being an active participant in the survey.

* Are you planning to publish professional psychiatric papers and publications to your findings? Or are you working on this project solely for your personal interest?

* If your research reveals a positive alternative to the current accepted educational norm, are you planning to actively advocate for change?

As you are aware, I can only provide you with my personal opinion on my educational experiences. I cannot speak for other E.R.O.S. members. Before I agree to undergo this case study, I wish to make it very clear that I only speak for myself. Under no circumstances will I undermine to reveal the actual names of people and places, or jeopardize their society and individual standing in any way. I am obligated to honor my oath of confidentiality and pledge never to reveal the true identity of the clandestine society. As long as you are aware of my pledge, I am happy to answer your questions to the best of my ability.

Although I have not known you for very long, I consider you a trusted friend. My intuition tells me you are a man of integrity. I have always trusted my inner voice and it has never failed me. I look forward to your next correspondence and your answers to my questions.

I hope all is going splendidly in your part of the world. Keep me posted on the progress of your gay organization. It is good to receive your emails as always.

Yours truly,
Young.

1967 Grand Canyon

After a vigorous day of whitewater rafting and scenic hiking, dusk settled at our campsite. The boys had built a campfire. We sat chatting, enjoying the amazing desert sunset, lowering its sleepy head over the mountainous horizon as the fading light cast a hazy glow over the majestic cliffs. Our entourage sat by the water's edge indulging in an enjoyable recollection of our last five days activities in Vegas and at the Canyon.

George had brought his guitar to serenade us with his favorite country and western songs. After puffing on a Marijuana joint, he began playing his guitar and singing his favorite folk songs. He sang a song I had never heard before and the melody and lyrics caught my attention. Tears welled up in my eyes. I missed my mother as I lay on Andy's lap, enjoying this melodic tune. Without a word, my guardian's loving hand reached down to brush away my rolling tears on my cheeks. He bent over, planted a gentle kiss on my lips and whispered in my ear, *"My sweet angel, I know what's going through your mind. We both miss home but you, Oscar, and I are now family. We'll take care of you."*

Words were not needed; I was content to be sandwiched between my lovers as we sat around our circle of loving friends. The emotive sound of music floated through my discerning ears, caressing my tender soul as I loved and cherished my newfound family.

After the guitarist finished playing, I enquired, "George, what's the name of the beautiful song you just strummed? I've never heard this ballad before. Who wrote it?"

"*I knew this song when I was a kid growing up in Maryland. It is an old folk song from my part of the world. As kids we sang it at social and family gatherings,*" the musician replied.

Oscar questioned, "*Which part of Maryland are you from? Is your family from there? I thought you told us you moved from Chicago?*"

"This song touched my heart and made me miss my mother." I quibbled.

He answered smilingly, "*I was born in in a small town near Blue Ridge Mountains. When I was growing up, my siblings played and swam in the Shenandoah River every summer. We sing this song all the time.*"

"But the lyrics said West Virginia, not Maryland!" I chimed.

George replied laughingly, "*The Blue Ridge Mountains touch the tip of West Virginia, and the Shenandoah River is in Maryland. I don't know why Maryland isn't mentioned in the lyrics.*"

"You are a very good guitarist. You should make this your song, famous. It has enticing lyrics and a rhythmic tune." I added.

He plunged into another song as we lay in repose around the campfire. After five days of frenetic work, I dozed off rapidly, wrapped in a warm blanket on my lover's lap. My Valet carried me into the tent that Oscar had erected earlier. That evening, Oscar spent the night in our tent after he had tucked Devaj into his sleeping bag. The three of us cozied up in love, warmth, and blissful contentment. I was grateful to be embedded between my handsome lovers. I knew then and there that home was where my heart belonged.

Breaking Dawn

While Oscar and Andy slept, the dim light of the glowing moon seeped through the cracks of our tent's entrance. I awoke to sentimental memories of my mother. Sleep eluded me. I quietly crept out of the tent to enjoy the sacred aloneness. I wanted to embrace my solitude, ravishing in my own perspicaciousness, to contemplate my life in the stillness of this enchanting moonlit night. I strolled to the pond, wrapped in a thick blanket to cover my nakedness. I leaned against a rock, enjoying the tranquility of the undisturbed night. As I cogitated over the numerous blessings in my life since leaving home, an unsuspecting hand touched my shoulder. Astonished, I turned in the direction of the intruder. He was hooded under his wrap and it was too dark to see his face. I could not identify the interloper. Before I could screech for help, he planted a kiss on my lips, prying my mouth forcefully open to receive his yearning tongue. I struggled for release, but his taut musculature pinned me against the rock. The mystery man constrained my hands above my head while French kissing my mouth. He bound my wrists to a branch above the rock. His mouth kissed me assertively preventing my screams.

My heart pounded to this unanticipated arousal. His raw manliness set my libido aflame and I was excited by his masculine dominance. My mind raced ablaze with unbridled fantasies. I played along to the man's demanding wishes. His primal instinct ignited a fiery passion I had not known. He had stirred my groin to hardness as his sensual lips nibbled demandingly on my burning nipples. This intoxicating sensuality was too tantalizing; I did not want this mysterious captor to stop his exigent actions. In the heat of the night my unknown lover had stimulated my libido to full attention, and I was ready to reciprocate his passionate urgencies.

Straddling above my face, he fed his curved stiffness into my receiving mouth. I desired his pulsating length and gladly surrendered my body to his rigorous postulation as he jammed himself into my desiring orifice. This ecstatic delirium sent fits of frenzied spasms into my being. Holding his hand behind my head, he pushed into me. My complete oral attention was his peremptory. Inhaling deeply, I sucked his pulsating length down my longing throat. After several strokes my mysterious amore shot jets of creamy liquid into my gagging passage. I drank every drop of his delicious feed, not allowing any to go to waste; I continued suckling his organ until it bobbed back to life. The uncircumcised rod was too exquisite for me to let go. I wanted more.

Turning me on my stomach, he entered me in a single stroke, driving himself into my buttocks. I moaned and groaned ecstatically, enjoying the feel of his quivering manhood pounding deep inside my lusting cavity. Kissing my mouth with urgency, my amorist tasted the tarrying seed he had planted in my oral opening. This sexual nympholepsy was too titillating for my ruminating mind. Soon, my shuddering erection released jets of spurting semen onto my spuming midriff. My covert lover shot inside me simultaneously, burying his engorged phallus in the core of my person. He laid his sinewy torso against my back while his groans of panting satisfaction slowly subsided. We kissed passionately, sharing the cum he had lapped from my heaving torso.

He had no desire to be released from my bondage. We made love again and again until the hint of dawn appeared over the horizon. Only then did he release me and go his merry way. My surreptitious amore was no other than the talented musician who had played those sentimental ballads at our campfire.

I needed my solitude, to ponder on the erotic adventure I'd just experienced. A 6 foot 3 inches figure walked towards my direction. It was my mentor. He had awoken at the first light of morning and came looking for me. As we looked into each other's adoring eyes, he planted a sweet kiss on my lips. He held my hand and gently led me to the pond for a morning dip. I was blissfully felicitous to have Andy as my Valet, lover, guardian, chaperon, and most importantly, as my mentor.

Second Week Of June 2012

My response to my ex-lover's message:

Hi Andy,

What exciting adventures have you been up to recently? You mentioned that you go on rowing expeditions; where have you been to lately?

Walter is an avid paddleboarder and he inquires if you paddleboard besides rowing. Although he doesn't belong to any paddling club or associations, he does go some distance out into the Pacific Ocean. Personally, I'm not into paddleboarding, although I have done it on occasion. It is not my idea of a work-out. I prefer swimming in our heated swimming pool and working out with weights. I've been doing that for years, ever since Nikee introduced me to the sport when I was at Daltonbury Hall.

I stopped working out after our separation as I was wallowing in the misery of losing you. When I met Jorge (my boyfriend for the next six years) in early 1972, he (being an Oxford gentleman) was never big on sports or any form of active physical activities. It was not until I lived in Hong Kong after my separation from Jorge that I returned to the gym with a vengeance. I will tell more as we continue our regular correspondence or when we have a chance to meet in person.

Bernard:

You wanted more information about Bernard, the adolescent boy from Belfast. He was from a middle class family of 5 children. Although I met his father a couple of times, he was quite a piece of work. An accountant by trade, he worked full time for a mining company. Like most Irish, he drank like a fish and was often found in his local watering hole. He wasn't a terribly responsible father to his children. There were times when Bernard would show up crying. When I asked what happened, he kept quiet, afraid to confide his secrets to me. As he got to know and trust me, he opened himself to me like a fresh bloom. Being his confidant and mentor, I promised not to betray his trust.

One day, he met me in the park with bruises and a gash behind his ear. I was concerned for his safety and pressed him for information. He finally disclosed that his father had beaten him in a drunken rage. He had found the boy playing with a doll upon his return from the pub. Having spent all his money on hard liquor, he was looking for an easy target to extricate his frustrations. Unfortunate for Bernard, he became the defenseless victim. His father flew into a rage and hit the boy until Bernard's mother stepped in to stop his unruly actions. By then it was too late; the adolescent had suffered his father's wrath and injuries. I was working on a design project in my hostel when Bernard called. We agreed to meet at a nearby park.

He had run out of his house, terrified of returning home. As we spoke, tears of fear filled his eyes. I had to embrace him until his trembling subsided. I told him I would call Pastor Rick to have a serious talk with his dad. Bernard refused my suggestion at first. He was afraid if the pastor spoke with his old man, he would receive another brutal beating when he went home, for calling for help.

We returned to my hostel and I called Pastor Rick. The compassionate Reverend came to my hostel to make sure Bernard was okay. He would pay a visit to the McGee household to speak to Mr. McGee. Bernard refused to return home with the Pastor. He was petrified of his father. I suspected there was more to his story than what he had told me and the pastor. I did not press the boy for further information, which he had no wish to divulge to the minister. I offered to accommodate Bernard; he could stay with me for a couple of days before it would be safe to return home after the dust had settled. Bernard ended up staying a week with me.

His father refused to accept his sissy son back into the fold even after Pastor Rick did his best to convince the man that he should accept his son no matter his orientation. Bernard's mother was devastated, but she was also under the care of her brutal husband. She had little choice and no voice to speak out for her beloved son.

Eventually, the Reverend found a temporary family that was willing to accept Bernard until the church could find a permanent accommodation for the kid. I was flabbergasted that Bernard's father could unleash such violence on his own flesh and blood. Saddened by this incident, I became Bernard's mentor just like you were for me. On that note, my beloved Andy, I will continue Bernard's story in my next email.

I am glad you haven't changed much over the years we have been apart. I continue to cherish your love and hope we will meet soon. Like you, I look forward to our correspondence. Tell me more about yourself in your next message.

Love and kisses,

Young.

66

Life Is An Experience

*"To a great experience one thing is essential;
an experiencing nature."*

Walter Bagehot

Second Week Of June 2012

Dr. Arius reply arrived the following day after I email him. His message read:

Hi Young,

Of course I'll be happy to answer your questions. I'm very curious to learn the nature of your secondary education at Daltonbury Hall. In my opinion, the current secondary school system is less than desirable, especially in the United States. As a psychiatrist I'm always interested in people and their experiences; be they positive or negative. Our experiences are what make us grow or slack as a well-rounded person.

Reading A Harem Boy Saga sparked an interest in me that the traditional and classical mentorship education between an erastês and an erômenos may have positive effects instead of the current accepted norm that it is a negative and damaging experience to an adolescent. I'm especially intrigued by the 'big brother' and 'little brother' mentorship program. Although I haven't read A Harem Boy Saga (the series) in its entirety, I am pique to follow your experiences to gain further insights.

At this stage of my research; if you are a willing participant, it will be for my personal knowledge, understanding, growth and wisdom. Maybe as we journey along and I gain further perspicacity to this project, I'll be in a better position to discern the direction the research may develop. If we agree that it is a relevent academic case study, then with your permission, I will publish my findings in professional psychiatric publications. Let's take this research a step at a time and treat this as a fun questions and answers project. Will this approach work for you?...

1967 Los Angeles

The SAQR landed smoothly at LAX shortly after takeoff from Las Vegas. The 1st thing I saw was the 'Theme' Building, announcing to arrivers that the 'jet-age' had arrived in the City of Angels. Reminding our entourage that we were embarking into a futuristic world of *2001 Space Odyssey*; a film released by Metro-Goldwyn-Mayer Studios; the same studio our entourage were heading after we deposited our luggage with the 'Beefeater' costumed concierge at the one year old Century Plaza Hotel. Our Cadillacs sped us towards Culver City.

Our set designers accompanied the two Italians, our Arab companions and the four Bahriji boys, me included arrived at the main entrance of MGM. After showing their respective identities to the entrance security guards, our set designer guides drove into the expansive studio lots where the final touches of a duplicate version of Saint Peter's Basilica loomed impressively ahead of us. Needless to say, I was impressed by the authenticity of the exterior facade until at closer inspection, did I notice the backside of the building were propped up by unpainted piped and wooden scaffoldings. This was a section of the set for *"Sacred Sex In Sacred Places"*.

As we walked to another part of the studio lot; partitioned sound proof warehouse-like buildings housed the interior of various sections of the faux fabricated Vatican our photographers had the designers recreate from photographs. I had never seen such a huge film studio and was spellbound by its vastness. The magnitude of the studios; the number of backstage workers trooping around on various duties they were called to perform; the actors, actresses and extras mingling around waiting to be called to action by their respective directors. Last but not least the busy costumers, make-up artists, stylist, set and prop hands making last minute adjustments, send my young mind spinning with excitement. It was a fantasy world I wanted to be a part of, especially in the wardrobe department. This experience was the 1st of many that left a memorable mark in my life. Besides my love for fashion, I also wanted to be a costume designer.

While the two Italians and our Arab companions were busy checking the sets and talking with set builders; Andy, Oscar, Devaj and I walked to the adjacent studio to see the motion picture that was being filmed. A hairdresser was putting the final touches to an actress hair. Oscar exclaimed suddenly, *"Its Mia Farrow!"* We turned towards the direction he was indicating. *"Let's go over and introduce ourselves, I want her autograph."*

Before anyone of us could reply my lover had whipped out a pen and paper walking towards his idol. Ms. Farrow was busy chatting with the hairdresser who looked familiar. I could not recall where I had seen his face. The three of us trotted behind Devaj's enthusiastic Valet.

"Ms. Farrow, I'm so delighted to have this opportunity to meet you. I'm an admirer of yours and loved your performance in Peyton Place." He extended his hand to shake Ms. Farrow's.

The actress taken aback by Oscar's forwardness was left speechless for several seconds. She stopped short her conversation with the hairdresser, turned to my BB and uttered, *"Uh, hello! Have we met before?"*

"I follow Peyton Place on British television and admired your acting greatly. You play the role of Allison Mackenzie to perfection," my lover replied.

Flattered by Oscar's compliments, the actress responded, *"Thank you! I'm glad to meet you. What's your name young man?"*

"I'm Oscar and these are my friends (turning to introduce us)."

Just then I noticed Mario, Gabrielli and our Arab companions walking towards us. My polite BB introduced each of them to Ms. Farrow. As soon as Mario's turn arrived, the photographer bent to kiss the lady's hand. I could tell she was flustered by such a gentlemanly gesture. She said smilingly, *"I'm happy to be acquainted with all you gentlemen. If you'll excuse me, I'll have to be ready before my role call."*

Mario taking the opportunity exclaimed, *"Hi Vidal, I didn't know you are in Hollywood doing Ms. Farrow's hair?"*

Putting his arm around Vidal Sassoon's shoulders, he embraced the hairdresser like an old friend he hadn't seen for ages. Before Mr. Sassoon could respond, Mario greeted the coiffeur with a big hug and spoke, *"Meet the world renowned Vidal Sassoon."*

We extended our hands to shake the stylist. Surprised by the news, I couldn't contain my fervor, I exclaimed, *"You are Vidal Sassoon! The man who styled Mary Quant's hair to a Bob!"*

Astonished by my sudden burst of jubilation he was caught off guard before regaining his posture. He answered, *"Well, eh yes. I'm Mary's London hairdresser."*

I continued, *"I love the 'Bob'! I had my hair bobbed before I entered Daltonbury Hall. The school had me cut it to a short crop. I felt so fashionable when I had the 'Bob'."* Stressing on the word fas-hion-able.

Mario chimed, *"What movie are you working on with Mia?"* He asked as if he had known Ms. Farrow for a long time.

"We are working on Roman Polanski's, 'Rosemary's Baby'."

"Is Roman here too, I must say hello! Where is he? We must get together, are you guys free this evening? Let's have a party!" The Italian voiced with conviction.

Caught off guard, the hairstylist coquetted, *"We are going to the Playboy Club. Roman is a key holder so he invited Ms. Farrow and me to join him this evening. Would you like to join us at the Playboy Club?"* Since he wasn't talking to anyone in particular, he motioned a flamboyant hand gesture, indicating to us that we were all invited. The stylist was put in an awkward situation by the Count to invite our entire entourage.

Mario seizing the opportunity agreed that all of us would love to join them. After we bid our farewells to Mr. Sassoon and Ms. Farrow, Andy enquired of Mario and Gabrielli, "Young and Devaj are underage. Are they allowed to enter the Playboy Club?"

Both Italians replied laughingly, "'Ka-ching' speaks louder than words. As long as you boys don't consume any alcoholic beverages, I'm sure Hefner wouldn't mind. After all we'll be there for dinner. Dress formal and leave the rest to us."

Second Week Of June 2012

Andy's reply arrive a couple of days after I email him. My ex-lover wrote:

Young,

Your emails bring joy to my heart. I'm glad you did the correct thing to help Bernard. I would have done the same if I were in your shoes. What happen to him after he went to a foster home? Did he adjust well in the home?

You asked me what happened after I left London for Christchurch. As I had mentioned in my previous correspondence, I plunged wholeheartedly into my engineering studies. The days were easier than the nights when I woke to dreams of you and missed the love we shared terribly. There were times I went for long walks when I suffered chronic insomnia. Much like you, out of incorrigible loneliness I went looking for love in the wrong places.

One evening I stumbled upon a cruising park near the university campus. After insouciant sex with different men in the dark whom I did not care to know afterwards; a horrendous sense of self-hatred often befell my person and I regretted endangering myself in these situations. The more I resisted the temptation, the more it became a habitual act. After the dark faceless encounters, I became lonelier than before. I was to a point of nervous breakdown when I noticed an attractive Portuguese Filipino student on campus who reminded me of you.

A Gxxm Boy's Saga XX: Unbridled

One day I saw him going into one of the lecture halls, I followed. I thought it was you when I first noticed him. I sat some distance away from the boy at the lecture hall. He was a freshman law student from a well to do family in the Philippines. I stalked him for a day before I introduced myself. Toby was new at campus and was finding his way around. We started hanging out after classes. He was attractive, charming and pleasant but lacked a certain je ne se quoi which you possess. As much as I like him I had a hunch that he wasn't altogether the kind of man I would be totally happy in a long term relationship. My loneliness and heartaches got the better of me and I pursued this relationship half-heartedly; thinking our emotional affinity would improve with time.

One evening, a week after we met we were at a pub celebrating a friend's birthday. I was intoxicated trying to drown my sorrows from missing you. He had a wee bit too much to drink at the celebration. We ended up in my flat with our clothes scattered around us. He had a beautiful physique like yours. I began seeing you in him when we became intimate. I longed for your sweet lips and wanted to believe I was making love to you instead of Toby. Ignoring my premonitions, I plunged full steam ahead. I kissed him passionately like I did you when we were a couple. With my eyes clammed shut, I imagine holding you in my arms, caressing you and submerging fully in you. I desired no other only you.

Toby was delirious from my amorous display of affection, he had never been made love to like the way we did together. Under the influence of my inebriation, I made love to the boy with ferocity, biting and kissing every part of his sinewy body. I desired him to be you; I longed to make sensual love to you, nibbling your soft earlobes, sucking the sides of your delicious neck, drinking the nectar from your tendinous veins, and leaving love bites to substantiate my love for you. His perky nipples stuck out like yours as I lapped at those tiny luscious knobs. He wanted me as much as I craved for him.

By now my manhood was throbbing uncontrollably, I needed to be inside him, the way you revered my hardness inside you. In a drunken daze, I unconsciously tuned out his crying moans. Instead I heard your groans emanating from his temulent breath. I had to be inside you to render you our perpetual love we so lovingly bestowed upon each other during our intimate moments. It was a criterion I later discovered that Toby and I did not share.

Unlike you who received me so readily and compliantly, I did not realize my length had caused him to shriek in pain during entry. I withdrew my quivering organ leaving me with pulsating dissatisfaction. He tried to accommodate my pleasure and in my bibulous state I saw your sweet yearning biophilia rather than his obliging bligation to please me. I would have terminated our liaison there and then if I was in my right mind. Knowing your infatuation for my unbridled sex and my hunger for you, ravaged my senses; I pounded into the boy despondently until I relinquished my load into his tightness. If I was with you, you would not have enraptured me to stop but craved for me to deposit my abundance into your core; staying inside until my stiffness rears its bulbous head, to ravish you again and again.

Unfortunately Toby isn't you; it hurt him if I stayed in his opening after my release. As his drunkenness wore thin, so did his ineradicable homosexual guilt from years of deep-rooted Catholic upbringing. He requested I leave without reaching a pleasuring crescendo himself. The following day we met on campus; I was surprised when he asked me if I'll be his boyfriend. My pity for my companion supplanted my sound reasoning and I reluctantly agreed to give the relationship a try.

Well my dearest Young, that's all in the past; after all life is an experience and to any great experiences, one thing is essential; an adventurous nature. That is an essence I love about you which Toby did not possess.

Your loving ex-Valet,
Andy.

67

The Playboy Club

"Playboy was a wonderful experience and a great opportunity for me."
Rita Mero

Mid June 2012

I was pleasantly surprised by Andy's candid email. During the years I was with my ex-lover he was a rather reserved gentleman of impeccable manners. I would never have guessed he would verbalize an unreserved monologue regarding his feelings for me and his early sexual relationship with Toby in a email. Maybe age and time has brought forth a sense of self-assurance that as teenagers we were often unsure of ourselves.

Locating Andy has been a revelation. Our renewed friendship and regular correspondence is a journey of self-discovery in and of itself. After all what is life but a journey of experiences? What better way to travel down this yellow brick road than to have companions that are near and dear, to share in our tree of knowledge and wisdom.

In response to my ex-Valet's email, I wrote:

Hi Andy,

I am surprised by your honesty and openness in relating your early relationship with Toby. I had not expected such frank soliloquy from a 'perfect' gentleman like you. Although we often discussed everything candidly in the old days, we had never written down our thoughts and opinions in black and white. Are we finally reaching an Age of Aquarius where truth and freedom are here to enlighten humanity? I am gladdened that we are able to communicate quickly and efficiently in this electronic age.

I know you are aware that I am writing my memoirs. Aren't you concerned that I may reveal the true nature of your feelings you confided to me in my writings? One thing I can promise you; I will never do anything unsavory or conduct myself in an ungentlemanly fashion towards those I love, respect and trust. My dearest Andy, I value your love greatly and laurel you in the highest esteem in my pantheon of cultivated beings. Moreover we are soul mates and as past E.R.O.S. members we also have a duty to our forebears to continue living spiritually and intellectually. To be illustrious examples in the chaotic world we reside...

1967 Playboy Club Los Angeles

The moment we stepped out of our limousines into the entrance of the first 4 floors of a ten story building at number 8560 Sunset Boulevard, there was a long queue of dressy revelers waiting to get into the famous Playboy Club. Since our entourage was accompanied by a renowned movie director, Roman Polanski we brushed through the crowd without harassment. The 'Door Bunny' made sure our host, a silver key holder gained entry with their invited guests.

Entering the club with several celebrities had its perks. We got to sit at the best tables and were served by several impeccably groomed and hospitable bunnies. The Bunny Mother made sure that our visit was flawless. She had allocated these top notch waitresses to attend to our tables. Gabrielli and Mario, especially the socialite Count, were up and about socializing with this movie star and that celebrity when they spotted them.

Aziz and Tahu (Bahir wasn't invited since he was hired help) went gaga over the leggy corseted bunnies. They were every male and I'm sure some females sexual fantasies come to reality. For the sexually repressed Tahu; his 1st time out of the Middle East, he was completely aghast gawking at these scantily clad females. He must have thought he had died and gone to Allah's paradise and served by an abundance of 'Houris' (Allah's paradise playmates). Although Aziz was a sophisticated world traveler, he too behaved as if he had just been let out of confinement and was craving for an evening of libidinous sex. Both our Arab companions devoured the bunnies with their ruttish eyes and mouth watering lascivious appetite; causing unnecessary modesty whenever the bunnies did their rounds at our tables.

While waiting for dinner, I turned to my gorgeous looking Valet and my incredibly debonair BB, said, *"I'm amazed to be inside a Playboy Club. I'd seen copies of Playboy magazines when I was eight and here I am looking at the 'real' bunnies!"* I exclaimed with ebullience.

Oscar astounded by my remark questioned, *"How did you get hold of playboy magazines at eight years old?"*

"I found them under my Brother James' bed. When he returned from London on his summer breaks, he would hide the magazines from my parents."

"How did you discover these girlie publications? Did he show them to you?" Andy enquired.

"I used to sneak into my brother's room when he's out and rummage through his things. I was curious to know what he brought home during his holidays to Kuala Lumpur.

"One day when I was in his room, he sneaked a girl into the house when Mother was out playing mahjong. Hearing their footsteps coming upstairs, I hide under his bed. That's where I discovered the magazines."

"Did they know you were under the bed?" Oscar inquired.

"While they were making out on the bed, I was busy browsing at pictures of naked bunnies. The photographs didn't do anything for me sexually. I was more interested in imitating their sexy poses in their next to nothing lingerie." I explained.

Both my lovers laughed at my confession. Suddenly, we heard a shriek from the bunny that was clearing the ashtrays next to Tahu and Aziz. Standing upright, she said sternly,

"Sirs, it is our club's policy that you can look but you can't touch. Please refrain from pinching my buttocks or touching me inappropriately. Otherwise, I'll have to inform Bunny Mother to remove your presence from this establishment."

Bunnies were trained to treat this kind of crude behavior with style and panache and soon had our Arab friends 'eating out of their palms', like obedient dogs trained to sit or move at the commands of their masters; in this case, their mistresses. It was an amusing scenario to behold since both men held dominant male positions in the Middle East but at the Playboy Club they were behaving quite the opposite.

The Fight

Who should descend the stairs while we were having dinner, but our friends Nirob and Kismat. The Nubian had obviously made haste to pursue Anya to Los Angeles who was seated next to her 'big sister' Dominique. Andy spotted the Nubian and waved for them to join us. After a round of 'kissy face' greetings, the couple joined us at the Playmate Bar for after dinner drinks, while Motown hits that were performed by no other than the *Supremes* themselves. I for one was completely enthralled watching my idol, Diana Ross perform live in this exclusive venue. Never in my young life did I imagine witnessing a live performance by the group, I had habituated one of their songs for my 'Slipping and Sliding' dance performance at the Methodist Boy's School variety show. It was a gay boy's dream come true to witness Ms. Ross singing for the 1st time *"Someday We'll Be Together"*, before this song officially became a number one hit in the Supremes *'Cream of the Crop'* album in 1969.

Needless to say I took to the crowded dance floor grooving to the rhythm of this fabulous melody. I couldn't care less whom I was dancing with, since our entourage went onto the floor together to have a fun time. I was flapping and twirling under my own hypnotic spell and cadencing in my dream world from this melodic tune. Unfortunately, this hypnotic experience did not last long. I was irrationally propelled back to the present by a vicious catfight playing out on the dance floor. Anya and Kismat were tearing away at each other's hair like a couple of wild cats in a heated fight. They were rolling around biting, scratching and pulling at each other.

The Bunny Stuffing

While the two belligerents were tearing at one another, Kismat accidentally threw a flying kick on a bunny carrying a tray of alcoholic beverages, sending the corseted 'rabbit' flying across the room. In the swirling process she knocked another bunny with a tray full of cigarettes around her neck, sending beverages and cigarettes spilling onto the stage.

That wasn't the only mishap that flew across the room; Kleenex tissues, absorbent cotton, cut-up Bunny tails, foam rubber, lamb's wool, gym socks and an entire host of other inflated objects, stuffed into the bunnies 34D and 36D bra cups came tumbling out of their respective bosoms. Their corseted tops flapped downwards revealing the two bunnies deflated bosoms. They did their best to cover their modesty with their hands while doing their best to pick themselves up from this embarrassing situation.

The crowd was stupefied by such a display of impropriety but was at once amused by this hilarious accident. I for one burst into laughter at such an unbecoming sight and so did those who witnessed that evening's drama at the Los Angeles Playboy Club.

The Fight Has To Stop

Stunned by such a display of vulgarity, the Bunny Mother, Nirob, Gabrielli and Mario intervened, doing their best to separate the two opposing entities. Finally, Bunny Mother and Gabrielli managed to pull Anya away from an angry Kismat.

She was screaming obscenities at the teenager on top of her lungs even-though she was held tightly by Nirob and the Count. The girls were soon led away in opposite directions before the music began again as if nothing unusual had happen.

Gabrielli, Dominique and Anya left the club post haste. Mother Bunny was talking to Nirob in a secluded corner while the Nubian did his best to bring equanimity back to Kismat's quivering body. Before long, they too left the Club, leaving the Count, our two Arab companions and we Bahriji boys dazzled; wondering what in the world had happened a few moments ago.

I couldn't help probing my lovers, *"What happened to Kismat and Anya? How did they end up fighting?"*

Andy shook his head before replying, *"Obviously, Kismat found out that Nirob was having an affair with our Bahriji girl. She got jealous when she saw her boyfriend dancing intimately with Anya and attacked her on the spot."*

"It's best not to mess with lady-boys; they can be extremely malicious when crossed." Oscar voiced.

"What's going to happen between Anya and Nirob, now that Kismat know about their illicit affair?" I asked with great curiosity.

"In my opinion, it's likely that our Black friend will terminate his relationship with the lady-boy and go with Anya." Oscar added.

Andy being the gentleman soon put a stop to our speculations. Since we have to start our photographic work early at MGM studio the following morning, we bid our celebrity movie director, actress and hairdresser farewell and called this eventful evening a night.

Mid June 2012

...Continuing Bernard's story, the adolescent did not adjust well to his first foster home. I spend time with him whenever I could. The poor boy was bullied relentlessly in school and I feared that the bullies, like KiWi and his gang of 3 would eventually drive the boy to suicidal attempts.

One day when we met he was crying uncontrollably. After inviting him to have high tea with me at my hostel, he finally confided his secret. Besides suffering the wrath of his father's drunken beatings; his older brother Jack was as much a tyrant like the old man. Jack had raped the adolescent when he refused his brother's advances. Bernard was afraid to tell the Reverend in case the minister confronts the brother and he was petrified that his older sibling would come for revenge.

By now Bernard was shaking uncontrollably. I had to embrace the boy to calm his distress. It was my duty to report this violent act to Pastor Rick which I did. The Reverend like me was astonished that there was so much abuse in the dysfunctional McGee household. Besides being afraid of his brother and father, Bernard was also bullied by an older boy in his foster home. Nick was taking advantage of the meek and genteel Bernard, ordering him around when his parents were not in the house. My heart reached out to my friend. I offered to assist him anyway I could. He ended up staying with me at the hostel for two months before I departed for London. By then, the Pastor had found the boy a stable family where he was well taken care of.

The two months that Bernard was my roommate, we became very close. I taught him photography which he took to heart. Years later, he became a professional photographer. My protégé came to visit me a month after my return to London. I introduced him to my compassionate Uncle James who kindly took the boy into his home until he introduced Bernard to a Scottish photographer friend in Edinburgh. My charge became the photographer's apprentice. Through hard work and determination Bernard rose in rank and become the photographer's assistant. I'm glad Bernard turned out unmarred after what he had been through. I visited him in Edinburgh a few years later when I was on a skiing trip in Scotland. By then he had found himself a mature lover. I was happy that Bernard had found someone who loved and cherished him as he is. That was the last time I saw my charge. We corresponded for some years but soon lost track when I became involved with Jorge (the Oxford graduate). My dearest Andy this is another episode which I will disclose at another time.

For now be well, be safe and take excellent care of yourself. I am yours truly always.

Love,

Young.

Xoxoxo

68

Pride & Prejudice

"They were concerned about the racial issue. They thought it was not a safe issue to go Asian, unfortunately."
Lucy Liu

Mid-June 2012

During my regular correspondence with Andy, my ex-lover's unequivocal frankness reminded me of the old days when we were close and open with each other about our experiences. Although there were times when I kept secrets from him, I was bound to reveal the truth sooner or later. We had always shared understanding and honesty in our relationship. It is also not in character for Bahriji students and E.R.O.S. members to do anything but be themselves. Therefore it came as no surprise when Andy wrote:

My dearest Young,

Your correspondence brings an abundance of joy to my heart. Although we've both grown older (and hopefully wiser), you are still the boy I knew and the boy I left behind many years ago in London. I love listening to your experiences after our separation. Keep them coming, it's like listening to your sweet voice all over again.

As I mentioned in my previous email, I should have ended my relationship with Toby before it began. Our four-year relationship lasted with a copious amount of quarreling, disgruntlement and resentment. I wanted to end the relationship three months after our sexual rendezvous, but Toby threatened suicide if I left. Those years were not easy for either of us. Pettifoggery often led to intense bickering, and he would sulk for days, waiting for me to kiss and make up with him. I resented having to admit that the squabbles were my fault and having to apologize to keep peace. These prolonged melodramas sent me into a psychological and physical tailspin. I had difficulty concentrating on my studies.

One day, I told the boy I wanted to end our relationship. He was devastated and immediately started to blame me for the pain I caused him. He did not listen to what I had to say before he stormed back to our lodging. I was speechless. I felt guilty for what I had done, even though it was the best solution for us.

I tried explaining that I loved you and I had mistakenly used him as a substitute, but it was no use. Toby proceeded to use this as ammunition, accusing me of perjury. Instead of being sound of reason, he turned the tables around, saying that I had falsely led him to fall in love with me. As you are well aware, it takes two to tango.

Toby reminded me of Oscar's charge, Srihan. Their parents spoiled them materialistically when what they most needed was love. Toby grew up not knowing how to love. Love, to him, was about taking; he knew nothing about giving. Unlike our relationship which was built on mature love, Toby's and my relationship was the complete opposite…

1967 MGM Studios, Los Angeles

Our photo shoot started early in the morning with short breaks in between sessions, where different shifts of models were on call. Ford Modeling Agency in New York had sent several Los Angeles male and female models for our photographers to select among. Mario, Aziz, and Gabrielli decided to hire two elegantly sassy females and a couple of sexy male specimens to join our entourage. While Ellie (one of the female models) was busy posing with Dominique and Aal (a Ford agency male model), Andy, Oscar, and I had a chance to chat with Elijah (the other male model). The good-looking 22-year-old took a sip of coffee said, *"You guys aren't from this part of the world, are you?"*

"We are from England," my Valet replied.

"I thought so. You speak with an English accent." Looking at Andy and Oscar, the model declared, *"Charming! You guys*

should register with Ford if you want to pursue a modeling career. I've been with their agency for a year and jobs have been trickling in regularly. Of course the girls get called more often than the guys, but with your looks, the two of you wouldn't be out of work."

Andy answered, "Thanks for the advice; I don't intend to pursue a full-time modeling career. I'm here because of this young man." Pointing his finger at me, "He's the one who's into fashion and artistic pursuits."

Shaking his head, Elijah responded, "I'm talking about the two of you (directing his gaze at my guardian and my lover simultaneously). I'm not talking about him (giving me a dismal look)."

I could tell that both my lovers were slightly agitated by the way Elijah had given me that look of distain. Oscar asked with annoyance in his voice, "What's the matter with Young? In my opinion, he is as good a model as we are."

The model responded indifferently, "He's Asian."

"So? What has his ethnicity got to do with his ability to model?" My BB asked with umbrage.

"He looks Asian and I haven't encountered any Asian male models registered with Ford."

Andy was getting flustered as their conversation developed. My mentor spoke, "If what you say is correct, I will definitely not sign with Ford, not that I care about modeling."

"Neither will I!" Oscar announced, "If the color of a person's skin clouds your judgment of his ability to do an excellent job, I suggest you take a good look at yourself in the mirror. Be careful what you say to my charge. I may do some collateral damage to you that you'll regret."

Elijah defended himself with a racist comment, "It is no wonder my father advised that the 'Chings' are here to take away our jobs. We Irish were here before they arrived." He pointed an angry finger at me.

By now, both my lovers were ready to defend me when Gabrielli arrived, just in time to dissipate the indignation. Overhearing the last segment of Andy's conversation with the rude model, my teacher announced sternly, *"Elijah, you are called by the photographers. Go take your position now."*

The scornful model left, but not before spitting on the ground in full view of our group. Without uttering a word, my professor hugged me tightly before releasing his grip. *"Young, you'll find that there are always some people like that, throughout your life. Don't let their closed-mindedness get to you."* With that comment, he patted my head and walked back toward his place.

That day was the last we saw of Elijah. He was replaced by Harry, sent to us by a brand new modeling agency, Wilhelmina.

Columbia Pictures Studio

Since our Los Angeles set builders had used different studio locations to build the various sets for *'Sacred Sex In Sacred Places,'* our entourage was bundled in a couple of shutter buses. We drove towards 1438 N. Gower Street, Hollywood, California, which happened to be the location of Columbia Pictures Studios in 1967.

Mario had the perfect opportunity to conduct his interviews with those involved in the production of *'Guess Who's Coming to Dinner.'* Meanwhile, Aziz was busy filming *'Sacred Sex In Sacred Places'* in one of the studio warehouses with Jane, Anya, Aal and Nirob. Our Nubian friend had sent Kismat packing after a belligerent break-up, about which he later confided to Andy, Oscar and me. He had to pay a hefty financial price for their separation. Kismat was not the sort of 'woman' who would give up a fight so easily unless a substantial monetary settlement was litigated. Only then would she relinquish her rights and free Nirob.

For now, the Count had secured an interview with the film's director, Stanley Earl Kramer. After formal introductions, Mario inquired, *"Mr. Kramer, you are well-known for directing 'message movies.' Can you shed some insights about your upcoming film, 'Guess Who's Coming to Dinner'?"*

As our group, which consisted of Gabrielli, Dominique, Andy, Oscar, Devaj, and me listened attentively, my mind drifted to my brother Hal and his Irish girlfriend, Joyce. When news broke that Hal, who was in an English architectural college, was going steady with an Irish girl, my parents were in an uproar. During my summer 1966 vacation in Kuala Lumpur, my father had expressed an undeniable dissatisfaction with my eldest brother's falling in love during the course of his studies. In my father's conservative mindset, his eldest son should be concentrating on his architectural studies instead of undulating around London with his 'fling.'

Mother, unsure about whether Hal was really in love or this affair was another of his habitual playthings, had some cause for concern as well. According to my parents, fooling around with a casual fling was acceptable for a respectable young man. But if the affair turned serious, it was quite a different matter. Up until 1966, no member of the Foong or Ho (mother's) family had dated a foreigner, let alone married one. This, to them, was rebellious and a sacrilegious act of defiance and was not an unacceptable proposition for either of my folks. They could not comprehend the thought of a white woman becoming a member of the Foong clan. Was this Irish girl a gold digger? What would the relatives think? How would their children be received by the Malaysian Chinese society? These were vital questions, and my parents had irrevocable doubts.

Much like the parents of Joanna "Joey" Drayton in *'Guess Who's Coming to Dinner'*, who had problems accepting their daughter's black fiancé, my parents had similar concerns about accepting their son's white girlfriend. This was a legitimate concern for my parents' generation. What will their upper-crust friends, neighbors, and relatives think? My parents were more concerned with keeping 'face' than with the happiness of their son or daughter. Racial prejudice was definitely an issue in those halcyon days. Thanks to Mr. Stanley Kramer and the resplendent acting and storytelling by three of the greatest actors of the 20th century, their important racial message eventually softened the hearts of many a prejudiced parent, including mine.

Little did my father or my mother know that Hal and Joyce had secretly gotten hitched in a civil ceremony in the heart of England! Unbeknownst to them, Joyce was already several months with child. Left with little choice, my parents finally succumbed and accepted Joyce into the fold. Otherwise, they feared, they would lose their eldest son and the chance to hold their first grandchild in their arms.

Joyce arrived in Kuala Lumpur, a city she had no knowledge of and in which she had no friends she could count on. The only family member with whom she could share her solace was her brother-in-law, *moi*. Although she could console her problems of missing Hal (who was back in England attending college) with me, the unbearable Malaysian humidity was especially taxing on the pregnant woman. It was little wonder that she could not wait to be on the next flight back to England.

I was eager to return to London and to the arms of my beloved Andy after weeks of having to put up with my father's incessant nagging and activities meant to "butch me up." I did not entrust my secrets to anybody because no one in my family would have understood what I was going through, especially since I was a gay adolescent, whom most would consider unable to make decisions for himself. Let alone the fact that I had a lover who was older and, atop of all these issues, I had been inducted into a clandestine sexual society. What was the adolescent thinking? He must be brainwashed by his mentors and sold into slavery to the uninitiated. How could they know I was having the time of my life, learning the wonders of the world whilst in the protection of benevolent benefactors who loved, cherished and adored me as I was? I had found my family away from home.

Mid June 2012

...*Young, as time passed, I missed you more than ever. My exasperation with Toby festered with each passing day. When I finally could not tolerate our tempestuous relationship, I confronted the young man. After a heated emotional argument, Toby left our unfinished discussion in a state of vexation. I did not realize he was using the age-old psychological threat of overdosing himself to obtain my attention. I found him unconscious, foaming at the corner of his mouth from consuming an entire bottle of sleeping pills. He was rushed to hospital. I would not have been able to live with my guilt if Toby had died. He recovered from this ordeal, but my respect for him had plummeted. Instead of loving him, I felt sorry and pitied him. This was a malignant sign of what was to come. To appease him, we often kissed and made up after impassioned disputes. I made false promises that I had no intention of keeping. These desolate pledges soon dissolved into self-abhorrence. I had allowed myself to be trapped into a situation, and I could not figure out a solution.*

Throughout this ordeal, I threw myself into my engineering studies, channeling my unhappiness into what I enjoyed best. I could not give myself fully to the boy, and had little respect for him. When we made love, I shut him out. Instead, I saw you in our sexual liaisons. Toby was merely a vehicle to satisfy my sexual desires to be with you. Throughout the years we were together, it was you I made love to, not Toby or anyone else. I could not and would not release you from my mind. The pain of losing you was too oppressive, until the fateful day I suffered a nervous breakdown. I ended up in a hospital, in the psychiatric ward. Aria and Ari came to nurse me back to health. Aria stayed for two weeks until I could commence classes again.

I knew I had to get away from this toxic relationship. The day I graduated I enrolled in a postgraduate program in Alberta, Canada. I desired to be as far away from New Zealand as possible; I needed to be away from Toby and to find myself again. I finally had a solid and legitimate excuse to separate from the boy. I was glad when Toby's parents demanded their son's return to the Philippines after his graduation so that he could take over his father's business. Toby did not wish to return to Manila, but had no choice. His father threatened to cut off his financial support if he did not return.

Thanks to universal intervention, my freedom was restored. I began a new life in Canada. That, my dearest Young, was the beginning of a new chapter in my life.

The rest will be revealed to you in our next correspondence.

For now, be happy, be well, and most importantly, be you at all times: the Young whom I love and cherish.

Andy,
Xoxoxo

69

War & Peace

"People always make war when they say they love peace."
David Herbert Lawrence

Mid June 2012

Good morning Andy,

I hope today brings you good cheer and bounteous energy. We certainly have been through some tough times since our separation. Back in the late 80s to the mid-90s, I too experienced a negative relationship like you and Toby. My relationship with Kregory, an American from Wisconsin, lasted for nine years. It came to a screeching halt one day in August 1996 when he suddenly disappeared from our apartment and my life. It was the best thing that ever happened to me. The universe had again intervened on my behalf when it was time for a new beginning. I will relate this life's chapter at a later date.

It breaks my heart to learn that you went through a difficult period with Toby. I'm glad those days are behind us. I believe that I emerged from those horrendous experiences to become wiser, stronger and better-equipped for life's challenges. You, my dearest 'big brother,' have always been my guiding light, and I'm positive that you, too, returned unscathed through adversities. I, for one, am grateful for my Bahriji education and treasured E.R.O.S. experiences. Without this priceless enlightenment and knowledge, my life would have turned out differently and would have been difficult to grapple with. Now that we have reconnected, it's also the beginning to a new friendship. If the universe chooses to bring us together again, time is our guiding star. For now, I'm gratified to be corresponding regularly with my ex-lover, Valet, mentor, and guardian.

1967 Invitation

Harry, Elijah's model replacement, proved to be an excellent sport. He was a charming 23-year-old who had arrived in Los Angeles three months ago to pursue an acting career. Having signed with Wilhelmina Modeling Agency, his career was slowly taking shape. The day our photographers assigned Harry, Andy, Jane, and me for a four-way liaison, we had a chance to talk on set.

Harry asked, *"Are you guys here to try your luck in the movie industry?"* as we pose naked for the photographers against a faux backdrop of the Sistine Chapel.

"Oh, no! We are friends of Aziz and Mario. We are amateur models from England doing a favor for our photographer friends.

"You don't sound American. Where are you from?" Andy inquired.

The model replied, "I am from Johannesburg, South Africa. My dad is an English diplomat and my mother is American from Kansas. It's my ambition to be an actor, and Hollywood is the best place to forge an acting career. Modeling for me is a stepping stone to meeting people in the creative field."

"Have you met people who can get you into the film industry?" I asked curiously.

"I'm getting there. In fact, tomorrow I've been asked to a private celebrity party in Bel Air. I met this guy Sam who is a talent scout and he invited me to tomorrow's event. He asked me to bring my good-looking male model friends to join the celebration. Sam is recruiting guys to attend this function. It's an impromptu introduction party for potential talents to meet movers and shakers within the film industry. Would you guys like to go?"

Before Andy could decline the invitation, I had agreed to attend. Since Andy was my chaperone, he had no choice but to tag along. So did Oscar and Vaj.

The Century Plaza Hotel

That evening, after a hectic day of filming, we headed back to our hotel to rest and relax. As we neared our destination, our cars were diverted to the back streets. All vehicles came to a halt when several traffic police officers advised us to turn around to leave the area or alight and walk to our terminus. Our entourage decided to head towards the hotel on foot. Little did we know we were heading into a clash between the police forces and an army of Vietnam War protestors, who were marching towards the Century Plaza Hotel.

As we rounded the corner to our lodgings, we came face to face with a large troop of shouting and banner holding war demonstrators. Arm in arm, they formed a human barricade, lock-stepping in tune to their anti-Vietnam war cries. The police, in full, armored regalia, were at the ready to protect the president of the United States, who was currently attending a fundraiser at our 5-star hotel. Without warning, several front-liners started throwing stones and rocks at a group of policemen who were trying to march pass the Beefeater uniformed doormen and into the hotel's main entrance. The protestors were there to disrupt the Democratic fundraiser and to confront President Johnson to end the Vietnam War. They wanted to bring home the American soldiers who were dying under the hands of the Vietcong in a war to which they saw no end.

Before long, thousands of demonstrators were in combat with the armed forces, throwing punches at the club-swinging police. Our entourage was stunned to witness such violence in the streets of Los Angeles. Quick-thinking Andy, Mario, and Gabrielli shouted for us to split into smaller groups and run to the back hotel service entrances. Andy, shielding my head with his arms, protected me as we moved to the rear of the building. As our group ran for shelter, police were hitting rioters with their fists, clubbing those unfortunates who happened to be in the way. Cries were heard along the crowded streets. Mobs ran in all directions, screaming from the violent blows showered upon them by the inexorable law enforcers. Tear gas was fired into the jeering multitude. The gas blinded my eyes, but I held my Valet's hand tightly as we rushed towards the hotel's service entrance. We arrived just before the staff locked all the doors to the building.

Andy, Oscar, Devaj, Aziz, Mario, and I made it into the hotel. The other missing people from our group were nowhere to be found. In a panic, we scattered in twos, looking for them in the hotel. Located by the kitchen service entrance, there was a group of the president's men, guiding Lyndon Johnson to a waiting helicopter stationed in the back parking lot. As the president made his way out, Dominique, Anya, Nirob, and Gabrielli made their way in, narrowly escaping the riot before the hotel staff closed all entrances and exits of the structure.

We breathed a sigh of relief as we made our way to our individual suites. Fourteen floors below us lay injured and bloody, battered bodies in a field of dissipating smoke. The sound of ambulances made its way to the rampage, carting the crushed bodies to be rescued and hopefully resuscitated in the nearest hospital around the vicinity. The police did not leave the premises until the last of the rioters had scrambled away from the atrocious scene.

Mid-June 2012

...Do you remember the arrogant male model who came to the Bahriji School to give a grooming course to us students when we were there? An evening after my return to London, while staying at Uncle James' home, I visited one of the London sex clubs. Uncle James was in Hong Kong and I had his town house to myself before I moved to my own lodgings in Ladbroke Grove, recommended by the Nottinghill Methodist Church housing project.

A Saram Boy's Saga IV: Unbridled

I was terribly lonely and needed company desperately. I ventured to "Heavens" located Under the Arches on Villiers Street, Charing Cross, a little before midnight. In 1972, this establishment was located in a large warehouse. For the uninitiated, the entrance was nondescript. It was dimly lit from the outside, and when a patron wished to gain entry, he pressed an obscure doorbell by the side of a huge aluminum sliding door. A pair of eyes would look through a peephole, checking to make sure that it was neither a police raid nor an underage client. If the patron was handsome and dressed like a macho gay man, he'd be asked for identification. Once approved, the green door would slide open to allow entry.

Inside "Heavens" was a different world. Throngs of leather and denim-clad patrons checked their belongings in the tiny cloakroom next to the cashier's booth. A small safety deposit box was then allocated upon request for each visitor to deposit his wallet or important documents for safekeeping. The safety deposit box key, attached to an elastic band together with the clothing claim tag, would then be handed to the patron to wear around his wrist or ankle. Most patrons were shirtless except for their jeans and leather pants. The uninhibited would strip down to their jock straps or sports undergarments. Their naked buttocks were ready to be in service for a night of unbridled debauchery.

I ventured into the dimly lit darkness towards the blaring disco music and crowded dance floor. The enclosure reeked of poppers (alkyl nitrites), a recreational drug often used by gay men to heighten their sexual arousal. The club was hopping with the latest disco hits from the popular disco queen of 70s, Donna Summer. Half-naked and almost naked men were crowding the dance floor, grinding their perspiring bodies against each other in a sensual and sexual trancelike state. Men in various stages of foreplay were gyrating their muscular and sinewy bodies against each other in preparation for impulsive back-room romps.

After taking to the dance floor for a couple of songs, I embarked on an exploration journey towards the back of the house. It was difficult to make out the abundance of naked bodies loathering in the dark in various stages of copulation. When I ventured into a large room with a sling in the middle, I heard a familiar, high-pitched groaning voice. It was a voice I had heard several years ago in class at the Bahriji School. It was a soprano voice that I could never get out of my head. Surrounding the voice was a queue of mesomorphically built men, waiting their turn to satisfy their sexual desires on an equally muscular hunk lying on the suspended, swinging sling. The man's legs were spread above his torso. They were strapped to either sides of the hanging chains and so were his wrists, tied securely above his head. Although the 'bottom' was blindfolded with a black kerchief, I instantly recognized him as none other than the famous supermodel, Rick Samuels.

I was dumbfounded to witness this specimen of male beauty in such a compromising position. I had never imagined finding the famous Rick Samuels in a dungeon, let alone in such a vulnerable and decubitus posture.

He was my visiting lecturer, who had advised me to be selective in posing pornographically and for high art. He specifically told me that he was careful not to associate himself in the porn industry. Here he was, lying bare among men whom he did not know or have the vision to see. They were using him as a sex object, gratifying themselves regardless of how he felt. The men took turns pumping their swollen instruments into both his orifices until they could stave off their cravings no longer before they released their loads into Rick's welcoming openings. He was the 'power bottom,' otherwise known to the gay underground community as a 'cum pig' or a 'pig bottom.'

That evening was an eye-opener and a reformation. It reaffirmed men's double standards in their words and actions for me. They were just like seasoned politicians, who promise a world of positive reforms before election. When elected to office, their promises are thrown to the wind. A set of new rules for personal gains then take effect. Thus is the nature of mankind.

That evening, Andy, I learned an important lesson that humankind has its strengths and foibles. It is therefore worth the effort to take a closer look at a person's character instead of embracing the superficiality that could often cloud a sound judgment.

My beloved ex-'big brother,' I am positive in my heart of hearts that you are an honorable gentleman of your word. From the first time I met you to our recent reconnection, you will always be the man I respect, honor, cherish, and, most importantly, LOVE.

Young.

70

Hollywood & Bore-ywood

"I am always looking for meaningful one-night stands."
Dudley Moore

1967 The Party

All of us packed ourselves into two Cadillacs and headed towards Bel Air to the Meet and Greet party with Harry as the head of our entourage. Harry's agent Sam had advised his client that he was introducing the aspiring actor to a group of Hollywood movie movers and shakers. We were invited because Sam had asked Harry to bring his attractive modeling friends to the celebration. I, being curious, had persuaded both my lovers to go. Mario came because he did not want to miss an opportunity to be acquainted with celebrities and to gather potential sexual conquests. Gabrielli tagged along to keep a watchful eye on his students since he had been assigned the task by the Wazir, to make sure the foreign exchange students were well guarded. As for Aziz and Tahu, they were simply inquisitive, and like me wanted to see what transpired at a fancy pool gathering. Since females were not invited, Dominique and Anya went out to dinner with Nirob and Bahir, their chaperones for the evening.

Mr. Henry Willson

By the time we arrived fashionably late due to the fact that we had lost our way finding the property, the party was already in progress. Sam was waiting by the expansive mansion's lobby for us. The first person he introduced our entourage to was the famous talent scout, Mr. Henry Willson, who's most famous discovery up until then was Roy Fitzgerald, otherwise known to the world as Rock Hudson. Henry was well known in the inner Hollywood circle for recruiting handsome, square-jawed "Captain America" type specimens for uses both personally and professionally. He would nurture the careers of his young finds, frequently coercing them into sexual relationships in exchange for publicity and film roles.

Willson was as gay as they come. He owned a talent agency which was known for cruising above and underground gay clubs and truck stops for potential recruits, and then transforming these strapping virile milk-fed and ready to go do Man-Things servicemen into wholesome Midwestern boys or rather men-next-door heart throbs and male stars; which post war audiences hungered for.

Willson would take these "Captain Americas," usually have sex with them, then strip them of their names, and rebuild them from the ground up. He would give them preposterous yet catchy stage names that somehow combined the very normal with the very unique. Arthur Gelien became Tab Hunter, Robert Mosely was renamed Guy Madison, and Orison Whipple Hungerford Jr. was now known as Ty Hardin. And so went the list with the likes of Rand Saxon, Clint Richie, Troy Donoghue, Race Gentry, Rory Calhoun, Chance Nesbitt, and the best star name of all time, DACK RAMBO. To him name repetition was not a problem. When a new "star creation" didn't take, Henry would simply pass the name onto his next endeavor. He'd bestow the star with "masculine" hobbies, such as football, carpentry, polo playing, and horseback riding and in the process rewrite their personal narratives to best appeal to what audiences in the 1960s seemed to crave; the romantic beefcake aspect of the Hollywood created male image.

Not all of Willson's clients were gay, although the majority was. He would put them in training to "eliminate" any stereotypically effeminate gestures. Swaying hips were straightened, limp wrists were slapped; in other words, they went to *"Straight Guy School."* His recruits learned how to light a cigarette "like a man," with a swift single motion or swoon like silent movie heros the likes of the infamous 'Valentino.' With the help of the fan magazines, audiences ate these guys up and made female fans deliquium with adoration; the same way that so many male stars these days that are on ABC Family and Disney that have that vaguely-Bieberish-yet-ambiguously-ethnic looks have done. Although few in Henry's stable became huge stars the way that, say, Clark Gable was; their images were too hollow to sustain the weight of actual superstardom, but for all of their derivativeness, they filled the B-list categories.

Needless to say, when Mr. Willson saw Andy, Oscar, Harry and Aal he was in 7th heaven. I'm sure in his mind he fantasied that 'fresh meat' was available to him in the form of these four handsome male specimens. Little did he know that both my lovers thought little of being in the limelight, let alone being celebrity movie stars; unlike Harry and Aal who ate up Henry's coaxing compliments to their engorged egos.

Pool Party

As we proceeded into the spacious living room overlooking a large open air swimming pool, groups of attractive looking and scantily clad 'beefcakes' were frolicking either in or out of the pool. They were either chatting among themselves or were enraptured and under the spell of their older, homely, and out of shape 'mentors.' Obviously these mature gentlemen were the ones that had the power to propel these eager wide-eyed sprites to stardom. Most were happy to exchange their youthful bodies as miniscule sacrifices to these old men in exchange for stardom or to be kept boys. After all, if they played their cards correctly, fame and fortune would be their ultimate reward. What better way to gain entry into the film industry then to be a 'trophy' boy to one of these well connected 'sugar daddies'?

Mario was the first to exclaim, *"Cary Grant and Randolph Scott are here! I see Tab Hunter and Anthony Perkins over there. I must go over to make my acquaintances."* With that statement, our photographer was off in the direction of the men, who held court with several hunky groupies. The Count was in his element since he was the perfect example of 'the man about town,' especially when it comes to falling prey to the images of good-looking Olympian "Gods," fabricated by the movie industry. Like a collector of beautiful objects, Mario was no exception to the rule, even if these sexual fantasies were only for one-night-stands.

As we mingled with the crowd, Andy and Oscar were getting more and more wary of the party by the looks of their body language. They stuck to Vaj and me like glue, not letting us out of their sights. Andy whispered when we sat on the comfortable couch, *"Good God! This is a stifling crowd. I'm ready to leave the party."*

I asked, *"What's the matter? Aren't you enjoying the attention showered upon you by all these 'demi-gods'?"*

"That my boy, I can do without. I can't carry a decent conversation with these guys. Their language and demeanor are so crude."

"How so?" Vaj chimed in.

"I feel the same way too. I have nothing in common to say to these guys no matter how good looking they are." Oscar reiterated.

"What's the matter with them? They are Hollywood celebrities, aren't they" I queried.

"The majority of them speak like lorry drivers and milk delivery boys. They are so shallow and hollow. Can't you tell that their main goal is to butter up a 'sugar daddy' or find a suitable contender to

groom them to be the next movie heartthrob? Neither of which I'm interested in," Andy replied.

"No offence to the 'rah-rah' celebrity stars, producers and directors, but this is one of the most 'air-head' party I've been to thus far." Oscar snubbed.

Before we could continue, Gabrielli had joined us. He said, "I'm ready to leave if you guys are." Without questioning my professor, I knew he felt the same way as my lovers.

I wasn't ready to leave, as I wanted to see what would happen when some of the handsome guys who were now frolicking in the pool took off their swimsuits to the shouts of 'take it off' encouragements from the mature camp. We all knew a night of licentious wantonness was soon to happen.

The persons in our entourage that stayed were Aal, Henry, Aziz, Tahu and you guessed it, Mario. Gabrielli, Andy, Oscar, Vaj and I drove back to our hotel to have our own passionate lascivious fun and games.

Third Week of June 2012

The questionnaire arrived via email from Dr. Arius. It read:
Good Day, Young!

Thank you for agreeing to be a candidate in my survey. As I mentioned previously, let's conduct this research like our regular correspondence. There is no pressure on your part to answer or not to answer my questions; it's entirely up to your discretion on the way you like to channel this analysis. There are no fixed rules or regulations on how you answer my queries. Be yourself and treat this study like you are talking with a confidant. Let's get started and begin from the beginning;

** In **"Initiation"** you said that as far as you can remember; as a baby you disliked your father. What was it that you didn't like about the man? Did he have a certain smell that repelled you or something conscious or subconscious that repulsed your connection towards him?*

* Do you think your overly protective mother had an influence on you disliking your father?

* When you were wearing pretty frocks and playing with dolls, did you feel less than a boy? How did you feel or react when you saw other boys playing with 'boyish' toys; like miniature toy soldiers or train sets, etc.?

* Did your mom try distancing you away from your dad?

* What did your brothers think of your parent's relationship?

* Did you have any boy pals or friends when you were growing up? If not, why is that? Would you have grown up differently if you had had guy friends?

Let's start with these questions and we'll proceed further with others, as we continue along in our future correspondence.

Now that you, Andy and Oscar have reconnected, I hope your newfound friendships are progressing well with both your ex 'big brothers and lovers. Keep me posted, as I'm interested to know the outcome.

Kind regards,

A.S.

Andy's Message

Around the time I received Arius' email, Andy's message arrived. He wrote:

Young,

I do remember Rick Samuels. I was at the seminar in the Bahriji when he came to lecture. Like you I was at once mesmerized by his style and beauty, which of course was a false image manufactured by the advertising agencies and sales promoters. I was surprised to hear your backroom story of him being gangbanged in the dungeon. We are not ones to judge since both of us had been down that negative road of self-loathing. This seems to be a common thread with people whom others considered good-looking or beautiful. In my opinion, it's a fake image that handsome people know they cannot live up to.

Instead of exterior beauty being an asset, it often becomes a psychological burden.

During the years when I was with Toby, I delved in some fashion modeling work in New Zealand. I ventured into this business because it was my subconscious way of reminding me of the days we posed for Mario and Aziz. It was also my twisted way of hoping to meet another person like me, with the hope of building a loving long-term relationship. It was also a desperate attempt to break loose from Toby's psychosomatic grip on my person.

Ian was his name and he was a very attractive 24 year old architecture student. He modeled to earn some extra spending money. We became fast friends, but he had this foreboding nature which often came on unexpectedly. A sentence or a word could trigger his depression, sending the otherwise cheerful man into bouts of non-verbal communication. It was like a brightly lit light bulb suddenly being switched off in mid-sentence.

We did have an affair while I was trying to patch things up with Toby. As delightful as our sexual liaisons were there was a hidden missing element, YOU! Much like my liaisons with Oscar, without your presence, our sexual communications took on a different dynamic which only you as the missing link could resolve. There were times during or after sex when Ian would abuse himself with negative thoughts and self-denigration. I tried to console him, yet I was deeply sorrowed about my own unresolved issues with Toby. It was like the blind leading the blind.

I was gravely saddened when Ian took his own life. Heavily drugged on prescriptive anti-depressant and a stomach full of extensive alcohol consumption, he fell off his ten story apartment building. He died instantly. This was the straw that threw me into a nervous breakdown. Thank God I climbed out of my despondencies with the help of Ari and Aria.

My dearest Young, I have a confession to make; you are the only person I have truly loved and will continue to love. All these years I've tried to forget you but I cannot. That said I am not trying to pry you away from Walter and have you return to me.

We are just getting to know each other yet I feel your spirit has never left. Please make sure that Walter understands that I'm not jeopardizing your wonderful relationship. I am happy for the both of you. You had asked jokingly if I was interested in a triplet relationship. Maybe when the time and opportunity arises it may happen, but now I'm enjoying my own company after Albert's passing. In a way it is nice to have my freedom after 8 years of building a life with Albert.

I love you my darling boy and always will. As always, I await your cheerful emails.

Andy.

Xoxoxo

Part Six

The United Arab Emirates, Abu Dhabi,

The SEKHAM Household,

Makkah, Mecca.

71

Questions & Answers

*"Do not be too timid and squeamish about your actions.
All life is an experience."*
Ralph Waldo Emerson

1967 Back at the Sekham

Normal studies resumed with the Sekhem children and Gabrielli after our two weeks of whirlwind photographic escapades in the United States. On the SAQR returning from Los Angeles to Abu Dhabi, I managed to sneak in a few quiet hours to fill in the blank pages of my already bulging diary. So much had transpired since I set foot at the Sekham household. It was a struggle for me to jot down my numerous exciting adventures, but when I started writing in my journal, memories began flowing out of my head onto the pages. The abundance of snapshots and photographs taken both by me (with my automatic camera) and our professional photographers enabled me to document my experiences during my Harem years.

My time at the Sekham was fast drawing to a close. My two remaining weeks in Abu Dhabi flew by rapidly. We spent three of those 14 days following Sayid and his brother to Mecca for their Hajj. The grand finale to my Sekham experience was Jasim's wedding ceremony to Ria, his 10-year-old cousin.

That was when I learned of my next Arab Household assignment.

Oscar's Announcement

One evening, while Oscar, Devaj, Andy, and I were enjoying a private dinner at the Maktub, Oscar said, *"I have* news for all of you. I've been accepted into the University of Vienna. I start in the fall."

I was surprised to hear the news, since my lover had never mentioned that he was planning to leave so soon. I queried, astonished, "When did you enroll? You never told us you are going for graduate studies!"

"I wasn't sure if my grades were good enough to be accepted into the prestigious Medizinische Universität Wien (The Medical University of Vienna), so I kept from telling anyone. I didn't tell anybody except my Daltonbury and Bahriji student counselors. My parents have no idea either. I figured that if I didn't get accepted, no one would know I applied," he announced.

"Congratulations Oscar! As much as we'll miss you, this is a great university to pursue your medical studies. M.U.W. is one of the best medical universities in the world. Well done, old chap!" Andy wrapped his arm around my BB's shoulders, giving him a congratulatory hug.

As delighted as I was for Oscar, I was sad that my lover would be leaving us after our Sekham service, which would happen in a couple of weeks. As I threw my arms around my lover to congratulate him, I couldn't help tearing up like I did when Nikee left for Saint Andrew's University in Scotland. I knew my time with Oscar was drawing to a close. Like Nikee, the chances of seeing this 'big brother' again would be rare, but life moves on, even though I wanted our loving relationship to last.

Andy, seeing my tears, came over and the three of us hugged, holding tightly onto one another while Devaj observed us with a saddened heart. He, too, knew that he would miss his mentor and guardian.

Invitation

That evening, when Oscar came to join Andy and me after Devaj had retired for the evening, my Valet asked, "Oscar, we have use of the Kahyya'm and the Simorgh. Will you join us for a cruise around the Greek Islands during the summer holidays?"

My BB leaned towards me and planted a sweet kiss on my lips before responding, *"Of course I will. It'll be fun to tour the Greek islands with the both of you before I go to Vienna. When's the trip?"*

Andy turned towards me for a response. Looking blankly at my Valet, I muttered, *"As soon as I can get away from Malaya and the clutches of my father. I have to return home during early summer break. But I can always tell my parents I have to be back at Daltonbury Hall two weeks before term begins. I guess we can go the 2nd week in August?"*

"That works for me," my Valet replied.

"That's fine with me, too," Oscar seconded.

"Great. Now that we have made our holiday plans, I'll ask Dr. Henderson to consult the Hadrah to check if those dates are okay for us to use his plane and yacht. I'll do that tomorrow. Tonight, we'll make love like there is no tomorrow!"

"That sounds fabulous!" My BB expressed vehemently.

"I'm ready whenever you are!" I said with a happy ring in my voice. As the famous John Updike once said *"Sex is like money; too much is never enough."*

End June 2012

In response to Dr. Arius' questions for his research, I wrote:
Dr. A.S.,

As always it is a delight to receive your emails. I'll be more than happy to answer your questions. I'll respond to them one at a time. Please bear with me if my answers are lengthy at times. If I veer off into a tangent, please feel free to eliminate or edit my response. I'm eager to find out the results your research will yield when you are done with the survey. I'm ready to begin.

Question one:

* In **"Initiation,"** you said that as far as you can remember, even as a baby, you disliked your father. What was it that you didn't like about the man? Did he have a certain smell that repelled you or something conscious or subconscious that blocked your connection towards him?

Answers:

Although I cannot provide you with definitive answers, I'll do my best to remember how I felt when I was with my dad.

a) Mr. S.S. Foong was a heavy smoker since the day I was born. I presume as a baby, the cigarette smell on his person repelled me. His aggressively loud booming voice did nothing to my gentle ears, either. Although he never shouted at me when I was a child, his stern demeanor deterred me from wanting to be near him. Moreover, his angry reprimands toward his subordinates when they had done nothing wrong challenged my respect for the man I called Father.

b) Maybe unconsciously I was imbued with a glamorized portrayal of the "ideal" family from western magazines, movies, and periodicals of the mid-20th century. I wanted a father whom I could look up to: a strong, kind man who understands the needs of his family and children. But this was a Hollywood invention. It doesn't exist, or it exists empirically in a small sector of the global population.

c) Since my dad was seldom at home (he was with his mistress and their children), it was difficult to have a loving relationship with the man, especially when he roared and rebuked me for my effeminate behavior over which I had no control. I was simply being who I was. His negative criticisms damaged my ego badly.

d) I could not relate to his air of superiority toward my mother. I resented that aspect of my father. I swore to myself that I would not grow up to be like my old man.

Question two:

* Do you think your overly protective mother had an influence on you disliking your father?

Answers:

a) The answer to this 2nd question is a resounding 'Yes' and a reverberating 'No.' My mother was protective of me because she had nurtured a deep, strong relationship with me. She loved me for who I was and not for what she thought I ought to be. It was her unconditional love which drew me to her, whereas my dad never provided me the moral or psychological support I needed from an understanding and encouraging father.

b) I was afraid of Foong Senior and I saw him as a dictator, which did nothing to endear me to the man. He wanted me to change into a person I was not and never will be. I could never ever live up to the image he had for me. In my eyes, I would never be good enough to gain his approval.

c) On the other hand, my mother raised me to think for myself. Never did she coerce me not to be who I was. She nourished me and encouraged me to work on projects I loved and felt passionate about. On the contrary, my father tried to 'butch me up' into what he desired his sons to be. I was a victim of his own desires and I felt no urge to participate. I went to the sports-related activities solely to salivate on the handsome macho men who were often my tutors or fellow team mates.

Question three:

* When you were wearing pretty frocks and playing with dolls, did you feel less than a boy? How did you feel or react when you saw other boys playing with 'boyish' toys like miniature toy soldiers, train sets, etc.?

Answers:

a) No, I did not feel any less a boy when I was dressed in girls' clothes. I thought girls' garments were more creative and imaginative than boys'. In fact, I often wondered why boys' clothes were so boring and mundane compared to what my mother dressed me in.

b) Playing with dolls came naturally to me. It might be because, from the moment I opened my little eyes, I was surrounded by dolls. I did enjoy playing dress-up with my doll collection, especially the Barbies, which in later years I saved my own money to purchase.

Round about ages 5 or 6, I began taking a keen interest in designing Barbie dolls' clothes.

There were times in the middle of the night, after I went to bed when the house lights were off, I would shine a light under the sheets to begin the process of making and dressing my dolls. I enjoyed doing that when there was nobody to bother me and I had all the time needed to craft these feminine creations.

c) Train sets, toy soldiers or 'toys for boys' never interested me. They seemed too mechanical and bloodthirsty, fighting and killing each other all the time. These warlike sports were not to my liking. I don't understand why boys take great pride in killing, beating each other. Is that what being manly is about?

Question four:
* Did your mom try distancing you from your dad?
Answers:

a) I think the answer lies not in my mum trying to distance me from my father but in my dad distancing himself from his family. He was seldom at home, so I saw very little of him. When he was home, he was often temperamental; no one dared get close to him. I was afraid I would be the next victim. I choose to distance myself from my father without my mother having to do it for me.

There were numerous occasions when he would shout at our gardener for not trimming the dividing hedges between us and our neighbors, trimming them too low or trimming them too high. Ah Choi (the gardener) would be under fire, or if Bakar (our chauffeur) did not bring the car to the Porte Cochere fast enough, the Malay man would suffer the wrath of his tyrannical boss. This was the nature of my father; he endeared himself to very few of his employees.

Question five:
* What did your brothers think of your parents' relationship?
Answers:

a) Both my brothers were studying in England. They were out of sight and out of mind. They were having a ball of a time away from my parent's domestic squabbles. As far as I remember, they didn't care one way or other.

That was another reason I could not wait to leave my family in Malaya and be as far away from my dad as possible. I wanted to create my own life where nobody could or would tell me what I could or couldn't do.

As I mentioned in **Initiation**, I wished my parents had gotten a divorce and Mother had married Uncle James. That to me would have been the ideal solution to my parent's problems. Unfortunately, women from my mother's generation and social standing would think divorce to be an insurmountable decrepitude to a marriage, let alone to the welfare of their children. After all, in their marriage vows my parents promised each other, "till death do us part." My parents' generation takes pledges and oaths seriously.

Their staunch "gentleman's word of honor" probably influenced me in upholding my personal pledge of allegiance and oath of confidentially to the Enlightened Royal Oracle Society to this day.

Question six:

* Did you have any boy pals or friends when you were growing up? If not, why is that? Would you have grown up differently if you'd had guy friends?

Answers:

a) As far as I can remember, my main playmate was my cousin Pinky. Although I remember my mother's longtime friend and confidant, Yin Yee; her son, Tuck would come to visit and play with Pinky and me, but I was never as close to Tuck as I was to my female cousin. Tuck loved to climb trees and I didn't really care for those kinds of rugged, outdoorsy endeavors.

b) I was extremely protected when growing up due to my wealthy parents' social status; they were afraid I would be a likely candidate for kidnapping. I was always accompanied by either a family member or hired help before and after school hours.

Since I didn't care for any of the afterschool sporting activities that most of the boys my age seemed to delight in participating in, I preferred to be at home playing with my dolls and with Pinky, my playmate.

c) Most likely if I'd had guy friends, the pressure of having to hide my homosexual inklings would be a greater burden than I could have dealt with. I would most likely have been bullied by the 'straight' boys like KiWi and his gang of three, or I would have ended up pining for their forbidden sexual gratifications. That would have ended either in disasters or, as it did in the case with KiWi, with unsatisfactory sexual doom.

Well, dear Arius, I did my best to satisfy your questionnaires. It has been fun; please keep them coming.

Until I hear from you again, best wishes to you and your doggies.

Kind regards,

Young.

72

The Secret Hideaway

"Muslims have a very bad attitude toward homosexuality: they are very tolerant."
Pim Fortuyn

1967 To Makkah

After travelling an hour on the SAQR, we arrived at the holy city of Mecca, the capital of Makkah Province, Saudi Arabia. Mecca was the birthplace of the prophet Muhammad; it was also the site of the revelation of the Quran. Our entourage consisted of Aziz, Tahu, Gabrielli, Sayid, Jasim, Jul, Isa (both were the boys' uncles), Oscar, Devaj, Andy and me. After checking into our 5-star hotel, Aziz and Gabrielli suggested we explore the city. We wouldn't be going to the Masjid al-Haram, which housed the Kaaba ("The Cube", "The Primordial House", "The Sacred/Forbidden House"), until the following morning.

Although non-Muslims are prohibited from entering Mecca, the holy city, Wazir Thabit had made special provisions with the Makkah authorities to allow the foreigners among us enter. If any pilgrim questioned our presence, we were to inform them that we were Muslim converts, there for Hajj.

Aziz joined us, mostly to secretly scout for suitable locations for *"Sacred Sex In Sacred Places"*. He had already done Hajj several times prior to this trip. Gabrielli, on the other hand, was there to make sure that his foreign students were well guarded, since the Wazir had instructed him to watch over our well-being throughout this experience.

Education

As we toured the souks and marketplaces near the hotel, my teacher took the opportunity to explain Hajj to his students, including Sayid and Jasim.

"*Do you boys understand the significance of this pilgrimage?*" He asked as we gathered round him.

Tahu was the first to answer, "*We are here to perform Hajj and to assume Ihram,*" he said. Ihram, I later learned, is the sacred dress of Muslim pilgrims for pilgrimage or for other acts of worship, especially the daily worship. "*We are not to have sexual relations with our wives, commit sins, or conduct unfair disputes because Allah is sure to know.*"

Before he could continue, Isa spoke, "*Hajj is the perfection of one's faith. It combines both the physical and monetary aspects of worship in Islam; an example is the Salaat (prayer), which pilgrims offer in the Kaa'ba. Hajj also encourages the spending of material wealth for the sake of Allah, which is the chief characteristic of Zakaat (an annual tax on Muslims to aid the poor in the Muslim community). By spending our wealth, we cleanse our hearts from the greed of this world. Hajj also builds generosity and develops in us a willingness to sacrifice for Allah.*"

"Very good explanation, Isa," my teacher congratulated him.

Before Gabrielli could utter a word, Jul explained, "*When I set out for Hajj, I disassociate myself from my home and dear ones in favor of Allah. I suffer hardship and self-restraint, fast and perform Itikaaf,*" he referred to a particularly commended pious practice — a period of retreat in a mosque for a certain number of days in accordance with the believer's own wish.

"*I am also to forget my material comforts. I'm to avoid using scented oils and perfumes, wearing only my Ihram. I can't cut my hair and nails. I busy myself worshiping Allah and carrying out the rites of Hajj. In other words, I abandon all my worldly desires and submit to my Lord with Ikhlas (sincerity), Ittiba (obedience) and humility. I call out to Allah, 'Here I am before You, My Lord; I'm a slave for you.'"* As the man spoke these sentences, a sly sarcastic grin crept onto his face.

I was beginning to wonder whether he believed in those words. I gave him the benefit of the doubt.

Tahu added, *"You may or may not be aware that the physical demands of the various Hajj rites far surpass those of prayers and fasting, thus enhancing the patient pilgrim's self-control, obedience and humility, which are required for his daily Eebadah (worship).*

"Therefore Hajj develops a man's spiritual and moral goals, allowing a deeply spiritual transformation to take place within the individual and resulting in the reformation of his life according to Islamic ideals. There are certain pre-conditions before this act of pilgrimage becomes compulsory. I believe these are Islam, soundness of mind, puberty and capability."

Directing his attention to the foreign students, Gabrielli advised, *"Boys, you must understand that Hajj is not meant to be a hardship. It is an act of devotional worship Muslims perform, but only if it is feasible and affordable for them to make the journey."*

Andy asked, *"What do you mean by feasibility for them to make the journey?"*

"Feasibility includes having the physical health, financial well-being, and sufficient provision needed to undertake the Hajj. Hajj is not obligatory for one who does not possess adequate money to feed his children during his absence. If he has to borrow money, he stays at home until he is financially able. Muslims with physical disabilities are not obliged to make Hajj unless they can pay others to carry them.

"Hajj is also not obligatory even if the journey to Makkah exposes the Haji's (pilgrim's) life to risk. In addition, a woman should have a Mahram (escort), since she is not allowed to travel alone without a Mahram. Therefore, a woman who cannot find a Mahram to accompany her is not obliged to make Hajj." Gabrielli explained.

Sapiosexual

We had been wandering round the souq for an hour before we found an outdoor cafe to rest our feet. As we continued our chitter-chatter, Oscar burst forth with a comment. "Professor, I, for one, am a sapiosexual: I'm attracted to your incisive, insightful and irreverent mind. I'm completely mesmerized and aroused by your intelligent philosophical discussion of the Hajj. It's an intellectual foreplay and I can't help but go 'ouch' to your witty sense of explanation."

Andy, quick to second Oscar's announcement, said amusingly, "I agree with Oscar wholeheartedly. I too, dear professor, am also a true sapiosexual!"

"What's a sapiosexual?" I interrupted.

My lovers and my professor laughed before Andy replied, "You, my darling, will soon be initiated to become a sapiosexual under the guidance of your excellent teacher and mentors."

Our Arab friends looked at us with blank stares. They, like me, had no idea what a sapiosexual was.

To The Souk

Since the evening was young, Aziz, who had been to Makkah suggested, "Let's have some fun. I'm bored sitting at the cafe. I am going to treat you guys, especially my nephews, to a special place I know in this part of the world. Who wants to join me on this special excursion?"

Since we were all jibber-jabbering about nothing, we agreed to the photographer's secret outing. Aziz would not disclose its whereabouts. He wanted it to be a surprise and to astonish us.

We hopped into several taxis following Aziz's lead and arrived in an old section of town, some distance away from our hotel. Alighting at a night souq, we ventured into a labyrinth of stalls filled with hawkers, vendors and shops selling knickknacks and trinkets. I had no idea where we were heading. I was glad Andy, Oscar, and my teacher were next to me. If I had gotten separated in this busy souk, I would not have been able to find my way back to the hotel. Street vendors were shouting at the top of their lungs to attract buyers to their kiosks while shoppers were busy bargaining on their purchases, looking for excellent deals.

The Secret Hideaway

Turning a corner behind a Persian-carpet vendor's stall, Aziz led us into a hidden passageway. I would not have known that such a secret alley existed if not for the photographer's guidance. Down the long arched corridor we proceeded until we came to an obscure wooden entrance. The Arab knocked several times before a turbaned Bedouin came to answer the door. Opening it a crack, our host spoke Arabic to the guard before the man guided us into a dimly lit foyer.

It took me a few seconds to adjust to the light. To my surprise, I had stepped back in time, into a 19th-century Arabian decorated interior. On the ceiling hung an array of Persian lanterns that gave off soft, sensual glows of ruby reds, emerald greens, topaz yellows, turquoise blues, and tangerine oranges. Brocade cushions and ornately embroidered pillows lay scattered around the waiting room.

The guard told us to wait while he hurried off to summon the proprietor. Before long, an elegantly dressed Arabian in traditional garb came to greet our entourage. Since we foreign students did not speak a word of Arabic, we relied on our Arab friends and Gabrielli to conduct the communications. After much cordiality and friendly greetings with the toothy, grinning salon keeper, we were ushered to a quiet back room with a floor-to-ceiling double sided mirror installed on one side of the wall. Next to the comfortable floor cushions and pillows were hookah pipes, at the ready to entertain the customers while they waited for the "line-up" to assemble in the adjoining chamber.

Since the foreign students knew nothing of what was to happen, we sat still as our Arab companions giggled grinning from ear to ear. My curiosity got the better of me and I asked my professor, "What kind of a place is this? Where are we?"

Gabrielli shushed me to be quiet and gave me a wicked wink. He said nothing. By now, I was too inquisitive to be quiet. I turned to my Valet and BB and asked, "What are we waiting for? What's going to happen?"

Both my lovers shook their heads, indicating that they did not know what was happening. Since we had no clue, the only choice was to wait for all to be revealed.

June 2012

Dearest Andy,

You haven't changed much over the years. I'm glad we can continue to relate to each other after such a long absence. Times of change had not vanquished my love for you either. You are always in my heart and I'll continue to cherish your love wherever I am.

You haven't heard the last of Bernard – at one time, he arrived to visit me at Uncle James. I had no idea he was in London when he showed up one afternoon. I had been out running a couple of errands. As I was unlocking the front door, I felt a tap on my shoulder and Bernard was behind me, looking as handsome as when we parted in Belfast. He had grown taller and more mature during our absence.

In Ireland he had worked some odd jobs to earn enough money for a one-way plane ticket to London. The only person he knew in London was me. He knew I would not turn him away if he called. Uncle James was in Hong Kong and I was the only one staying in the house; I took the boy in, making him promise that he would have to leave when I moved in 3 weeks to my new lodgings in Ladbroke Grove. He did as promised and was a splendid house guest. When Uncle James returned a week before my move, he was charmed by the adolescent. Bernard made a good impression on Uncle James.

A Harem Boy's Saga IV: Unbridled

The boy had run away from Belfast and planned a fresh start in London. During the course of the 3 weeks, he successfully secured himself as a newspaper delivery boy in the mornings and also worked part-time in a Deli near the house. To top it off, five evenings a week he was a bus boy in an Italian restaurant. Both Uncle James and I were impressed by his industrious tenacity. James decided to help him obtain an apprenticeship with a professional photographer in Edinburgh, Scotland.

One sleepless night shortly after the boy's arrival, I was going through a tough time, missing you. Bernard heard my sobs and crept into my bed. We held each other close. I could not help but relish his intimacy and his warm body next to mine. Wrapping my arms around the boy, we were aroused by the passionate auras surrounding the both of us. As an experienced 'big brother' I took charge. I kissed his tender lips before planting soft kisses on his closed lids, and soon I was nibbling at his delicate earlobes. He groaned with pleasure, desiring to do the same to me. Before I knew it, we were taking turns caressing each other's nipples. Our seductive foreplay lasted for a long time until we could stave off our sexual urges no longer. He engulfed my manhood, licking, suckling and engorging mouthfuls of my rod. I could hold back no longer. Pressing his head against my crotch, I released my abundance into his orifice with forceful intensity. Yet he continued to nourish himself on my length; unwilling to relinquish his feed, he greedily guzzled the last drop of my seed down his yearning throat. His sensuality propelled me to share my lingering sustenance from his delectable tongue. We French kissed until we were drunk with the elixir of love.

His youthful beauty did not fail to arouse me to another bout of sexual vitality. As I flipped him on his stomach, he lifted his derriere to receive my pulsing organ. He hungered for my entry and I – I was deliriously ready to feed this angelic sprite with my protruding protraction. Gently and lovingly I submerged myself into his person, gyrating slowly to the rhythmic flow of our entangled bewilderment.

He opened willingly to my warmth as I plunged inside him, at times fast and furious and at others slow and gentle. In the process I ground his manhood onto the bed, coercing him into ecstatic moans before giving in to cries of whimpering ecstasies. My hand reached around his slender torso, working his hardness to the point of no return. He could not hold off any further. Jets of oozing cum shot onto my stroking palm. His sexiness sent my ejaculation spewing deep inside his opening as he swallowed my dripping seed between his pining fissures. He devoured his own seed from my fingers as I planted caresses on his amorous mouth, sharing every creamy bead of his milkiness between us.

He wanted me in him, like I did you, long after our tantalizing desires had subsided. Our friendship took on an intimate significance that night, which we shared over and over again during our time together before Bernard left for Scotland and I to my new dig.

Keep your news coming, Andy. Like you, I look forward to receiving your uplifting messages.

Love and kisses,
Young,
Xoxoxo

73

The Profane & The Profound

"The only way to get rid of a temptation is to yield to it. Resist it and your soul grows sick with longing for the things it has forbidden to itself."
Oscar Wilde

1967 At the Secret Hideout

We didn't have long to wait before a row of bright overhead lights lit the adjoining room to our otherwise dimly lit ambiance chamber. We saw a line-up of a dozen scantily dressed females. Some were bare-breasted, covered modestly with their long, flowing locks. The bright lights blinded the girls' eyes for a second, as if they had come without warning. Although they could not see our entourage, we saw them clearly through the large double sided mirrors. Our grinning proprietor was busy chatting with our Arab companions. Not understanding a word of Arabic, I could only decipher by his hand gestures that he was explaining each females' assets to our Saudi friends. Obviously our companions were deciding on their picks for the evening. Jul and Aziz selected five girls to accompany them.

Through an intercom, Abdullah, our host, announced the selected girls' names. As rapidly as the twelve girls had appeared, the rejects left the room in a hurry, disappearing through a curtained side exit as if dismissed by their director from their role call. Two burly Bedouin males stood guard in the women's room. Three male musicians took their places at a corner and began playing their musical instruments while each woman took center stage one at a time. They began their sensual belly dances for their unseen audience. The women had no idea for whom they danced. As their dancing progressed, the few items of clothing left were soon discarded, revealing their vernal forms to our salivating Arab assemblage. Grinding and gyrating to the rhythmic sound of the drumming, these women seemed lost in a trance. The Arabians in our entourage were getting hornier and hornier by the second as they watched the performing prostitutes.

Jul was the first to name a price, informing our host of his picks. Abdullah happily told the chosen females to proceed immediately to one of the upstairs chambers to entertain their distinguished guest.

Isa and Tahu each chose one woman while Aziz, accompanied by Sayid, disappeared into a chamber with three females. Aziz had intended for Jasim to join them but he wanted to stay with Andy, Oscar, and me. After our companions had vanished, the toothily grinning owner turned to us and addressed us in broken English, *"You no like woman for sex?"* Not knowing that Gabrielli could speak fluent Arabic, he continued, *"You like boys? We got boys. You want see boy sex?"* He inquired, as if it was an everyday occurrence for him to play the role of a match-maker.

The Best Whorehouse this side of Mecca

Oscar was the first to reply, *"Thank you very much. We are good. We'll wait here for our friends to finish, if it's alright with you?"*

Gabrielli answered in Arabic, which came as a surprise to the brothel owner. My teacher spoke. *"We didn't know our companion Aziz was bringing us here. We are here for hajj. If I had known, I would have stayed in our hotel and let them come by themselves."*

The innkeeper answered in Arabic, *"No worries! While you are here, you should have fun! Most of our customers are here for their pilgrimage. You can obey the laws of Allah, not to have sexual intercourse with your wives during hajj. But the law doesn't say you cannot copulate with other women or boys!*

"*Besides, it's after sundown. Fast is broken; eat, drink, and be merry, my friend. There is always time to be pious the following day at the Masjid. Meanwhile after sunset you can be sanctimonious at my establishment. Relax, enjoy, and have a good time. Isn't that what life is about?*"

"*I've nothing against our friends having a good time but we are pretty happy to wait for them to finish their business. Maybe we'll take a walk to the souk for some beverages,*" suggested my professor.

Before we had a chance to leave, the friendly proprietor continued, "*How about this young man here?*" He directed his gaze at Jasim. "*Doesn't he want to have some man-woman or boy-boy experience?*"

The Italian replied on his student's behalf, "*This young man is getting married in a week. He is betrothed to his cousin Ria.*"

Before Gabrielli could continue further, the Arab interjected, "*Oh! More reason for him to have his experience here before his wedding night. Here is the perfect opportunity for him to sow some wild oats, so he'll know what to do with his soon-to-be wife.*

"*Our girls will be delighted to teach him some tricks. Would he like to give them a try?*" He was obviously hoping to coerce Jasim into being one of his clients.

My teacher asked Jasim, "*What would you like to do? Do you want to stay with your uncles or go with us?*"

Jasim thought for a while before replying in Arabic, "*I'd like to see what the boys look like.*"

Abdullah said laughingly, "*That can be arranged, young man. Give me a moment to gather our batchas (dancing boys) so you can take your pick. They are here for your enjoyment.*"

We had little choice but to wait for Jasim. Personally, I was curious to see what sort of boys this establishment offered. Before long, the lights in the adjoining room came on bright and a group of ten boys had lined up in a row. They ranged from twinkie-looking adolescents to older teenagers. To my discerning eyes, they appeared unkempt and rough around the edges. I couldn't help leaning against Andy as I whispered, *"They certainly don't look anything like the Bahriji boys or girls that we know."*

Gabrielli heard my comment and spoke softly into my ear, *"No! They certainly don't. I'll fill you in on their status when we leave this place."*

We waited for Jasim's decision as he scanned the line-up. It didn't take him long to shake his head with the answer 'No.' The Arab continued trying to persuade the adolescent to hire a boy for a trial run, but the adolescent had made up his mind. He was going with us to the souk.

The Profane & the Profound

As soon as we set foot outside the main entrance, I found myself back in the hustling and bustling marketplace. Looking aimlessly at the various stalls, I fell in step with my teacher. I couldn't help but ask, *"Professor, you said you would fill me in about the batchas when we were out of the inn. What are you going to tell me?"*

"Let's find a café and we can talk over a cup of Arabian coffee."

After we ordered our beverages at a nearby coffee shop, Gabrielli turned to Jasim and asked, *"Jasim, why did you not pick a batcha for some fun?"*

"I don't need to have fun with the batchas in that place. They don't look clean and they are not as good-looking as Andy, Oscar, Devaj, and Young. I already have the best teachers here to teach me."

Our educator smiled and gave Jasim a pat on his head before shaking his head sadly and saying, *"I feel sorry for those girls and boys working in the brothel. Most of them are runaways or kids who were captured and sold as sex workers to these kinds of secret brothels. They are often abused by their owners and work for pittance. They are the unfortunate products of human traffickers."*

Andy and Oscar looked shocked by the professor's information. Oscar enquired, "How do you know they were the products of human traffickers?"

"Oscar, if you observe them closely, they have a sad, frightened look on their faces. The majority of them are smuggled into the Emirates from third world countries like the Philippines, Thailand, India, and other neighboring countries. These poor souls are from destitute families who couldn't afford to keep them. In order to survive, their uneducated parents are forced to sell their children to sex traders, hoping that they will have sufficient food. It's a way out of poverty for their children. More often than not, these youngsters end up worse off than their parents had anticipated."

Andy asked eagerly, "Why doesn't the local government clamp down on such atrocities?"

"As much as the government has the best of intentions, there are those in authority who are as corrupt as the human traffickers. It is a case of the profane verses the profound. As is often the case, powerful people here in the Emirates live double lives. On the surface, they portray themselves as Allah-fearing devotees, but in the secular world they operate with their own set of values.

"Due to the intensity of the gender segregation, men and women seldom have opportunities to meet each other to bond in any form of platonic or intimate relationships before marriage. You boys are well aware that "normal" males and females require regular sexual releases; it's especially so for hot blooded Arab males. The only release they have without being frowned upon is either to visit a secret brothel or have 'Bacha Bazi' ('boy play' or 'playing with boys') with an adolescent, which is an accepted Arabian tradition.

"During Ramadan and Hajj, devotees are to refrain from sex with anyone, let alone their wife or wives. How then do you expect virile males like our Arab friends to restrain their natural bodily functions? They must defile their strict religious laws and go underground to perform that which is in every person's inherent DNA."

We were beginning to understand the truth. Yet I couldn't resist asking, "It is one thing to have the right to consensual intercourse but quite another for human trafficking to exist. This is 1967; we are not living in the dark ages anymore."

"Young, you are right to bring up this issue. As Wazir Thabit's business partner, I have been trying to convince him to work on a legislature to curb this act of inhumanity. It is not an easy process and he has encountered many obstacles along the way with fellow government officials. Hopefully, human rights laws will one day stop this egregious monstrosity."

It had been close to an hour and half since we left the whorehouse. We were ready to reunite with our Arab friends and to return to our comfortable 5-star hotel for a good night's rest. We had to be up at the crack of dawn to be physically and spiritually prepared for an active day at the Masjid al-Haram.

Last week of June 2012

The next set of questionnaires arrived from Dr. Arius sooner than I had anticipated. The good doctor inquired:

Dear Young,

Thank you for being honest, truthful and straight to the point with your answers. I appreciate you taking the time to respond to my queries. Here's the next set of questions for you to ponder.

* How did you react when you were in your father's presence?

* Did you get to meet or know his mistress Annie? If so, how did you find her as a person? Was she the kind of woman that your aunties said she was? How was your rapport with her and vice versa?

* Did you ever try to resolve your differences with your dad in later years?

* How did you feel when you entered Daltonbury Hall? Was your life in Malaya very different from your life in England? How did you cope when you first arrived in the United Kingdom?

* What were your reactions when you were suddenly assigned to a good-looking and understanding 'big brother'? During your early

days at the boarding school, did you open up immediately to your 'big brother' Nikee or to other 'big brothers' in your House?

* Were you unreserved by nature or was it a learned trait?

As always, I enjoy our regular correspondence. I feel like I already know you even though we have not met. I hope one day, in the not-too-distant future, I'll have the opportunity to talk with you in person.

Take excellent care of your good self.
Best Wishes!
Love,
A. S.

74

The Pilgrimage

"Motives and purposes are in the brain and heart of man.
Consequences are in the world of fact."
Henry Geaye

Early July 2012

Young,

    I started reading your blog, "Life Of A Harem Boy," and it brought back memories of our time together. As much as I am not in favor of you writing about our E.R.O.S. experiences, I applaud your bravery and the honest approach in your stories. Your courage to tell all has somehow convinced me to add my point of view to our adventures together. My dear, you sure have cogent ways of softening my stances in providing credence to your narrations. One thing I'm glad you didn't do is tell your story as an exposé to discredit the positive experiences of our clandestine society, of the people involved and the schools we attended. For this I laud you.

    If you are open to my retelling of your stories through my experiences, we may at some point arrive at a juncture where we can be co-authors in one book of your Harem Boy series. This collaboration will provide further credibility to our escapades. I'd be happy to team up with you if you are open to me being a co-writer of one of your 5 books. Since I am semi-retired and have time to kill, it will be an excellent opportunity for me to recount part of my life story in conjunction with you. In many ways, I am glad we reconnected. Maybe the time is ripe for us to work on a joint project (which we had the intention of doing many years ago). Do you remember how we discussed a collaboration but never got around to it? This may be the perfect project. We can tell a similar story from different angles and points of view. I think we'll also be able to rekindle our friendship more deeply. Let me know your thoughts.

1967 Masjid Haram Sharief

We arrived at the Al-Haram Mosque, also known to Muslims as Mecca's Haram Sharief. Besides being the largest and most popular mosque in the world, it is also the holiest and the main destination for Hajj pilgrims. This massive structure covers an area of 356,800 square meters, and it accommodates close to 820,000 worshippers during Hajj. The Masjid al-Haram ("Holy Mosque") is the only mosque in the world that has no qibla direction, since Muslims pray facing the Kaa'ba in the central courtyard.

Nestled among the mountain passes of central western Arabia, fifty miles inland from the Red Sea, lies Mecca, or *makkat al mukarrama* (the honored Mecca). Imbued with holiness before the rise of Islam, *al-haram al makki* (The Holy Site of Mecca) has served as the most sacred congregational place for the Arabian Peninsula tribes since the erection of the Kaa'ba. According to Islamic tradition, God commissioned Ibrahim (Abraham) with the help of his son Isma'il (Ishmael) to build an edifice (the Kaa'ba), where people would gather to worship only HIM. Allah, the Exalted ordered Ibraheem (alaihis-salaam) to build 'the Cube,' calling the faithful to walk around it, to stand up or to bow down to make prostration (in prayer) to the one and only Almighty.

Whoever performs Hajj is required to worship Allah sincerely and to seek His help, forgiveness, and Taqwa (the Islamic concept of self-awareness, which in a broad sense involves thankfulness and respect for God and his creation).

The VIP Enclosure

As our vehicles drew close, huge crowds of worshippers were already lining the entrances to the complex. Aziz, who had performed the hajj several times, advised us to alight and walk to this massive structure. I was beginning to wonder how in the world we would get in through the guarded gates if we had to queue behind the thousands of pilgrims waiting to gain entry.

Needless to say, privileges were secretly granted to society's wealthy and elite. Although hajj was meant for all worshippers to be equal in their pursuit of godliness, the powerful and the well-connected still have priority on earth.

Aziz ushered us towards an obscure doorway guarded by security personnel. After a brief conversation in Arabic, we passed through the entrance without any hassle or fanfare. Once inside, another guard, who had been instructed by the masjid officials of our imminent arrival, led us through a series of private staircases leading to a private balcony overlooking "The Primordial House." Much like a royal box in a performance theatre or a stadium, this esoteric space was allocated for our use the entire time we were at Al-Haram. It had been specially designated for our entourage, so that we could rest our tired feet when we needed to get away from the maddening crowd.

I was later told by my professor that this was one of several 'royal' enclosures designated for Hajj VIPs for rest and recuperation after circling around the Kaa'ba numerous times in devotional prayers.

The Hajj

After our Arab friends had changed into their Ihram (the sacred dress of Muslim pilgrims), an attendant who had been allocated specially to our booth proceeded to give our Muslim pilgrims a prep talk on the true journey of Hajj, which Gabrielli later translated into English as a lesson for us foreign visitors.

The attendant began, "Dear Hajis (pilgrims), this journey should act as a reminder to you that our life in this world is temporary and that we will sooner or later return to Allah. Then will he judge our deeds. Our life in this world is misleading; remind yourself that it is our Afterlife that's everlasting and permanent. Every soul will taste death. Millions have come before us and not one body lived longer than its appointed time. But a soul will live beyond the body. Therefore perform good deeds, O Haji, and may you meet Allah laden with good deeds. Our time on this earth is short. Our prophet Muhammad was not the first of prophets but he (peace be upon him) was the last of all prophets. He showed us a sign of the Final Day.

Let the Hajj be an avenue of self-examination. Renew your allegiance to the Book of Allah and the Sunnah of His Prophet (peace be upon him). O Hajis, we are currently going through trials and tribulations. Our Islamic faith is being tested. We are called upon to abandon our beliefs and our worship, and an ever-changing immoral lifestyle with man-made laws is being promoted as an attractive replacement for the laws of our Creator. For sure, Islam – Allah's religion – will not be affected, but our faith and our destiny could be affected if we do not hold firm to the Book of Allah and the Sunnah of Prophet Muhammad (peace be upon him)."

He continued, "Allah says: 'It is not for a believer when Allah and His Messenger have decreed a matter that they (the followers of Islam) should have any option in their decision. And whoever disobeys Allah and His Messenger, he has indeed strayed in a plain error.' (Qur'an, 33:36)

"Therefore be pleased and submit to the message that Allah and His Messenger have advised, for that is Islam and Islam will be victorious. Lastly O Haji, make lots of Du'a (invocation) for yourself, for your relatives, and for the Muslim Ummah (nation or community) worldwide. Ask Allah to guide all Muslims to the path of righteousness and bring glory to them. When you, Insha Allah (God willing), return, spend your time seeking Islamic knowledge, practicing it, and calling people towards it. This is the path to success."

After his announcements, he led the hajis downstairs to begin their pilgrimage around the kaa'ba while we waited in comfort for their return. I couldn't help but take photographs of this once-in-a-lifetime experience.

Chance Encounter

Aziz was the first to return after disappearing for not too long. In tow, he came with a couple of friends he had encountered while walking round the kaa'ba. After introducing Najib and Ismile to us, Aziz said excitedly, *"I haven't seen the two of you since Islamic school. What are the both of you doing these days?"*

"It's great to see you too, Aziz. As you know, Ismail and I were inseparable at school. I'm attending law school at the University of Pennsylvania and this one," he indicated Ismile, *"is working on his graduate studies in dentistry. We decided to come for hajj on our 23rd birthdays. What are you up to, Aziz?"*

"As you both are aware, my passion is photography and that is what I'm doing these days. I'm working on a special project with these boys here."

Ismile inquired, *"That's great! Let's get together this evening and catch up on news. We haven't seen each other for nearly three years.*

"I know a great place we can rest and relax after our full day of paying homage to the Almighty. Shall we meet for dinner and proceed to this exclusive venue?"

"Sure! What a great idea!" Aziz exclaimed delightedly. *"For now, I'll let you guys return to your pious activities. We'll see you at seven this evening at my hotel."*

First Week of July 2012

After taking a few days to review Dr. Arius' second set of questions, I replied the good doctor:

A Harem Boy's Saga JV: Unbridled

Good day Dr. A.S.

As always, I'm delighted to receive your correspondence and I'm more than happy to answer your new questionnaire;

You asked how I reacted in my father's presence:

Not too well, I'm afraid. I could never fully be myself in his company. He struck terror within me that I could not fully comprehend, even though I was never abused. It was probably his domineering manner and booming tone of voice that frightened me. I did not know how to act when he was around. I became a timid boy in the presence of a fire-spewing dragon. I'd rather hide than face what I considered at the time to be a monster of a man.

There were times when he drove me to the Methodist Boys School and I had to sit next to him. I would ease myself to the passenger door, desperately trying to avoid eye contact with the man. One day he said to me, "Yoong, why are you so afraid of me? Am I really that frightening?"

I wanted to say yes, he was, but I did not utter a word. He continued, "Son, you are either very stupid or you are a quiet creative powerhouse in the process of becoming a genius. I don't understand you."

I was too scared to answer. I sat quietly throughout the entire journey while he babbled on, mainly about nothing.

In response to your second question, whether I met or know Annie, his mistress – the answer is yes. There were a couple of times when father assigned Annie the task of driving me to school (when mother was not in our house). The lady was as friendly as she could be. I did get to know her and she didn't come across in the way that my aunties and cousins described her. She was quite pleasant to talk with, but I didn't feel the need to build any solid rapport with her because I did not want to upset my mother by being too chummy with the woman who had brought her many heartaches and discontentment.

In answer to your third question, whether I ever tried to resolve my differences with my dad in later years:

I'm afraid the answer is no. I was simply thankful that my dad and I were finally oceans apart. The one thing I'm forever grateful to my father for: he provided me an education that forever changed the course of my life. For this I am truly appreciative of Foong Senior.

How did I feel when I entered Daltonbury Hall?

I was excited, elated and filled with anticipation to be in England. This was a country wherein I had wanted to be located since I was six years of age. As a teenager, I was fearless and dying to explore new, uncharted territories. Daltonbury Hall was precisely the relief I craved after my Methodist Boys' School bullying experiences. To have a handsome, caring 'big brother' twenty-four seven as my guardian was a dream come true for this gay boy.

Was my life in Malaya very different from England?

Very much so! To me, England was a completely different planet. I felt as if I had landed on the Moon. Instead of a planet filled with ugly rocks, it was a planet filled with good-looking boys (especially those I came in contact with as I was secretly groomed to enter E.R.O.S.). The boys I befriended were well-mannered and aristocratic in more ways than just being born into wealthy homes.

E.R.O.S. selected candidates that had a certain je ne sais quoi about them. That made a big difference to me; they weren't like the 'regular' boys I encountered at the Methodist Boys School in Malaysia.

You asked how I coped when I first arrived in the United Kingdom.

I was homesick for the first few weeks but I adjusted to my new environment quickly. Daltonbury Hall provided me with a fresh start, a new life. A life I was happy to leave behind when I left Kuala Lumpur. Everything was exciting, even at times when I was uncertain about my capabilities in my studies. The 'big brothers' were always available to assist, to comfort and encourage the freshmen and juniors when we faced difficulties in our educational and private lives.

In my opinion, the BB and BS program should be installed in regular schools. I believe this will eliminate the current dysfunctional school system and reduce school bullying as well as suicidal behavior in students. More often than not, adolescent boys look to an older and more experienced guardian for guidance and mentorship. I blossomed under Nikee, Andy, and Oscar's tutelage.

What was my reaction when I was suddenly assigned a good-looking and understanding 'big brother'? During my early days at the boarding school, did I open up immediately to my 'big brother' Nikee or to other 'big brothers' in my House?

I was like a fish swimming happily in water. I took to my 'big brother' Nikee like I had discovered gold in a hidden treasure trove. All the 'big brothers' had undergone special educational training before being assigned to a 'little brother'. They were trained in the art of listening to the needs of their charges. Even for the BBs that were not E.R.O.S. members, the boarding school had training programs for 'regular' students who wanted to mentor the juniors following in their footsteps. All BBs and BSs (in our sister schools) had been through a one-year mentorship training program before becoming BBs and BSs.

Therefore, whenever I had a problem and I needed advice, I was able to go to any BB of my choosing and confide to him. Most boys tended to disclose their quandaries to their allocated BBs because they seemed to understand us best.

The answer to your last question, was I unreserved by nature or was it a learned trait?

The answer is both. As much as I am a happy-go-lucky person, I also learned many methods and techniques to come out of my shell. Daltonbury Hall, Bahriji and E.R.O.S. turned me, in part, into the person I am today. This valuable training helped me pursue my dreams through the art of positive human relations. This is one of the main objectives of the Enlightened Royal Oracle Society: to be responsible citizens of the world.

Dr. Arius, I'm ready for your next installment of queries. Keep them coming.

With love and affection,
Young.

75

The Hammam

"The big difference between sex for money and sex for free is that sex for money usually costs a lot less."
Brendan Francis

1967 Najib & Ismile

True to their words, Najib and Ismile arrived at 7 P.M. at our 5-star hotel. Although their conversation flirted between Arabic and English, I soon learned that Aziz's friends were a gay couple. They had been together for five years since Islamic school in Abu Dhabi. They had enrolled at the University of Pennsylvania and were accepted into the law and dentistry department simultaneously. As far as their family members and religious leaders knew, they were platonic friends. It is officially proclaimed by the U.A.E. that there are "no" homosexuals in any of the Middle Eastern countries. Little did they know that these two best of friends were lovers!

Those who knew them knew they were inseparable. *"They're like Siamese twins,"* they would often comment. If they saw Najib without Ismile or vice-versa, they'd ask, *"Where's your missing half?"* Unlike today, when gays are widely accepted, in 1967 homosexuals lived a hidden existence. Homosexuality was kept underground, especially in ultra-conservative Islamic countries like the United Arab Emirates. It came as no surprise that the exclusive venue Najib and Ismile took us to was a clandestine destination frequented by closeted homosexuals. Only people who were in-the-know and part of the 'club' knew the places to go to meet other like-minded individuals.

The Hammam

Located on a side street a block from the infamous Masjid al-Haram was an obscure doorway. Above it, an inscription in Arabic calligraphy read, *"Hammam"*. When translated into English it means, "Spreader of Warmth".

Najib knocked five times on the wooden door before a pair of eyes appeared behind a small cubicle opening. The eyes surveyed our entourage before handing Najib a piece of paper and pen to write his secret Arabic password. If the password matched the club member's identity, entry was allowed. Not surprisingly, we gained entry after Najib's first try. He had gotten the password from a fellow homosexual friend who frequented this establishment.

Each of us had to sign our names in their guest book before paying the entrance fees. An adolescent Abd led the visitors to an upstairs changing room, where rows of lockers were situated. Individual lockers were supplied for us to store our clothes and valuables. Clean towels were located in each locker or at the changing room shelves.

Tellaks

An individual 'Tellak' (bathing attendant) was assigned to each of us. These boys looked cleaner, better-groomed and better-mannered than the ones I encountered at the brothel the evening before. Since the time of the Ottoman Empire, tellaks had played an important role in bath houses. Traditionally, they were adolescent boys recruited from the ranks of non-Muslim subjects from the vast Turkish Empire. Their function was blatantly sexual, serving their male customers in various ways. Supposedly, this tradition died upon the modernization of the Arab nations, but during the reign of the Ottoman

Empire, this was an acceptable form of service at any Turkish baths. While sodomy was forbidden by Islamic law, other types of homoerotic relationships were not. Tellaks were not slaves; on the contrary, they were paid well for their services and in some cases these good-looking boys formed close bonds with their customers. Tellaks were also tax exempted.

Our tellaks also acted as our personal attendants and guides, introducing us newcomers to the establishment and showing us the facilities. They stood quietly next to us while we stripped down, and they handed us towels to wrap round our waists. Much like an Abd, they assisted us in folding, hanging our clothes, and storing our shoes into our allotted lockers. They then handed us identical locker keys; they kept one key and we the other. If anything was reported stolen by the customer to management, the assigned tellack would have to answer for it. These boys were chosen for their honesty and trustworthiness. Therefore, at the end of each visit, their respective clients would reward them handsomely for their impeccable services.

Social Chat Rooms

Like the Roman baths, the hammam was also a place to socialize. In this case, this hammam provided a comfortable venue for Aziz to catch up on news with his friends. After we changed, our 13-man entourage split into smaller groups to explore this expansive space to our individual inclinations. Ismile, Najib, Aziz and Sayid (Aziz's favorite nephew) headed to the cafe lounge where nonalcoholic beverages and light desserts were served. A generously sized seating area allowed customers to talk without disturbance while their tellaks stood some distance away in case "other" services were required by their clients when they grew weary of conversations with their friends. Curtained private cubicles were located nearby the chat room.

Isa, Tahu, Jul and Jasim went in the direction of the dining room. They obviously wanted to fill their rumbling stomachs after not having eaten the entire day. It was time to break fast, and this they did at the scrumptious buffet table, laid out with all kinds of Middle Eastern edible goodies; they satisfied their hungry tummies before an evening of wanton sexual debauchery.

Oscar, Devaj, Andy, my teacher, and I gravitated towards the cascading swirl pool to cleanse our perspiring bodies after our day under the hot Arabian sun. Although our VIP enclosure was air-conditioned, as soon as we stepped out into the open, we fried.

As we relaxed, Gabrielli said, *"Did you know that Muhammad believed that the heat of the hammam enhanced fertility so Muslims could multiply?"*

Oscar laughed at the comment, *"What makes you think that, professor?"*

In all seriousness, my teacher replied, *"Until the hammam caught Mohammad's fancy, Arabs used only cold water and never bathed in tubs, which they considered bathing in one's own filth. But when the conquering Arabs encountered Roman and Greek baths, Islam's holy men adopted the pleasure of hot air bathing, perhaps to compensate for the joys of alcohol forbidden by their religion.*

"As Arabians picked up the foreign bathing habits, they tailored them to their ways and hammams gained religious significance; each became a kind of annex to the mosque. Did you know they used bathing to comply with the Islamic laws of hygiene and purification? Physical and intellectual developments were deemphasized, allowing only massage services to remain."

Andy asked amusingly, *"Not in this hammam. I don't see any signs of physical or intellectual developments being deemphasized. Quite the contrary, our tellaks are standing by to assist us physically and intellectually, to some extent, as we speak."*

"Andy, Andy, Andy, as you are fully aware, this is a secret homosexual establishment and not a run-of-the-mill hammam. Regular Islamic bath houses are very much a part of a town's social life and are frequented by the wealthy, who often own private baths. Traditionally, they chose public bathing to show the town's folks they were clean. Although baths were usually built under the auspices of mosques or the government, they were often constructed by wealthy individuals as a status symbol and as an outward sign of their devotion to Allah. To them, building a hammam was a venture that pleased The Almighty as well as the people. The rich elite heeded the advice of a certain Yusuf B. 'Abdalhadi, an early Arab writer, who wrote, 'Whoever has committed many sins should build a bath as penance.'

Our learned professor continued, "The oldest hammams were those of the Camayyad caliphs who subscribed to a semi-Bedouin way of life, despised the regularity of towns, and preferred nomadic life in the desert. Consequently, the first hammams were erected outside the cities, often in the wilderness. One of the oldest baths, the Kusair'Aman, rose unexpectedly from the flat, barren plain near the Dead Sea.

"As the Islamic faith spread, so did the hammams. Conquered temples, churches, and baths were often converted into bath houses."

I was curious to know what other facilities hammams offered, so I asked, "What other services do hammams provide besides bathing and sex?"

Gabrielli proceeded to give his students another Middle Eastern lesson. He replied, "The baths were always one of the few places open to everyone from early morning to late at night, and sometimes until dawn. You could visit the barber here, too. He shaved faces, cut hair, let blood, and, like the tellak, massaged and washed bodies. An important task of the barber was scrubbing the soles of bathers' feet to remove callouses. It was believed that de-calloused feet not only allowed bad vapors to escape but also drove away migraine headaches. When the bather stood, fatigue and other undesirables flowed down and out through their feet. Barbers were privy to town and travel talk and were the hub of news and gossip.

"Aside from treating oneself to the pleasure of bathing and chatting, people went to the hammam for religious cleansing. Before donning new clothes, after a long journey, convalescence, or recent releases from prisons...these were good times to clean up and check in with Allah." Our professor lectured while enjoying the water tumbling above his head.

Devaj asked, "Is it clean to have so many people bathe in the same water?"

The Italian found this question amusing. He said laughingly, "Order and cleanliness are essential to any hammam, and certain rules and regulations are enforced by law. Health inspectors are assigned the task of making sure that the baths are washed frequently, which entails scrubbing the stone surfaces to remove dirt and slippery traces of soap. The inspectors also check the water quality. Aside from cleaning the place, the tellaks and attendants burn incense daily for purification. Hammams are required to be fully prepared before dawn so people can bathe before Morning Prayers.

He added, "Massage attendants rub their hands with pomegranate peel to harden them and give them a pleasant scent. Attendants also make sure no beans or peas were eaten in the hammam and no lepers were allowed in. Not only are hammams pleasurable, but an old adage claims that they bring good luck: 'Whoever goes to the bath on forty consecutive Wednesdays will succeed at anything they do.'"

Since we had hardly eaten throughout the day as no food had been served at or near the mosque, our famished group headed towards the enticing buffet table, where Isa, Tahu, Jul and Jasim had had their fill and had left in search of their own alluring adventures.

Ginn, The Spirit of The Hamman

According to Islamic lore, the Ginns are spirits who dwell in the water of springs and in the darkness of caves. They find the damp darkness of the hammam ideal. And what does one do when one encounters the Ginn? Etiquette is provided in the Figh (Islamic law). One should speak the Balmala, which is an invocation that means "In the name of Allah." The Ginn should leave after hearing these words, but if he doesn't, one is urged to postpone one's visit. Otherwise, the Ginn might slap the visitor in the face, which will either render the visitor's voice useless or dislocate his jaw.

I found my first Ginn after my ambrosial dinner. Andy and I went exploring while Oscar and Vaj made their way to the massage rooms. We entered a dimly lit heated steam room. I could hardly see my way before a seductive hand reached to grope my groin. Thinking the hand belonged to my beloved Valet, I whispered, *"I can barely see anything in this darkness. What are you doing?"*

No reply. Another hand reached to fondle my sensitive nipples, causing my libido to stir under the arousing titillation. I reached for Andy, instead I felt a hairy chest against my palm. Before I could back away, a towering figure loomed in front, yet I could not see who this mysterious person was. This steam was too thick for me to make out anything. My heart thumped rapidly after I had heard Gabrielli's tale of the malevolent Ginn. My mind began to spin fantastical tales of an ugly, pernicious spirit molesting me while hitting me in the face, rendering me speechless before dislocating my jaw. I struggled under the pair of forceful hands, but a tongue had plunged into my mouth, keeping me from crying out for help. Pinned against the hot, slippery wall, I had little choice but to surrender to the man's fervent kisses. His longing tongue pried opens my oral orifice, demanding my reciprocation. Surprisingly, his luscious lips tasted peevishly sweet and his pressing kisses were those of a youthful vaquero. Yet my disquieting mind beseeched me to utter the 'Balmala,' which my teacher had taught me if by chance I encountered an evil Ginn. As much as I wanted to call out the invocation – "In the name of Allah," I also longed for his passionate kisses not to leave my heaving orifice.

Having also been advised by the professor that not all Ginns were malicious, there are those who show themselves to be benevolent. These phantoms would recite love poems in the visitors' ears. Could this be a lovey-dovey spirit I had chanced upon? Was this one of those rare eidolons of which Gabrielli had spoken so eloquently? I decided to give him a try.

I relinquished control and allowed this 'Ginn' permissible access to my sinewy frame. His masculine mischievousness was too overpowering for my resistance. Before long, I had subdued my irrational thoughts and succumbed to the manly phantom eating and licking at my squirming neck. His sensual foreplay was too tantalizing. I did not want this sensuality to end so soon. He thrust me against a wall before lifting my legs round his waist to gain access into my tenderness. In a forceful stroke, he entered me. The natural steaminess had opened me sufficiently without causing any discomfort or pain. Besides, his persuasive amorality provided more than sufficient erotic stimulation, satisfying my indecisiveness and giving way to an affirmative desire, which I surrendered to surreptitiously.

His strong, piercing ferocity brought me to a point of no return. I spewed all over my belly as my intruder pounded incessantly into my tenderness even after my rapacity had subsided. He continued his ravenous sexuality until my hardness grew once more under my captor's capricious onslaught. He desired me in every way and I, I was his willing accomplice in his every wish. His carnal prowess was too captivating for my defiance. I did not want him to stop, but he could hold off his urgency no longer. I knew he was ready when his heaving foray gave way to grunts and triumphant groans. Pushing my buttocks against him, he unloaded, planting his abundance deep inside my compliant perforation. Burying his handsome face against my youthful chest, he plunged a final kiss into my yielding mouth. Unmistakably, this sexy 'Ginn' with a heavy after-five shadow revealed Najib's identity. To this man I would gladly offer myself, if and when he was ready for another round of licentious copulation. It happened several months later at P's palatial residence.

76

Missing You, Missing Me

"Sometimes when one person is missing, the whole world seems depopulated."
Bernard Tristan Foong

Early July 2012

In one of my email response to Andy, I wrote:
Hi beloved ex-Valet,
I'm glad you expressed interest in co-writing one of the five A Harem Boy Saga books. The fourth book will be the best to commence our collaboration if you are serious about working on this joint project with me. I'll be more than delighted to incorporate your valuable opinions and I'm positive your voice will add credence to the series.

The first 3 books center on our first three Arab Household experiences and the numerous interesting and varied characters we encountered during our services. The fourth book is devoted solely to our loving relationship and functioning as a gay couple within the E.R.O.S. context in the late sixties and early seventies epoch. This will be "our" book; a tell-all about our love, our heartaches, our separation and our recent reconnection. This will also give us time to map-out and brainstorm the topics we'll like to include in the manuscript. Are you are open to my suggestions?

I have a few chapters left to complete A Harem Boy Saga – Book II that I had originally considered titling Passion. Recently a more appropriate word has manifested and that word is Unbridled. Maybe we can use Passion for the book we'll co-write together?

Tell me more about your life in New Zealand. As always I love to catch up on your news after our separation.

I eagerly await your next correspondance.

Forever Yours,

Young.

1967 Who Are You?

The benevolent *'Ginn'* miraculously disappeared as quickly as he had appeared. I was left alone salivating in the afterglow of our passion within the confines of the steamy chamber. I wondered what happened to my Valet after we had entered the steam-room? Since then he was nowhere to be found and nowhere to be seen.

I headed towards the shower facility to cleanse my already clean body.

Lining the circular wall were a series of shower cubicles, each with individual curtains to shield the bather from public view. In the center of this circular section was a series of communal showers. A 6 foot high circular tiled wall divided the curtained area from the communal showers. This divide was obviously erected for exhibitionist to display themselves to voyeuristic counterparts during the cleansing process.

Since there was nobody stationed at the communal shower stalls and I only required a quick wash, I ventured to use the un-curtained center arena. It was a quick in and out rinse before proceeding to find Andy. Little did I realize that when my back was turned, a hand was brushing against my backside? Startled, I turned to see whom the hand belonged. To my surprise several voyeurs had gathered around the circular periphery where I was showering ogling at my nakedness. An older man stood under the shower next to mine. His devouring eyes were glued to my boyish physique. I had to get away from this group of onlookers which none I desired or fancied sexually. Most were out of shape or for a lack of a better word, 'slimy' in demeanor.

It was time to find my guardian. Grabbing a dry towel to wrap around my waist I headed down a long corridor.

Where Are You?

I had absolutely no idea where I was heading. My tellak was nowhere to be found. Along one side of this dimly lit corridor was an open courtyard while the other consisted of a series of curtained rooms. The sound of sex emanated from the chambers. I figured these must be private and communal playrooms. The corridor got narrower and dimer as I ventured further. Men were loitering about naked or toweled, waiting for their catch to enter one of these rooms. Hands reached out to touch me but I did not respond. My focus was to make it to the end of the corridor to find my Valet. I was lost without him. I finally made it safely to my destination where a half-naked statue stood erect on a pedestal under a dimly lit halogen light. On either side were exits to an outdoor garden surrounded with a high wall overgrown with jasmine. I was glad to be out in the night air, away from the unsavory characters lurking by the corridors.

I found an empty bench to catch my breath. No sooner was I situated, a hand reached from behind the shubberies to caress my shoulders. I had little choice but to be on the move again. I journeyed into a jasmine maze hoping that I would be left alone. There were couples or groups in various stages of copulation round every bend I turned. Now, I was more determined to find either of my lovers, but most of all I wanted Andy. I needed his protection and his loving aura to aegis me from these repugnant men that kept reaching to touch my body. Where is my protector when I needed him most?

Andy Is That You?

Just when I was at a lost, I noticed a triplet coveting near the center of the labyrinth. A tall figure with his back to me resembled the man I was looking for. He was mounting his tellak doggie style while the youth suckled on an engorged phallus attached to none other than my *'Ginn's'* lover, Ismile. My immediate reaction was to separate their passionate union. The green eyed monster had unsuspectingly reared its ugly head. Its fiery eyes were urging me to disrupt their coition.

Suddenly Andy's words of wisdom loomed before my burning mind, *"Conquer the negative and transform your fears and jealousies into positive experiences."* I stopped in my tracks just as I was about to lunge at the tellak. I wanted to give this licentious boy a fist full of my fury like I had so unashamedly beaten Timothy at Havasupai Falls yet I stood unmovable. Instead, I slowly backed away. I did not want to be noticed. I wanted to hide, to think, to ponder and most importantly to calm my rage from the sudden onslaught from this covetous emerald dragon. I had to get away, far away from this sexual avariciousness. I did not want this lubricious beast of jealousy to devour me alive. I did not hanker for the beast virid slime to apprehend my soul and to debauch my person into a wretch of a man. *"Walk away and don't look back. Go!"* My still small voice confronted me. *"You are an enlightened being. You, Young are a valued member of the Enlightened Royal Oracle Society!"* I backed away from the formidable scenario to find my way out of this unnerving maze while my body stammered in a cataleptic fit.

It was one thing to have multiple liaisons with my lover's involvement but quite another when he was soliciting sex without my presence. I slumped to the ground to close my weary eyes. I tried to block out the hurt my injured ego was suffering.

"Weren't you doing exactly the same thing as Andy a few moments ago in the steam-room? Were you not also in the throes of

passion with Najib, your benevolent 'Ginn'? If you have the sexual freedom, why shouldn't your Valet experience the same? Why do you throw a jealous fit when he is with others? My pensive thought declared judiciously.

"Grow-up Young! Grow up! Have you already forgotten the lessons your Valet taught you about the art of loving? Now is the time to practice what you have learned. Pick yourself off the floor, you stupid boy. You have one of two options; you can either be negative and confront your adversary (the green-eyed monster) or be positive and befriend your foe. The choice is yours." My guardian angel advised. "The ball is in your court. Remember to choose wisely because there are consequences to the choices you make."

My Guardian Angel

Just as I was at an emotional and mental cross road, a voice called out my name from behind the shrubberies, "*Young, where are you? Vaj and I have been looking for you. Answer me if you are in the labyrinth.*"

I responded in the direction of the voice, "*I'm here! I'm here!*"

Before I had time to wipe away my tears of sorrow, Oscar was already embracing me in his arms. He said, "*Thank God you are safe. We were worried about you. We didn't know where you had disappeared? Vaj and I saw Andy half an hour ago and he like us was looking for you all over. We decided to split into two groups to find you. I'm so glad you are alright. Where were you?*"

Clearing my throat, I uttered, "*I was in the steam-room. I thought Andy was next to me when we entered. I'm also looking for him.*" I did not confide to Oscar what I witnessed inside the maze. I knew I had to confront my jealousies alone. I had to face my fears head-on and to subdue the emerald beast back into the abysmal confines from whence it abruptly materialized. This was not an easy task but over time I did learn to keep this Brobdingnagian creature at bay.

My guardian angel in the likes of my lover Oscar had conspicuous appeared to guide me to safety. Much like the angel in my dream six months ago who promised to be by my side in times of trials. Both my BBs had kept their promises to keep me safe in times of tribulations. All I had to do was to call out their names.

What Happened?

As Oscar, Devaj and I sat waiting for our entourage at the chat room, I couldn't help but ask, *"How was the massage service? Were you guys well looked after?"*

Devaj asked, *"You'll never guess who our masseuses were. We both had big burly men giving us a full body scrub and a soap rub down. My masseur tried shaving my face until Oscar told him that service was not required, since I don't have any facial hair. He then proceeded to shave my armpits and pubic hair which my Valet also told him that I don't required that service either."* The boy laughed.

"Oscar did get a good clean-up. Couldn't you tell? He's now a sparkling person." Devaj joked of his guardian.

"After the hefty masseuses finished, our tellaks took over to wash the soap off our bodies. While drying us they proceeded to work our organs to give us a 'happy ending'. Since I didn't want the evening to end so rapidly, I omitted that service. I went exploring on my own before Oscar found me in the garden. That was when we started to search for you."

"What did you do?" Devaj inquired of me.

Since I wasn't up to relating my steam room sexcapade, I told them I had been looking for Andy. I also failed to inform them of my experience inside the labyrinth. Instead I remarked, *"I wonder where Andy disappeared to? It's so unlike him to leave without telling me."*

Just then I noticed my Valet walking towards us. I stood on the pretext I needed to order some beverages at the service bar even though I could have had our tellaks do the ordering. The truth be told I was not ready to face Andy and to pretend

I didn't know what had transpired in the maze. I needed time to gather my thoughts and be civil to my beloved.

Andy followed me to the bar. He stood beside me and said, "We need to talk."

"About what?" I replied nonchalantly.

"Don't pretend you don't know what I'm talking about. I saw you backing away in the maze. Give me a chance to explain."

I kept quiet when my Valet began, "When we were changing out of our clothes, Najib asked privately if he could have you for himself. He also asked if I would go with Ismile since his boyfriend wanted a tryst with me and my assigned tellak. Both Najib and Ismile have an "open relationship" agreement. They both know in order for a long-term relationship to work eloquently, both parties have to allow each other a certain amount of sexual freedom to pursue other men, if and when the right circumstance arises. Tonight was a good example.

The reason I didn't tell you Najib's request is because I wanted to see if you are mature enough to decide how best to handle a situation you had witnessed, if it happens again, which without doubt it will. Like any excellent E.R.O.S. recruits you handled an otherwise explosive situation well. This I give you credit. I'm beginning to be assured that you truly love me unconditionally through your actions this evening.

"I've said it before and I will repeat it again; mature love says: "I need you because I love you." And what does immature love says?"

Before my lover could finish speaking I interjected, "Immature love says, "I love you because I need you"."

"Very good Young! I'm proud of you. Are you beginning to understand the true meaning of unconditional love we had discussed in the Bahriji at the 'Hanging Gardens of Babylon'?"

"Yes Andy! I need you because I love you." I truly was beginning to understand my lover's love for me. In order for him to love me, he must release and allow me to soar. Only then will I return out of my free will to love him more. From that moment forward I vowed I would love him unconditionally like he did me.

Early July 2012

True to his words, questions from Dr. Arius continue to arrive as quickly as I responded to his queries. In one of his emails he wrote:

Dear Young,

You are certainly diligent in answering my questions. Like you, I had similar experiences with my father in that we had a love/hate relationship. If I am not mistaken Andy's relationship with his dad was very much the same, am I correct? According to my analysis after years of psychiatric research in the field of homosexuality; close to 80 percent of gay boys had or continue to have love/hate relationships with their fathers. It is often the patriarch who has difficulties accepting the feminine aspect of their own machismo attributes. Patriarchs are often threatened by the effeminine energies that co-exist in all human beings. As is usually the case, when confronted by a gay son/sons or lesbian daughter/daughters, it upsets the traditional supercilious male dominance in the animal hierarchy; thus throwing the father figures off the balance scale. Some dads choose not to deal with their own fears which they unconsciously project onto family members closes to them, especially their homosexual children. On the other hand for those fathers that choose to reject their gay children; disowning their flesh and blood, they are on many occasions afraid to face their own fears head-on. In the majority of cases, throughout my research dads or parents with conventional religious background also have difficulties accepting their homosexual children due to religious indoctrinations.

Although we are currently living in a more enlightened moment in the history of mankind, age old customs and traditions continues to exist in conjunction with new ideologies. I believe your stories will assist to further enlighten our society and culture, propelling us humans towards a new dawn to understanding the future. As the saying goes; "It is a necessity to learn from the past to live in the present, in order to choose where we want to go in our future."

77

A Time for Us

"Experience is not what happens to a man. It is what a man does with what happens to him."
Aldous Huxley

Early July 2012

Doctor Arius's questions continued to arrive and I answered them as truthfully and diligently as I possibly could. The doctor inquired:

Hi Young,

Thank you for your honesty in answering my questions. I'm enjoying our correspondence. Your spontaneous, bubbly personally reminds me of the young protagonist in A Harem Boy Saga. I feel like I already know you intimately without having met you in person. Please do not take this as an insult; rather, it's a compliment – your childlike exuberance is within your DNA. It is refreshing to communicate with someone who hasn't lost his dynamic, playful ebullience. Maybe that is the reason I'm attracted to you.

Enclosed is the next set of questions;

** In one of your early chapters in **Initiation**, you mentioned that your father had the intention of sending you to a homosexual reform institution. Why did he not go through with it? Did your mother take drastic measures to stop him from following through, or did Uncle James play a role in the reversal of his plans?*

* In your writing, I got the impression that Uncle James played a vital advisory role in persuading your parents to enroll you into Daltonbury Hall. Was he very close with your mother?

* Why did you take such a liking to Uncle James?

** In **Initiation**, you wrote detailed descriptive scenes and settings of the boarding school, yet did not confide to your readers*

how you felt when you went from bustling London to the quiet Isle of Wight countryside. I for one would like to know your thoughts, feelings and reactions towards the change from city to country life.

* Why, in your opinion, is the presence of a 'big brother' or a 'big sister' (for the affiliated sister schools) vital to the growth of your education and well-being? I'd like to know your opinion about the BBs & BSs programs.

* As 'perfect' as you made out your BBs to be, there must have been moments of 'imperfection,' arguments or disagreements between the BBs and their 'little brothers'. Can you relate some negative examples to your readers, rather than just the positive situations you described so eloquently?

After reading **Initiation**, I want to know more about your personal feelings and sentiments as much as your descriptions of the surroundings you found yourself in. Tell me more about how you felt during your experience!

Love and blessings,
A. S.

1967 Sheikh P

The week after Hajj was as hectic as the weeks prior to Tahu and Mais' wedding ceremony. We Bahriji students were on the last leg of our Sekham service. The entire household was once again making a joyful noise, this time more so than the last, since it was the matrimony of the Wazir's adolescent son, Jasim, to his first cousin, Ria, a close relative of the Abu Dhabi Al Nahayan Royal Family.

Preparations went according to plan and the Big Day arrived with great fanfare. As Mais' wedding reception was, Jasim's ceremony was held at the Ai Gin Palace Hotel. This time around, there were more guests, mainly friends and family of the royal household. Without doubt, Hadrah Hakim's entire harem was present. Needless to say, P and his personal entourage arrived with pomp and circumstance. After all, he held a distinguished position in a line of heirs to the Al-Khalifa dynasty of Bahrain. A distant relative of the Al Nahayan Royal Family. Although the Prince wasn't next in line for the throne, he was a close runner up. As a member of a ruling family, he was obligated to perform official civic duties when called upon.

Sheikh P was educated in Dubai and later the United Kingdom, where he graduated from Eaton College and the Royal Military Academy of Sandhurst. When we met at the Sekham, he had just obtained a business degree at Cambridge University. In his twenties, he was also an active adviser to the sheikh Mohammed bin Rashid Establishment for Young Business Leaders and possessed a strong interest in economics.

P was also well known for his poetry, especially his romantic and patriotic poems. The art of poetry is highly regarded within the upper-crust Arabian societies, and the majority of wealthy elites are expected to have some skill in this creative art form. His skills in poetry and equestrianism made him pretty popular within the Arabian Peninsula Sheikhdoms. Outwardly, the prince seemed to have inherited a great sense of decorum and responsibility from his upbringing; only those within his inner circle knew this aristocrat to be otherwise.

At The Reception

The Wazir and Aziz were busy talking with the prince before the wedding ceremony began. Thabit waved Andy and me over when he saw us in the great hall. Politely obliging my Master's summons, we proceeded to greet the animated trio. After formal greetings to our hosts and His Highness, Thabit said, *"Young and Andy, I'm sad that your time at the Sekham is drawing to a close. You'll both be greatly missed, especially by my brother."* He nodded at Aziz as he spoke.

"That is correct. I will definitely miss my two hardworking models and apprentice. I hope I can loan you guys from your next Household, if your host is agreeable," the photographer said deviously, directing his gaze at P.

Since I had no idea where Andy and I would be located on our next assignment, I did not utter a word. The Prince asked, "What photography project are you working on with these two young men?"

"I'll be more than delighted to share the nature of my project with your Highness. Maybe we can set up a meeting so I can inform your Highness." Aziz replied.

"Sure, I'll like to learn more of your project. Let's set up a meeting after the wedding." P replied.

Just then other guests had arrived to greet the aristocrat. Giving me a naughty wink, the prince smiled and excused himself to attend to his official duties. Thabit and his brother were equally busy welcoming well-wishers who had circled around to greet the groom's father. Andy and I politely excused ourselves to return to our assigned seats. I could not help but ask my guardian, "Do you know where and to which Household we'll be allocated next?"

Andy commented, "I don't know, but I have a funny feeling we may be going to the Prince's palatial home."

"Whatever makes you think that? He didn't mention anything."

"Although I don't know for sure, I have a gut feeling that we'll be part of the Prince's harem. Meanwhile, we have three months of summer vacation before we are allocated to the next household. You don't have to worry your pretty little head for a while yet. I'm certainly looking forward to our cruise around the Aegean in the merry month of August," my Valet responded cheerfully.

Just as he was completing his sentence, we noticed the Hadrah, so we proceeded to pay our respects to my ex-Master. After formal greetings, Andy complimented Hakim, "Sir, you are looking well. It's a delight to see you again."

"I'm happy to see the two of you, too. You guys are looking more handsome than ever. Professor Henderson asked if you boys could have the use of the Simorgh and the Kahyya'm in early August. That shouldn't be a problem. The Kahyya'm will be docked in Monaco the entire summer. I'm attending a major yacht show in Cannes. I'll inform Captain Kasim that you will be using the Kahyya'm for a week. He's a great captain and will sail to any of the Greek islands you wish to visit." Hakim replied.

Andy spoke on our behalf, "Thank you, Sir! It's most generous of you to let us have the pleasure of using the Simorgh and Kahyya'm. Is it alright if our companion Oscar joins us on the cruise?"

"Of course, Andy. I'm sure your friend is a responsible young man like you. That shouldn't be a problem."

"Yes Sir. Oscar is also a Bahriji student. He is here at the reception, if you'd like to be acquainted with him." My Valet mentioned.

"Certainly, I'd like to meet him. If you boys would like to attend the yacht show, I'll be happy to have you join me." Just then, a group of the Hadrah's business colleagues arrived to greet the patriarch, leaving Andy and me to our own devices. During the course of the matrimonial reception, we did introduce Oscar to the Hadrah. He was more than pleased to be acquainted with our lover, and we agreed unanimously to attend the luxury boat show with Hakim before we sail to the Greek islands.

Early July 2012

In one of Andy's responses, my ex-lover wrote,

Young,

That sounds great! I look forward to co-writing the fourth book of A Harem Boy Saga with you. This will provide us time to map out the outline of our joint project during the course of our correspondence. As much as I'd love to work with you on this project, I want to be sure that Walter is okay with us going into this venture together. I have no desire to upset your loving relationship and certainly have no wish to be an unwelcome intruder into your lives. Let me know if he agrees.

When I was in hospital recovering from my nervous breakdown, I met Jack, a 24-year-old nursing student. He cared for me during my recovery. We dated for several months before his transfer to a hospice in a different city. I did not have the courage to tell Toby that Jack and I were dating. I was afraid Toby would threaten suicide again, until the fateful evening when he discovered Jack and me making out in my flat.

My caregiver and I had proceeded to my lodgings after a scrumptious dinner one evening. After several glasses of wine while watching television, Jack leaned his head against my shoulder. His dreamy, doe-like eyes looked adoringly at me, reminding me of your beautiful Asian eyes staring at me during our intimate moments together.

Our kisses soon led to lingering sensual foreplay. Before long, our clothes were scattered all over. Jack went on his knees, eagerly caressing my growing hardness and wrapping his luscious lips around me under my briefs. Easing down my underwear, he went to work. His sweetness stirred my longing for you. Closing my eyes to savor his warm fallation, I reclined against the comfortable sofa and enjoyed the pleasurable sensation showered upon my erection. He engulfed my pulsating manhood, suckling away as if to satisfy his hunger. It was similar to the way you used to relish my hardness for hours on end. Like you, he pleasured me with deep, devotional worship; I was overwhelmed by his sexual imperativeness, wanting his warmth to wash over my entirety. His expert titillation did wonders for my soul, causing me to spasm involuntarily. He devoured my length as if deprived of nourishment while I nurtured my feed into Jack's bobbing head, pressing him against my quivering palpitations.

Just as I was on the verge of release, loud banging was heard at the front door, rudely jolting us back to reality. Desperately adjusting my spinning vision to normality, I saw Toby fuming in front of our nakedness. The boy was shouting obscenities at Jack and me. That was the straw that broke the camel's back; I had enough of Toby's erratic behavior. I commanded him to leave my flat, and our relationship terminated from that moment forward. I had no wish to see this irrational guy again. I was no longer responsible for his childishness, even if he threatened suicide. By now I had enough of his stupidity and told him that was none of my business if he decided to take his own life. Toby stomped out of my lodgings, cursing and hurling profanity at us. This offensive episode had ruptured our evening of blissful sexuality.

Jack and I decided to take a hiatus. I also needed a respite from Toby's drama. My four-year on-again-off-again relationship with the Portuguese Filipino ended that very evening. I had been holding on to that relationship, hoping I would uncover a glimmer of your positive traits in the boy. I learned that people don't change; what changes is our perception of them.

Toby slowly relinquished his suicidal absurdity over time. Our friendship remained cordial despite all that had transpired. He continued to try to reignite our passions, which to me had passed the point of no return. I never looked back after I left for Canada to pursue my postgraduate studies. That was the final chapter to my relationship with Toby.

Well, Young, here we are, reminiscing about the past when we have the present and the future to enjoy each other's company.

Be well, be good, and don't do anything I wouldn't do.

Love you always,

Andy.

78

Ma'a salama مع السلامة — Goodbye Sekham

*"There is no such thing as a moral or an immoral book.
Books are well written or badly written."*
Oscar Wilde

1967 The Time has Come to Say Goodbye

My time at Wazir Thabit's household had drawn to a close. I was sad to leave the Sekham. During those three months, I had come to enjoy the company of Sayid, Jasim and several members of the Sekham's household, most notably Sabiya, Mais, and her half-sister Naira. Although Andy, Oscar, Devaj and I were often on the road with Aziz and Gabrielli working on *"Sacred Sex In Sacred Places,"* I had learned much while in the Sekham service.

The Wazir had been most generous to the Bahriji students. On the final day before Andy and I left to return to the Oasis school, Thabit summoned us into his private chamber to thank us for assisting his brother Aziz in his photography project. His brother, his two sons; Sayid, Jasim, and Gabrielli were there to bid us farewell.

Araka fi ma ba'd أراكا في ما بعد Wazir Thabit
(See you later, Wazir Thabit)

Thabit, the patriarch, was the first to speak after Andy, Oscar, Devaj, and I had assembled in his private office. *"Three months have flown by, and you boys are already leaving the Sekham to seek new adventures. On behalf of my household, I thank you for your contributions during your time here. Although you saw little of* me due to my busy business schedules, your presence has provided much joy to my family, especially to my brother and my sons.

"The four of you have done much to harmonize Sayid and Jasim's brotherly affection. My boys are now better behaved and better educated in the art of loving."

Andy spoke on our behalf, "Sir, we have been honored to be of service to your family. Thank you for providing us the opportunity to experience life in your household, Italy, and America, and for the chance to work with your brother on 'Sacred Sex In Sacred Places.' Young and I are very grateful and appreciative of your Excellency's generosity. We will miss the members of the Sekham household greatly."

"You are so humble, Andy. You boys were hand-picked by your school to have the opportunity to experience our way of life. My family enjoyed your company very much."

The Wazir handed each of us an envelope before he continued, "Please accept our token of appreciation from my family. I hope to see you again soon. Knowing Aziz and Gabrielli, they will find ways to loan you boys from your new Master to continue working on 'Sacred Sex In Sacred Places.' I know my brother will not let you off the hook easily," Thabit joked.

Just then, the photographer chimed in, "I will definitely miss the four of you, but I'm sure I'll be seeing you soon enough. You guys will not escape my clutches," he said amusingly. "I'll find you soon (directing his gaze at me)." Aziz gave me a mischievous wink before leaning to give each of us a bear hug and kisses on our cheeks. He also handed us a large brown envelope each. "Open these on your way back to the Bahriji. Bon Voyage!"

The last time Andy and I saw the Wazir was at the Cannes yacht show in the summer of 1967. Thabit was there to purchase a luxury boat. The Hadrah had mentioned my assistance in the renovation of the Kahyya'm to him, and my ex-Master asked my advice on the interior design for his new purchase, which he named *Bettawfeeq (Good Luck)*. I was delighted to be of help, as *Bettawfeeq* was an elegant, custom-designed luxury yacht.

Aziz, The Photographer

Our Sekham parting was not the last Andy and I saw of the photographer. We did meet when I was in service at my next Household. He managed to borrow my Valet and me for a few weeks to continue work on *"Sacred Sex In Sacred Places."* We bid our final يعادو (farewell) a year and half later, at the end of 1968, when Aziz and Mario launched the first of their photography exhibition in West Berlin, Germany. Andy and I were invited to the lavish photographic exhibition and book launch. It was the first in a series of *"Sacred Sex In Sacred Places"* exhibitions. I continued to assist both photographers throughout the course of my four years of harem services whenever I was available. We travelled to many exotic locales. I garnered an abundance of knowledge and grew richly in my life experiences, and I am grateful to Aziz for selecting me to be a part of *"Sacred Sex In Sacred Places"* photography project. Andy and I were the lucky ones who saw this controversial venture to completion.

Needless to say, *"Sacred Sex In Sacred Places"* caused much controversies and 'boo-ha-ha' among the conservatives at the West Berlin show. The liberals loved the exhibition and came in droves to view the polemic photographs, while conservatives demonstrated outside the art gallery where the exhibition was held. Both photographers could not sign enough copies of their books. It was a sold-out event. The European paparazzi had a field day interviewing our friends. They appeared on West German talk shows before working their way to other major European cities, where they autographed numerous copies of their erotic books for voyeurs and art critics alike.

Over the years, Aziz became a well-known photographer in the western world, especially in the European continent, while remaining an unknown photographer in the Middle Eastern sheikhdoms. It was to his advantage; otherwise, a

Fathwah would have been issued by extremist Islamic clerics for my friend's death. His photographic depictions of copulating orgies and couples in the throes of passion, some taken in famous mosques and masjids, would have been considered a sacrilegious act against the Islamic faith.

Mario, The Man-nizer

My infatuation for the Count waned after accompanying the photographer to numerous photo shoots. I discovered soon enough that this Italian 'Casanova' belonged to many and Andy was my true love. We were inseparable. Mario was just a passing phase in my adolescent life, while Andy lived on within my heart forever. As was with this man-izer, he grew in fame and fortune as an established fashion and erotic photographer and as a classy erogenous film consultant. He advised the creators of numerous erotic films. He worked with Franco Zeffirelli in *Romeo and Juliet (1968)*, with director William Friedkin in *The Boys in the Band (1970)*, with director Stanley Kubrick in *A Clockwork Orange (1971)*, *Barry Lyndon (1975)*, with director Bernardo Bertolucci in *Ultimo tango a Parigi*, more famously known as *Last Tango in Paris (1972/1973)*, with Just Jaeckin in *Emmanuelle* and *The Story of O (1975)*, and with director/writer Serge Gainsbourg's debut film, *Je T'Aime Moi Non Plus (aka I Love You, I Don't – 1976)*, which was banned in the United Kingdom when initially released. This movie was often accused of perversion because of unnecessary emphasis on anal sex. It also contained an explicit reference to fellatio (in a scene of the consumption of gooey cucumbers). Mario had also worked with the outspoken homosexual writer/director Derek Jarman in his debut homoerotic cult film *Sebastiane (1976)*, and, last but not least, with fellow photographer and "master of erotica," director David Hamilton, in his directorial film debut *Bilitis (1977)*. It was composed of soft-focus, photographic quality images of sexual awakening. The list of erotically charged films the Count consulted on seemed endless.

At the height of his fame in 1980, he met an untimely demise while on a private plane flying from Italy to Utah. It crashed into the Pacific due to severe weather conditions. His body was never recovered. I was sad when I read the deplorable news in a European tabloid magazine. As Johnny Depp so rightly said, *"There are four questions of value in life... What is sacred? Of what is the spirit made? What is worth living for? And what is worth dying for? The answer to each is the same. Only love."* Count Mario Conti certainly lived life fully and unconditionally. He lived for what he truly and sacredly believed, that which was worth living and dying for. Love set the free-spirited 'Casanova' free in the end.

In truth, I believed he died making love above the clouds with a handsome male model, rumored to be his new beau, with whom he had fallen madly in love. According to the news article, the two were on their way to the Sundance Film Festival for the premiere of William Friedkin's notorious, gay grisly slasher-thriller, *Cruising (1980)*, for which the Count acted as a movie consultant.

I will always remember the Italian aristocrat in his prime as a virile male specimen who believed himself to be created in the image of the God of gods. Like Zeus, Mario's mission was to empower the male species with sexual prowess that knew no borders or boundaries. He is greatly missed by *moi*.

Best Wishes Tahu & Mais

Mais gave birth to two beautiful twin boys and remained a devoted housewife to her beloved husband, Tahu. During my continuing sojourn with Aziz and Mario on *"Sacred Sex In Sacred Places,"* Tahu had various liaisons with others (males and females), away from the prying eyes of his family. He was soon elevated to a senior position in Aziz's photography business after his marriage into the Wazir's family.

The last I saw of the former photographer's assistant was at the end of 1968, after *"Sacred Sex In Sacred Places"* drew to a close. We had been working on this project for close to three years and had travelled to many parts of the globe. Even today, this man, Tahu, remains an enigma to me. A quiet and reserved person by nature, he kept many things to himself. He spoke only when spoken to. On the contrary, his wife was the dominant partner in their relationship. It is often true to surmise that "Opposites attract!"

All the Best, Gabrielli & Sabiya

My ex-teacher married Sabiya a year after Andy and I left the Sekham. Surprisingly, Thabit gave his blessing without any objections. His business partnership with the Italian (now his son-in-law) lasted many more years before Gabrielli and Sabiya returned to Rome to raise a family. She produced four heirs: three girls and a boy. Of course, Thabit doted over his grandchildren, especially Rafiq, his grandson, who lived up to his name of being kind and friendly. The boy, well versed in both Arabian and Italian cultures, followed in his father and grandfather's footsteps. He was educated in the best schools and colleges within the Arab Emirates and Italy. Fluent in several languages, Rafiq grew into a competent humanitarian, obtaining a degree in liberal arts before joining his father's and grandfather's companies as their international liaison. My professor traveled with us to several of our photo shoots whenever he could get away from his busy business schedule. The last time I saw him was in October 1968, when we were filming at an Islamic sacred site in the Indonesian island of Java. He was then preparing his permanent return to Rome after spending a week with us on location.

Sabiya obtained a degree in Oriental Studies at the Sapienza (Sapienza University of Rome). The Wazir gave his favorite daughter a fanfaronade wedding, both in her native homeland of Abu Dhabi and in Rome, her husband's prominent family fatherland. She worked with her husband for several years before becoming a full-time housewife, taking care of their four children.

Good Luck, Sayid & Jasim

These two brothers couldn't be more different than night and day. While Sayid forged his way as yet another Playboy of the Middle Eastern world, Jasim grew to be a stoic intellectual. Although his arranged marriage to Ria caused much friction, the man showed little remorse. He did what was expected of him by his family while his wife did what she pleased when she pleased. 'Genial' is probably the best word to describe their relationship. Although Jasim never admitted publicly that he preferred the company of males to females, he was, like many of his Arab peers, often seen in the company of men (especially older Caucasian men who seemed to dote over the soft-spoken, handsome young buck).

Although both brothers received a sizable family trust fund when they came of age at 21, Sayid lived a life larger than his inheritance could support while Jasim was careful with his money. Some may even have labeled him as parsimonious. As wealthy as Jasim was, it appeared that he preferred to be a 'kept boy' when in the company of mature gentlemen.

Like Ubaid, his distant cousin, Sayid kept a growing male and female harem in later years. He spent a large part of his time travelling the world, garnering sexual experiences and expanding his father's many businesses globally. His brother was the home body, stationed in Abu Dhabi. He was the responsible entrepreneur who traveled under the auspices of "business" to meet with his mature male clients and business associates. Jasim kept a private penthouse in New York and a secluded home along the French Riviera.

What Happened to Young?

In the early months of June 1967, I returned home to spend a couple months with my family. Father continued to 'butch me up' sending me to gymnastics, body-building and swimming classes at Chin Woo (the sports stadium Foong Senior owned). I was enrolled back at the Methodist Boys' School to continue classes, as if I'd never left Kuala Lumpur. Although I had no wish to participate in the grand scheme of activities that Father had so painstakingly arranged for me, I went along with it to please Mother and avoid further friction between my parents. After all, I was home for eight weeks and I looked forward to returning to Andy's loving arms with each passing day.

My summer homecoming was pleasant enough, if only to see my mother and female relatives. I had nothing much in common with them, but they were a welcome diversion from the daily drudgery Father was putting me through.

At my old school, I met a nice boy named Charles. He acted as my protector when I was being bullied. We became friends. Little did I guess that Charles was gay! He displayed no signs of epicene behavior. On the contrary, he behaved like an ordinary boy. It was years later, when he paid me a visit in Hong Kong from Sydney, that he told me the truth of his sexual inclination.

Back then in the summer of 1967 and in subsequent summers, Charles was a good friend who came to my rescue when I needed help keeping the bullies at bay. Lucky for me, I was only at the Methodist Boys' School for eight weeks before returning to London.

I was overjoyed to be with Andy again the first week of August 1967. We stayed at Uncle James' townhouse for several days before boarding the Simorgh, flying to Cannes to join Hadrah Hakim at the yacht show. The week spent cruising the deep blue Aegean Sea was one of the best times of my young years, about which you, dear readers will read in great detail in the third book of *A Harem Boy's Saga*.

My experiences in my third assigned Arab Household helped me grow as a person by leaps and bounds. My third Household Master was as aberrant and eccentric as they come. Besides being a man of great distinction, he embraced life like there was no tomorrow. He lived by the book of the present. To him, the present was the only moment worth living in. Andy and I were whisked along with him as if in an endless tornado, circling to the whims of His Highness. He was indeed a character to be reckoned with, and I was part of a 3-month whirlwind that lifted me off solid ground much like Dorothy in the *Wizard of Oz*. Those few months were a fun time, which I thought would never end; but, like Dorothy, I was eager to get home – not to Kansas but back to England, where my heart belonged.

Young.

Author

Bernard Foong is, first and foremost, a sensitivist. He finds nuance in everything. To experience the world he inhabits is an adventure which is mystical, childlike and refreshing. He has a rare ability to create beauty in a unique fashion. His palettes have been material, paint, words and human experiences.

By Christine Maynard
(screenwriter and novelist).

Bernard Tristan Foong alias Young, is an accomplished fashion designer. After graduating from The Royal College of Art, London, England; he worked as an in-house bridal wear designer for Liberty's of London for four years.

The Hong Kong Polytechnic/University offered Mr. Foong a fashion design professorship for the next six years. He was a founding member of The Hong Kong Fashion Designer's Association. Consultant to numerous fashion companies in Hong Kong; ranging from lingerie, furs, womens-wear designs to his specialty: romantic and ethereal bridal ensembles.

During his lecturing sojourn in the United States of America, he was recruited by The University of Wisconsin, Madison as an associate fashion professor. He was also a visiting lecturer at The Minneapolis College of Art, Minnesota.

In 1994 to 1996, The Singapore Temasek Polytechnic recruited Mr. Foong to organize the school's fashion design and merchandising department. He was also the acting fashion development manager for Parkson Grand department stores in Kuala Lumpur, Malaysia.

The designer was offered a scholarship to complete his Master in Theatre Costuming at The University of Hawaii in 1996. Since then he has made Hawaii his home. He resides in the beautiful island of Maui with his life partner of sixteen years, Mr. Walter Bissett and their *'Goddess'* daughter, Ms. Kali Durga (a fluffy Himalayan).

He is a full-time writer and is currently working on his third book, **Debauchery**; the sequel to **Initiation** and **Unbridled**.

A Harem Boy Saga is a series seven books, documenting the designer's life.

Acknowledgements

In January 2011, an interminable urge overtook me to document a segment of my adolescent life which had been kept secret for forty-two years. I was compelled by an unseen power to write *A Harem Boy Saga*.

Ms. Marji Knowles, a friend and confident, intrigued by my story, encouraged me to proceed. Not only did she offer me assistance in editing my manuscript, she also provided sound advice and suggestions throughout my writing process. I am grateful for the months of hard work she devoted to **A Harem Boy's Saga – Book I – Initiation.** Her cogent arguments spearheaded my determination to complete the first in a series of *A Harem Boy Saga*.

Ms. Christine Maynard, my editor in chief manifested from Louisiana. She is a genius in keeping my youthful voice intact while transforming my story onto the pages of **Initiation** and **Book II – Unbridled**. I have grown to cherish and love this amazing woman during the months we spent editing. We laughed, cried, and sometimes cursed but forgave, as we cleaned and scrubbed this manuscript to perfection. We have since become close friends. A quote by William Blake:
   "Opposition is true friendship."
In the process of editing Unbridled, I've the privilege to come to know my other editor, Ms. Ellen Fishbein from New Jersey. She did a superb editing job and provided valuble suggestions to improve my writing skills. For this I am thankful to her.

I'm grateful to Ms. B K Wright. Her advice and valuble assistance gave me the incentive to continue on this long and winding road to complete my second book in the series of *A Harem Boy's Saga*.

At this juncture, I would like to say, "Thank You" to all my friends and supporters who continue to support my revelations during the past years of grueling work, before the **Initiation** and **Unbridled** came to fruition.

Last but not least, I am deeply appreciative to my life partner, Mr. Walter Bissett for his steadfast unwaivering support, encouraging me to tell my story truthfully. In his words;

"The truth will set you free."

Young.

young@aharemboysaga.com
www.aharemboysaga.com